White Ferocity

This book is part of the CODESRIA Book Series.

White Ferocity
The Genocides of Non-Whites and Non-Aryans from 1492 to Date

Rosa Amelia Plumelle-Uribe

Foreword by Samir Amin & Louis Sala-Molins

Translated from the French by Virginia Popper

Council for the Development of Social Science Research in Africa
DAKAR

© CODESRIA 2020
Council for the Development of Social Science Research in Africa
Avenue Cheikh Anta Diop, Angle Canal IV
BP 3304 Dakar, 18524, Senegal
Website: www.codesria.org

ISBN: 978-2-86978-723-0 (P)
ISBN: 978-2-86978-981-4 (E)

All rights reserved. No part of this publication may be reproduced or transmitted in any form or by any means, electronic or mechanical, including photocopy, recording or any information storage or retrieval system without prior permission from CODESRIA.

Typesetting: Daouda Thiam
Cover Design: CODESRIA
Cover Image: Nineteenth century engraving in *L'abolition de l'esclavage* by Guy Fau
Distributed in Africa by CODESRIA
Distributed elsewhere by African Books Collective, Oxford, UK
Website: www.africanbookscollective.com

The Council for the Development of Social Science Research in Africa (CODESRIA) is an independent organisation whose principal objectives are to facilitate research, promote research-based publishing and create multiple forums for critical thinking and exchange of views among African researchers. All these are aimed at reducing the fragmentation of research in the continent through the creation of thematic research networks that cut across linguistic and regional boundaries.

CODESRIA publishes *Africa Development*, the longest standing Africa based social science journal; *Afrika Zamani*, a journal of history; the *African Sociological Review*; *Africa Review of Books* and the *Journal of Higher Education in Africa*. The Council also co-publishes *Identity, Culture and Politics: An Afro-Asian Dialogue*; and the *Afro-Arab Selections for Social Sciences*. The results of its research and other activities are also disseminated through its Working Paper Series, Book Series, Policy Briefs and the *CODESRIA Bulletin*. All CODESRIA publications are accessible online at www.codesria.org.

CODESRIA would like to express its gratitude to the Swedish International Development Cooperation Agency (SIDA), the Carnegie Corporation of New York (CCNY), the Andrew W. Mellon Foundation, the Open Society Foundations (OSFs), Oumou Dilly Foundation, Ford Foundation and the Government of Senegal for supporting its research, training and publication programmes.

Contents

About the Author vii

Foreword to the English Edition – Ferocity of Whites,
    Ferocity of Capitalism ix
    Samir Amin

Foreword to the French Edition – Gorée xvii
    Louis Sala-Molins

Preface xxix

Acknowledgements xxxiii

Introduction 1

I
The Exclusion of Non-Whites or the Institutionalisation of Barbarity

1. The Destruction of Native Americans 11
2. The Annihilation of Black People 27
3. Saint-Domingue 59
4. From One Continent to Another 69

II
The Ideological Weight of White Supremacy

5. From the Exclusion of Non-Whites to
   the Exclusion of Non-Aryans 91
6. Business Comes First 113

7. The Weight of Racist Ideologies 129
8. The Racist Tradition of the United States 147
9. The Consequences of Normalisation 181

III
Apartheid – A Crime against Humanity... But the Other One

10. When Nazism Becomes the Sort of Thing With Which One Can Associate 197
11. Back Full Circle to the Exclusion of Non-Whites 215
12. Never Again! Well..., Not in Europe Anyway 227
13. They Did Not Realise Blacks Are Humans 241

Conclusion 259
Bibliography 265
Index 273

About the Author

France-based lawyer and essayist Rosa Amelia Plumelle-Uribe was born on 24 December 1951 in Montelíbano, Colombia. Towards the end of the 1970s, in Bogota, the capital of Colombia, Rosa Amelia Plumelle-Uribe was part of the "Black Culture" group, where she became aware of the position of Blacks in the history of humankind. From then on, she has focused her work on denouncing crimes and injustices perpetrated under the banner of white domination and oppression and the racial discrimination of other groups, including the slave trade, slavery, massacres of indigenous peoples by settler populations, colonialism, Nazism and apartheid. Through her work over the years, she continues to build a different North–South relationship.

In 2001, Plumelle-Uribe's research and reflections over many years came to fruition with the publication of *La férocité blanche. Des non-Blancs aux non-Aryens : génocides occultés de 1492 à nos jours* (Albin Michel), and a German edition published in 2004. Another work *Traite des Blancs, traites des Noirs : aspects méconnus et conséquences actuelles* (L'Harmattan, 2008) focuses essentially on how on one hand Arab-Muslim slave traders exported Africans to Asia, Europe and the Middle East, and on the other hand how Europeans had continued to sell themselves to one another.

In recent years, the demand for reparations for the crimes of the slave trade has triggered great hostility among the powers implicated in those crimes. Confronted by the opposition to reparation by all those that felt threatened by the very idea, Plumelle-Uribe published *Victimes des esclavagistes musulmans, chrétiens et juifs. Racialisation et banalisation d'un crime contre l'humanité* (Anibwé, 2012) to demonstrate the responsibilities of the players, benefactors and beneficiaries of slavery and the slave trade.

Following the deadly terror attacks of November 13, 2015 in France, Plumelle-Uribe published *13 novembre 2015. Victimes innocentes des guerres* (Anibwé, 2016) to analyse the historical circumstances and causes that have made civilian populations vulnerable and jeopardised everyone's security. She examines elements that help to understand that, in the new reality of the twenty-first century, the reciprocity of violence is such that military interventions in the South are no longer feasible without compromising the security of civilian populations in the North.

Plumelle-Uribe has also contributed to several collective works such as *Esclavage, colonisation, libérations nationales* (L'Harmattan, 2000), *Déraison, esclavage et droit* (UNESCO, 2006), *Crimes de l'histoire et réparations : les réponses du droit et de la justice* (Bruylant, 2004), and *50 ans après, quelle indépendance pour l'Afrique* (Philippe Rey, 2010) among others.

Foreword to the English Edition

Ferocity of Whites, Ferocity of Capitalism

Samir Amin

Rosa Amelia Plumelle-Uribe's book needed to be written; now it must be read. The crimes against humanity perpetrated on a huge scale since 1492, centuries before the Nazi crimes – the genocide of the Native Americans, the Atlantic slave trade and slavery – are known, or should be known, to everybody. But any reference to these crimes is immediately buried in the complacency of the public today, at least the citizens of the United States and of Europe. All this belongs to the past, albeit a sad, sickening one, but nonetheless a page of history that has fortunately, *definitively,* been turned (my emphasis).

We now live in the best of all worlds, striding forward on the radiant path of full respect for human rights, for all humans, on the road towards democracy (for all). It is the "end of history" we are told by Fukuyama: liberal democracy has written history's last chapter and there will be no more hereafter because this system is capable, by peaceful, nonviolent means, of solving all the problems faced by humanity. It already allows access and will increasingly allow access to all the benefits of civilisation both material and ethical. This nonsense is unfortunately the daily fare of some hundreds of million human beings: probably a majority of the 15 per cent of humanity that lives in the United States and Europe (to which I would add Japan, it being "honorary Whites" in the eyes of the apartheid regime!), and a small number of those who live elsewhere on the planet, i.e. "Western" facsimiles.

The magnitude of the crimes described in detail by Uribe is not disputed, as she points out in her preface. There may be here and there some eminent specialists (and I am not one of them) who could add some details, maybe correct some errors (that escaped my notice). That could be, but no researcher could, in good faith, claim any more than that.

As for me, I do not know exactly what the definition of a "White" is. Ideology – and the law too, alas – categorises human beings in the United States as "White" (I have no idea why, as "Caucasians"! Perhaps to please Stalin!) and "Coloured" (everyone else). Everyone else! In the case of Blacks and people of mixed Black ancestry: in the United States, a "single drop of black blood" downgrades you – I nearly wrote *degrades you*. But how about the emigrants that came from Asian India, those who have a "white" skin and furthermore speak an Indo-European language, just like the "Caucasians"? And how about the Hispanics who are not from the indigenous peoples: Iberians and Italians? Are they "White Caucasians" or "Coloured"? In Europe there are those who are snow white in the North, and the dark-skinned Whites of the South. Are they as dark-skinned as the Arabs (White or not White?). Steve Biko, confronted with his torturer, disguised as a judge, who asked him a question about his colour, good-humouredly answered: "Why do you call yourselves white? You look more pink than white." And the Jews – for whom the criteria for belonging to this so-called "community" I am unable to define – are they as white as the Europeans, or are they dark-skinned like their Semitic Arab cousins? Any individual can be good-looking or ugly, intelligent or stupid, kind or criminal, regardless of his or her skin colour. And very fortunately, I am not the only one to believe this. To definitively set aside some sort of para-theory about "human races" (be they three or fifteen matters very little) – at least in stated principles if not in the actual perceptions of all the individuals that inhabit our Earth – is in my view certainly a step forward. But it should not be an excuse to forget history and the questions that still affect the reality of our world.

The year 1492 in the subtitle of Plumelle-Uribe's book is not a random date. Not the year of the "discovery of America" (in Eurocentric parlance), since I suppose that the human beings that lived there at the time had discovered it earlier. But if a date of birth had to be found for capitalism, this would be it. Along with a number of others, I talk about the six centuries of the history of capitalist modernity (1492 to the present day). Here is not the place to go into any further detail about our understanding of those six centuries.

Let me just recall what I have already said (and before me, Karl Marx and others): 1492 is when the conquest of the Americas by the Europeans from the Atlantic coasts – the Spaniards, Portuguese, British, French and Dutch – began. I call this "conquest and destruction", destruction of the societies of American Indians (and therefore massacres methodically organised for that purpose) and then reconstruction of new societies shaped to serve the development of capitalism at the time in Atlantic Europe. The subjection of the surviving indigenous peoples and their reduction to the status of inferior beings – quasi-slaves – followed by the establishment of plantations based on slave labour supplied by the Atlantic slave trade (the second genocide studied by Plumelle-Uribe) can only be meaningfully interpreted in the light of the analysis of what "historical capital" truly is.

It is a fact that historical capitalism originates in Atlantic Europe. I have put forward the thesis that the transition of forms of social organisation that pre-dated capitalist modernity had begun earlier and elsewhere, and that there is another explanation for the belated but decisive advance of Europe in this area than the legends built up by Eurocentric ideological historiography ("the European miracle" that comes after the "Greek miracle", etc.). But again, this is not the topic of this foreword. Because historical capitalism emerged from the "Atlantic European" world, an equal sign might come to mind: capitalist equals European (hence "White"). This reduction/confusion still prevails.

The ferocity of the capitalism of what was called the mercantilist era (roughly 1500 to 1800) arises from the demands of what Marx refers to as "primitive capital accumulation". This extreme ferocity was practised not only in the colonies of America and indirectly in Africa, which supplied the reservoir of slaves, but also in Europe itself, through the destruction of the ancient peasant economy, condemning millions of peasants to extreme poverty. Marx's pleadings as a young lawyer in defence of the "wood thieves" of the Rhineland eloquently demonstrate this relationship between capital accumulation and ferocity. In England, the starving masses were caught for petty thefts and were lucky if they were sentenced only for deportation to Australia as convict labourers.

Does this ferocity abate with the passage from mercantilism and its accompanying primitive accumulation to the accomplished form of capitalism with the industrial revolution in England and the political revolution in France at the end of the eighteenth century? Certainly not, although it takes on new forms that emerge in Europe and the United States concurrently, as well as in the Iberian Americas and India, which by then was British, and later on in the African and Asian colonies.

In the case of Europe, ferocity characterises the exploitation of the new working class, which Engels describes in an explanation of what the implications of deploying the capitalist rationale are. One might be tempted to say all this belongs to the past. In many ways, yes, thanks to the victorious struggles of European workers that deserve respect and should be congratulated, and certainly not deplored!

An epitome of ferocity was reached with the expansion of capitalism in the United States throughout the nineteenth century. The extension westwards went hand-in-hand with what was no doubt one of the greatest genocides in history, the organised, methodical massacre of all indigenous peoples in the region. And films that glorify cowboys who slaughter indigenous peoples are still served to educate children in this savage country almost to this very day. The British treated the indigenous peoples of Australia almost the same.

By comparison, neither the French of old Canada nor later on those of New Caledonia, the Spaniards in Latin America or the Russian Tsars planned the genocides of the peoples they conquered. In Latin America, the indigenous communities already decimated by the vicious conquest, dispossessed of their best land, the brutal, barbarian methods of subjection, survived nonetheless. So did the Kanaks and the Samoyeds. The Soviet Union, heir to the empire of the Tsars, gave the Samoyeds huge territories in Siberia and protected their culture. The United States and Canada have not even contemplated recognising that they were the perpetrators of unparalleled crimes against humanity. They are in no position to preach to others.

How can this special brand of barbarity of the Anglo-Americans be explained? Certainly not through their genes that can be speculated to be more criminogenic than those of other "White" peoples. No, the reason is that capitalism – because it was more advanced in its modern forms in the United Kingdom and the United States compared to Spain, France or Russia – proved to be systematically more efficient in its will to destroy the obstacles to its expansion.

In the United States, the triumphant new capitalism that started out from New England had no problem in accommodating the ferocious slavery of the southern states. After that, it turned the abolition of slavery to its advantage to subject the new proletariat – now supplemented by an additional black component – to an exploitation which "whether ferocious or not", remained fundamentally associated with entrenched racism.

There was a parallel development in Latin America where the Creole ruling classes (Whites or pseudo-Whites) debased the indigenous peoples, reducing them to abject conditions.

The only revolutions experienced by the continent are the Saint-Domingue revolution (Blacks liberated by Blacks, not waiting for the "abolition of slavery") – concomitant with the French Revolution (and commended by the *Montagnards*: the slaves of Saint-Domingue fought and won their freedom, they are citizens); and the later revolution of Mexico (1910–1920) followed by Cuba, where memories of slavery were still fresh.

Again, all this belongs to the past. At least, that was what was said in Europe during the first Belle Époque, 1890–1914. Savagery was over and done with. This discourse is very similar to the one in the second Belle Époque, a century later (1990 to the present day and beyond) with "the end of history" discourse). Needless to say, at the time (1890), the voices of the Africans subjected to the colonial conquest went unheard. And anyway, the purpose of going there was to "civilise" them, to pull them out of poverty and from the ferocity of their internecine strife. Just as today NATO intervenes only to establish democracy… as clearly is the case in Libya.

In the meantime – between the first and second Belle Époque – there was Nazism. Plumelle-Uribe is right to say that the ferocity of the Nazis is not an anomalous, inexplicable occurrence. It is integral to the rationale for implementing ferocity, which, I once again stress, is inherent to capitalism. She and I both see that the ideology of "Western" countries does not always go in the best, the most humane direction, quietly advancing on the right track. On the contrary, its progression laid the foundations for and led to Nazism.

The eighteenth century Enlightenment was not uniformly racist, far from it. The anti-slavery movement, the preoccupation with defining genuinely universal values, occupied the thoughts of the best minds. Undoubtedly, that thinking remained Eurocentric. The "European miracle" was not attributed to the race, to the genes (whose existence was yet to be discovered), but rather to the "Greek ancestor", the "Greek miracle". This is a mythological construction, so be it. I have pointed out, along with the author of *Black Athena,* that ancient Greece was not the ancestor of Europe. Ancient Greece belonged to the ancient Orient. I have shown that Eurocentrism was built up from formulations originating from the Enlightenment.

It was in the nineteenth century that racism systematically took over the place of the Greek ancestor, thereby founding the new myth of European superiority (the superiority of Whites). This is a French invention: Arthur de Gobineau was the first to formulate this new "theory of races". It was a resounding success. Influential politicians such as Chamberlain immediately adhered to this miserable new philosophy of history.

It is amusing to read the classifications of race popularised by these intellectual leaders of the last two centuries. The Germans rank themselves at the top, followed by the other Anglo-Saxons; the English have the same list, but put themselves above the Germans; the French justify their top position with an argument that I must admit is likeable: they are the heirs of the Revolution… which they nonetheless betrayed. The middle positions of the lists were consistently taken by more or less the same dark-skinned inhabitants of Southern Europe and Latin America. What about the "Asians"? The Chinese were at the bottom but the Japanese at the top. Baffling. The Indians of India, down at the bottom in spite of their "Indo-European" language. The Muslims felt closer to Jews than to Christians, which is why they have never been "anti-Semitic". Nowadays, it is taboo to mention that the Israelis (and hence the Jews) were placed way down the list of course, with the Arabs in a miserable position. Right at the very bottom, needless to say, as nearly always, the Negroes (as they were called at the time); no doubt because their status had been synonymous with that of a slave, an animal that speaks.

The hierarchy in these classifications was in line with the colonial conquests for which Black people (Africans) were the prime victims. Where it was possible, such as in South Africa, they were subjected to a particularly savage and humiliating regime of discrimination. Apartheid was not invented by the Boers, who were content with driving the Blacks off conquered land, but by the British Governor of the South African Union, a cultivated admirer of Plato's praise of slavery. The new "Boer" state did of course inherit and apply the system on a large scale. This was no aberration, no remnant from the past, but a truly efficient system for the functioning of capitalism. The dominant media would have us believe that the ideology of the "liberals" was anti-apartheid. No. Apartheid was able to avail itself of the support of the United States and European countries until its very last gasp. Political apartheid was routed by the battles of the country's Black people, and no one else. Hitler did not come up with anything very new in this area. His crime was to treat other "Whites" in the same way as the "races" categorised as "Coloured" were.

Césaire very rightly calls attention to the fact that what the Nazis were criticised for was that they extended to "Whites" a treatment that had hereto been confined to others. An anecdote: I was watching the British film *Bridge on the River Kwai* again and I jumped when the British officer complained to his Japanese jailer that "they treat us like Indians!".

To understand where this ferocity originates, look at the logic of capital: accumulate and accumulate, regardless of the price (in human terms). Capitalism is a system, indeed the first system that is founded on the principle whereby "wealth is source of power". The love of money – to which utter devotion is owed because it is vital for the system to reproduce itself – "drives you to crime". A crime hardly perceptible to the "stay-at-homes" who, although they might not join the ranks of the ferocious combat squads, keep quiet about the crimes perpetrated because they derive some tiny material benefit from the situation. And they know it. Individual crimes of all sorts committed by those that wield power: swindling, abuses (sexual) against employees, etc. But also crimes against humanity ordered and carried out by politicians in positions of command, both past and present. These men (and a few women) know what they are doing and the consequences of their decisions: they protect high finance and nothing else.

This is why, in spite of the "liberal" discourse, which indiscriminately sings the praises of modern times, ferocity is still on the daily agenda and ever more menacing. The revived popularity of fascism in Europe bodes of nothing that can justify optimism in this respect.

But at the same time, one should be aware that people under domination do not always respond with intelligible, noble resistance to the ferocity of the instruments for their oppression that they are confronted with.

There are innumerable examples of this type of sorry reactions, in particular in Latin America, precisely because this huge region of the South was shaped by capitalist colonisation earlier than the others. As a result, the entire continent of the Americas, from Alaska to Tierra del Fuego, is still today marked by a particular brand of barbarian violence, as illustrated by the example of the planned assassination of street children in Brazil.

We all know the criminal and stupid descent into organised massacres between peoples in the peripheries, such as Yugoslavia and many countries in the Middle East, Africa and South East Asia. These ferocious massacres were sometimes visibly ordered by the leaders of the world ("Western" or more precisely by those empowered to take political decisions in the major imperialist countries), or else sneakily or openly supported by the latter. For what reason? These absurd "conflicts" serve the cause: perpetuating the domination, not of the "West", but of financial capital. An analysis of the reasons and mechanisms behind this ferocity is necessary, but it should not be used as an alibi to excuse it. It must become a means for mobilising peoples to end it.

While Uribe's work deals with ferocity from 1492 onwards, I believe it is useful to dwell a little on ferocity preceding capitalist modernity because ferocity, alas, is as old as the world. It is important to know the reasons that foster it and hence the mechanisms through which it operates, so as to be able to better fight it.

Ancient violence was rooted in the battle for power, not money. With capitalism, money became a source of power. Previously, power was the source of wealth. There are innumerable examples of barbarian ferocity perpetrated by conquerors in the past: the hundreds of thousands of human heads cut off under the orders of Timur, for instance. These misdeeds were committed no less by Blacks, Asians, or people of other colours than they were by Whites. And generally the victims belonged to their own "racial group" (assuming this term is in any way meaningful), quite simply because the means at the time did not permit military expeditions to be carried out at the fringes of the planet.

The difference between the ferocity motivated by the battles for power of the Ancients and the ferocity motivated by modern accumulation of capital arises from the means available to the societies concerned. There is unfortunately no comparison between the means the Ancients had and the weapons of mass destruction of modern times. This is why those who have responsibility for the decisions to make use of these means are today the most colossal perpetrators of crimes against humanity ever to have existed, with the presidents of the United States in the lead.

How can this inclination for crime be explained? By the genes specific to the peoples associated with perpetrating them? By those of the individuals that give the orders for their perpetration? Certainly not. So what then? To the carnality inherent to the human race as a whole, as some anthropologists suggest? I am not qualified to settle this question. I would conclude simply by saying that this inclination, assuming it exists, must be fought and to do so requires questioning the modus operandi of the dual rationales of capital and power. A utopian struggle for the reconstruction of mankind and of society? Maybe… but a creative utopia, the only one that is worth devoting all one's strength, both ideological and political, too.

Foreword to the French Edition

Gorée

Louis Sala-Molins

Anchored to the deep sea, spreading crescent-shaped over the blue ocean very close to the sands of Dakar, the narrow strip of Gorée also testifies forever to absolute horror.

The fort, the village, the slave house. The African continent a few metres eastward. The island vertical to the noontide light. At sundown, the immensity of the sea. Every day, from the pale glimmer of dawn to the blazing sunset, the sun of Gorée journeys from the Senegalese plains to the pier, and from the pier westward to the end of where the sun sets, tracing the route that hundreds of thousands, millions and millions of men, women and children for centuries were forced to take to satisfy the rapacious greed of the European nations of Christianity, the White American nations of Christianity.

Gorée and the extreme stupor of the captives who ended up there, their necks in the grip of yokes, their ankles chained. Gorée, the attempts to break free foiled by swords or by gunpowder. Gorée, under the blistering sun, the smell of burnt flesh as branding begins. Gorée, the solemn Introit for the grand liturgy of the whip whose last crack kills right here, or else during the crossing, or over there, in Saint-Domingue. Gorée, two hot coals on each face, all those eyes widened in terror.

Gorée, and then suddenly like a thunderbolt, the instant shift from being human to being animals. Gorée, the smothering of lives by the wrenching of hearts. No more husbands or wives, no more brothers or sisters, no more children. No more names. Just "pieces" and "bits of ebony," and "bucks" or "niglets." Gorée, Black people turned to livestock: measured, felt, weighed, estimated, palpated, frisked, branded.

What they took on board in Gorée were not men, women and children. In Gorée, what the Christian White nations loaded was livestock. And the innocently functional cattle ships inflicted unspeakable torture on their cargo. Relentlessly, without respite, throughout the entire, interminable crossing.

Beneath that route, the dark abysses of the seabed are guarded, as Édouard Glissant recalls, by a procession of standing corpses that swing to the rhythm of the currents from the African coasts to those of the West Indies and the Americas. From Gorée to Saint-Domingue, Christian White nations turned the abyssal line into a Dantean necropolis. The men and women whose rebellion at sea designated them as the targets of the slave drivers' rifles. The men and women who, to cast off their irons, chose to end their lives. The men and women whose bodies were slowly but surely destroyed by the criminal rigours of deportation. The men and women, who by the shipload, at one time towards the end, had to be disposed of when the trade was outlawed, once Christian Europe was well established in Asia and in the hinterland of the southern continent. Standing blind, all those corpses of children of Africa mount guard along this linear necropolis. From Gorée to Saint-Domingue. From Africa to the Americas. The "losses," those thrown overboard: some fifteen per cent of the deportees. How many is that for a good fifteen million overall? The gruesome count is easy: two million and a quarter. Next to nothing: more or less the population of inner Paris in the year 2000.

Gorée is just one barracoon among others along the western African coast. Saint-Domingue is just one destination among others on and off the coasts of the West Indies and the American continent. And there were other piers in eastern Africa where the same livestock was herded, celebrating for the Mascarene islands the same liturgy for the same lust for money.

Rationalising the wholesale dehumanisation of an entire continent, a feat so successfully accomplished through knowledge and faith, degrading all Blacks to the status of animal by mere reason of being black, lays the foundation for making it lawful to enslave any Black because of his blackness and for reducing the relationship between the slaver and the Black, the colonist and the Black, the colonists' and slavers' princes and the Black, the colonists' and the slavers' priests and the Black, the White peoples of the colonists and of the slavers together with their priests and their princes and the Black, to that of an owner towards his property. Naturally, the law spelt out that will to power, which as usual brought to heel both belief and science.

Under the fiery sun, Gorée tells that story. Gorée screams out that story like so many other African piers. Saint-Domingue in chains, with maroons toiling to grow sugar cane, rising up, rebelling, failing, illuminating the few pages of the book of every Black's life with a thousand deaths and ten thousand acts of torture, every day crushed, at last triumphant, only to be immediately subjugated, tells of all of this. Saint-Domingue roars it out. Go to Port-au-Prince. Stand facing the bronze sculpture depicting the Maroon with the conch shell. Be White: a good citizen from a good Christian nation, say France. You do not waver. Tears do not wash down your face. You are not engulfed by rage or by shame. Are you a monster? Not even that. What is, who is a Maroon? And why is he blowing into the shell? Since when have there been Maroons and conchae in the "Handbook of the Duty of Remembrance" for Whites?

Gorée. We arrived there as a group. About twenty of us. All of us – of all colours – had stayed up many evenings poring over the many aspects of the history of the slave trade. We were all of us accustomed to daily discussions about the manifold ways – and a single one – in which the nations of Christianity supervised absolute horror on the flesh of Blacks. We all knew everything there is to know about it, nothing could possibly surprise us. The place locked us into silence and slashed our hearts. We dispersed, looking for a corner where we could quietly weep. Each of us terrified that by catching sight of another, or uttering a syllable, we might disturb the other's huge sorrow. Gorée bellows out the ghastly infinitude of a catastrophe of exemplary banality, the episodes of which are counted in centuries and the victims by millions and millions.

No longer are there any slaves in Gorée today. No longer can you smell charred flesh. No longer can you hear moans or twitching. The heavy silence of meditation is made heavier with time by a half-smothered sob or suddenly broken by a visitor whose chafed soul cannot repress a lament.

But how about the victims: were they dozens or hundreds of millions? Starting from the beginning to the end of the genocide of slavery and the trade, or else from well before then until this morning?

If the language of the technicians of history was appropriate to the shocking account that I am so bold to preface, I would say that Rosa Amelia Plumelle-Uribe, Colombian-born and black-skinned, is set in the very long term. And if I wanted to play the clever little game of literary erudition,

I would add that this woman, to hammer out her message, has chosen to combine the reading convenience of diachrony with the rhetorical tools of synchrony. More simply, "From 1492 to the modern day," Plumelle-Uribe casts light on every circle of her descent into the hell of anti-Black racism with the dismal glint of the previous and following circles. She wants us to understand fully the ideological, profit-motivated perfection of the uninterrupted spiral of horror and easily grasp the reduction of the crime of crimes – the dehumanisation of others – to a matter of tending quietly to day-to-day business. And where was this quietness? In Gorée? In the whole of Black Africa. In Europe. In America. Over there, in Barbados? No. All around the Mediterranean, from Spain to Israel, from France to the four corners of the Sahara.

More clearly still, Plumelle-Uribe does not begin her account the day when the sons of Jacob decided that a lucrative transaction was to be preferred to fratricide and sold their brother Joseph as a slave to a caravan. Nor, further back in time, to the day when Yahweh, using Noah as his mouthpiece, enslaved Canaan, who was blackened and dehumanised by Jewish, and then Christian, posterity. Nor, in somewhat more recent times, to the day when Plato and Aristotle proclaimed in unison that slaves were "calves." All this happened way before the birth of baby Jesus who, as everyone knows, came along and turned everything upside down. The author mentions in one sentence only the genocidal torrents of the trans-Saharan slave trade of the Arabo-Islamic brand. Plumelle-Uribe begins her account the day the world perceived by Christianity extended westwards. The day when the indigenous peoples, who were living on their land and who came from nowhere that had any value for the science and faith of the time, were sent back into nothingness by those who know and believe. The day when, once that annihilation had been completed, the trade in Blacks, from the African coasts to the Iberian Peninsula and Europe, rolled out westwards, took hold of the ocean and swelled to the gigantic proportions we know of. Whether the Black slaves were taken from their places of servitude in Spain and transported to the West Indies by Christopher Columbus on his second voyage or whether it was not until 1502 that experiments began over there to see if they bore up better than the indigenous peoples to the infernal pace of the work in the mines does not matter. Without overstepping the boundaries of her account further back in time, the author establishes an inescapable truth: when the conceptual broth of knowledge and faith coagulates into an image of a divided world (us, and all the others) or of a hierarchy of races (from the most perfect to quasi-monkeys) and when laws and customs give a free rein to the "race of masters," inevitably subjugation, banishment from humanity of those others comes about through the sheer momentum of the initial repulse. It takes on dramatic effect by unleashing imagination that goes to any length to make sure that contempt is not just useful for conducting daily business and deadly in the longer term, but refined through constant debasement, by brutal separations, by specially designed torture and punishments. With one and only one imperative: immediate benefit for the "race of masters," and in the last instance only, the outright annihilation of "sub-humans," once the anticipated ideological, political and economic benefits have been reaped. Not only must the "masters" subjugate and enslave, they must also debase for as long as they derive benefit and in the end annihilate what are no longer people, not even animals, just things.

Having established this, as noted above, and reiterated it each time we descend into the next circle of this agonising spiral, should the investigation not have ended in 1945, without bringing it laboriously all the way to the present day? After all, we all know that in secular but nonetheless Christian Republican France, the civilised Christian nations launched a dynamic movement in Nuremberg with definitive effects that led to the unchallengeable condemnation of anti-Semitism, racism, eugenics and consequently anti-Black phobia.

Yes, that would be the right place to stop if we considered Auschwitz to be such a monstrous aberration in the history of humankind, this radical question need to be asked: "Is thought still possible after Auschwitz?" We know what the answer is. We were thinking before; we will be thinking afterwards. And even though Heidegger thought, while it was going on, Auschwitz is unthinkable. And nothing that thought has produced, nothing that this combined mass of science and belief has produced to inspire the powers that be can be compared to it. Never before had man been to this extent dehumanised, reduced to sub-human status, objectified, annihilated. Humanity learns this at Nuremberg, assimilates it after Nuremberg, and willy-nilly erases forever from its references the concept of "race" and at the same time definitively condemns eugenics. Never again!

But never again what?

"Yes, it would be worthwhile to study, clinically, in detail, the approaches used by Hitler and Nazism, to reveal to the highly distinguished, highly humanist, highly Christian bourgeois of the twentieth century that in him *dwells*, unbeknown to him, a Hitler; that Hitler inhabits him, that Hitler is his *demon*, and if he rails against him, there is no logic to it, for fundamentally, what he reproaches Hitler for is not the *crime* in itself, *the crime against humanity*, it is not *the humiliation of humanity itself*, it is the crime against the White man, and the fact that Hitler applied colonialist processes to Europe, to which only the Arabs of Algeria, the 'coolies' of India and the 'Negroes' of Africa had thus far been subjected." This is what Aimé Césaire said in 1955. In the spirit of his *Discourse on Colonialism*, of which Plumelle-Uribe's entire book is an unbearable illustration, what is never again to be is the transposition to Europe and within the White world of this division of the world, this hierarchy of races the inevitable effects of which have just been recalled. Never again this, the unbelievable suffering inflicted upon Jews and other White groups of *untermenschen* guilty of being born, admittedly into the White world, but outside the circle of the "race of masters" which, this time, does not include all Whites as previously, but only Aryans. Was this suffering inflicted on a whim? No. Ultimately, it was required by the conclusion derived from a litany of syllogisms which form a logical chain but which could have been deduced from the first proposition universally accepted – at least in the White world – throughout the long decades of triumphant racism and eugenics that extended from the nineteenth to the twentieth century. This proposition is that it was the task of the superior race to control and civilise the others, it was its task to ensure that its necessary pre-eminence be maintained, and again and finally, it was the duty of that race to use any means to preserve its biological and cultural integrity.

In other words, wasn't this turn-of-the-century tenet the very same one which, under the flags of first Christianity and the Spanish Empire, and then Europe, produced the ideological legitimation of the American disasters that were inaugurated in the late fifteenth century, and laid the foundation for the identity of a "race of masters" over there and all the way up to and including the twentieth century? How else was segregation over there, legitimised before and after 1945? And, in South Africa, what was the underpinning for the primarily racist policy that culminated in the political, cultural and biological barbarity of apartheid? What sort of catechism did the very Catholic King of the Belgians hear, what were his scientific references as he mixed the mortar of his Congolese empire in a lake of blood? What was the price for the dismembering of Africa in the nineteenth and twentieth centuries by Christian White people? What were the educational and political objectives of Republican France – the birthplace of human rights, etc. – when it exhibited animals alongside "savages" at its Colonial Exhibition; when it sent Black people to the

1914–18 mass graves; when it "recruited" them in 1940 and hid them away during the homages and victory parades; and, when, after they had been brought back home, they were generously peppered with machine-gun fire in Thiaroye, Senegal?

Using a variety of means depending on the epoch, concocting a range of casuistry – the simple schematic of dichotomy (us, and them), or the more convoluted ranking of races governed by the contradictory effects of "perfectibility" and "degeneration" (our dear Buffon, our cherished Enlightenment) – the white kingdom was globalised and the need to enslave, humiliate and sacrifice negritude was made to seem self-evident. (Yes, I know. Anyone can easily line up some wonderful writings coming from such and such a man from such and such a predatory nation, censuring the polices of enslavement, death and annihilation. Righteous people come from all over the place. While admirable writings make for admirable anthologies, purposeful policy makes for tragedies, and ideological popularisation for catastrophes and genocides.)

This trickery of the dichotomy and hierarchical ranking at the heart of what until then – and in spite of the anti-Judaism tradition – was a homogeneously white kingdom. That and the necessary effects, in the heart of the white kingdom, that dichotomy and racial hierarchy had produced before, then and after, on negritude. One fundamental difference did exist however. Everywhere laws publicly stated, without anyone being bothered, that the duty of the Black man is to serve and to die. Practices of annihilation of non-Aryans were secret; whether or not this was a well-kept secret is not the issue here.

Plumelle-Uribe forces her readers to admit what they so ardently wish to forever ignore: while, for some, Nuremberg was definitive, for others it was just a mundane episode with no major implications. The "never again" so solemnly proclaimed up by the victors' tribunal is illuminated by nauseous compromises that allowed humiliation, enslavement, killing and lynching to continue in full legal probity, all while the tribunal was celebrating law. Terse and clear was this "never again" for some and that was justice; for others, it was "more and more of the same, as it was before, now and ever shall be as needed" and that was the very paradigm of injustice. Follow, for instance, the "jurisprudential" pathway taken by Judge Gros, who in Nuremberg first and then again at the United Nations expressed the voice of France. Nuremberg tinkered about so that Auschwitz and its contiguous archipelago could be condemned, but Gorée and its gulag were not dismantled? No connection? A hideous comparison of the incomparable?

I come to what is most unbearable in Plumelle-Uribe's narrative: the uncovering of everyday racism and its viscous trace in the American administration of justice where the ideological drive of Nuremberg has altered nothing, demonstrating more than any subtle or abrupt argumentation, that the Whites in the United States, one of the powers that defeated the Third Reich, are by no means willing today to recognise their fellow Black countrymen as full-fledged human beings. Everyone thinks he knows it all. The rigorous description of the concatenation of reasons and facts, the calm assertion of the historical connection between popular support for the lynching of Blacks because they were black right until the day before yesterday and the parodies of justice in which Blacks are the actors today, the consciously repetitive manner used by Plumelle-Uribe to lead her readers into the heart of the labyrinth, back there where the Black man is up against the Minotaur – most readers will realize that they knew far less than they thought. Beyond Nuremberg, the genocidal absurdity of Gorée undergoes a cruel metamorphosis in the American courtrooms. I am enslaving you because you are Black is what one used to hear in Gorée. I am convicting you because you are Black is what is said today in the name of the American people. And here again, Plumelle-Uribe has no need to belabour either the texts or the sources to throw into the face of the reader for the umpteenth time the uniformity, over the centuries, of the previously described ideological substrate that legitimates the murderous effects of the eviction of Blacks from the human race or, its political equivalent, i.e. their banishment to the lowest possible level, down and out.

We would here reach the heights of the scandal were we to content ourselves with comparing the passion for justice displayed by the American judges at Nuremberg who alongside their Allies condemned the Nazi genocides with the solidly instrumentalised carelessness of the racist dislike exhibited by American judges at home. But after all, by virtue of what supreme virtue might one day demand that the virtuous of one day should forever remain the model for all virtue? As our classical doctrine would have it, justice does not issue forth from the principle of the law: justice is virtue.

And so precisely: if the fluttering lightness of virtue is suitable for dealing with the memory of Gorée, an island among so many others in that tricontinental, multi-centennial immensity of organised crime constituted by the most ruthless utilitarian genocide, then how can one expect that a fraction of an ancient people restructured in the form of a State after Auschwitz would treat winged justice with the heaviness of law? Everything should have induced Israel, a prime witness of racist cruelty, to rear up at the front line of the fight against the South African Neo-Nazi regime. Everyone remembers the connivance of the Westerners with this murderous regime. Everyone remembers that fanatical supporters of Hitler democratically took power there and equipped racism with all the legal, political, economic, military and biological finery we know about. There were many combatants: one name – Mandela – is enough to evoke the stubborn example of a struggle that so many hoped would end in triumph. But how promptly did we forget the scandalous, unspeakable constancy of Israel teaming with the others, then Israel shouting louder than the others and finally Israel alone against the others in supporting the loathsome regime of apartheid! Whether it was left-handed, right-handed or ambidextrous, the Israeli government, legitimatising itself daily by calling on its often tragic history and the genocide of its people, claiming to be the sole heir to the consequences of that genocide, was an accomplice to this crime against humanity whose victims still filled the air with their shrieks less than twenty years ago. This scandal lasted from the time Israel emerged in history, with smoke still rising from the ashes of Auschwitz, until the passage (read "Resurrection") of Mandela from prison to power.

This realpolitik subordinated justice to the interests of a state legitimised by its chosen ideology. This policy glorified or at the very least accepted the repulsive cohabitation between Israel and South African neo-Nazism. Dare to say it, in a single stroke you excuse each and every one of the major crimes in history. I repeat *each* and *every* one of them. So you no longer dare... I can only wish that this momentary confusion and hesitation brings tears to your eyes and causes you to weep for Gorée as you do for Auschwitz.

One day, President Mandela went to Senegal. This man of extraordinary stature whose courage the South African jails never managed to break, went to Gorée on a pilgrimage: there he broke down and sobbed.

Gorée. Spare us the arguments about the precise location of the barracoons on the island. Spare us the transformation of this site into a banal place under the pretext that some Blacks helped the Whites to shackle other Blacks more effectively and put them in irons. Whites were the torturers, Whites were the beaters, and Whites were the victims of the Nazi genocides. Don't argue with a sly smile that in Saint-Domingue and elsewhere, there was a whip wielded by Blacks between the colonists and the plantation slaves.

In Auschwitz and elsewhere, the escort parties all the way to the doors of the gas chambers were White; the musicians that accompanied those being escorted for their last few steps were White, and they knew that they too would soon be under escort. Just as the flagellating kapo of Saint-Domingue was, when the time was ripe, sliced to the bone and hung up by a rib. The intentional vilification of the victims of any penitentiary, forced labour or genocidal system was not something invented by Hitler in Germany, nor by the King of the Belgians in the Congo. To set oneself apart from the victims, get closer to the tormentors – this was a gamble on a chance of survival. Has anyone ever had the effrontery to criticise the victims of the Nazi genocides in this way? Conversely, has anyone ever refrained from criticising, for the very same reasons, the prey of the multifarious Black hunt that spanned several centuries?

Am I mixing everything up? Being White myself, am I prohibited from understanding the black prose of Plumelle-Uribe? Who can prevent me from reading Césaire, from listening to Fanon, from pondering over Malcolm X? Or is it that the racist dogma is so far gone today that I should be forced to join arms with the powerful of the same colour as when in the more remote past, in the recent past and now as well as earlier, they planned the subjugation of all by the vilification of the many? White, I speak about Whites and Blacks. And if to do so I needed a *nihil obstat*, I would not expect to get it from Hotzenplots, the robber with the seven knives, since each syllable of Césaire, each word of Fanon, each sentence of Martin Luther King gives it to me. Did I not recall above the black words of Césaire condemning with marmoreal coldness the perpetual schism between Whites and the others, that heritage of white ferocity that it would be pointless to deny?

No one, on the left (and who cares about the right) could find the slightest bone to pick with Plumelle-Uribe for what she has the courage to write except at the cost of misrepresenting her words or pretending not to feel the irony, the sarcasm and the understatements wherever they appear. Her work will be stricken down – in a manner also frequent in literary circles that lean left (and who cares about the right?) – by those who glancing through it will form their opinions on the basis of the table of contents, and those who spending just a little more time, but not much, will in one fell swoop disallow that this Black woman speaking about Black people has the distance allowed to anyone speaking about the history of the calamities that happened where he or she comes from. To be sure, there will be the inevitable: "Blacks exaggerate", "Blacks don't understand their own history." Because anti-Black racism, in the form of contempt, is almost unimaginably insidious and pervasive and – too bad for the paralogism – unbelievably innocent. Here is an example.

Lately, I was reading *O Vous, Frères Humains* by Albert Cohen [translated as *O Humans, My Brothers*] and shivered with him as he remembered his tenth birthday when he ran to hide his shame and despair for having been pointed at and mocked as a Jewish child by a fine trader from his good city of Marseille. "Is it a sin to be born?", wonders the little boy. The same Albert weeps his eyes out feeling "condemned, set apart, guilty, criminal, incomprehensibly criminal, and irrevocably criminal for having been born." He dries his nose and eyes on his sleeve, he replays the scene in his mind: the throaty laugh of the customers in the shop who had heard the mocking and seen him scuttle through the door imperiously pointed at by the shopkeeper: "Oh, they were happy those bad men. Oh they were bad, those happy men." Put a small Black boy in the place of little Albert. Or else... Between two radio newsflashes reporting the tragic situation in Palestine (this was October 18, 2000), I was reading *Churchill d'Angleterre* written by the same Albert Cohen, a generous soul if there ever were one, describing everyday life in London in June 1940, with its quiet streets in spite of Hitler's furious air strikes : Well no, it doesn't work – here the peddler's 'yid' and Cohen's 'nigger' are not interchangeable. And it's not Cohen's fault. Just that, like everyone else, he does not apparently know where, at which syllable, the language of contempt for Black people begins. While Auschwitz will always conveniently keep you on your toes so that you don't slip, Gorée is useless to you. One last piece of evidence?

In her agonising descent into the hell of anti-Black racism, Plumelle-Uribe says very little about France. In France, Gorée means something. The same applies to Saint-Domingue. And the Island of Réunion, and the Antilles. It has meant something (or should mean something) since 1999 and 2000, when first at the National Assembly, then at the Senate, and once again at the National Assembly, the members of parliament, White and Black members of parliament of the "land of human rights" unanimously voted in favour of a law that characterises the combination of slavery and trade as a "crime against humanity." Christiane Taubira, a Black woman and member of parliament for French Guyana, was the initiator of this law named after her. But there is a big difference between the calm protest in the wording she proposed to the Laws Commission and the left-wing government and the grandiloquent text which was subsequently approved. To be precise: the wording proposed by Taubira demanded condemnation, remembrance, justice and reparation. Indoctrinated by the government, the left-wing and the Laws Commission translated this into: condemnation, education and repentance. And so, at zero risk, everybody, Black or White, left or right, unanimously voted in favour of a law whose insignificance is to the Code what the gentlest of the Atlantic waves is to the pier of Gorée or the wharves of Saint-Domingue. So, on set dates, France will symbolically sniffle and cope with her immense debt towards the descendants of those she deported from Africa and dispatched through all the harbours along the coasts of the continent, Gorée in Senegal included.

I indignantly asked about the fiasco masquerading as a triumph of this draft bill to someone who was deeply involved in the initial drafting and the chaotic reception it was given by the government and the Laws Commission. The answer I got was this: "I tend to believe more and more that in April 1998, not a single member of the French government was willing to recognise that the slave trade and slavery were a crime against humanity, even after the journalists had asked their questions; and officials' minds were content with singing the praises of abolition and merely remembering Schoelcher's heroic deed, thus hushing up the centuries of abominable oppression that preceded it."

Eternal glory unto the French lawmaker, so true to its prestigious history. A teardrop in France is worth at least a flood of tears in any other land. One teardrop, just one. What if it were true that, after Gorée, thought could continue unperturbed just as it did while Gorée was happening? Rosa Amelia Plumelle-Uribe is convinced that the answer is no.

Preface

The French edition of *La férocité Blanche. Des non-Blancs aux non-Aryens: génocides ocultés de 1492 à nos jours* was published in 2001. A German translation came out a few years later. In the interval, several European readers let me understand that they had felt a certain unease during and after their reading of this book. Some said they had been shocked at the idea that I had actually written that "the Nazi atrocities committed in Europe against European victims during the Second World War were an integral part of an old Western tradition of enslavement and dehumanisation of other, non-European peoples." Yet to this day, none of these readers has, to my knowledge, challenged the accuracy of the facts upon which I founded my main argument. Neither has anyone denied the cogency of my reasoning.

At the time I finished my book, I had no idea that during the first half of the nineteenth century, long before German scholars entered the business of rationalising colonial domination, certain British, French and North American scholars had been at work on a common project: finding scientific justifications for the extermination of so-called inferior or backward peoples defined as obstacles to the progress of civilisation. No wonder. Even now, surprisingly little is known about this sinister phase in the history of the international scholarly establishment.

The item that brought it to my attention was the outstanding work of the Swedish writer Sven Lindqvist on the genesis of the European genocide. Whether one agrees or disagrees with the author's conclusions, his book has the incontrovertible merit of giving the discerning reader a set of particularly valuable bibliographical references. These include publishing data on books cited, conference proceedings, and minutes of seminars, round table conferences and debates where scholars of the 1860s, putting their heads together in all serenity, coolly contemplated the extinction of inferior races that happened to be living on lands necessary to empty to facilitate the advance of civilisation.

Following the publication of the German edition of my book, I was invited to give a series of lectures in Germany. Of my numerous encounters there, I remember one in particular, with a man whose behaviour had me thinking a great deal about the power of cultural alienation induced by the ingestion of commonplace prejudices. I had agreed to a private meeting with this man. It was clear that he had read, reread, underlined and annotated his copy of the German edition of *La férocité blanche*. He scolded me roundly for imputing utilitarian motives to the Nazi policy of extermination, "as if the crimes committed by the Third Reich could be placed in the same category as other crimes constituting the common narrative of history." I protested that I had nowhere in my book overlooked the Nazis' ideological motivations, and that the data supporting my identification of utilitarian motives were verifiable historical facts, not figments of my imagination.

Using the historical approach of the German researcher Gotz Aly, whose work I had recently read in French, I listed a number of social reforms promulgated by the Nazi government, which Aly had examined and analysed in one of his books. The book states that on account of these reforms, "Hitler was able to enlarge his support base well beyond the circle of his immediate followers and his direct electoral constituency."

The purpose of these reforms was to raise the living standards of the Aryan population. They were funded with money confiscated from Jews under an anti-Semitic program referred to as Economic Aryanisation. If, as the book notes, "some 95% of Germans, along with Austrians, benefited from this Aryanisation," it would be absurd, to say the least, to claim that anti-Semitism was the exclusive motive that drove Germans to support the Nazi government. In conclusion, I added that I did not see how, in bringing these facts to the notice of readers, I could be said to be cheapening the memory of atrocities committed by the Nazis, or to be making them more palatable.

The man's only answer was to lecture me on the horror of Nazism and the use of science and modernity in the service of a criminal enterprise. Perorating, he asked me if I really was not aware that all the arguments in my book could be used by ill-intentioned persons to gloss over the Nazi horror.

His question caught me short. It took me back to a painful episode, seventeen years in my past. In France in the late 1980s, during the bicentenary of the French Revolution, I had met a history professor who seemed receptive to the idea of a study of slavery in general, and of the Atlantic slave trade in particular, following a less Manichean approach than usual. At the appropriate juncture, I gave him a status report on my research, focused on the dehumanising assault on Blacks in the concentration-camp environment of America. My outline indicated the similarity of this earlier experience to the dehumanising Nazi programme during the Second World War, apart from the detail that it lasted several centuries.

I knew my research was breaking new ground. Since this professor had expressed an interest in the subject, I awaited his comments with a measure of nervous apprehension. When he asked me whether I had considered the possibility that this kind of research might be "inopportune," I thought I had misheard him. He must also have sensed that I had not really got the full meaning of his question. So this good history professor, whose decency I had never doubted, undertook to explain to me, in an atmosphere now charged with tension, that this type of argument could be used by persons with ulterior motives to challenge the singular status of Nazi atrocities….

My work, in 2006 as in the late 1980s, has been aimed at gaining recognition for the fact that the slave trade, the oppression of Blacks and the barbarous experience of colonialism, all constituted crimes against humanity. It seems, though, that for the opinion makers of our time, however painstaking my scholarship, however accurate the historical information adduced in my analysis, and however cogent my argument, all of it counts for much less than certain received notions concerning a "crime impossible to explain."

Still, I note that among the victims of white supremacy, thanks to the advancement of knowledge, increasing numbers are beginning to challenge supposedly eternal truths that, on examination, turn out to be nothing grander than common prejudices.

At the end of the Second World War, the victorious colonial powers decreed that the Nazi horror was incomprehensible, because behind its atrocities there was no rational economic motive. Since utilitarian considerations have always been invoked to rationalise dehumanising assaults on non-European peoples, it was absolutely necessary to strip the Nazi enterprise of any possible utilitarian motive. Hence the reductionist approach that isolates Nazism from the common stream of human history, the better to focus attention exclusively on atrocities committed by the Nazis, while overlooking other factors without which this terrible disaster would never have taken on the enormous proportions it did.

This mystification of Nazism has worked for a considerable time now. But with the passage of time, as more and more historical data get uncovered, fresh information confirms the proven insight: that the Nazi assault on humanity was no singularity. It was part of an uninterrupted flow of historical atrocities which included the slave trade, with the barbarism of the colonial period serving as a link in the chain of continuity.

A Word of Thanks

I would like readers of this English edition to know that it was made possible only by the tenacious determination of Dr Dialo Diop, supported by Virginia Popper, whose skill and patience have been exemplary. I hereby express my deep friendship and gratitude to them.

Acknowledgements

I grew up in a society where inequalities in all fields of life including death were such that they caused and continue to cause consequences so terrifying that even those who believed they had escaped destitution had very little opportunity to enjoy their material comforts without losing some of their humanity. The slightest human feeling was enough to trigger conflict with a system that was controlled by just a few families whose wealth was comparable to that of the largest fortunes of the West. This system was determined to maintain the status quo and as such willing to criminalise any sort of social demand.

In this context, in the 1960s and 1970s, many people in the countries of America and elsewhere in Africa and the Asian continent, including teenagers, became aware of what economic alienation meant. They became committed alongside the most disadvantaged. I must pay a tribute to my mother because, while she did not share all of my choices, she always supported me even when, against her will, she paid the consequences of my activism.

What I want to underline is that, in spite of the fact I gained awareness at a fairly early stage of economic alienation and of social inequalities, I nonetheless reached adulthood without realising what racial alienation meant.

I owe Amir Smith, Vicente Murrain and Amilkar Ayala in Bogotá in 1977 my discovery of Aimé Césaire's *Discourse on Colonialism*, Frantz Fanon's books, Malcolm X's autobiography and *Tambours del destino*, Peter Bourne's work on the Haitian revolution. It was not until then that I became aware of our particular position in the history of humanity. A position, as remarked by Césaire, that goes back to a time when millions and millions of women, men and children, were driven from their homes, chained up like animals, and compelled to cross the Atlantic and be stripped even of their human dignity under the skies of America.

I would like to thank Jovina Teodoro for introducing me to the deeply moving book *O genocidio do negro brasileiro* by Abdias Do Nascimento.

At that time, thanks to a United Nations international awareness-raising campaign, under the combined pressure of African and Eastern European countries, I became informed of the crime against humanity constituted by apartheid, which I had not heard of anywhere, whether in my political circle or elsewhere.

I was lucky in France to be put into contact with Jacqueline Grunfeld, a former French Resistance fighter, anti-apartheid activist who, until she died in 1993, fought against all forms of racism. To this brave and generous woman I owe my ability to discern between Judaism and Zionism.

I also derived great benefit from my encounter with Denise Mendez whose intellectual honesty and strict ethical standards were of great help to me in my endeavours.

When I read *Le Code Noir ou le calvaire de Canaan* by Louis Sala-Molins, I felt the need to meet the author and hug him very warmly on behalf of my people.

I also derived great benefit from my meetings with Régis Doumas who, despite not sharing my beliefs, was able to enter into a debate with me which over the years have become a true dialogue, for which I am extremely grateful to him.

I had the good fortune of meeting Christiane Rémion-Granel who I would like to thank for her perseverance in this struggle for human dignity and who greatly stimulated me.

I want to extend my very special thanks to Frédéric Plumelle, my husband, to whom this work owes a great deal. Without the generous help he gave me for over fifteen years, I would never have conducted the research that was essential to my work. Furthermore, he was also willing to act as my sparring partner to whom I submitted the results of my analyses and thoughts. His always well-founded criticisms and suggestions for wording enormously helped my progression. I am therefore very grateful to him because, thanks to his support, I was able to carry through to the end this contribution I owed to the memory of my people.

I also want to thank our three children, Corinne, Henri and Jean-Gabriel, who in their own way helped me and who often had to suffer the consequences of my unavailability while I was preparing this work.

Introduction

There is a dynamic relationship between the destruction of the indigenous peoples of America, the annihilation of Black people and the policy of extermination introduced in Europe by the Nazis in the first half of the twentieth century.

In parts 1 and 2 of this work, it will become apparent that during the three and a half centuries of mass deportation and enslavement of Africans, one conspicuous feature stood out from the start, then developed and gradually became an element of culture. This was the eviction, the banishment of Blacks from the human family, for which the White race became the gold standard on a planetary scale. To evict a group from the human family is to annihilate it. When a group is banished the victims are seen as belonging to a different species and the process of annihilating them can proceed in a climate of almost utter indifference. Eviction from the human race was a constant feature of the entire African American genocide. But this abomination continued well beyond that genocide because it actually blazed the trail that later led to the annihilation of other human groups, including the victims of the Nazi policy of extermination.

The shift from the exclusion of non-Whites to the exclusion of non-Aryans was a process that spanned several centuries. During that time, a culture of annihilation – the corollary to the genocidal practice – grew and developed.

When the very same practices were introduced into Europe, the European cultural fabric had already integrated a well-structured discourse, supported by a frame of reference and stereotypes, accrediting the idea that inferior beings existed and could be annihilated. The widely accepted hierarchy of races and a sense of belonging to a superior group were part of the collective consciousness of Whites. Their frame of reference had integrated the exclusion of human groups considered to be racially inferior. As such, the Nazis' overt racism and their calls for exclusion could not, as a matter of principle alone, generate hostility or be rejected in Germany or anywhere else in the Western world.

That is why the full thrust of Nazi propaganda centred on the "otherness" of the Jew, portraying him as a different and dangerous being that belonged to an inferior race. Although it was just theory, this discourse was sufficient to prevent first the Germans, and later many of the citizens in the countries occupied by Nazi Germany, from identifying in any way with the Jews who were being persecuted, robbed, imprisoned and deported in an atmosphere of practically complete indifference. After 1945, some authors had the indecency to explain and sometimes justify this indifference under the pretence that no one could possibly imagine and hence know that these Jews – who were first outlawed from society, openly hunted down and stripped not only of their property but also of their dignity by being treated like livestock – would end up, at least those who were able to survive this horrendous ordeal, in gas chambers. This amounts to saying that, with the exception of the gas chambers, all the atrocities inflicted upon the Jews before were acceptable or at least tolerable!

In the third and last part of this work, it will become clear that not all crimes against humanity are apparently equally reprehensible nor do all victims deserve sympathy, far from it. One thing is the crime against European humanity in the setting of Europe itself. Thanks to the military defeat of its perpetrators, this crime was given a legal characterisation and its victims recognised as such. The recognition turned that crime into the supreme crime, the crime of crimes. Another thing is the crime against the other humanity, the crime that took place outside and often far away from Europe. Those who fell prey to this crime lack both the power and the legal standing to be recognised as victims today, i.e., the status wielded by the victims of the Nazi genocides or their descendants.

We must remember a horrifying reality, post-1945, when the Nazi episode came to a close, the same policy was applied elsewhere by former Nazis with the support of the Allied powers, i.e. Germany's former enemies. It is in this way that apartheid, a crime against humanity, became official in 1948 when the former pro-Nazi activists came into power in South Africa. Family squabbles were soon settled and normal racial business was quickly resumed, i.e., the exclusion of non-Whites, the only form of accepted and traditionally applied racial segregation until the Nazi adventure temporarily disturbed the routine.

It is important for the reader to remember that the relations of destruction and subservience established by the Europeans on the American continent were to determine the attitudes and relationships of domination they imposed on all the other non-European peoples for centuries. It is commonly accepted that the desire to gain riches, i.e., the profit motive, took a great leap forward during the conquest of America. There was practically no limit to the power of money since it could be used to acquire honour, nobility, the hallmarks of dignity and respectability, public recognition and much more, all of which were already highly coveted in Western societies in the fifteenth century.

New concepts emerged and developed in pace with the new interests of the conquering countries. For instance, racial hierarchies were established to meet the ideological necessity of rationally, objectively, explaining the annihilation of other, non-White peoples in America, Africa or Asia, in any case in very remote places far, very far from Europe. In this way, while money had the power to elevate a great many causes, undertakings and situations, and to suppress reservations and misgivings, the profit-making motive itself slowly acquired a hitherto inexistent power of legitimation and justification in the mind-set of Western societies. Gradually, horror came to be measured using a hierarchy that mirrored the racial classifications established by Western thinkers and scientists.

Because this yardstick for differentiating crime became an integral part of the European cultural fabric, the response to barbarian deeds was inevitably restrained. Such deeds were assessed not on their face value but through the prism of what motivated their perpetrators.

When later they acquired the status of commentators and judges, how did Europeans see the atrocities they had committed? Well, historians, thinkers and writers defined these deeds as some of the "inevitable" collateral damage in any battle for power and riches. Consequently, those who committed these deeds, the perpetrators of the atrocities inflicted upon the victims of the conquest and of colonisation from the end of the fifteenth century were never, even to the present day, ever referred to as "persecutors." History books were to describe them as "ambitious" men, at worst greedy. Describing them as persecutors, loathsome beasts or monsters is never contemplated.

On the hierarchy of atrocities, a persecutor and an ambitious person are two quite different categories. The monstrosities committed by a persecutor cannot be compared with the "excesses" or "blunders" of an entrepreneur, although their deeds may be very similar in nature. In one case, we are dealing with barbarity that is inherently gratuitous, frightening, and inexplicable which only a monster can perpetrate. In the other, we are dealing with deeds, which, although reprehensible and certainly unfortunate, are nonetheless explicable since their underlying motivation is the pursuit of profit. These are deeds committed by entrepreneurs who are willing to commit any crime and confront any danger as long as they anticipate deriving profit therefrom.

In the meantime, the profit-making motive gained recognition in Western societies. As the hierarchy of atrocities became entrenched and the profit-making motive acquired enormous power of justification and legitimation, Western historians came to describe the slave-trader who peddled human flesh as a man who,

> must combine the qualities of a sailor capable of ensuring the safe passage of a modest schooner over the 7,000 miles that have to be covered to twice cross the Atlantic ocean, with those of a businessman and an ambassador. He had to be clever in choosing trading posts, skilful in his relations with the African kings, firm and patient when bartering with the Black brokers, cautious in transactions with the settlers and, in the event of unfortunate encounters, capable of putting up a fight with a hand gun, a sword, or even his bare fists.[1]

In other words, he was a remarkable man in many respects.

Profit-making was presented as a mitigating circumstance when explaining the destruction of other peoples, and became a powerful form of justification in Western culture. This forced transformation of an ideological explanation into a standard, a truth that professes universality, formed the basis of a misunderstanding, which, in spite of the passing of time, still shapes mentalities and how knowledge is approached and interpreted. This is what perpetuates the ideological domination that enables the heirs of former persecutors to prevaricate and bend the interpretation of history to suit their own needs. So commanding is this domination that even the victims embrace what is often put forward as the only objectively valid interpretation of history.

The difficulty in adopting a more subtle approach is immediately apparent. A young woman to whom I was speaking about the unacknowledged debt that white supremacy owes to deported Africans and their descendants forced into slavery in America replied (without a trace of hostility) that in this area responsibilities were shared because Africans had themselves contributed to hunting down and selling their own brothers. This begs the question of whether she would accept the idea of shared responsibility with Nazi Germany for the outrages committed in occupied France because the collaborators eased matters for the Nazis? She – just as I do – construed the horrendous way in which the Nazi persecutors used their victims to speed up their own destruction as an aggravating circumstance, in contrast to the African victims whose contribution to their own destruction is construed as a circumstance that mitigates the responsibility of Europeans.

Western historians never fail to call attention to the fact that,

> it must be admitted that Africans were in part responsible for their own misfortunes. […]. Trade with the Whites brought wealth and power to Dahomey and the Ashanti community. […] The entire trade (of human flesh) was in the hands of Africans who shrewdly played off the European powers one against the other, even entering into full-fledged treaties with them.[2]

At a round table meeting dealing with "the need to do the work of remembrance," a young man based himself on a first-hand account given by Simone Veil to explain the unforgettable trauma experienced by victims of Nazi barbarity and the necessity of remembrance, part of which is the recognition of their suffering. He read out a poignant passage of this account and we in the audience were deeply moved.

When the contributions came to an end, I called attention to the fact that in spite of the topic of the round table, the various presentations we heard had not once mentioned the destruction of the indigenous peoples of America, nor the massive deportation of Africans and their banishment from the human species as non-Whites. I went back to the passage by Simone Veil which had clearly distressed the participants – a passage I was already familiar with since I had read it in the book *La Concurrence des victimes* by Jean-Michel Chaumont:

> In addition to the awful trauma of the arrival, of the separation from the greater part of the convoy, the children and the older women and the men, we were spared no humiliation – tattooing, heads and body hair shorn, exposed naked for hours on the pretext of disinfection. Humiliation was permanent: clothed in rags, starved, exhausted by lack of sleep and gruelling hard labour, we felt we were losing our identity, that we were becoming sub-human.[3]"

The question I asked was: had anyone ever even once realised that for three and a half centuries in the concentration camp universe of America this indeed dehumanising treatment was inflicted on a specifically targeted racial group, on millions of women, men and children merely because of their racial status. These people's crime was that they were not White, that they were non-Whites. Had any consideration been given to the trauma of these millions of men, women and children that were legally stripped, because they were black, of any human dignity and positively nailed into a state of sub-humanity that white supremacy perpetuated from one generation to the next through the centuries. I added that it was high time, at least in places of remembrance, to restore their humanity to the victims of white supremacy, for Nazi barbarity cannot be effectively condemned unless the barbarity against non-Whites that preceded and laid the foundations for it is itself formally and explicitly condemned.

Once more, I found myself in the minority. One of the speakers took the floor and, with the fine assurance of the righteous, explained to us composedly and impassively that there should be no mixing of apples and pears and one should only compare what is comparable. He took his time in explaining to us that the purpose of the trafficking of Black people was not to kill the victims but to create monetary gain, the economic profit that derived from it, whereas the Nazis actually wanted the death and total destruction of their victims. He warned against the danger of playing down the Nazi atrocities, adding that one crime cannot justify another.

We had come round full circle and I was disappointed by this refrain I hear every time I attempt to explain to Western listeners that the Nazi barbarity was a European variation – an extension of another barbarity. To those Western humanists, even with the best intentions, who cannot live without the hierarchy of horror that satisfies the needs of white supremacy, I would like to say this:

> Stop considering a small part of this Earth as being the whole of the Earth, get rid of your time-honoured tendency to believe that your own ideological constructions are universally recognised truths just because, as a result of being useful to you, they were unanimously accepted amongst yourselves. Of course, might has always been right and so in spite of being a small minority, you had the power to define and impose on the remaining 80% of mankind those interpretations that are best suited to your needs, cloaked in the mantle of objectivity and sometimes science. Take the famed profit-making motive. You bring it up at will to mitigate the gravity of the crime or even to dissolve it altogether. That is why for instance, in spite of clear evidence to the contrary, you have determined that the Nazis were not motivated by profit.

Introduction

I experienced this control over forms of expression at a round table on the slavery and the slave trade in October 1998. I had spoken about the "mass deportation of Africans as a crime against humanity." When I returned to Paris, a history professor at the University of Orleans, very amicably suggested to me that "one should not use the word deportation in the case of the slave trade so as to avoid any misunderstandings." I stared at him uncomprehendingly. He added that if I really felt that I could not forsake the word deportation in writing, then I should put it between quotes and insert a footnote specifying the connection with the slave trade. To justify his position, he went on to say:

> At the time of the slave trade, the word deportation was never used. History books and historians never use the word deportation in relation to the slave trade. Occasionally, the word importation or transportation is mentioned. The word deportation conjures up the deportations that took place in Europe under the Nazi domination and so it would be intellectually dishonest to misapply it.

It dawned on me that we are not even allowed to call the most massive deportation of human beings in the history of mankind by its name, on the grounds that the slave traders, their descendants and their historians, at the time and ever since, never used and never authorised the use of the term deportation to characterise their doings. Are we seriously expected to follow suit simply because the perpetrators of these barbaric deeds preferred the use of euphemisms such as "trade"? This monopoly over words and their definitions is no accident. It is part of the process of manipulating history and maintaining control over its interpretation. Seen in this light the significance of legal characterisation becomes strikingly obvious.

When Western historians – i.e. those who for centuries were the only ones in a position to write their history and ours – engage in research on Nazism, they very carefully sidestep the fact that Hitler simply revealed an already entrenched racist savagery that dated back well before the twentieth century, a racist savagery, a system for annihilating man which, until then, had been applied only to colonised peoples.

As for philosophers (needless to say, Western), after 1945, they set about convincing us that Nazism, Nazi Germany and the Nazi genocides cannot be understood using the conventional principles and criteria of Western philosophy. These more Cartesian-than-thou gentlemen enamoured of logic, cannot comprehend that because there was the genocide of indigenous American peoples, because there was the mass deportation and enslavement of Africans, Auschwitz cannot be perceived from outside Europe, by non-Europeans in the same way as it is in Europe by Europeans. And hence, while a European philosopher might wonder, in the wake of Auschwitz, "is thought still possible?" a descendant of deported Africans not remotely resembling a philosopher, might explain to the latter that Gorée, and moreover, Saint-Domingue did not disturb "philosophical thought" and so it should suffer no worse a fate from the atrocities that it lived with for as long as the victims were from latitudes very remote from those of "Philosophy."

It is urgent and necessary for Blacks at least to be aware that the alleged difference that serves as the foundation for the paradigm shift when moving from the African American genocide to the Nazi genocide is derived not from facts, but from their legal characterisation and the status of the victims. Once that is accepted, it becomes perfectly clear to anyone in good faith that, in history, the definition and characterisation of facts, together with their historical substance are a question of power.

The genocidal policies of European powers against Africans and their descendants in America lasted for as long as it was in the interests of the metropolitan powers to pursue them. For instance, rather than arising in relation to the victims of the genocide, the question of compensation arose in relation to those who perpetrated it. As it turned out, this aberration contributed importantly to developing a reductionist interpretation of the genocide.

In contrast, the genocidal policy of the Nazis lasted up to the point that Germany was defeated, when it was militarily crushed. In the final analysis, it was because its firepower was not up to the test that Germany found itself in the dock. This resulted in Germany having to pay the penalty for its policies, whereas we endured the same for centuries, without any of the guilty parties ever being bothered in any significant way. Thanks to this "circumstance," i.e., the defeat of Nazi Germany, the issue of compensation did arise, but in this case for the victims of the genocide.

Notes
1. Crété, Liliane, *La Traite des nègres sous l'Ancien Régime*, Paris, 1989, pp. 63–64.
2. Ibid, p. 9.
3. Quoted by Jean-Michel Chaumont, *La concurrence des victimes*, Paris, 1997 p. 27.

I

The Exclusion of Non-Whites or the Institutionalisation of Barbarity

1

The Destruction of Native Americans

Atrocities a little less repulsive

> When the Europeans in the fifteenth century came upon America, an unprecedented form of modern day fascism was unleashed. Except that historians did not speak of fascism but of conquest and the names of the conquistadores were inscribed into the annals of History. What did this conquest really mean? The Europeans brought only death and desolation to the indigenous peoples of the Americas. In North America, the Native Americans, the Sioux, Iroquois, Comanches, Hurons, and Cherokees were slaughtered, the kingdoms of Central America (the Yucatan, the Mayas, the Aztecs, the Toltecs, etc.) were annihilated and those of South America (the Chimu, the Incas, the Tukuna, the Tupi), etc. were crushed in a bloodbath. With the subsequent mass emigration of European settlers, European fascism was strengthened and succeeded in entirely eliminating the indigenous peoples. How many tens of millions perished under the occupation by European migrants? For nearly five centuries now the history of the Americas has been the history of the European conquerors and theirs alone. In the United States, the Native Americans that escaped annihilation have been parked in reservations and are grudgingly considered a national minority. Not only have their kingdoms been destroyed, but also their civilisations and even their personality.[1]

When I read these lines in Kum'a N'Dumbe's book for the first time nearly twenty years ago, I was rather disturbed by his use of the word "fascism" with reference to the twofold disaster caused by the arrival of Europeans in America and the relations of domination thereafter established. I wondered whether it was appropriate to use this word which probably began to appear in dictionaries in 1922 to describe Benito Mussolini's regime in Italy, whereas the events he is referring to took place three, four or five centuries beforehand. After pondering this question, I realised that the word "fascism" [just as the word "genocide" which did not enter dictionaries until 1948 and said to be coined by Raphael Lemkin in his book *Axis Rule in Occupied Europe* (1944)] describes and reports very ancient deeds. Deeds that, to this very day, continue not to be taken seriously simply because the victims have never confronted their torturers from a position of power in a way comparable to that of the victorious allied forces in 1945 in respect to Nazi Germany. I had studied the history of European colonialism a little since school, but this was the first time that I had read any comment coming from someone who was neither a European nor a Westernised intellectual from the Americas, who inevitably, and sometimes unwittingly, reproduced an interpretation which, by virtue of its subtle racism and perfect integration into the cultural fabric, is eminently insidious. In other words, the reason I found it difficult to understand his writing was because it was clearly different from the conventional Eurocentric writing we are accustomed to.

As a rough idea of the destruction of the indigenous population of America, Todorov states that in 1500 the world population is estimated to be around 400 million, of which 80 million inhabited the Americas. In the mid-sixteenth century, of these 80 million, only 10 million remained. Taking Mexico alone, just prior to its conquest, the population was approximately 25 million. In 1600, it was 1 million. "If the word genocide has ever been applied to a situation with some accuracy, this is the case here," he writes.

> It constitutes a record, not only in relative terms (a destruction in the order of 90% or more), but also in absolute terms since we are speaking about a population diminution estimated at 70 million human lives. None of the large-scale massacres of the twentieth century can be compared to this mass hecatomb.[2]

Many of the countries of the American continent have tended to obscure this mass destruction. Some very different schools of thought, stemming from conflicting ideological foundations, have contributed to erasing not so much the destruction of Native Americans but the associated atrocities as well. The extermination of some 70 million human beings has been passed off in the pages of history as the inevitable collateral damage in a process that had its good side, too.

The South-American elites, for instance, in spite of being descended from Native American and White peoples and therefore of mixed blood, are contemptuous of the latter. At the beginning of the 1980s, I remember that textbooks approved by the Colombian Ministry for Education, taught pupils that the history of their country began with the "discovery," i.e., the arrival of the Europeans. This reflects the tenets of white supremacy whereby nothing historically worthwhile occurred prior to White people coming on to the scene. Wholly consistent with this Eurocentric version, pupils had to learn that the great periods of their history were the "discovery" and subsequent conquest, the colony up to independence and then the period from the Republic (following independence) to the present day.

According to this conception, during the conquest, the Europeans displayed a warring spirit and sometimes indomitable courage when fighting the Native Americans who, with their poisoned arrows, let alone the risk of being eaten by those savage cannibals, were formidable opponents. The colony was the period when the colonisers – prevalently Spaniards so it is claimed – proved their generosity by willingly mixing their blood with that of indigenous women, to produce mixed bloods. The wholesale raping of indigenous women, their sexual exploitation and the trauma and humiliation they suffered as a result are portrayed to schoolchildren as a heroic act that saved their country, which would otherwise would have become a Native American reservation.

But there is more: language and religion are construed as gifts for which the conquered country owes gratitude to the former colonial power.

In Colombia, since independence and the inception of the Republic, the class that holds power has never been very kindly inclined towards Spain. However, while the country is highly circumspect towards the former colonial power, it is even less appreciative of the Native Americans. Many otherwise open-minded people would consider it an insult to be mistaken for a Native American.

In reaction to this interpretation of history, a number of progressive intellectuals who support the few remaining Native Americans undertook to provide a different reading, one aimed at restoring their humanity and the rights they have unendingly claimed. This approach produced a legend that portrays the Native Americans as defying the Spaniards in their attempt to impose slavery upon them, preferring to die standing up for their freedom rather than bow down under the yoke. Although it is moving, this story fails to address the atrocities inflicted on Native Americans and, in so doing, consolidates another legend whereby Black people are purported to have "accepted" slavery because they, in contrast to the Native Americans, were accustomed to bowing their heads.

Bartolomeo de Las Casas is known for his struggle in the defence of the Native Americans. In spite of this, he is not much in favour with the revolutionaries who, in South America in the 1960s, 1970s and beyond, joined ranks with Native Americans to uphold their rights. In truth, these were the only left-wing organisations that took any interest in defending the rights of Native Americans not to be kicked out of the places where they had been parked after being robbed of their best lands every time the interests of the large landowners so required. These rights' activists criticised Las Casas because he never gave up his efforts to evangelise the Native Americans. As a result, so they say, he did the colonial power a very great service, since evangelisation is considered to be one of the pillars of colonisation.

At the beginning of the 1970s, for instance, the commonly accepted view among sympathisers to the native cause was that Las Casas' struggle was far more a cunning ploy than a humane reaction or position in comparison with the blind greed of the conquistadores. In other words, the latter who were more miserly than they were intelligent failed to comprehend that it was neither in their interest nor in that of His Most Catholic Majesty to kill the labour force which, if properly handled, could actively contribute to producing incalculable wealth. It was therefore utterly wasteful to hound the indigenous peoples whereas they could be usefully turned into vassals of the Crown. This rather approximate and curt explanation is unlikely to arouse sympathy towards Las Casas. The reason for this is very simple: in the former colonies, a revolutionary must be anticolonialist. At the beginning of the 1970s, the struggle of organised peasants to defend their most basic rights was in full swing in the countries of South America. Some people believed that the peasant movement in Colombia was about to stir up a true revolution. A number of leftist leaders had been successful in coordinating their struggle with that of the indigenous peoples on the basis that they had a common enemy, i.e., the power of the large landowners supported by the repressive organs of the State including the army in defence of a minority. At that time, a number of European intellectuals with leftist leanings, attracted by what was referred to as "the historical process of the revolutionary movement" that Latin America was going through, liked to go there on vacation. Often very favourable to the indigenous peoples, they were vaguely familiar with Las Casas' condemnations and could not understand why his name did not come up in connection with the struggle against the injustices unendingly endured by the Native Americans.

In fact, the atrocities inflicted upon Native Americans and denounced by Las Casas were not taken up by the revolutionaries that fought alongside Native Americans quite simply because according to their analysis of colonialism, the dichotomy of oppressed vs. oppressor and exploited vs. exploiter is fully explanatory. Because the conquest and subsequent colonisation were pure violence, any colonial enterprise could be nothing but murderous. No attempt is made to analyse the sadistic, perverted behaviour, sometimes taken to the extreme by the conquistadores, because these are seen as the inevitable conduct inherent to any process of domination and subordination of one group by another, stronger, group. In short, it is colonialism's intrinsic nature to be so. And where a European humanist might see excessive cruelty, a formerly colonised anticolonialist militant simply sees the true essence of colonialism to the extent that to speak of atrocities perpetrated by the colonialists would be tautological. After all, has there ever been a single instance of an endeavour to conquer and establish colonial domination that forsook these prerequisite atrocities? This interpretation rejects the cheap literary notions that would have one believe that there were nasty colonisers as opposed to other nice colonisers. There were neither good nor bad colonisers. There was colonisation, its agents and all the consubstantial barbarity.

This interpretation, which in principle I share, seems to me nonetheless a little scanty and may interfere with understanding patterns of conduct which were introduced during the conquest, institutionalised throughout the colonial period and continued after the colonisers departed. It is precisely because oppression of Native Americans did not cease when colonisation ended that to this day they must still fight just to have their right to be alive recognised. Additionally, to the best of our knowledge, not all citizens in the former colonies have become anticolonialist activists. In the matter of colonialism, while there is no need to state the obvious for the benefit of activists, there is a need to do so for the majority who, through the effects of cultural domination, continue to believe in the benefits of colonisation "in spite of its excesses," since colonisation brought with it the language and a "superior civilisation." Thanks to this civilisation, we Colombians, are not a country of Native Americans.

A policy of destruction

The American continent was conquered at the cost of the destruction of the Native Americans. Similarly, the cost of colonial domination that institutionalised barbarity in America up to modern times was the annihilation of the imported Africans and their descendants in America. The bloodthirsty conduct that accompanied the beginning of the conquest of the New World was allowed to unfold and flourish throughout the colonial period becoming part and parcel of the ways and customs of the European colonisers. The gradual transformation of that bloodthirsty conduct into a cultural element that is quintessential to the methods of subordination used by colonial powers marked the beginning of the moral collapse of decent European society. However, this moral collapse of the "superior race" (discovered incidentally just after 1945) was unimaginable as long as those atrocities were committed in a setting far away from Europe.

During the conquest, when the Whites occupied a village, Native Americans that had not been massacred on the spot were sent into slavery, thus postponing their death very briefly. That was how the trade in human flesh began in America: the Whites would seize upon the Native Americans and sell them to other Whites, who in turn bought them and either sent them out to work themselves to death in the mines or else sold them to yet other Whites. These dealings in indigenous peoples were liable to occur in rapid succession, and at every change of tormentor, victims would have their faces branded with the initial of their new owner with a hot iron. Thus, and in spite of their very short life span, the faces of Native Americans often looked like the alphabet.

In his *Very Short Account of the Destruction of the Indies*, Las Casas narrates the claims of a man who boasted, even in the presence of a 'venerable clergyman' that he had done his utmost and continued to do his utmost to impregnate as many indigenous women as possible so as to be able to sell them for a better price.[3] The purpose of this practice was twofold. On the one hand, White people could satisfy their biological needs in spite of the scarcity of White women by raping Native American and Black people who were at their beck and call. And on the other, pregnancy had the effect of raising the market price of the enslaved women. Some people claim these cases were few and far between. Maybe, but their mere possibility should cause one to pause and think. Moreover, the fact that the perpetrator of such a monstrosity should boast of his feats in public is chilling. Two centuries later we discover the narrative of Jean-Gabriel Stedman who tells us how a Dutch captain had claimed a higher price for a Black woman whom he had made his mistress on account of her being pregnant. These facts argue in favour of a far more widespread practice than is readily admitted. We know that all the slave owners used the women that belonged to them sexually but that the children born of this intercourse were nonetheless enslaved and often separated from their mothers and sold.

Thomas Jefferson, for instance, one of the founding fathers of the United States, the second president of that country, sexually exploited the Black women he owned in the same way as other slave drivers. The children that resulted from those sexual relations were as many little piccaninnies that augmented his human chattel. Certainly, Thomas Jefferson felt no animosity towards Blacks since "in his will he emancipated them all, as well as his Black mistress and her illegitimate children.[4]"

In spite of being driven by the desire for riches, the conquistadores were careless about labour that could be gained from the indigenous peoples they enslaved. The manner in which the Native Americans were moved to the places where they were to work themselves to death reflects an utter contempt for them. Their lives were not even worth the labour they could offer. This contempt is remarkable in that five centuries later we still find it, practically intact and as murderous as ever.

Las Casas mentions in detail, also in the *Very Short Account of the Destruction of the Indies*... the conditions under which the Native Americans were taken to the mines, which were turning into death camps. This was the beginning of what would very soon turn the American continent into the largest concentration camp intended for non-Whites, under the administration and supervision of the Whites. In the chapter devoted to "the province of Nicaragua," Las Casas mentions an official who sent his men to raid Native Americans and at the same time loot and rob anything that might be useful. Having been shackled by the neck and linked one to another by a long chain, the indigenous peoples were forced to walk and additionally carry a load that weighed approximately two arrobas (i.e., 50 kg). Because these marches were often long, the conditions bad and food scanty, one or several Native Americans were liable to collapse. To avoid losing any time unchaining them, they were beheaded just above the iron collar. Their heads would fall off to one side while the body was left on the other and the party could continue onwards.[5] Such a simple solution.

As early as 1519, this conduct was denounced by a group of Dominicans in a report sent to M. De Chèvres, a minister of Charles I (future Charles V), quoted by Todorov. This report relates to events that took place in the Caribbean islands, but it is common knowledge that everywhere the conquistadores acted in the same manner:

> Each time the Indians were transferred, there was so great a number of them dying of hunger on the way that the wake they left behind the ship would have sufficed, one might think, to guide another landing party to the

port. [...] More than eight hundred Indians having been led to a harbour of this island, known as Puerto de Plata, there was a wait of two days before they were made to go down into the caravelle. Six hundred of them died, who were flung into the sea; they rolled upon the waves like logs.[6]

There is something astonishing about the consistency of this pattern of behaviour by Whites towards non-Whites, regardless of whether they were Spanish, British, Portuguese, French, Dutch or other nationalities, and be it in America or in Africa. Wherever nothing was to be feared from the courts, torture, massacres and exterminations were perpetrated time and again, even by people who, in the environment they originated from, would never have dreamt of infringing the law or the standards dictated by propriety.

In the report mentioned by Todorov, the Dominicans illustrated the special treatment administered to children using specific examples:

> Some Christians encounter an Indian woman who was carrying in her arms a child at suck; and since the dog they had with them was hungry, they tore the child from the mother's arms and flung it still living to the dog who proceeded to devour it before the mother's eyes. [...] When there were among the prisoners some women who had recently given birth, if the new-born babies happened to cry, they seized them by the legs and hurled them against the rocks, or flung them into the jungle so that they would be certain to die there.[7]

More than two centuries later, from the statements of Jean-Gabriel Stedman,[8] an eye-witness, it can be inferred that not only had this special treatment for children not been banned, but it had become almost commonplace for perfectly decent White ladies who had absolutely nothing in common with convicts. What Stedman says about Mrs S. (he conceals her name, no doubt so as not to offend her sensibilities or those of her honourable family) indicates that she is neither frenzied nor even impulsive. She is simply a White person who, due to her skin, is permitted to do anything she wishes to non-Whites. Clearly, she loves the tranquillity and silence on board a boat. But her Black maid's baby is always crying. So Mrs S. does the only thing she believes will be effective: she orders her maid to bring over the baby and holds it under the water until it drowns, and then sets it adrift to go with the current. There! Its cries will no longer be heard and thankfully she will be able to rest.

And barbarity becomes entrenched

It is significant that the time interval between the arrival of the Christians in the New World and the development of the barbarity that shaped the subsequent behaviour of the victors over vanquished groups was so short.

Las Casas describes an event to which he was more than just an ordinary witness. This was the massacre of Caonao, in Cuba, perpetrated by the troops of Narvaez whose chaplain he was. This account is found in the excellent Spanish edition of his *History of the Indies* supervised by Augustin Millares Carlo, and published together with a preliminary analysis by Lewis Hanke. The French version of this account is taken from Todorov's book. The Caonao massacre was a statistic, just one of the many massacres perpetrated by the conquistadores. What makes it instructive is the absence of any pretext that might explain the event: there was no real or apparent danger, no false alarm or misunderstanding that might have provided grounds for anticipating hostilities. Nonetheless, the violence and cruelty that ensued were unbearable:

> You need to know that on the day of their arrival the Spaniards stopped to have lunch in the dried up bed of a torrent which still held a few puddles of water and which was filled with whetstones; this gave them the idea of sharpening their swords.
>
> Having reached the village after this picnic, the Spaniards decide to test whether their swords are as sharp as they seem. A Spaniard, in whom the devil must have clothed himself, suddenly draws his sword. Then the whole hundred of them draw theirs and begin to rip open the bellies of the villagers, to cut and kill those lambs, men, women, children and old folks, all of whom are seated quietly and astonished, watching the horses and foreigners. And in the space of a few minutes, not a man among all these people remained alive. The Spaniards then enter a large house nearby, for this was happening on its threshold, and in the same way, with cuts and stabs, begin to kill as many as they find there, so that a stream of blood is running, as if a great number of cows had perished.
>
> To see the wounds which covered the bodies of the dead and dying was a spectacle of horror and dread: indeed, since the devil, who inspired the Spaniards, furnished them these whetstones with which they sharpened their swords, on the morning of that very day in the bed of the stream where they broke their fast, everywhere where they wielded their weapons upon these stark naked bodies and this delicate flesh, they cut a man quite in half with a single blow.[9]

Las Casas obviously believes that the devil has his part in this. Others think that the Spaniards undoubtedly had a murderous streak, just as some have claimed about the Germans in 1945. Clearly, devils had nothing to do with it and, in my opinion, the Spaniards are no more inclined towards murder than their British, Portuguese, French, Belgian, Dutch or German counterparts.

It seems to me that complete, limitless power of life and death of one group over another inevitably distorts the view that the dominant group has of the dominated group and of all those related to it. This idea that is engendered by the relationship of the powerful to the weak, a relationship that becomes synonymous with superiority versus inferiority, is an essential premise in any enterprise aimed at conquest, at colonisation; in short, at the domination of some humans by other humans who are convinced they belong to a superior species. It is the conviction that they were dealing with inferior beings that drove the Whites into this vicious circle where I kill you not only because you are inferior but, also because at best you are a pig, and at worst, a scourge, a plague. By killing you, not only am I protecting myself but, moreover, I am helping to cleanse society by removing some of the trash that contaminates it. It is solely by virtue of this firm conviction that men and women, who in all other respects were fine people, were able to commit or dispassionately witness all sorts of murders and destruction of human beings without losing the attributes that gave them an aura of dignity and respectability amongst their own kind.

The Schutzstaffel (SS) staff who, four centuries later, on May 1st, 1943, as testified by Eugen Kogon,[10] slaughtered or wounded a number of prisoners simply to find out who among them was the best shot used an excuse as absurd as the Spaniards who wished to test the sharpness of their swords. The Germans are no more carriers of a criminal streak than the Spaniards although some have alleged otherwise. What they did have, which explains a great deal, is the unlimited power of death over their victims. The similarity in behaviour – less the gas chambers – every time relations of superiority/inferiority, humans/sub-humans have taken root, the fact that these similarities have travelled across borders and through the centuries whatever the nationality of the so-called superior or master group, these are the features in situations that inevitably engender atrocities.

One may wonder why such great hatred is expressed not only through the deeds but also through the words of the self-termed superior group towards the whole group they consider inferior. Whether the events occurred in America, Africa or more recently in Europe under Nazi rule, the language of the group that rules as absolute master pitilessly heaps every failing upon those it annihilates. In actual fact, hatred is not necessarily construed by the superior group as that feeling we might harbour against a person who has inflicted the worst evils upon us. For these ladies and gentlemen (Whites or Aryans depending on whether they were outside or inside Europe), it was more a matter of preserving themselves, or in any case preserving their self-image. There can be no question of crediting those you must crush or those you are already in the process of annihilating with the noblest qualities and the most highly developed intelligence. It is essential to do the reverse for that is how relations of subordination are established.

Except for pathological cases of depraved individuals, members of a superior group (non-Aryans in this case and non-Whites in other circumstances) that take part directly in reducing their victims to bestiality, or who derive profit from them albeit without direct contact, need to believe that they are rightfully entitled to behave as they do towards the inferior group. It is in this way that preconceptions acquire the status of inescapable truths. Those who in their description of the world legitimise atrocities committed by the superior world are the most charismatic in their group and claim to speak on the basis of science or reason, giving their words an aura of truth that needs no further demonstration.

Todorov quotes two accounts that he chose among many others because of the special social status of those witnesses. One was that of a clergyman (the Dominican Tomas Ortiz) and the other that of a scholar of science and literature (Fernandez de Oviedo y Valdés, aka Oviedo), i.e., people who belonged to social groups who at the time tended to be more kindly disposed towards the Native Americans.

These two narratives are of particular interest to me because in addition to the prestige and charisma of their authors who were not criminals, they also verify the following tragic fact: Ortiz and Oviedo's portrayal of Native Americans, the impression they give of them, the perception that emerges from what they say, hackneyed and passed on by the officials of the colonial power is perfectly mirrored in the image that prevails four and a half centuries later in the countries of America, particularly among culturally more backward groups.

This is what the Dominican Ortiz tells the Council of the Indies:

> On the mainland they eat human flesh. They are more given to sodomy than any other nation. There is no justice among them. They go naked.

> They have no respect either for love or for virginity. They are stupid and silly. They have no respect for truth save when it is to their advantage. They are unstable. They have no knowledge of what foresight means. They are ungrateful and changeable... They are brutal. They delight in exaggerating their defects. There is no obedience among them, or deference on the part of the young for the old, nor of the son for the father. They are incapable of learning. Punishments have no effect upon them... They eat fleas, spiders and worms raw, whenever they find them. They exercise none of the human arts or industries. When taught the mysteries of our religion, they say these things may suit Castilians, but not them, and they do not wish to change their customs. They are beardless, and if sometimes hairs grow, they pull them out. [...] The older they get, the worse they become. About the age of ten or twelve years, they seem to have some civilisation, but later they become like real brute beasts. I may therefore affirm that God has never created a race more full of vice and composed without the least mixture of kindness or culture. [...] The Indians are more stupid than asses, and refuse to improve in anything.[11]

Father Labat was to publish *New Voyage to the American Islands* in 1722 upon returning from the West Indies. It is unlikely that this French Dominican ever read his Spanish counterpart, but nonetheless, two centuries later, he says precisely the same thing, but not about the Native Americans (who, first with their suffering, and then with their destruction, had already paid a very heavy toll to white supremacy), but about the Blacks who during the Enlightenment were still paying the toll of white supremacy in the enormous concentration camp that the American continent had become for them.

Let us now read what is said by Oviedo, the historian who, as Todorov rightly states, does not bring the Native American down to the level of a horse or a donkey (or even just below) but rather places him somewhere in the class of building materials, such as wood, stone or iron, or in any case inanimate objects. "And so when one wages war with them and comes to hand to hand fighting, one must be very careful not to hit them on the head with the sword, because I have seen many swords broken in this fashion. In addition to being thick, their skulls are very strong.[12]" Todorov notes that Oviedo is an advocate of the "final solution" for the "Indian problem", a solution for which he would like the God of Christians to take responsibility for: "God will soon destroy them. ... Satan has now been expelled from this island; now that most of the Indians are dead, his influence has disappeared [...] Who can deny that to use gunpowder against the pagans is an offering of incense unto Our Lord?[13]"

Remembrance trampled upon

We all remember the outrage of the Colombian bourgeoisie when General de Gaulle, on a visit to Colombia, ineptly said that he was delighted to be in "one of the most Indian countries of America." While the French claimed they did not understand why it caused so much outrage, Colombians, particularly the most acculturated, who are also the most conservative, could not understand why the General had insulted them for no reason. What a humiliation for anyone who has read Voltaire, Montesquieu, Diderot, Rousseau and all the others to be treated like a despicable Indian!

Years later, I had the opportunity to see that this type of touchiness is, unfortunately, very widespread among the formerly colonised people of America. In 1982–1983, as a foreign student at the Paris Censier University, one of my fellow students was a young Brazilian woman who had been trained as a psychologist and whose husband was a medical intern at the Villejuif hospital. Her son was in nursery school in Paris. The child's teacher knew where he came from and decided to talk about Brazil, explaining on which continent it is located and which language is spoken there. She ended saying that there are many Native Americans in Brazil. The child must have been intrigued because he went back to his parents and asked them whether it was true that there are a lot of Native Americans in Brazil. They gave him several postcards of Brazil for his teacher "so that she realises that there are more than Native Americans in Brazil". When my friend was telling me this, I froze. No Native American, or Black person appeared on any of the postcards. She had left her country only a year before; I was the first Black person with whom she had anything to do who was not either a servant of hers or of a friend.

This conversation with this Brazilian psychologist brought to mind the image of a friend of mine, also Brazilian, and very much aware of what living in a racist society means. After completing a thesis at the Sorbonne, she went back home with her doctorate and struggled to obtain a position at the university. In the former colonies of America, a degree from Sorbonne, Oxford or Harvard is still highly regarded. And because in addition to Portuguese, she was fluent in French, Spanish and English, she managed to get the position. She bought an apartment in a well-to-do neighbourhood in Brasilia. One day, she heard the doorbell ring. She found herself face-to-face with a Black youth selling premium quality scents and cosmetics. He asked her whether her masters were in. My friend explained to him that she was the mistress of the house. The young man smiled and said he liked jokes particularly ones that are not unkind.

Hoping to have an educational influence, she invited him in. She explained to him that the apartment belongs to her, that she was not kept by a White and that she paid for it out of her own salary. When he was about to go and she was taking him back to the door, she said "I could see in his eyes that he didn't believe me." This speaks eloquently of the little esteem there is for Blacks in Brazilian society. What is most distressing about the ideological domination of white supremacy is the way in which it has caused so many Blacks to identify deeply with this degraded self-image.

I also observed the contempt for indigenous peoples in the countries of America at a playground in Sceaux, an affluent suburb south of Paris. I had taken my two children there and was speaking to them in Spanish when I heard someone say to me in the same tongue: "You speak to them in Spanish?" I was somewhat startled as I looked at the young woman who had just spoken to me because it was the first time I had set eyes on her. She had not greeted me and immediately used the familiar form of address. There was no doubt in her mind that she was superior to me. Before I answered her, she asked me what country I came from. I put on the vaguely dense look I thought was appropriate to the situation and said I was from Colombia. She pointed to a little boy playing in the sandbox and said to me: "I'm looking for somebody to look after him, someone who will speak Spanish to him." Using the polite form, I asked her where she came from. Slightly surprised and somewhat reluctantly, she told me she was born in Peru but that her grandfather was French, that her parents had studied in France, that everybody in her family spoke very good French; that, naturally, her husband was French and she therefore was of French nationality. She added: "I always dreamt of having a blond, blue-eyed child, which is what I did and so I won't have any more." I asked her if she was afraid that a second child might not be as blond as the first and she answered "yeah," but immediately went on to add that it would be surprising because in her family they were all White. So this unfortunate Peruvian, a descendant of Native Americans, married to a Frenchman and mother of a blond, blue-eyed child, dismissed the possibility of a second child just in case she might give birth to a child who is not blond and possibly – God forbid – has Native American features.

I wondered if there was anything worth salvaging from someone so deeply brain-washed, verging on idiocy. I was becoming more and more convinced of the urgent need for better knowledge of every aspect of the destruction of Native Americans because, as it turns out, cultural alienation and a pervasive contempt for the indigenous peoples on that continent have been continuously perpetuated.

Notes

1. Kum'a N'Dumbe III, Alexandre, *Hitler voulait l'Afrique*, Paris, 1980, p. 9.
2. Todorov, Tzvetan, *The Conquest of America: The Question of the Other*, Oklahoma Paperbacks, 1999, p. 133.
3. Las Casas, Bartolomé, *Brevisima relaciòn de la destucciòn de las Indias, Del reino de Yucatàn*, Buenos Aires, 1966 (Translation).
4. Paraire, Philippe, *Les Noirs américains, généalogie d'une exclusion*, Paris, 1993, p. 37.
5. Las Casas, op. cit., *De la tierra firme*.
6. Todorov, op. cit., p. 139.
7. Ibid, p. 139.
8. See pp. 41–42 of chapter 2.
9. Todorov, op. cit., p. 141.
10. See p. 37 of chapter 2.
11. Todorov, op. cit., pp. 150–151.
12. Ibid. p. 151.
13. Ibid.

2
The Annihilation of Black People

Concentration camp settings

In twentieth century Europe, the National Socialist state of Germany was the perfect example of what can happen in a society where crime is permissible. As long as people are sure to go unpunished and run no risk of coming up against the judicial and legal system that governs their society, people who are not predestined to operate outside the law will willingly do so.

In the various concentration camps established by the National Socialist regime, every single SS member, right down to the lowest in rank both socially and in his own party, had an unassailable right over the lives and especially the deaths of thousands of human beings who in many respects were superior to him. This unrestricted faculty to harm could only encourage criminal arrogance and worsen the plight of victims, who were stripped of their every right.

For several centuries, on the American continent, millions of human beings, because they were black-skinned, were placed outside the rule of law thereby making it impossible for them to stand up for themselves and thus depriving them of their very humanity. Concomitantly, any white-skinned merely by being White, however stupid he might be, was entitled to obedience from Black people everywhere and at all times. As I learned more and more about the German concentration camp system – its rules, the practical implementation of barbarity there, the day-to-day life and death routine – I was struck by the resemblance between two seemingly remote worlds. When reading the testimony of a survivor of the camps, I was sometimes under the impression of déjà vu, as if I was re-reading an account about the nineteenth century concentration camp setting created in America strictly for Black people.

What I had yet to comprehend was that equivalent historical circumstances foster similar patterns of behaviour ending up the same way.

For the torturers to be able to exercise their power without the slightest hindrance, two conditions must be fulfilled: their victims have to be robbed of their every right and prevented from defending themselves in any way. The only way the torturers' right founded on violence could be perpetuated and maintained was by the rule of terror. It was crucial for terror to quell the slightest inclination among victims to resist. That is why relentless terror was the backbone of the concentration camp setting that functioned in America for more than three centuries.

The rule of terror needed justification and a semblance of legality or even legitimacy. Victor Schoelcher aptly summarises this, stressing that

> Any legal system based on violence is inevitably condemned to use violence to perpetuate itself. Logically, all societies have to find ways of protecting themselves. When a society runs counter to nature, it can only maintain itself by resorting to laws that go against humanity. The more difficult it is to expect the obedience that is demanded, the more ruthless must be the punishment meted out to those who disobey.[1]

That is why it was not enough to reduce Black people to the condition of animals (after all, some people are fond of animals). It was furthermore necessary to heap every depravity upon them thus making them repulsive in a way that made it easier, i.e. safer and entirely legal, to brutalise them without offending either the sense of propriety or individual consciences of White people. This explains the barbarity of the American plantation, nay concentration camp setting, and specifically why people who were neither monsters nor acting in pursuit of monetary gain – a notion so dear to the experts – often perpetrated these deeds.

When this system was applied to contemporary Europe, it was referred to as "totalitarianism." To this day, European researchers refuse to acknowledge that there is anything in common between the American concentration camp setting and certain aspects of the German concentration camps. To justify the use of terror, the Nazis strove to convince themselves that the victims were degenerate beings and that to kill them was in the interests of social hygiene. In the concentration camp setting that plagued America until the start of the second half of the nineteenth century, the extreme violence, absence of the rule of law, and especially the discourse used as justification correspond to the experience of those who lived in German concentration camps.

Blinding similarities

Of course, you will always find scholars who are able to view relations between victims and their tormentors as bordering on the idyllic. Take for instance the brochure by Armel de Wismes, published in 1984 under the title *La Traite Négrière vers le Nouveau Monde* where the author refutes testimonies about the hell designed especially for Black people. He avails himself of "other testimonies that are just as irrefutable showing us Blacks who lived peacefully with *good masters*."[2] He might as well say that there are "irrefutable" testimonies showing victims of Nazism living peacefully with the "nice SS men" at Buchenwald, Dachau or any other German concentration camp. This is a measure of the liberties that can be taken with truth on the topic of remembrance and the suffering of non-European victims. This is how a crime against humanity is insidiously conventionalised as long as it does not take place in Europe and its victims are not Europeans.

For the German concentration camps, I have chosen the account of an Austrian sociologist, Eugen Kogon. He was arrested several times by the Nazis and finally deported to Buchenwald in 1939 until freed in 1945 by the Allied troops after enduring more than six years in the camp. In the case of America, I refer to the testimony of Victor Schoelcher, the most consistent of French abolitionists. I also quote statements by Joseph Eleazar Morenas, an officer of the King who worked in various colonies for more than 20 years. Morenas, whose account, *Précis Historique de la Traite des Noirs et de l'Esclavage Colonial*, was published in 1828, was not an abolitionist. As far as I know, he never challenged the principle of slavery. What he did express, in fact very courageously, was his hostility towards what he referred to as "the excesses of the slave trade, the excesses of slavery." Morenas went before the King and the Chamber and argued in favour of easing the concentration camp setting of America. This cost him his appointment. In contrast to Schoelcher, he never fully understood the fact that this system could only perpetuate itself through terror.

In this comparative approach, I have not considered the Soviet concentration camps. The reason for this is simple: the initial motives and the hackneyed ideological discourse put forward to justify the Stalinist policy were not only different but actually the opposite of the motives and ideological discourse developed to vindicate, first the concentration camp setting of America and then, decades later, the National Socialist government policy in Germany. It will be the task of other researchers to understand how and why a political plan initially motivated by the generous aim of achieving well-being for humankind eventually took such a criminal turn. Such a study goes beyond the scope of this book.

Among examples of barbarity that prevailed in the German camps, Kogon narrates the following event:

> In the spring of 1938, a Gypsy tried to escape. Commandant Koch had him placed in a wooden box, one side covered by chicken wire. The box was only large enough to permit the prisoner to crouch. Koch then had large nails driven through the boards, piercing the victim's flesh at the slightest movement. The Gypsy was exhibited to the whole camp in this cage. He was kept in the roll-call area for two days and three nights, without food. His dreadful screams had long since lost any semblance of humanity. On the morning of the third day he was finally relieved of his sufferings by an injection of poison.[3]

This type of torture may not have been a daily occurrence but the fact that it could happen at all to someone in the concentration camp population speaks volumes about the terror that ruled.

When Morenas denounces "colonial justice" and pleads for the system to be "eased," he feels the need to specify:

> I am not speaking here about those poor creatures who are put into ovens to be roasted or those who have been devoured by dogs; or of the Blacks that have been made to die from starvation or whipped to death, or shot down for the sake of passing the time; nor of those wretches who were tortured by passing a burning torch back and forth across their bodies or by burning their genitals with red hot coals. What I wish to draw attention to here is the barbarity the courts resort to in the name of justice.[4]

In his petition to moderate the special laws applied to non-Whites in the French part of America, Morenas reports the following case:

> A court in Guadeloupe, by judgment of the 11th Brumaire of the year XI (1803), sentenced Millot de Girardière to be exposed in the square of Point-à-Pitre in an iron cage until death ensues. The cage used for this form of torture is 8 feet tall. The person imprisoned in the cage stands astride of a sharp blade. His feet rest on a type of stirrup and he must stand on tiptoe to avoid injury from the blade. Before him on a table within his reach are placed food and drink. But a sentinel is on guard day and night to prevent him from touching them. When the victim's strength begins to ebb, he falls on to the edge of the blade and suffers deep, cruel wounds. The terrible pain causes the unfortunate person to raise his body again but immediately

he falls back again onto the sharp blade, suffering awful injury. This torture is inflicted for three or four days.⁵

Perhaps this too was not a daily occurrence, though obviously it occurred more than once since we are apprised of the fact that it lasts three or four days depending on how strong the victim is.

There was therefore a time when atrocities, similar to those that decades later the SS performed in relative privacy for only the concentration camp inhabitants to see, were committed out in the open and quite legally against non-Whites in the American concentration camp setting. That is a fact. Nobody can seriously dispute this and because it cannot be disputed, nobody talks about it. What is disturbing here is that these atrocities were just part of the landscape, that they were committed in the name of the law and a certain conception of justice, that judges could allow such horrifying acts to be performed quite legally provided they were directed against the "racially inferior" group. One has to stop and wonder if what we are looking at is not methodical, sustained and cold-blooded barbarity.

The institutionalised practice of barbarity necessarily develops a culture of destruction. Once this culture becomes firmly entrenched, it can continue to evolve independently of the reasons from which it stemmed, especially once it has flourished as an institution for a long period. The lawfulness (even the legitimacy) of this barbarity lasts as long as the system itself does.

> By judgment of the Senior Council of Martinique on June 17, 1679, several Negroes were sentenced to having a leg chopped off, several Negresses to having their noses cut off and all of them to having their foreheads branded with a fleur-de-lis mark using a hot iron as punishment for attempting to escape. In their judgment, the judges declared that they had been indulgent and that similar cases in the future would incur the extreme penalty.⁶

The scope and consequences of this reality have been systematically covered up. In a debate where I emphasised that we can no longer afford to continue in this way, another participant replied that those were cruel times and our perception of human rights as we advocate them today did not exist at the time. Objectively, that difference between seventeenth and nineteenth century standards does exist. However, once that difference has been established, it remains that the institutionalised barbarity legally implemented in the concentration camp settings of America and its targets, the non-Whites, did not change, and yet in the meantime the Declaration of Human Rights had been proclaimed.

Times may have been cruel but there was never any question of applying to Whites the special laws devised strictly for non-Whites. In fact, to apply the same penalty to Whites and non-Whites for a similar offence was explicitly prohibited. This would have contradicted the racial policy whose clearly stated purpose was "in no way to undermine the contempt that the Whites have for the Negro race."

The method of terror aimed at containing the Blacks was very cleverly combined with a policy that successfully established the belief among Blacks that their race was inferior to that of the masters.

> By judgment of the Senior Council of Martinique on October 20, 1670, a Black was sentenced to having a leg cut off and exhibited on the gallows because he had killed a foal that belonged to a White. A few months later (May 10, 1671), the same court sentenced a White called Brocard to pay a fine of 500 pounds because he had burned a Black woman's genitals with a burning coal.[7]

Surely one day we need to take stock of the impact on humanity of this institutionalised barbarity that extended into modern times dressed up in legal disguise and proudly supported by a hackneyed doctrine for more than three and a half centuries. It cannot possibly have disappeared without leaving a legacy, particularly since it ended without a crucial element: recognition of what it was, i.e., a genocidal policy.

> In 1741, a Black man from Leogame (Saint-Domingue) shot his master dead with a rifle. The court sentenced him to redeem his misdeed by ordering him to be placed, hatless, wearing a shirt and with a rope around his neck in front of the main door of the city's parish church, where he was to be taken and led to a dustcart by the executioner of High Justice and there, hatless and on his knees, to be made to declare that he maliciously killed and assassinated his master by shooting him for which he repents and seeks pardon from God, the King and justice. This having been done, he is condemned to have his fist cut off on a post, and this to be hung on to the door of the said church from whence he is to be taken and led by said executioner in the same cart to gallows to be set up in the city square, where his arms, nipples, thighs and shins are to be pierced with red hot tongs. Unto the wounds thus made by the tongs, molten lead is to be poured before he is thrown alive on a burning stake to be reduced to ashes, the latter to be thrown to the winds.[8]

A century later, although the message of the Enlightenment had already travelled around the world several times, the Whites in America continued to apply special laws to non-Whites who were still considered to be less than human.

In 1822, a Provostial Court was instituted in Martinique to ward off the risk of a Black insurrection. The investigating judge, a certain Davoust, began to travel all over the country with his auxiliaries so as to administer justice on the spot.

> He had absolute powers, travelled if needed, took the Negroes suspected of sedition from their quarters, judged them on the spot, without appeal, without recourse, ordering their heads to be cut off. The intent of these formidable examples of the King's justice was to instil terror in Blacks. Before leaving, Davoust had two axes forged: a large one for beheading and a small one for cutting hands off. But he grew weary of these expeditious instruments and instead one day had 16 Black people burnt alive one after the other on the public square in Lamentin before a crowd of more than 20,000 Blacks who had been forced to assemble there.[9]

The reason Morenas in 1828 went to the trouble of denouncing law and justice as applied to non-Whites in the portion of the concentration camp setting of America under French supervision is that here the French government was in a position to engage in reform. That does not mean that elsewhere, in the territories under British, Portuguese, Dutch or Spanish supervision, the system spared non-Whites these terrifying atrocities. In spite of the scant means of communication compared with those we know today, there was a degree of uniformity in America. Whether in the territories under English, Portuguese, Dutch, Spanish or other rule, practices and legal norms were the same because the goal everywhere was to perpetuate the debasement of non-Whites. The terror tactics were therefore the same. The hypocrisy of literature that makes fine distinctions between good and bad torturers depending on their nationality is obvious to all. In actual fact, there were neither good nor bad Whites; there was simply a system based on the negation of the other. To perpetuate itself, this system was compelled to deny systematically the slightest iota of humanity in its victims.

Inevitable destruction in the concentration camp setting

The German concentration camps were places where, for twelve years, Nazi barbarity reached unimaginable heights. These camps,

> were a training ground for the SS. There they were taught to free themselves of their more humane emotions and attitudes, and learn the most effective ways of breaking resistance in a defenceless civilian population; the camps

thus became an experimental laboratory in which to study the most effective means for doing that. They were also a testing ground for how to govern most "effectively"; that is, what were the minimum food, hygienic, and medical requirements needed to keep prisoners alive and fit for hard labour when the threat of punishment took the place of all normal incentives.[10]

This statement by Bettelheim who was an eye-witness at Dachau and Birkenhau incidentally reminds us that the same causes can produce the same effects: The colossal power that Whites had over Blacks, that unlimited power to torture and to kill that they wielded for so long contributed to shaping a European culture and European patterns of behaviour that the SS reproduced.

In the Nazi system, the Führer was placed at the top as the guarantor of the supremacy of the race of masters, a portion of which is embodied in every SS man. The top layer in the concentration camp setting of America is white supremacy for which each White is a representative by virtue of belonging to the race of masters. In the German camps and likewise in America, the victims are stripped of their humanity and placed in a position where they cannot defend themselves.

Some myths die hard. One of these would have us believe that the Whites, although they negated the humanity of Blacks in America, nonetheless kept them in relative comfort. Their survival in animal terms, so it is claimed, was rather well provided for. The idea is that because Blacks were an investment for Whites, they took some care of them. And so, the story goes, the Blacks were relatively well fed and housed. In other words, they allegedly enjoyed living standards that many peasants in Europe at the time would have envied. The Whites themselves propagated this myth, not the Blacks who, incidentally, had no say. A scrutiny of the facts provides no support whatsoever for this theory.

Of course, the rationality used in the German concentration camps to calculate meticulously the minimum food ration needed to keep prisoners alive and capable of hard labour under the threat of punishment was not something completely new to Europeans who supervised the concentration camp setting of America. In an account published in 1856, after meeting with several planters in the United States, Frederick Law Olmsted states:

> Without actually wanting to starve their slaves, some planters took pains to determine the smallest amount of food that would enable them to supply the labour they expected from them. Above that amount, there was no immediate improvement in yield, so there was no point in their view in increasing it. The

half hands or quarter hands (the elderly, women, children) were therefore given half portions. Rations were distributed on Sundays; often, before the end of the week, they had been exhausted and slaves had no option but to beg, steal or pilfer to feed themselves for the remainder.[11]

We know how many lashes of the whip a Black person accused of theft was liable to receive and how effective each lash was in causing blood to spurt from the lacerated backs of the victim. And still in spite of this, Blacks would steal a piece of salted pork, poultry or potatoes.

In an anti-slavery work published in Lyon in 1798, a Swiss clergyman, Benjamin Frossard stated:

> Mr Newton assures me that according to a planter in Antigua, to whom his ship had been consigned, very detailed calculations are made to determine the most beneficial choice for owners, as between giving slaves a moderate amount of work, plentiful supplies and treatment liable to prolong their lives, or else driving them to death and then buying more to replace them; and that the result of these fine calculations was that the latter method was the most profitable. He adds that he could name several plantations on the island of Antigua where slaves rarely survive more than nine years.[12]

As it so happens, if a Black person committed any offence against the laws on property, he paid for it with his life whereas his master was paid compensation for his loss.

In 1798, *Description de la Nigritie* by Pruneau de Pommegorge, a former member of the Sovereign Council for Senegal, was published in Amsterdam and Paris. It states:

> It is surprising that for a century now we have brought 30,000 to 35,000 Blacks on average every year into our colonies in Saint-Domingue, Martinique, Guadeloupe, Saint-Lucia... the figures are frightening, in that there still is a necessity to send for more from Guinea and our colonists continue to experience a scarcity. But looking closely at what is going on in that country, one's surprise soon subsides.[13]

When he inquired about why colonists took so little care of Black slaves and made them work themselves to death so swiftly whereas their interests should dictate that they be kept alive as long as possible, one colonist answered quite simply that "as long as a newly acquired Negro lasts him one year, he earns for him his value, that is to say the price he paid for him."[14] Even at that time many observers were confronted with this paradox that made Frossard argue: "[The planters'] interest should dictate that they should maintain their Black slaves as long as possible: I agree. Nonetheless, often they do all it takes to lose them."[15]

And he concludes from this:

> if they were less dazzled by the pursuit of immediate gain, they would rapidly conceive that the very same reason that induces them to be sparing in their use of the horses that draw their fine carriages or the oxen that toil to plough their fields, should persuade them to take special care of their slaves whose preservation makes for their prosperity.[16]

The trouble is that one year was enough for a White to recoup the cost of a Black.

Bettelheim was arrested by the Gestapo and interned in a concentration camp. Confronted with the modus operandi of Nazi barbarity he notes:

> ... the Gestapo had several varied, though related purposes. One major goal was to break the prisoners as individuals and to change them into a docile mass from which no individual or group act of resistance could arise. Another purpose was to spread terror among the rest of the population, using prisoners as hostages and intimidating examples of what happened if you did try to resist.[17]

The rationalised, methodical application of terror that was essential to prevent any attempt at rebellion amidst a population that was twenty to thirty times greater than that of its torturers had already proved its worth in America. The reason Europeans there took barbarity beyond what words can express is that at all costs, literally, they had to intimidate a population they saw as insufficiently docile. Father Labat, a missionary in the French West Indies, presumably not particularly inclined towards unwarranted cruelty, considered intimidation of Black a necessity because "they are always ready to revolt, to do anything and commit the most horrible crimes to win their freedom."[18]

Father Labat was no doubt right. If the subordination of Black people had not been as absolute as it was, it is hard to see how the Whites would have been able to entrench their racial supremacy. The argument of the racial inferiority of their victims would certainly not have been enough on its own. Barbarity had to be taken far, very far, to such an extent that it lasted all the way down to modern times. This is what, so to speak, provided certain legitimacy to the administration of torture; it was endorsed twice over: both formally and as an everyday practice.

Seen in this light, even the most unimaginable forms of torture perpetrated by the SS personnel give an impression of déjà vu for anyone who takes the trouble to make a little foray into the history of the concentration camp setting of America. Kogon states:

> The penal companies, especially, were assigned to the quarries, as were certain selected victims. These pits were the hunting preserves of notorious SS sergeants and prison warders. On May 1, 1943 […], the SS men at Buchenwald placed bets of six cigarettes or two glasses of beer apiece as to who could kill a prisoner in a given group by throwing stones at him from above. When their throwing marksmanship grew poor, they lost patience and simply started shooting. The result of this 'pastime' was seventeen dead and wounded.[19]

When I read this account, it reawakened the memory of the shock I had felt twenty years previously when I read about something that happened in Saint-Domingue in the 1780s in Peter Bourne's *Drums of Destiny*. A planter named Marylis one day invited several friends to come and play bowls at his home. He chose a number of Blacks amongst his slaves and buried them alive up to their necks leaving their heads as targets. To kill them all, down to the very last, took them over an hour. From that day onwards, his friends considered Marylis to have more money than he had sense. If what he had wanted was to get rid of a few slaves, he could have sold them.[20] This type of spectacle is inevitable in any system built on the negation of the humanity of whole groups. To begin with, these deeds are intended to terrorise the victims but then, generation after generation, they end up shaping the mentality and the behaviour of society in general.

On this topic, Frederick Douglass's account is telling. Douglass was born on a plantation in the United States at Tuckahoe, near Hillsborough, about 12 miles from Easton, in Talbot County, Maryland. His mother was an enslaved Black. According to what he had heard the Whites on the plantation say, he was born in approximately 1818. Although Blacks were explicitly prohibited from learning to read, Douglass secretly did so. In 1838 he escaped and became free. In 1845, as a tireless advocate for the freedom of Black people, he published his autobiography:

> I speak advisedly when I say this, that killing a slave, or any coloured person, in Talbot County, Maryland, is not treated as a crime, either by the courts or the community. Mr Thomas Lanman, of St. Michael's, killed two slaves, one of whom he killed with a hatchet, by knocking his brains out. He used to boast of the commission of the awful and bloody deed.

Douglass goes on to add:

> The wife of Mr Giles Hicks, living but a short distance from where I used to live, murdered my wife's cousin, a young girl between fifteen and sixteen years of age, mangling her person in the most horrible manner, breaking her nose and breastbone with a stick, so that the poor girl expired in a few hours afterward. She was immediately buried, but had not been in her untimely grave but a few hours before she was taken up and examined by the coroner, who decided that she had come to her death by severe beating. The offence for which this girl was thus murdered was this: – She had been set that night to mind Mrs Hicks's baby, and during the night she fell asleep, and the baby cried. She, having lost her rest for several nights previous, did not hear the crying. They were both in the room with Mrs Hicks. Mrs Hicks, finding the girl slow to move, jumped from her bed, seized an oak stick of wood by the fireplace, and with it broke the girl's nose and breastbone, and thus ended her life.[21]

This "harshness," as the Europeans described it, is found from one end of America to the other. Everywhere, they outdid themselves in inventing means for inflicting pain designed to secure the docility of their victims.

In a letter from Martinique dated May 24, 1712, Governor Phelypeaux appeals to the King to moderate certain practices, giving several examples:

> The naked subject is attached to a stake close to an ant-hill and after rubbing him with some sugar, ants by the spoonful are poured onto him from the top of his skull to the soles of his feet taking care that they should enter into all the orifices of his body. Others are tied up naked to stakes in places where mosquitoes swarm, these being exceedingly stinging insects and causing a torment greater than any other. For others, strips of iron are heated until red hot and then applied and tightly bound to the soles of their feet, around their ankles and over the arch of the foot – a torment that these torturers repeat hourly. Today still, six months after this act of torture there are Negroes and Negresses who cannot take a step.[22]

Apparently, the Governor was not very successful as can be deduced from the enactment, many years later, of laws, decrees and orders designed to codify the "harshness" of Europeans. An administrative regulation in Saint-Domingue dated February 9, 1779 indeed orders:

> We exhort all people of colour, whether freeborn or emancipated, male or female, to display the greatest respect not only for their former masters and drivers, together with their widows and children, but furthermore to all Whites in general under penalty of being taken before special courts

if the need arises and punished ... including by loss of freedom, if the misdemeanour is such as to deserve it.[23]

Earlier, in 1767, the Council of Port-au-Prince (Saint-Domingue) orders a free coloured man to be whipped, branded and sold as a slave for having struck a White. The metropolitan authorities seem to consider these measures inadequate. In 1778, the minister sends

> several copies of a decision of the Senior Council of the Île de France dated August 18, 1777 sentencing a free Negro to be hung for insults and premeditated attack on the person of Mr Foucault. As it is necessary to maintain free and enslaved Negroes in subordination, the intention of his Majesty is for this order to be made public in Saint-Domingue. By order of the Council of Cape dated June 9, 1780, two free coloured women who indulged in a lively exchange with a White woman are sentenced to being tied by iron collars to a stake specially set up for this purpose at Clugny square on a market day and to remain there from seven in the morning till ten with a sign in front of them bearing the words "mulatto guilty of insolence towards White women.[24]

There is a plain determination to make clear over and again that even the most backward of Whites possesses tremendous powers over non-Whites such that the wisest of the non-Whites owes obedience and submission to the most dim-witted White. The fact that these oppressive measures were publicised is intended to reinforce the Europeans' awareness of belonging to a superior race and the non-Europeans' awareness of their inferiority and hammer in the need to behave with extreme humility towards Whites, even when they come under attack from the latter. Children too must learn how to behave at a very early age. All non-Whites, young or old, owe White children obedience. If, for instance, a White child has a tantrum, he is allowed to "get it out of his system" by dealing the piccaninny allotted to him a few blows with a stick. As for the piccaninny, he or she is well-advised to understand at a very early stage that there can be no defending oneself or running away. As is to be expected, they each conform to their respective role at a very early age. "It was a common saying, even among little White boys, that it was worth a half-cent to kill a 'nigger,' and a half-cent to bury one.[25]"

It is significant that in spite of the distance that separated the colonial metropolis from the Americas, the concern for subduing the victims had to be so forcefully expressed by the authorities from the metropole. Every single law directed at reducing Blacks to the status of animals, at casting them into sub-humanity, was instigated by the metropolis. Even the most abominable sentences delivered by the courts located in the concentration camp setting of America conformed to the higher law of the metropolis. Furthermore, magistrates that represented the law and administered justice in the colonies were frequently from the metropolis.

Even women who, it is thought, are more liable to feel compassion and be less inclined to violence and torture, surrendered to the depravation of the unlimited power they had over their non-White victims. In Douglass's words:

> Directly opposite to us, on Philpot Street, lived Mr Thomas Hamilton. He owned two slaves. Their names were Henrietta and Mary. Henrietta was about twenty-two years of age, Mary was about fourteen; and of all the mangled and emaciated creatures I ever looked upon, these two were the most so. His heart must be harder than stone that could look upon these unmoved. The head, neck, and shoulders of Mary were literally cut to pieces. I have frequently felt her head, and found it nearly covered with festering sores, caused by the lash of her cruel mistress. I do not know that her master ever whipped her, but I have been an eyewitness to the cruelty of Mrs Hamilton. I used to be in Mr Hamilton's house nearly every day. Mrs Hamilton used to sit in a large chair in the middle of the room, with a heavy bull's pizzle always by her side, and scarce an hour passed during the day but was marked by the blood of one of these slaves. The girls seldom passed her without her saying, "Move faster, you – black gip! –" at the same time giving them a blow with the bull's pizzle over the head or shoulders, often drawing blood. She would then say, "Take that, you – black gip! –" continuing, "If you don't move faster, I'll move you!" Added to the cruel lashings to which these slaves were subjected, they were kept nearly half-starved. They seldom knew what it was to eat a full meal. I have seen Mary contending with the pigs for the offal thrown into the street. So much was Mary kicked and cut to pieces, that she was oftener called "pecked" than by her name.[26]

Always and everywhere, regimes that are bent on achieving the total submission of individuals exhibit the same depravity. Bettelheim describes the SS attitude towards suicide in the process of the depersonalisation of victims noting that:

> … the main goal of the SS was to do away with independence of action and the ability to make personal decisions, even negative ways of achieving it were not neglected. The decision to remain alive or to die is probably the supreme example of self-determination. […] The greater the number of

prisoners that committed suicide, the easier was the task of their guards. But even there, the decision must not be the prisoner's. An SS man might provoke a prisoner to commit suicide by running against the electrically charged wire fence, and that was all right. But for those who took the initiative to kill themselves, the SS in Dachau in 1933 issued a special order: prisoners who attempted suicide but did not succeed were to receive twenty lashes and prolonged solitary confinement. Supposedly this was to punish them for their failure to do away with themselves; but I am convinced that it was much more to punish them for an act of self-determination.[27]

One of the testimonials presented by Isabelle and Jean-Louis Vissière was given by Jean-Gabriel Stedman, already mentioned above, and was published in 1796 upon his return from Surinam. This Dutch colony was contending with a rebellion by Blacks fighting for freedom. The metropolis sent out an Expeditionary Corps. One of the mercenaries in that corps was an English officer, Captain Jean-Gabriel Stedman. He states:

> Mrs. S. was travelling to her plantation in a covered boat accompanied by a Negress who was suckling her child. This woman was sitting at the front; the child was crying and could not be soothed. Mrs S., disturbed by the cries of this creature, ordered her slave to bring the child to her. She grasped the child by the arm and held it under water until it drowned and then let it go leaving it to drift with the current. The desperate mother immediately threw herself into the river determined to put an end to her days. But she was prevented from doing so; a party of oarsmen dove into the water and brought her back on to the boat. Upon reaching the plantation, her mistress ordered her slave to be lashed three or four times to punish her for the harm she had wished upon her mistress by putting an end to her days.[28]

One might think Mrs. S. wished to preserve the property in which she had invested, but considering how willingly Whites caused Blacks to perish, I am convinced that it was simply a reminder that even the very act of breathing lies within the purview of white supremacy.

Human beings as a commodity

> Both the concentration camps and the death camps, and what happened in them were an application beyond reason of the concept of labour as a commodity. In the camps not only human labour but the total person became commodity. People were 'handled' as if they were made to order. They were used and changed according to the desires of the customer, in this case the state. When no longer useful, they were discarded, but with care so that no salvable material was wasted.

> ...Athenian prisoners of war were 'worked to death' too, in the quarries of Syracuse. But there again it was a state that exploited slave labour, not private capitalists. Nevertheless, the analogy between the quarries of Mauthausen and Syracuse, separated by more than 2000 years, is appalling.[29]

I would add that there is no need to go that far back in time to establish this analogy as noted by Bettelheim above. It is enough to take a glimpse at the concentration camp setting of America. But the willingness to do so would require that three and a half centuries of mass deportation of Africans towards America and the negation of their humanity resulting in the institutionalisation of barbarity had made its way into the collective memory of Europeans. In point of fact, the destruction of these millions of women, men and children, who were sacrificed because they were black, has never penetrated into the Western collective memory. In the twenty-first century, their descendants continue to hope for, seek and see justice administered to the victims of white supremacy, i.e., they seek recognition of their humanity and consequently of the crime against humanity of which they were the victims.

One of the testimonies presented by Isabelle and Jean-Louis Vissière came from Paul Erdman Isert, a German surgeon. According to Vissière, in 1786, the king of the Ashanti, whose sister this physician had cured, offered to show him his kingdom after which he returned to Europe by the slave traders' route, giving him an opportunity to visit the Indies. The letters that he sent to his family were published in 1788. One of the deeds he had witnessed first-hand on the island of Sainte-Croix, described in his letter of March 12, 1787 to his father in Christianstadt, has stayed in my mind:

> The quantity of stones makes working the land more difficult than it is ordinarily. Since a plough cannot be used, everything is done with a hoe and the toil of these Negroes. The cruelty with which these wretches are treated in that country, mainly those who by misfortune fall into the hands of a farmer, is inconceivable. [...] I saw that for very trifling mistakes, often mistakes just imagined, they are publicly tied to a stake whereupon their flesh is torn into pieces by a whip. Their backs are scarred for life! And yet it is still not enough for their skin to be so pitilessly lacerated – no! Their suffering would be far too short lived! Some way must be found to sting them even more so that they feel it for even longer; and so their bleeding wounds are rubbed with salt and hot pepper! So, one is tempted to ask, what is generally the crime committed by this petty villain? He wants to run away, shouts the master, he wants to live as the savages do, the dog! Put him in an iron collar with a pair of horns so that everyone knows

what he is! Means for tormenting Negroes in the colonies are infinite. But nobody excels more in these abominable inventions than the noble breed of mulattos, those creatures that are somewhere between a Negro and a European! The wife of one of these in my area had a Negro who had broken some sort of utensil. To make sure the misdeed was painfully avenged, she had him stripped naked, his hands tied and hung him on a nail. Then she took a needle, which she slowly stuck in him, piercing all the parts of his body. The unfortunate fellow gave forth strange cries but she went on performing her operation for a whole hour...

I saw a bizarre contraption intended to rid Negroes of their taste for brandy, which, alas, is their sole consolation amidst all their misfortunes. It is a tin mask that covered the whole head of a woman and was clasped round her neck by means of a lock. It has holes on a level with the eyes and nose so that the person can see and breathe. But the woman cannot take any sort of food without permission, for the mask must be opened. She was compelled to wear this muzzle day and night![30]

Isert's account explains how it came to be that religion deludes one into believing that routine acts of barbarity are done in a charitable spirit. From there stems the benevolent explanation produced by (European) historians who are willing to accept that by pouring lemon juice, salt and pepper on the bleeding wounds of Blacks, Whites were concerned that the wounds should not become infected. I have even heard a Black lawyer, who was seeking justice for the victims of the concentration camp setting of America, quite seriously explain that at the time the habit of putting salt and pepper on wounds caused by whip lashes was intended to avert gangrene. This justification has accomplished the feat of making even the cruellest manifestations of barbarity acceptable. Fortunately, we have the first-hand testimony of Erdman Isert who could see this was neither curative nor preventive but simply cruel.

The sophistication of the cruelty perpetrated on this coloured woman is a sign of how institutionalised barbarity was able to shape mentalities. Combining terror in its most violent form with a discourse on racial superiority was to have the most disastrous consequences. The so-called mixed bloods, i.e., people born through sexual exploitation or rape, strove to keep their fate separate from that set aside for other Blacks. In general, they desperately sought closer ties with Whites. Unhappily for them, Whites were wholly unreceptive and gave no consideration to the fact that these were their own offspring fathered under illegitimate circumstances. As testified by Jean-Gabriel Stedman, "I met with a Dutch captain who argued that because a Negress whom he had temporarily made his mistress was pregnant she should fetch a higher price, thus trafficking in his own flesh and blood.[31]" This speaks eloquently of the moral collapse of respectable European society.

The closer mixed bloods are to the White man, the greater is their contempt for their Black mother or grandmother to whom they owe the stigma of the cursed race. They might concomitantly also hate their White father who refuses to recognise them as one of his kin. This tragic downward spiral whose repercussions – by the way – continue to be felt to this very day, led to some ostensibly incomprehensible conduct amongst many mixed bloods, including the case mentioned by Isert.

The role of the victims

For a Black person embarking on the study of the system of violence in the concentration camp setting of America, it is somewhat disturbing to discover that, when a White decided to have a Black tortured, the act itself was generally carried out by a Black. Many historians have gleefully underlined the fact that often the atrocities suffered by Blacks were even more appalling when their torturers were themselves Black. In these cases, no attempt is made to disguise the violence so that the reader gets the unpleasant impression that if Black people had been a little more mutually supportive, the system would not have lasted nearly as long as it did. In short, the victims are the ones responsible.

Certainly, the Whites could make use – and did make use – of their victims to better crush them. There was no way any Black person could possibly object. Jean-Gabriel Stedman illustrates this:

> The first act of barbarity that awakened my compassion was the execution that I witnessed in a nearby plantation. A beautiful Samboean slave, aged about 18, completely naked, was tied to a tree by her arms. Hanging there, she was so cruelly lacerated by the whips that two Negroes were wielding that blood streamed down her from head to toe. The poor wretch had already received two hundred strokes when I noticed her head lolling down on her chest, presenting the most atrocious sight. I ran to the overseer and begged him to free her immediately since she had already received her full allocation of the punishment. But he answered me that to prevent strangers from interfering with his administration, he had set himself a strict rule that the punishment should be doubled if any such person were to intercede in favour of the guilty party. Thus the barbarian ordered the execution to be immediately repeated. I attempted in vain to stop him, he declared to me

that any delay far from softening his resolve would only make his vengeance all the more implacable and terrible. I had no choice but to flee from this hateful monster and leave him to satisfy his thirst for blood like a rabid beast. When I tried to find out the reason for this barbarity, I learnt with certainty that the only crime that this unfortunate had committed was to persistently reject the caresses of her vile tormentor.[32]

The power that Whites had over the Black population was boundless. This was no clandestine or covert power, exercised from behind the scenes. It was a power so inordinate that it had nothing to fear from inquisitive eyes.

The witness went on to add that when he went back to the plantation where he was staying, he learnt that the master of the house, Mr Ebber, had behaved likewise in a similar situation:

> A Black prisoner had fled into the forest and Mr Ebber in a fury turned on the two slaves who let the prisoner go and had them tied up in the carpenter's workshop. Under his orders they were so cruelly thrashed that Captain Tulling felt he should ask for them to be pardoned. But with no greater success than I. His intercession produced the opposite effect to the one he anticipated. The humming of the whip lashes and the excruciating cries of these unfortunate persons could be heard for more than an hour and a half and this barbaric punishment did not stop until one of the two had died.[33]

The Nazis too, who built on past experience, used their victims to speed up the process of their own destruction. Bettelheim notes:

> It was almost impossible for prisoners not to cooperate with SS efforts to reduce them to passivity inside a de-individualised mass. Both the prisoner's self-interest and SS pressure worked in the same direction. To remain independent implied dangers and many hardships; to comply with the SS seemed in the prisoner's own interest, because it automatically made life easier for him.[34]

Just as the Europeans had previously done in America, the Nazis in Europe utilised their victims' right up to the last moment. The rule of terror ensured that they obeyed and obedience in turn kept the system running smoothly. In Poland for instance, as early as 1939, the German authorities decreed the principle of forced labour. The Jewish organisations were put in charge of organising "the Jewish units" that the Germans were to use as and when needed. Hilberg quotes a German eyewitness in 1940 who stated: "Today in the Gouvernement général, one can see Jewish troops, spades on shoulders, marching without any German escort through the countryside. At the head of the column marches likewise a Jew.[35]

The Nazis' total subordination of human beings in Europe, although directed at victims whose status was different, produced the same result as the total subordination of human beings by Europeans in America. This sheds light on the reasons that Blacks "facilitated" their own annihilation.

> In Upper Silesia, where the Jewish population is concentrated in the cities of Sosnowiec, Bedzin and Dabrowa, Regierungsprasident Schmelt, acting in his capacity as Regional Plenipotentiary for non-German labour, sent several units of 10,000 Jews to industrial plants, we are told by Hilberg. They were separated from the non-Jews and compelled to work for pay that was 30% less than the normal salary under the command of Jewish foremen who were paid a little more. Schmelt took care to describe the method to the Slovak delegation and explained that if a Jewish supervisor did not achieve the production targets, he was demoted to the rank of labourer. Consequently, he told his visitors, these privileged people drove the other Jews using 'brutal means'.[36]

It cannot be overstressed how carefully the Nazis drew on past experiences to build their system. It is known that the Europeans in America were careful to avoid bringing groups of Africans that spoke the same language or came from related communities to live on the same plantation. Freshly imported Africans who were put up for sale at public auction were systematically separated, including brothers from sisters, husbands from wives and even children from parents. The official reason put forward at the time for this dispersal was that although painful it was necessary to avoid rebellion.

In the concentration camps, to prevent cohesive groups from forming, the Nazis established several categories of prisoners on the basis of their actual or presumed affinities. By mixing them, the SS exacerbated the tensions and used them to better establish their authority. Kogon notes:

> On the other hand the intermingling of the prisoner categories was to serve the principle of "Divide and Rule." Conflicts were to be pointed up, every sense of solidarity undermined, so that a few could control the many. Control of each camp was in the hands of a very small group of picked death-head officers permanently assigned to the commandant. They used different prisoner categories for their purposes in turn, playing one off against the other. In view of the motley character of the prisoners, the SS had no trouble in finding and planting their ever-present informers. Coupled with the merciless exercise of terror, these methods enabled a handful of men to keep even the largest camps in check.[37]

Prey for the dogs

Just as the Europeans had done in America, the Nazis in Europe put dogs to good use. There are countless accounts of how the SS enjoyed having their prisoners savaged for the sake of cultivating their dogs' ferocity. Kogon, for instance, reports: "Many of the guard battalions had special dog platoons, consisting of bloodhounds and police dogs trained to attack men in striped clothing. They were used outside the guard line – on railroad construction sites and the like – and did a great deal of mischief.[38]"

In the concentration camp setting of America, dogs were trained to drink the blood of Blacks and feed on their flesh. The Spaniards were undoubtedly some of the best breeders of these animals, but they were not the only ones. All the European nations used the ferocity of these Black-eating dogs. The Europeans came up with the idea of using those who were the intended victims of these savage beasts to train them.

Towards the end of the 1920s, a survey was conducted in the United States among a handful of people who had survived slavery. They had been born on plantations and freed at the end of the American Civil War. These surveys were published under the title *Slave Narratives*.

> Then, one day along come a Friday and that an unlucky star day and I playin' round de house and Marster Williams come up and say, 'Delia, will you 'low Jim walk down de street with me?' My mammy say, 'All right, Jim, you be a good boy,' and dat de las' time I ever heared her speak, or ever see her. We walks down whar de houses grows close together and pretty soon comes to de slave market. I ain't seed it 'fore, but when Marster Williams says, 'Git up on de block,' I got a funny feelin', and I knows what has happened. I's sold to Marster John Pinchback and he had de St. Vitus dance and he likes to make de niggers suffer to make up for his squirmin' and twistin' and he the bigges' debbil on earth.
>
> We leaves right away for Texas and goes to marster's ranch in Columbus. It was owned by him and a man call Wright, and when we gits there I's put to work without nothin' to eat. Dat night I makes up my mind to run away but de nex' day dey takes me and de other niggers to look at de dogs and chooses me to train de dogs with. I's told I had to play I runnin' away and to run five mile in any way and then climb a tree. One of de niggers tells me kind of nice to climb as high in dat tree as I could if I didn't want my body tore off my legs. So I runs a good five miles and climbs up in de tree whar de branches is gettin' small.

> "I sits dere a long time and den sees de dogs comin'. When dey gits under de tree dey sees me and starts barkin'. After dat I never got thinkin' of runnin' away.[39]

If a Black child playing the part of a fugitive was unable to climb up a tree before the dogs caught up with him, he would be devoured. This was no great loss: just a routine part of the dog training.

The destruction of families

This determination to break down any bond arising from family ties amongst victims is a constant feature.

> I had a brother, Jim, who wuz sold ter dress young Missus fer her weddin.' De tree am still standin' whar I set under an' watch'em sell Jim. I set dar an' I cry, specially when dey puts de chains on him an' carries him off. An' I ain't neber felt so lonesome in my whole life. I ain't neber hyar from Jim since, an' I wonder now, sometimes, iffen he's still livin'.[40]

This is clearly a standard practice. A Black child was not allowed to experience what was set aside for White children alone: the joy of nestling against their mother's breast. The dimensions and consequences of this crime have never been studied.

The chains of slavery were not made lighter for women who gave birth to mixed blood infants fathered by their master, nor did the circumstance of rape alleviate the sufferings of slavery for the child born of this forced intercourse. Indeed, often matters were made worse. Douglass's testimony in this respect is enlightening:

> My father was a White man. He was admitted to be such by all I ever heard speak of my parentage. The opinion was also whispered that my master was my father; but of the correctness of this opinion, I know nothing; the means of knowing was withheld from me. My mother and I were separated when I was but an infant – before I knew her as my mother. It is a common custom, in the part of Maryland from which I ran away, to part children from their mothers at a very early age. Frequently, before the child has reached its twelfth month, its mother is taken from it, and hired out on some farm a considerable distance off, and the child is placed under the care of an old woman, too old for field labour. For what this separation is done, I do not know, unless it be to hinder the development of the child's affection toward its mother, and to blunt and destroy the natural affection of the mother for the child. This is the inevitable result.

> I never saw my mother, to know her as such, more than four or five times in my life; and each of these times was very short in duration, and at night. She was hired by a Mr Stewart, who lived about twelve miles from my home. She made her journeys to see me in the night, travelling the whole distance on foot, after the performance of her day's work. She was a field hand, and a whipping is the penalty of not being in the field at sunrise, unless a slave has special permission from his or her master to the contrary – a permission which they seldom get, and one that gives to him that gives it the proud name of being a kind master. I do not recollect of ever seeing my mother by the light of day. She was with me in the night. She would lie down with me, and get me to sleep, but long before I waked she was gone. Very little communication ever took place between us. Death soon ended what little we could have while she lived, and with it her hardships and suffering. She died when I was about seven years old, on one of my master's farms, near Lee's Mill. I was not allowed to be present during her illness, at her death, or burial.[41]

In fact this was standard practice. The Portuguese, Spaniards, French, Dutch, and English developed the habit of mixing business with pleasure: To satisfy their often depraved sexual instincts, Black girls or women were raped as a matter of course. This often produced a mixed blood infant who not only increased the master's chattel, but also sold for a higher price. Later on, the apostles of white supremacy and historians took cynicism to the extreme and would have us believe that as long as these crimes were committed in the pursuit of profit they were not crimes against humanity. It was along these lines that a discourse developed that alleges that there are policies designed to annihilate whole groups but not intended to exterminate the victims and that such policies cannot be characterised as a crime against humanity – anyway, what is the connection between humanity and Blacks? – and certainly not as a genocide. Why? Because what was behind this policy aimed at annihilating Blacks in the concentration camp setting of America was the pursuit of profit. Never mind that it cost the lives of 20 or 200 million child victims. It was for a good cause, the cause of profit that was so beneficial to white supremacy. Then there is a separate, altogether different category – major crimes – in which from the start the intention was extermination. These are crimes against humanity.

Whatever the intentions were here or there, when Europeans in America separated parents from their children, they had no more qualms than the SS did on the arrival ramps at Auschwitz. Except, some might object, for the difference that in Auschwitz the victims faced immediate death, whereas in

America a recently acquired Black slave must live at least one year before his master was able to recoup the price paid. I prefer to dwell on the similarity in content that denied humanity in both of these cases.

The suffering and anguish of the Blacks who were forever separated from their children, their wives, their husbands, their brothers and sisters and parents, who were debased, dehumanised, treated like animals and commodities, was as heart-rending and distressing as that of the victims of Auschwitz upon being parted from their nearest and dearest. These were all agonising wrenches in the face of death. The reason these comparisons are so shocking to Europeans is simply because Auschwitz is part of their collective memory whereas the torture, suffering and death of these millions of women, men and children who lost their lives for the sake of white supremacy have never entered the collective memory of the Western world.

Have the doubts Europeans entertained about the humanity of Blacks completely disappeared today, after those three and a half centuries of uninterrupted dehumanisation? The European nations responsible for this disaster have yet to seek pardon from their victims. They procrastinate and have appropriated a right that even defeated Germany would not have dared claim: the right to characterise their own crimes, and decide, in lieu of their victims, what, if any, is the historical significance of the event.

A well-oiled system

The concentration camp setting of America did not operate unplanned and of its own accord. A whole arsenal of measures was established to regulate the life of non-Whites down to the very last detail. To insure total subjection of Blacks, White power had to be absolute. The rules set out every detail – at what time the Blacks had to be up and how many lashes of the whip they would receive if they were late. Blacks were not allowed to travel unless they had a written authorisation from their masters, and their jailers kept their movements to a strict minimum. Under no circumstances were they to be allowed to learn to read or write – just imagine, a Black might forge an authorisation, not only for himself but for other Blacks, too. The punishment for a Black caught red-handed in the act of reading was twenty-five to fifty lashes of the whip. Never before had a totalitarian regime taken the subordination of other men to this extreme. Even the people taken into slavery by the Athenians some 2000 years ago were not deprived of the right to read. There is only one other instance of such a ban. It occurred, post-1948, in South Africa, where the Whites managed to apply a treatment that Hitler had developed specially for non-Aryans. We shall return to this later.

The meticulous, almost obsessive way in which Europeans managed the concentration camp setting of America was not very dissimilar from the single-mindedness typical of the Nazis when seeking to control the existence of their victims. Blacks were not allowed to meet without permission from Whites. They were prohibited from carrying any form of weapon including sticks. Every detail was regulated, including the type of cotton material they used to clothe themselves and the names they called themselves. A whole array of punishments were defined for Blacks whose behaviour in any way contradicted or attempted to elude their predetermined status as sub-humans at the beck and call of the race of masters. These ranged from different forms of mutilation to hanging. These methods of destruction became integral to European domination so that when the concentration camp setting of America collapsed and European domination became established in Africa, Africans who were disinclined to obey were similarly punished, i.e., by cutting-off their fists or noses, and piercing ears.

In North America, for instance, Whites sometimes had the "good taste" to allow the victim to choose the particular mutilation to which he would be subjected. A runaway Black might be free to choose whether to have his penis or foot amputated. The Spaniards decided for themselves which organ to cut-off a non-White. A Coloured man guilty of having helped a fugitive received a punishment "of a hundred lashes of the whip the first time, castration the second and death the third.[42]"

Hiding a fugitive, giving him a little food or helping him in any way was considered to be a particularly serious offence. The price being so heavy, it was unusual for solidarity towards victims to be contemplated in any form. All the way through to the end of the first half of the nineteenth century, there continued to be cases where free or emancipated Blacks accused of helping a fugitive were cast back into slavery together with their families and subsequently sold-off separately.

In Lima, any Black guilty of having helped a fugitive was liable to be emasculated. The fugitive himself might suffer the same punishment. "In 1572, Francesco de Toledo acknowledged that in Lima a number of fugitives had been castrated under Marquis of Cañete.[43]" Cases of emasculation of Blacks were not confined to Peru alone. According to Tardieu, it was believed that this practice was found all over Tierra Firme, a territory spanning the Panama isthmus and the coasts of Colombia and Venezuela.

Whipping was the most widespread form of punishment in the territories under Spanish control, as well as everywhere else.

> Flogging was often combined with other forms of cruelty. In Tierra Firme, the penalty for a guilty person who had gone missing for more than eight days was to be locked in irons (calza for the feet, and ramal for the neck) each of which weighed twelve pounds, for two months. If he removes them, he receives 200 lashes of the whip the first time, as many the second and the penalty is prolonged to four months.[44]

The collateral damage of some forms of mutilation, such as severing a Black's hand or foot, was loss of productivity. Some masters were heard to protest. In one instance, the French government found a solution that was welcomed by the Whites. Article 40 of the 1685 decree, more commonly known as *Le Code Noir*, specified that: "Slaves sentenced to death following denunciation by their masters, providing the latter were not accomplices to the crime will, prior to being executed, be evaluated by two principal citizens of the island appointed by the judge. The assessed amount will be paid to the master. The amount shall by levied by the bursar on a per taxable head of Negro basis, the dues to be collected by the tenant of the *Domaine royal d'occident* ["Royal Land of the West"] to avoid weighing on the public purse." Since the very purpose of mutilating Black people and hanging them was to terrorise them and thereby deter them from rebelling or fleeing, it was neither reasonable nor right that the loss of the punished party be borne by the owner alone, whereas peace and public safety were beneficial to white supremacy as a whole. In this way a sort of provident fund was set up, to pay damages to the masters for each lawfully tortured Black. The most spine-chilling consequence of this bureaucratic measure was that it allowed Whites to order the punishment of sick or weak Blacks who had become useless mouths to feed, with the added bonus often of receiving compensation above the market price. Two centuries later, in the 1820s, this measure was still dealing out destruction to Blacks. Many Black women and men, worked to the point of collapse, were brought before the Provost's court in Martinique and accused – not of having wanted to escape, because they did not have the strength to run – but allegedly preparing poison or plotting to poison children the names of whom nobody even bothered to mention in the presentation of charges. This presented fine opportunities, in addition to the compensation obtained, for masters to get rid of, not just useless mouths to feed, but also any rebellious spirits who might cause trouble in the workshops. This convenient method of denunciation by the master was considered as sufficient evidence for the court to order severe punishment. Morenas, who at the time was brave enough to criticise this premeditated culling, emphasises:

> The owners of slaves protested vehemently against maiming for as long as the master was not paid the value of the Black, who more often than not died as a result of the punishment. But ever since £2,000 per head of Negro punished has been awarded, they find that maiming of arms and legs, severing of ears, noses and hamstrings are a natural and necessary means to maintain law and order.[45]

Published judgments handed down by the Provostial Court of Martinique gives an idea of the substance of colonial justice:

> By judgment of this Court on November 27, 1822, the slaves Prosper, Jean-Noel, Lazare, Calixte, Marcel, Offort, Catherine, Reine, Xavier, Saint-Paul; the free mulattos Déade, Régis and Jean-Baptiste accused of having administered poison and used it against animals; Charlotte, Marie-Thérèse aka Zo and Thérésine Hippolyte, accused of using poison to cause the death of animals and children (unnamed); Reine, Laurent and Romuald aka Laurette accused of having prepared and administered poison are condemned to decapitation.
>
> Judgment of the Provostial Court of July 1, 1823: Ambroise and Pierre for having poisoned livestock and men (unnamed); the Negro Parfait, for having poisoned livestock are condemned to decapitation; Elize, Zenon, Manette, Modeste and Joli-Coeur for having prepared potions and spells are sentenced to be branded, to the whip and sent to the galleys for life.
>
> Judgment of the Provostial Court of December 2, 1823: Raymond, a coloured man, seriously suspected of complicity in the poisoning of animals and people, of using by superstition human bones to perform and conceal the misdeed; the Negro, Régis, for having made and administered poison are sentenced to the whip, to be branded and sent to the galleys for life.
>
> Another judgment of this court sentenced the Negroes Placide, Beau, Charles and Maximum, to the whip, to be branded and to the galleys for life without specifying any reason for the punishment. The judgment orders that it is appropriate to multiply the punishments to deter the crime.[46]

Endless numbers of examples could be quoted: it is estimated that this court targeted twenty victims every month and was not abolished until 1827, by order of the Department of the Navy.

The Eurocentric vision of history would have one believe that these facts, while admittedly wrong, cannot be compared with the atrocities perpetrated by the Nazis because, in America, Whites were in pursuit of monetary gain, whereas in Europe, the Nazis were allegedly driven only by their criminal instincts. Louis Sala-Molins has convincingly demonstrated that: "Extermination is not done for extermination's sake. It is done because the perpetrator is confident that he will derive a supreme gain from the extermination.[47]" There is no such thing as a utilitarian genocide as opposed to a wanton genocide; there is just the crime of genocide.

The race of masters and their laws

It is significant that not one among European historians, legal experts and researchers that investigated the legal system of the Third Reich, found it worthwhile to explore the connections between the segregationist laws of Nuremberg and those instigated by the slave-trading powers in earlier times, in spite of the glaring similarities.

The racially based legal arsenal of the concentration camp setting established in America by the slave-trading powers for non-Whites alone includes countless laws and decrees that are patently intended to produce irreversible debasement of non-Whites. The purpose of these laws was to banish in Blacks any thought or sense of belonging to the human species. Blacks were cast out of humanity and kept well away from it. That is how white supremacy and the racist doctrine were able to reach a position of domination rivalled only by Hitler's[48] later exploits. Strangely, this connection has never come to the notice of the specialists.

One of the most deleterious effects of racial domination by Whites was that they were successful in getting the victims themselves to share the contempt that was heaped upon them. Thus, it was common for individuals whose grandmother or great grandmother was Black to ostentatiously express their contempt or even hatred for the Black race while asserting the inheritance of their White fathers and the pedigree thereby established. To no avail. Indeed, those who believed that they would gain official status as Whites after four generations without a single drop of black blood being re-injected were in for a surprise. When, in 1766, the Governor of Cayenne asked the Minister of the Navy how many generations were required before a Coloured man could claim to belong to the White race, the answer, according to Cohen, was categorical: "Those who descend from (Blacks) can never enter the class of Whites. For if there were a time when that could happen, they would then enjoy all the privileges of Whites, which would be against the constitution of the colonies.[49]"

Casting out a human group of people from public life on the grounds of their racial inferiority was an invariable feature of the legal arsenal of the slave-trading nations. A royal ordinance relating to the Windward Islands in 1733 states:

> The order of the King is that any inhabitant of mixed blood is prohibited from taking on any office in the judiciary or in the militia. It is also His will that any inhabitant who shall marry a Negress or a mulatto woman shall be banned from becoming an officer and from taking up any position of employment in the colony.

Years later, this ordinance was supplemented by an order of the Senior Council of Martinique dated May 9, 1765, applicable to all the Windward Islands. It "bans notaries public, registrars, bailiffs and prosecutors from employing coloured persons in their offices: considering that duties of this type can be entrusted only to peoples whose probity is recognised, which cannot be assumed to be the case in anyone of such lowly birth as a mulatto.[50]"

This order was once again compounded by article 3 of the ordinance of the Governor and Intendant dated November 25, 1783:

> Considering that His Majesty is intent on not destroying the difference that nature has set up between Whites and Blacks and that previous political determination has carefully maintained a degree of distance that coloured people and their descendants must never trespass; that, finally, it is important so as to maintain law and order that the state of humiliation attached to the species be cultivated in all respects; previous determination that is of special use because it is found in the very hearts of Blacks and contributes importantly to the very peace of the colonies, [...] His Majesty is determined to maintain the principle that forever removes coloured persons and their offspring from all the privileges attached to Whites.[51]

This does not differ significantly from the grounds presented by the legal experts of the Third Reich when it came to driving out the Jews from public life. The April 7, 1933 Law for the restoration of the professional civil service states:

> This law governs the statute for civil servants. It provides for dismissals, retirement, and demotion of some officials who do not offer the required professional, moral, political guarantees [...]. Civil servants who are not of Aryan descent must be pensioned off. If they are honorary officials, they must be dismissed.

Jews offered no more moral guarantees to the Nazis than mulattoes did to the Whites. And probably so as to cultivate the state of humiliation attached to the species of non-Aryans, these gentlemen of the Third Reich came up with the June 30, 1933 law, amending the civil servant statute. The incapacities were thereby extended to the spouses of Jews: "Civil servants of Aryan origin who marry persons of non-Aryan descent must be dismissed. Any person seeking appointment as a civil servant must prove that his or her spouse is of Aryan descent."

In the concentration camp setting of America, non-Whites were banned from any position that was socially valued or economically worthwhile as part of a deliberate design to exclude them. The only equivalent instance of such a scheme is found in the Nazi laws designed to exclude Jews from positions coveted by many Aryans who believed the key to a successful career lay in evicting their Jewish colleagues.

Such was the determination of the power structure to reinforce the state of humiliation in which non-Whites were placed, that they even ruled on names that non-Whites were entitled to use. The Governor and Intendant Ordinances of January 6, 1773 and May 4, 1774, spell this out:

> Ban people of colour, whether born free or emancipated, from bearing the names of Whites because misappropriation of a name of the White race casts doubts on the status of a person, causes confusion and finally destroys that intangible barrier that public opinion has established and that wise government maintains.[52]

The Nazis took a similar line by requiring Jews to use the forenames Sarah for women and Israel for men.

Notes

1. Schoelcher, Victor, *Des colonies françaises*, Paris, 1842, p. 86 (Translation).
2. de Wismes, Armel, *La traite négrière vers le Nouveau Monde*, Rennes, 1984, p. 26.
3. Kogon, op. cit., *L'État SS* (Seuil, 1970) traduit d'allemand *Der SS-Staat, Das System der deutschen Konzentrationslager*, 1946; première édition et trad. française en 1947 sous le titre: *L'Enfer organisé – Le système des camps de concentration*, La Jeune Parque), p. 104.
4. Morenas, Joseph Elzear, *Précis historique de la Traite des Noirs et de l'esclavage colonial*, Paris 1828, p. 251.
5. Ibid; pp. 251–252.
6. Ibid; pp. 317–318.
7. Ibid; p. 317.

8. Gisler, Antoine, *L'esclavage aux Antilles françaises*, Paris, 1981, pp. 84–85.
9. Schoelcher, op. cit., p. 133.
10. Bettelheim, Bruno, *The Informed Heart – Autonomy in a Mass Age*, Avon Books, 1979, pp. 110–111.
11. Presented by Fabre, Michel, *Esclaves et Planteurs*, Paris, 1978, p. 91. Note that the quote from Frederick Law Olmsted translated herein was taken from a French translation and not the original English.
12. Quoted by Isabelle and Jean-Louis Vissière, *La Traite des Noirs au siècle des Lumières*, Paris, 1982, p. 106.
13. Ibid, p. 78.
14. Ibid.
15. Ibid, p. 101.
16. Ibid, p. 107.
17. Bettelheim, Bruno, op. cit., p. 110.
18. Cohen, William B., *The French Encounter with Africans: White Response to Blacks, 1530–1880*, Indiana University Press, 2003, p. 57.
19. Kogon E., Ibid pp. 95–96.
20. Bourne, Peter, *Drums of Destiny*, New York, G.P. Putnam's Sons, 1947.
21. Douglass F. http://sunsite.berkeley.edu/Literature/Douglass/Autobiography/04.html
22. Gisler, op. cit., p. 43.
23. Ibid, p. 95.
24. Ibid, pp. 95–96.
25. Douglass F. http://sunsite.berkeley.edu/Literature/Douglass/Autobiography/04.html
26. Douglass F. http://sunsite.berkeley.edu/Literature/Douglass/Autobiography/06.html
27. Bettelheim, Bruno, op. cit., pp. 150–151.
28. Vissière, op. cit., p. 143.
29. Bettelheim, Bruno, op. cit., p. 238.
30. Vissière, op.cit., pp. 127–128.
31. Ibid., p. 138.
32. Ibid., pp. 139–140.
33. Ibid., p. 142.
34. Bettelheim, Bruno, op. cit., p. 136
35. Hilberg, Raul, *The Destruction of the European Jews*, New York, Harper & Row, 1961, p. 163., translation *La destruction des Juifs d'Europe*, Paris, 1988, p. 218.
36. Ibid.
37. Kogon E., op. cit., pp. 36–37.

38. Ibid, p. 56.
39. See http://bellsouthpwp.net/g/o/goodoowah/afram/Green2.htm; Mellon, James, *Bullwhip Days*, Grove Press, New York 1988, p. 299.
40. See http://www.gutenberg.org/files/31219/31219.txt
41. See http://sunsite.berkeley.edu/Literature/Douglass/Autobiography/01.html
42. Tardieu, Jean-Pierre, *Le destin des Noirs aux Indes de Castille*, Paris 1984, p. 284
43. Ibid. p. 290.
44. Ibid. p. 289.
45. Morenas, op. cit., pp. 318–319.
46. Ibid, pp. 325–327
47. Sala-Molins, Louis, "Le racisme et le microscope", in *Lignes* No. 3, Paris, June 1988, p. 19.
48. Some will argue that the circumstances were very different. Yet it seems obvious to me that in both cases, denying the other's humanity leads to his destruction.
49. Cohen, William B., *The French Encounter with Africans: White Response to Blacks, 1530–1880*, Indiana University Press, 2003, p. 105, quoting Lucien Peytraud, *L'esclavage aux Antilles françaises*, Paris, 1987.
50. Morenas, op. cit., p. 233; Schoelcher, op. cit., p. 177; Gisler, op. cit., pp. 92–93.
51. Morenas, op. cit., p. 235; Gisler, op. cit., p. 97.
52. Schoelcher, op. cit. p. 177; Morenas, op. cit., p. 232; Gisler, op cit., p. 98.

3

Saint-Domingue

Human suffering at its most acute

In 1791, the Black population of Saint-Domingue rebelled. Blacks under the leadership of François-Dominique Toussaint Louverture fought a desperate battle for freedom for all. For the first time, an armed battle deployed in military style was successfully conducted against the concentration camp setting of America.

As soon as the Amiens peace treaty was signed between France and the United Kingdom in 1802, Bonaparte decided to send in troops to Saint-Domingue to force the Blacks back into slavery. The expedition led by General Leclerc arrived in February 1802 to face a population that was up in arms, clearly prepared to die in battle rather than return into bondage.

Despite the Napoleonic armies' military excellence, the battle was so fierce that Leclerc realised the defeat of the people of Saint-Domingue was by no means a foregone conclusion. On May 5, 1802, a peace treaty was signed between Toussaint Louverture and Leclerc, who promised to abide by the freedom of Blacks and leave the government of Saint-Domingue in their hands. He undertook to act solely as the representative of France and appointed officers to positions commensurate with their rank. In fact Leclerc was setting up the conditions for restoring slavery that Napoleon adamantly called for. Once the peace treaty was signed, Toussaint Louverture announced the fact to his men, commended their courage and thanked them for their devotion to him. To bid them farewell, he embraced his officers. "The whole population was happy with the peace. What both citizens and soldiers wanted was freedom and they had faith in Leclerc's vow to abide by it.[1]"

But both the First Consul and Leclerc saw Toussaint Louverture as an obstacle that had to be removed before forcing Blacks back into slavery. He must be removed or made powerless. It was then that they began a plot, which was to lead to his demise. The troops swarmed into the area of Ennery harassing the farmers at every turn. Toussaint Louverture was forced to seek out Leclerc and demand that the soldiers stop making trouble with the population. Some of Toussaint Louverture's friends secretly warned him of the danger he was facing. "When he was advised to make provision for his own safety, he answered: 'Putting my life at risk for the sake of my imperilled country was a sacred duty; but to trouble my country to save my life would be an inglorious act.'"[2]

Toussaint Louverture's complaint about the disturbances caused by the troops gave Leclerc an opportunity to lay him a trap. He wrote to Toussaint Louverture asking him to reach an agreement with General Brunet on how to solve the problems raised by the troops in the area. General Brunet himself wrote a letter to Toussaint Louverture in the following terms:

> The time has come, Citizen General, to make the General in Chief unequivocally aware that those who mislead him about your good faith are contemptible defamers. You must assist me.
>
> My Dear General, we must make a number of arrangements together that cannot be made by letter but for which one hour's conference would suffice. Were I not overwhelmed with work and troublesome details, I would have brought the answer in person; but since I cannot venture out in the coming days, do so yourself. If you have recovered from your indisposition, come tomorrow; when what is at hand is to further good, it should suffer no delay.
>
> You will not find all the creature comforts in my country home that I would have wished to have at the ready for your visit, but you will find here the sincerity of a gentleman who has no other desire than the prosperity of the colony and your personal contentment. It is my dearest wish to meet Mrs Toussaint and I would be delighted if she were to join you on this trip. If she needs horses, I shall send her mine.
>
> Once again, General, you will find no friend more sincere than myself. With trust in the Captain General, with friendship for all that is subordinate to him, and you would enjoy tranquillity.[3]

From testimonies given at the time, cited by Métral, Césaire and others, a number of French officers at the Ennery garrison assured Toussaint Louverture that they had been told by one of Leclerc's aide-de-camps who was seconded to General Brunet that the latter had received orders to arrest him. In view of all these warnings, Toussaint Louverture must have been distrustful of General Brunet. He nevertheless agreed to go to Saint-Georges.

Following these two letters and in spite of being ailing, I gave into the entreaties of my sons and other persons and left that very night to meet with General Brunet, accompanied by two officers only. When he invited me to enter his room, I told him I had received his letter together with that of the General in Chief asking me to concert with him and that was the purpose of my visit; that I had been unable to bring my wife as he would have wished since she never ventured out or into society and tended solely to her domestic affairs; that if, on the occasion of a tour, he were willing to honour her with a visit, she would be delighted. I informed him that because I was unwell I could not remain very long with him and so begged him to expedite our business as quickly as possible so that I could go back. I showed him General Leclerc's letter.

Once he had read it, he told me that he had yet to receive any order requesting him to concert with me on the subject of this letter; he then made apologies saying that he was compelled to go out for a minute; and indeed he left, after having called in an officer to keep me company. As soon as he had gone out, one of General Leclerc's aides-de-camp came in accompanied by a large number of grenadiers who surrounded me, seized me, tied me up like a criminal and led me on board the frigate *La Créole*.

I called on General Brunet's word and the promises he had made me but to no effect. I saw him no more.[4]

That very night of June 7 to June 8, 1802, *La Créole* drew alongside *Le Héros*, which immediately set sail to France.

A predecessor and a precedent

Napoleon Bonaparte, the criminal governing France at that time, was in many respects the French predecessor of Adolph Hitler. The different treatment given to the two figures by official historiographers is just the outcome of two, reciprocating and complementary historical circumstances: on the one hand the crushing victory of the allied powers in 1945, and on the other, the proven impotence of the earlier victims of Napoleonic France, victims who have yet today to be recognised as such and to secure the reinstatement of their contested humanity. It is hence clear why Sala-Molins says: "If the losers were those who wrote the history of their defeat, the winners would read it without for a single moment imagining it to be a description of their victory.[5]"

Napoleon himself stated that he was willing to put to death anyone who spoke of freedom for the Arabs or the Blacks, that 'cursed race', and that he would exterminate if they refused to go back into bondage. Hitler[6] allowed a few Jews (albeit Jews who had been declared honorary Aryans) in his entourage and according to Hannah Arendt: "If interventions on behalf of 'prominent' Jews came from 'prominent' people, they often were quite successful.[7]" In other words, it was less risky to plead the cause of an eminent Jew with Hitler than to argue for the freedom of Arabs or Blacks with Napoleon.

In his *Le Consulat et de l'Empire*, Thibaudeau narrates a sitting of the Council of State on 21 Ventôse of the year XI (March 12, 1803). Irritated by Truguet's hostility towards the settlers of the islands [a hostility stemming from the "Anglophilia" of the settlers who were purported to prefer their property to their country"], Napoleon angrily replies:

> It is assumed that the settlers are for the English; but I can assure you that in Martinique there are some very good citizens. Those who are for the English are known. There are few of them... You see only supporters of the English in our colonies to have an excuse to oppress them. Monsieur Truguet, if you had come over to Egypt to preach the liberty of the Blacks or Arabs, we would have hanged you on the mast of your ship! Your Black friends delivered all the Whites in St. Domingue up to the ferocity of the Blacks! I am for the Whites because I am a White man! This is reason enough. How could Frenchmen dream of granting liberty to Africans, to men who had no civilisation, who did not even know what was a colony and what a mother-country? It is quite clear that those who want liberty for the Blacks want the slavery of the Whites. But again, do you believe that, if the majority of the National Convention had known what they were about, and had understood the colonies, they would have freed the Blacks? At present nothing but self-conceit and hypocrisy can make people cling to those visionary principles.[8]

Napoleon's contemptible behaviour towards the imprisoned Toussaint Louverture taken is entirely consistent with this shabbiness of spirit. Toussaint Louverture went on shore at Brest and was taken to the Joux Fort where he was to see no-one and was not allowed out of the room to which he was confined. With Toussaint Louverture under lock and key, Napoleon thought the time was ripe to restore slavery in Saint-Domingue. But Leclerc was confronted with a problem: How could he maintain the loyalty of the indigenous generals? When the peace treaty was signed with Toussaint Louverture, Leclerc had agreed to employ Black officers in accordance with their rank. Among those generals, there were people such as Christophe, Dessalines, Paul Louverture, Toussaint's brother, Charles Belair, Lamartinière, Jacques Maurepas and others. Before coming under French command, they had fought the expedition with a bravery that forced the respect of the Napoleonic armies. It was for this reason that Leclerc was preoccupied about their possible reactions to the kidnapping of Toussaint Louverture and to the news that was coming in from Guadeloupe and Martinique about the Consul's policy of re-enslavement.

Maurepas was of particular concern to Leclerc and his men. He had inflicted a serious defeat on the French and enjoyed the utmost respect from the troops.

Toussaint Louverture, who appreciated his bravery as much as he did his outspokenness, put him in charge of Port-de-Paix, a small coastal town:

> Upon seeing the French who had come ashore at that location, Maurepas, after burning the town withdrew to the gorge of Trois Rivières. The French led by Humbert, one of the army's most fearless generals, twice attacked him in this gorge and were twice forced back, which caused a powerful diversion to Leclerc's manoeuvres as he was compelled to detail a contingent of troops and to send General Debelle with fifteen hundred men by sea as reinforcement to Humbert. Maurepas vigorously fought off the two French generals. Leclerc was determined to bring him to heel and launched the Desfourneaux division together with fifteen hundred men from the Hardy division against him.[9]

The French generals, particularly General Debelle, would never forgive this scorching humiliation inflicted by a 'nigger'. Leclerc attempted to explain to the Black generals that Toussaint Louverture was plotting against the peace that it was to avoid disorders that he had been compelled to arrest him, and that part of the troops must now be disarmed. Tensions increased. General Charles Belair rebelled and other Blacks, frightened at the prospect of slavery being restored, joined him. Leclerc, who was not about to shrink from another betrayal, decided to set a trap for Maurepas. He wrote to him asking him to

> go to Cape with his whole family and his troops and assume the command of the city of Cape as a reward for his loyal services. No sooner had he complied with this invitation that his soldiers and himself were betrayed, arrested and disarmed. General Rochambeau ordered the installation of the machinery for a pompous and barbaric punishment so that he would perish before the four hundred Blacks that made up his troops. And then, it was deliberated as to whether his infant children would be killed so they would not remain to avenge their father...

> After being tied to the mast of a ship that served as gallows, Maurepas was humiliated in a dreadful farcical way – an old general's hat and epaulets were put on him, cruelly attached by means of nails. At the same time, his soldiers were brought before him and his wife and children were drowned before his very eyes. They averted their gaze so as not to watch his face distorted by agony. They were all buried at sea. Maurepas was the final one to breathe his last and the most pitiful.[10]

Maurepas's children were therefore put to death as a precautionary measure. The Consul had given orders to that effect: Blacks who displayed an immoderate taste for freedom had to be eliminated whether or not that might require the colony to be repopulated with other Blacks who had not been infected by the virus. Now if for reasons of state security, adults who were likely to become awesome enemies had to be killed, then it was also necessary that their children, even infants, be also put down to avoid leaving behind time-bombs. This was a case of tackling the problem at its inception.

A century and a half later the leaders of the Third Reich adopted the same attitude and procedure, albeit on a much larger scale and using up-to-date technology.

From the champions of the enlightenment to Saint-Domingue

As a result of this war of extermination triggered by Leclerc and continued by Rochambeau, who took over when he died, Saint-Domingue became the setting for what Hannah Arendt much later described as the "banality of evil" in her essay *Eichmann in Jerusalem*.

Rochambeau was one of those Frenchmen who crossed the Atlantic to stand up for the ideal of freedom and carry the spirit and message of the Enlightenment to North America. He also went to Saint-Domingue but on a far less honourable mission this time. His task there was to quell any attempts by Blacks to break free, using any means including extermination. When he took over from Leclerc, and was faced with the resistance of the people of Haiti who were willing to die rather than go back into slavery, Rochambeau took a decision that should attract the attention of those who try to identify some characteristic mental disorder in the Hitlers, Stalins and Pol Pots of this world. He decided to buy six hundred bulldogs – raised and fed on fresh blood and flesh, a system perfected by the Spaniards – with the intention of using them to crush the resistance of Blacks. It was the Viscount of Noailles in person who travelled over to Cuba so as to bring back these ferocious beasts. He was the first, on the 4th of August 1789, to generously throw feudal entitlements on to the table of the Menus Plaisirs, inspiring all the constituency to follow suit. The episode put an end to the privileges of the French nobility. In Saint-Domingue, all that generosity vanished. The arrival of the Viscount's ship brimming with its cargo of black-eating dogs at Cape harbour was greeted with joy and glee by the White population waiting there. It was determined that the dogs should be tested during a public display. "A victim was first designated, and the venue – the courtyard of a convent – was chosen. Here an amphitheatre, reminiscent of Roman circuses, was erected. The mob crowded there to witness the spectacle. The Black was fastened to a post. As soon as they were released, the starved dogs, driven by their unbearable hunger, tore the wretch to pieces.[11]"

Having proven their efficiency, Rochambeau then allocated the dogs to various detachments. This is the wording of a letter he sent on 15 Germinal to General Ramel who was at Tortue:

> My dear Commander, I am sending you a detachment of 150 men from the Cape National Guard under the command of Mr Barri, along with twenty-eight bulldogs. These reinforcements will enable you to complete the operations fully. I must inform you that you will be allocated no allowance or rations to feed these dogs. They must be fed on niggers. Fond regards. Signature: Rochambeau.[12]

Faced with such a campaign of destruction, death and extermination, the Blacks fought with the desperate strength of those who expected no humanity from their assailants. On November 19, 1803, Rochambeau capitulated. In their generosity, the victims allowed him and his men to pack up and board the ships in harbour.

On July 1, 1804, the Blacks of Saint-Domingue proclaimed the Republic of Haiti which they declared to be the "land of the New World Africans and their descendants.[13]" Saint-Domingue gained its freedom, but at a heavy price. According to Schoelcher, of the 900,000 Blacks living in the colony on the eve of the rebellion, only 400,000 remained at liberation. Not only were the atrocities committed against these people never characterised as crimes, but furthermore – and here one is dumbfounded – the French, who did not have the law on their side but did have the strength, were able to compel the Haitian survivors to pay compensation to the Whites. Indeed, it was their "sacred" right that they should not to be reduced to poverty as a result of Blacks acquiring freedom. Article 2 of the King's Order reads:

> In Paris on April 17, 1825, Charles, by the grace of God, King of France and of Navarre, wishing to provide for what the interests of French trade require and the misfortunes of the former settlers of Saint-Domingue, etc. The present inhabitants of the French portion of Saint-Domingue shall pay into the Caisse d'Epargne et de Consignations de France [...] the amount of a hundred and fifty million francs by way of damages to former settlers who shall claim compensation.[14]

The grounds for compensating the perpetrator instead of the victim were that:

> however important the position of the Blacks may be, however sanctified their misfortune must be in our eyes, for it is our doing, it would be unjust and imprudent to be concerned with them alone. [...] If the Negroes have the right to become free, it is incontestable that the colonists have the right not to be ruined by the freedom of the Negroes.[15]

Tocqueville, a democrat and abolitionist, in this speech was apparently not quite sure that Blacks were entitled to freedom. On the other hand, this humanist was certain that the Whites had a right not to be ruined by the freedom of Blacks. The banality of evil earned its letters of nobility long before Hitler's time!

The survivors of Nazi atrocities were never and cannot be adequately compensated. However, on account of Germany's military defeat, the notion of entitlement to compensation was re-interpreted for their benefit. For this radical change to happen, it was necessary for the crimes to have taken place in Europe and for the victims to be Europeans.

The normalisation of atrocity

These atrocities inflicted on Blacks because they were Black were normalised. It was not an offence to present arguments to justify them. Justification for the genocide of African Americans was provided a posteriori, at times in more subtle terms but most often quite crudely. Because they had defeated the Blacks, the Whites were incapable of feeling any shame or discomfort vis-à-vis the survivors, in contrast to what was required from the Germans. Prior to the emergence of the Nazi policy of racial domination, it was common to address the survivors of the African American genocide and later their descendants in terms exemplified here:

> You who have reaped nothing but benefits from our civilisation, how is it that you look at your past only to curse it and that you see your former masters solely as persecutors? [...] If you had been White like us and forced into bondage by conquest or oppression, this later gift of freedom would

soon have raised you to the level of your former oppressors. This prejudice you complain of is rooted in the inferiority of your race, in the unalterable difference between yours and ours, as well as – need it be said? – in the unwillingness amongst those of you who have enjoyed the benefits of an education to elevate your minds![16]

At the time, the only Frenchman, among those able to voice opinions, to speak out against this type of discourse was Schoelcher, the most consistent of the French abolitionists.[17]

Eugéne Augeard's *La Traite des Noirs avant 1790 au point de vue du commerce nantais* (The Black Slave Trade before 1790 Seen from the Standpoint of Trade Flows to and from Nantes) was published in 1901. Its title alone is fairly representative of a general tendency to reduce the African American genocide to a description of the changes that took place in large European cities as a result of the crimes perpetrated against Blacks. Eugène Augeard went unchallenged when he said: "To write the history of the Black slave trade is therefore to write the history of one of the most brilliant pages of our trading history.[18]"

The most gigantic deportation of human beings ever to take place in the history of humanity is summed up as being one of the most brilliant pages in the trading history of the slave-trading powers! Talk about "a detail" in the infamous words once used by Le Pen, leader of the French far-right party, with reference to the German concentration camps!

Notes

1. Schoelcher, Victor, *Vie de Toussaint Louverture*, Paris, 1889, p. 345 (quote translated from the French).
2. Métral, Antoine, *Histoire de l'expédition des Français à Saint-Domingue*, Paris, 1825, p. 132 (quote translated from the French).
3. Césaire, Aimé, *Toussaint Louverture, la Révolution française et le problème colonial*, Paris, 1981, pp. 309–310 (quote translated from the French).
4. Ibid, pp. 313–314.
5. Sala-Molins, Louis, *Le Code Noir ou le calvaire de Canaan*, Paris, 1987, p. 206 (quote translated from the French).
6. See Hilberg, op. cit., p. 48–53 for a description of what a Jew might do to try to obtain Aryan status.
7. Arendt, Hannah, *Eichmann in Jerusalem: A Report on the Banalization of Evil*, Penguin Books, New York, 2006, p. 134.
8. Thibaudeau, A.C., *Le consulat et l'empire, ou l'histoire de la France et de Napoléon Bonaparte, de 1799 à 1815*, Jules Renouard, Paris, 1834. See https://ia801209.

us.archive.org/4/items/bub_gb_sYM29xtgcQcC/bub_gb_sYM29xtgcQcC.pdf pp. 332–330.
9. Métral op. cit., p. 86; Schoelcher, op. cit., p. 332.
10. Métral op. cit., pp. 171–172; Schoelcher, op. cit., pp. 368–369; Césaire, op. cit., p. 334.
11. Métral op. cit., pp. 182–183.
12. Schoelcher, op. cit., p. 373.
13. Ibid, p. 379.
14. Métral op. cit., p. 342.
15. Tocqueville, Alexis de & Pitts, Jennifer, *Writings on Empire and Slavery*, Johns Hopkins University Press, Baltimore, Maryland, 2001, p. 221.
16. In *La défense coloniale*, February 1882 (quote translated from the French).
17. Schoelcher, Victor, *Polémique coloniale*, Vol. I, Paris, 1882, pp. 9–10.
18. Augeard, Eugène, *La Traite des Noirs avant 1790 au point de vue du commerce nantais*, Paris, 1901, p. 12, quoted by Vissière, op cit. p. 12, and by Hoffmann, Léon-François, *Le nègre romantique*, Paris, 1973, p. 52.

4

From One Continent to Another

A consistent pattern of conduct

It is astonishing to discover there is a consistent pattern of conduct wherever whole groups of people have been subjugated by another group in a position of absolute power. What is truly remarkable is that this behaviour is consistent not only between very different actors but also over time. Differences in religion, customs or languages between jailers do not substantially affect the way in which those groups of "sub-humans" are treated. A close look at the African continent provides evidence of this disquieting persistence of barbarian practices.

Take the Congo "In September 1876, in pursuit of the humanitarian ideal, that great benefactor King Léopold II convened an international geography conference in his palace. Its purpose was to 'open up to civilisation the only part of our planet where it has not so far penetrated'.[1]" At the end of this meeting, the participants agreed to form the International African Association (AIA) and appointed King Léopold as its chairman. In 1877, a gold star against a blue background became the Association's flag and it was soon renamed International Association of the Congo (AIC).

In 1884, in the run-up to the Berlin Conference that was to decide on the partitioning of Africa, King Léopold II was busy obtaining the recognition of the powers involved. On April 22, he gained recognition from the United States, and on October 16, from Germany; two months later England granted its recognition and then on February 5, 1885, France.

On February 26, 1885, the International Association of the Congo, on behalf of its founder Léopold II, notified Bismarck of its approval of the Berlin Conference resolutions. Bismarck responded by concluding his speech with these words:

> Gentlemen, I believe I echo the feelings of the gathering here when I express our satisfaction with the AIC's stance and take note of its approval of our resolutions. The new state of the Congo is expected to become one of the main custodians of the enterprise we have planned. Let me express our heartfelt wishes for its prosperous development and the achievement of the noble aspirations of its eminent founder.[2]

The day the independent State of the Congo was formed, it became King Léopold's private property. Its inhabitants were to live, or rather to die, in unison with the "noble aspirations of the King of the Belgians." The professed goal of this allegedly philanthropic undertaking was to end slavery in central Africa, prevent the advance of Islam and win as yet unexplored regions over to civilisation.

The publication of Adam Hochschild's book *King Leopold's Ghost* in 1998 has given us a better view of how Belgians ruled and acted in the Congo. Four centuries in between at the conquest of Latin America, the conduct of the Belgians was much the same as the Spaniards' had been towards the indigenous populations of the Americas. The Belgians and other Europeans in the Congo learned to live with horror there just like other Europeans forty or fifty years later who also learned to live with the everyday horror of the German concentration and death camps.

A very significant number of Europeans spent time in the Congo between 1890 and 1910. Very few of them were shocked by the barbarity inflicted by the authorities of the Congo Free State, thus making the testimony of those who did object even more valuable.

Let us examine the case of a woman named Ilanga whose story was recorded by a Swahili-speaking American government agent, Edgar Canisius. According to Hochschild, when Canisius later met the officer and soldiers who had captured her, he concluded that she had indeed spoken the truth. Here is her story:

> Our village is called Waniendo, after our chief Niendo. [...] We never had war in our country, and the men had not many weapons except knives. [...]
>
> We were all busy in the fields hoeing our plantations, for it was the rainy season, and the weeds sprang quickly up, when a runner came to the village saying that a large band of men was coming, that they all wore red caps and blue cloth, and carried guns and long knives, and that many White men were with them, the chief of whom was Kibalanga [The African name for Oscar Michaux, a Force Publique officer who once received a Sword of Honour from King Léopold's own hands.] [...]

The next morning, [...] soon after the sun rose over the hill, a large band of soldiers came into the village. [...] the soldiers rushed into the houses and dragged the people out. Three or four came to our house and caught hold of me, also my husband Oleka and my sister Katinga. We were dragged into the road, and were tied together with cords about our necks, so that we could not escape. We were all crying, for now we knew that we were to be taken away to be slaves. The soldiers beat us with the iron sticks from their guns, and compelled us to march to the camp of Kibalanga, who ordered the women to be tied up separately, ten to each cord, and the men in the same way. When we were all collected – and there were many from other villages whom we now saw, and many from Waniendo – the soldiers brought baskets of food for us to carry, in some of which was smoked human flesh [...]

We then set off marching very quickly. My sister Katinga had her baby in her arms, and was not compelled to carry a basket; but my husband Oleka was made to carry a goat. We marched until the afternoon, when we camped near a stream, where we were glad to drink, for we were much athirst. We had nothing to eat, for the soldiers would give us nothing. [...]

Until the fifth day, [...] when the soldiers took my sister's baby and threw it in the grass, leaving it to die, and made her carry some cooking pots they found in the deserted village. On the sixth day we became very weak from lack of food and from constant marching and sleeping in the damp grass, and my husband, who marched behind us with the goat, could not stand up longer, and so he sat down beside the path and refused to walk more. The soldiers beat him, but still he refused to move. Then one of them struck him on the head with the end of his gun, and he fell upon the ground. One of the soldiers caught the goat while two or three others stuck the long knives they put on the end of their guns into my husband. I saw the blood spurt out, and then saw him no more, for we passed over the brow of a hill and he was out of sight. Many of the young men were killed the same way, and many babies thrown into the grass to die.[3]

It could just as well have been four centuries earlier, when the Spaniards' grisly adventure began in America. The same method of destruction was used, with, alas, the same devastating consequences. Raids were conducted against the indigenous people to force them into slavery. Once they were captured and tied up, they were forced to go on long marches carrying the heavy loads that would have exhausted their persecutors. Those who collapsed, like Kitanga's husband Oleka, were finished off so that they did not hold up the march.

At the dawn of the twentieth century, some other Europeans on another continent, replicated the same horrifying deeds and prolonged barbarity, introducing it into modern times. There too, many babies were thrown into the grass and left to die. There too, not a thought was given to concealing the corpses. Civilisation was so far away that anything was permissible. In Léopold's Congo, people who, in their own homes in France, Belgium, Switzerland or England, would never have dreamed of stepping outside the law, learned to live with the annihilation of the indigenous populations, or worse still, heartily contributed to this enterprise. Some of them waded in their victims' blood; others (worthy civil servants, or bureaucrats as they were called many years later) tended to their business and were deaf to the howls of the victims and blind to the corpses exhibited on stakes.

Barbarity masquerading as something else

Starting in 1885, when the Congo Free State became King Léopold's personal property, many Europeans and North Americans travelled there. Amongst them was George Washington Williams, an African American journalist and historian who, according to Hochschild, was the first to take an interest in what the indigenous people thought of White domination. It was Williams' dream that Blacks from the United States work in Africa because they would have opportunities and career prospects they were denied in their own country by white supremacy.

President Chester Arthur, for whom Williams had campaigned, introduced the latter to an envoy from King Léopold II. For Williams this was the opportunity to further his dream of having African Americans settled in the Congo. It transpired that these Blacks were not particularly enthusiastic about going to work in Africa. Since Williams himself knew little about the country, he decided to go there to find out more hoping to come back with convincing arguments that would induce the Blacks from his own country to endorse his plans. Before travelling to the Congo, Williams interviewed King Léopold II and, just like many before and after him, was dazzled by a man whom he called "one of the noblest sovereigns in the world; an emperor whose highest ambition is to serve the cause of Christian civilisation, and to promote the best interests of his subjects, ruling in wisdom, mercy and justice.[4]"

For six months, Williams travelled through the Congo and what he saw horrified him. He did what no-one else had dared to do: he sent the king an open letter.

> Good and Great Friend, I have the honour to submit for your Majesty's consideration some reflections respecting the Free State of the Congo, based upon a careful study.
>
> Every charge which I am about to bring against your Majesty's personal Government in the Congo has been carefully investigated; a list of competent and credible witnesses, documents, letters, official records and data has been faithfully prepared. The documents shall be kept until such time as an International Commission can be created with power to send for persons and papers, to administer oaths, and attest the truth or falsity of these charges.

Hochschild, who points out that Léopold's establishment of military bases along the river had caused a wave of death and destruction, because the African soldiers who manned them were expected to feed themselves, stresses that:

> These piratical, buccaneering posts compel the indigenous people to furnish them with fish, goats, fowls, and vegetables at the mouth of their muskets; and whenever the indigenes refuse, [...] White officers come with an expeditionary force and burn their houses.

Williams continues his pleadings:

> Your Majesty's Government is excessively cruel to its prisoners, condemning them to the chain gang for the slightest offenses. [...] Often the ox-chains eat into the necks of the prisoners and produce sores about which the flies circle, aggravating the running wound.
>
> White officers were shooting villagers, sometimes to capture their women, sometimes to intimidate the survivors into working as forced labourers, and sometimes for sport. Two Belgian Army officers saw, from the deck of their steamer, an indigenous man in a canoe some distance away [...] The officers made a wager of £5 that they could hit the man with their rifles. Three shots were fired and the man fell dead, pierced through the head.
>
> Your Majesty's Government is engaged in the slave trade, wholesale and retail. It buys and sells and steals slaves. Your Majesty's Government gives £3. per head for able-bodied slaves for military service [...] The labour force at the stations of Your Majesty's Government in the Upper River is composed of slaves of all ages and both sexes.[5]

It is therefore a fact that from America to Africa, and from the sixteenth to the late nineteenth centuries, methods for annihilating indigenous populations remained unchanged. That having been ascertained, a second fact can be verified. Between the time the Congo Free State was formed in 1885 and the year 1890, the only visitor among the innumerable Europeans and Americans who came to the Congo to be distressed, terrified and permanently traumatised by what he saw with his own eyes was a Black man, George Washington Williams. Journalists, entrepreneurs, middle-ranking and senior government officials found nothing to offend their sensibilities inasmuch as the victims were so different and hence necessarily inferior. In other words, they were sub-human. Williams cannot comprehend how other men who witnessed the same spectacle as he had seen could continue to sing the praises of King Léopold's administration of the Congo. This form of insensitivity is also true of Nazism. As Kogon notes:

> For camp doctors to conduct despicable experiments, experiments on women, or for jailers to commit all sorts of acts of cruelty and for NCOs to wade in pools of blood, and for these very same men returning home to play with their children or kiss their betrayed wives: all these are pathological phenomena well known in the human soul. In order to resist the pressure of what is counter to nature, before it produces a split consciousness, madness or descent into darkness, human nature establishes a system of fully watertight compartments of impressions. It flees, slips or proudly advances from the compartment of terror to the compartment of simplicity, from the chambers of horror to a home of illusions, peace, love and goodness. Many criminals, murderers and torturers have loved innocent children. Why should Goering not pass a law against vivisection, why should Hitler not have especially loved receiving bunches of flowers presented to him by little girls, why should Himmler not have praised the honest lifestyle of the standard Germany family, and why should each and every SS member not feel affectionate towards his children and dogs? All this is abnormal, sick, perverted. It is the obvious hypocrisy of assaulted, rejected, oppressed consciences – but all this is not new, no newer than venality, which flourishes among those who do not possess firmly anchored moral beliefs but are free to live under control while following their sanctified sympathies.[6]

No, there is no psychological quirk typical of SS members to be uncovered, nor anything very new under the European sun apart from a barbarity that runs through the centuries and across borders. There is no enigma either in the Congo of Léopold.

It is easy to understand the terror felt by Williams when he discovered this enterprise of destruction against the population. Particularly since this enterprise led by the king of the Belgians was named a "contribution of Christian civilisation to the indigenous development of the Congo." His anguish is tangible in the report he sends to the President of the United

States and his letter to the American Secretary of State. He repeats that the United States has a special responsibility towards the Congo because it had "introduced this African Government into the sisterhood of States." He underscores the urgent need to put an end to the "crimes against humanity of which King Léopold's Congo State is guilty.[7]"

To no avail. Crime is primarily a legal notion. A number of conditions relating to power must exist for this notion to become operative. Consequently, even the most horrifying atrocities can go unpunished for as long as their perpetrators are in a position of strength and absolute or near-absolute power over the other groups. Another fifty years went by before the legal characterisation of crimes against humanity became effective at the Nuremberg trials in an effort that professed to be universal.

Terror again

The rubber king, likewise elsewhere the cotton king, vindicated the use of terror. In Hochschild's words:

> Rubber is coagulated sap; the French word for it, caoutchouc, comes from a South American Indian word meaning "the wood that weeps." The wood that wept in the Congo was a long spongy vine of the *Landolphia* genus. Up to a foot thick at the base, a vine could twine upward around a tree to a hundred feet or more above the ground, where it could reach sunlight. […] To gather the rubber, you had to slash the vine with a knife and hang a bucket or earthenware pot to collect the slow drip of thick, milky sap… Once the vines near a village were drained dry, workers had to go ever deeper into the forest until, before long, most harvesters were travelling at least one or two days to find fresh vines. As the lengths of vine within reach of the ground were tapped dry, workers climbed high into the trees to reach sap. Furthermore, heavy tropical downpours during much of the year turned large areas of the rain forest, where the rubber vines, grew into swampland.[8]

It is therefore unsurprising that people did not come forward in large numbers, eager to go deep into the forest for several days to collect the rubber that His Majesty King Léopold was demanding in ever increasing quantities. To compel the peoples of the Congo to become pack animals for the Whites, it was necessary to hunt them down, raid, tie them firmly, and drive them with the lashes of a bullwhip to carry heavy loads on their heads or backs. In the case of rubber, the system of terror was refined further. A newly introduced modality was to take hostages. The troops would arrive in a village, begin by plundering and ransacking it, and then they would capture the women. The price their husbands had to pay for them to be freed was a certain quantity of rubber set by the Force Publique officer or any other official in charge of collecting rubber. In the meantime, the women taken hostage were forced to satisfy the sexual appetites of the soldiers. Often, they died while they were held captive.

Hochschild quotes a semi-official instruction book, a copy of which was given by the administration to each agent and each government post in charge of enforcing terror.

> In Africa, taking prisoners is… an easy thing to do, for if the indigenous people hide, they will not go far from their village and must come to look for food in the gardens which surround it. In watching these carefully, you will be certain of capturing people after a brief delay. … When you feel you have enough captives, you should choose among them an old person, preferably an old woman. Make her a present and send her to her chief to begin negotiations. The chief, wanting to see his people set free, will usually decide to send representatives.[9]

From that moment onwards, the fate of the indigenous population was sealed. The village chief was made an agent of the Belgian government and compelled to supply captives. It was he who chose the victims, sometimes aided by the soldiers. Structures were set up so that the village chief, now a puppet at the service of the administration, could perform the dirty deed. Wherever the aim pursued was to subjugate and destroy, the dominant group knew that it would gain control over the entire population by gaining control over the leader or leaders of the group it sought to dominate. This was one method whereby the Europeans turned some of their victims into fearsome accomplices in Africa.

We also find this chilling practice of compelling victims to actively take part in their own destruction in Europe under Nazi rule. SS members pursued the same goal through the dignitaries in the Jewish populations that had come under their control. They conquered the Jewish community through their leaders. As demonstrated by Hilberg, they succeeded in all the countries under Nazi rule. Hilberg analyses the role played by the Reichvereinigung (National Union of German Jews) and the considerable benefits gained by the Nazis from this cooperation.

> The Germans had not created the Reichsvereinigung and they had not appointed its leaders. Rabbi Leo Baeck, Dr Otto Hirsch, Direktor Heinrich Stahl, and all the others *were* Jewish leaders. Because these men were not puppets, they retained their status and identity in the Jewish community

throughout their participation in the process of destruction, and because they did not lessen their diligence, they contributed the same ability that they had once marshalled for Jewish well-being to assist their German supervisors in operations that had become lethal. They began the pattern of compliance by reporting deaths, births and other demographic data to the Reich Security Main office and by transmitting German regulations in the publication *Jüdisches Nachrichtenblatt* to the Jewish population. They went on to establish special bank accounts accessible to the Gestapo and to concentrate Jews in designated apartment houses. Toward the end, they prepared charts, maps, and lists and provided space, supplies, and personnel in preparations for deportation. The Reichsvereinigung and its counterparts in Vienna and Prague were the prototype of an institution – the Jewish Council – that was to appear in Poland and other occupied territories and that was to be employed in activities resulting in disaster. It was a system that enabled the Germans to save their labour and funds while increasing their stranglehold on the victims. Once they dominated the Jewish leadership, they were in a position to control the entire community.[10]

A grisly task

Whether in King Léopold's Congo or Nazi-ruled Europe, in spite of the underhand dealings of their leaders, some people were not amenable to control and were anxious to seize any opportunity to flee and escape their torturers. That is why the administration of the Congo Free State decided to exterminate the indigenous people that tried to evade forced labour. The idea was for the victims themselves, supervised by some White officers of course, to perform the dirty deed. In other words, Africans of the Congo themselves, often enlisted into the army by force, were the ones to track down and slaughter other Africans of the Congo. But there was a problem nevertheless: The government agents and officers were distrustful of the Blacks. They feared that they might take advantage of the ammunition they were given to turn against their masters. A particularly savage "precautionary measure" was devised to counter that risk. Black soldiers had to justify every cartridge used by presenting the right hand of the person killed!

Reverend William Sheppard, a Black Presbyterian minister in the United States, after much insistence, eventually gained permission from his Church to go to the Free State of the Congo as a missionary. He arrived there in May 1890, accompanied by a White missionary who was to be his superior. Clearly, the Church was not prepared to dispatch a Negro to head its mission in the Congo. The two missionaries settled in the area of Kasai, not far from the land of the Kubas. It would seem that the Kuba king was initially able to protect his people from the devastation perpetrated by the Whites in their quest for slave labour because of the geographic isolation of his kingdom. But in the end, Kasai just like so many other regions in the Congo, was annihilated by the Belgian troops.

> The rain forest bordering the Kasai River was rich in rubber, and William Sheppard and the other American Presbyterians there found themselves in the midst of a cataclysm. [...] Armed men of a chief allied with the regime rampaged through the region where Sheppard worked, plundering and burning more than a dozen villages. Floods of desperate refugees sought help at Sheppard's mission station.

> In 1899 the reluctant Sheppard was ordered by his superiors to travel into the bush, at some risk to himself, to investigate the source of the fighting. There he found bloodstained ground, destroyed villages, and many bodies; the air was thick with the stench of rotting flesh. On the day he reached the marauders' camp, his eye was caught by a large number of objects being smoked. The chief "conducted us to a structure of sticks, under which was burning a slow fire, and there they were, the right hands, I counted them, 81 in all." The chief told Sheppard,

> See! Here is our evidence. I always have to cut off the right hands of those we kill in order to show the State how many we have killed. He proudly showed Sheppard some of the bodies the hands had come from. The smoking preserved the hands in the hot, moist climate, for it might be days or weeks before the chief could display them to the proper official and receive credit for his kills.[11]

It was therefore purely by accident that Sheppard discovered what Hochschild considers "one of the most grisly aspects of Léopold's rubber system."[12]

More than three and a half centuries have gone by since Bartoloméo de Las Casas in America found out that the Spaniards could quite unconcernedly roast a few indigenous people selected from amongst the community's nobility so as to make a deep impression and effectively instil terror. He himself had the opportunity to witness the agony of a number of indigenous chiefs being roasted alive on makeshift gridirons.

> Generally they kill the chiefs in this manner: using wooden poles, a grill is improvised to which the people are tied. A low-burning fire is lit beneath the grill to slowly roast the victims. Once I saw four or five Indians screaming from pain being roasted on the grills. Their screams disturbed the captain's sleep and so he ordered them to be drowned instead. But the executioner

> who was in charge of roasting them (and whose family I knew in Seville) preferred to stifle their cries by stuffing pieces of wood into their mouths.[13]

Some people have claimed that Las Casas invented these monstrous deeds. Others, using the allegedly "scientific" approach, have declared that these "isolated cases" should not be considered as representative of the conquista. Today, more and more people, especially among the victims, are beginning to grasp just exactly what makes up the "scientific" approach of officially recognised historians. Las Casas was not a historian. He did not have the "scientific approach" adopted by the historian Oviedo y Valdés whom I quoted in the chapter on the conquest. He was just appalled by the atrocities perpetrated against the indigenous peoples before his very eyes by Christians, whereas he, Las Casas, was convinced that the indigenous peoples were full-fledged members of the human race and could potentially even become "true Christians."

In the Congo, just as in the Americas, barbarity was by no means an isolated occurrence; it was a deliberate policy. Of course, an official researcher, inspired by the "scientific approach," would say that nowhere do we find any order written and signed by King Léopold demanding that the right hand of Blacks killed by other Blacks enlisted into the army be presented.

Activities of the most gruesome sort can be meticulously organised and prosper in the accommodating shadow of barbarity. We know that in the German extermination camps, the Nazis set up teams to "recover" gold teeth and objects from the corpses before dispatching them to the incinerators.

> Metals and valuables were collected from the corpses at the incinerators by the Sonderkommandos who worked in close cooperation with the SS: these 'special commandos' were gassed and replaced every four months. These recorded facts provide insight into the hideous reality of the dialectic of the master–slave relationship. Temporarily spared, the slaves were in charge of conveying the corpses from the gas chambers to the incineration facilities, and searching and stripping them. In this way, they were able to lay their hands on part of the gold that ended up in Auschwitz which they could use to bribe the guards, fraternise with them and live in comfort. But every four months, the masters killed the Sonderkommando members and set up a new team.[14]

When he grasps the "hideous reality of the master–slave relationship", Poliakov puts his finger on the horror and monstrosity that can develop every time this kind of relationship takes hold.

In the Congo for instance, "in some military units there was even a 'keeper of the hands;' his job was the smoking.¹⁵" Hochschild provides information that gives an idea of the magnitude of this gruesome practice:

> In 1896, A German newspaper, the *Kölnische Zeitung*, published, on the authority of a 'highly esteemed Belgian,' news that 1308 severed hands had been turned over to the notorious District Commissioner Léon Fiévez in a single day. The newspaper twice repeated the story without being challenged by the Congo State. Several additional reports of that day's events, including some from both Protestant and Catholic missionaries, cited even higher totals for the number of hands. On a later occasion, Fiévez admitted that the practice of cutting hands off corpses existed; he denied only, with great vehemence, that he had ever ordered hands cut off living people.¹⁶

In 1899, an officer named Simon Roi, perhaps not realising that one of the people he was chatting with was an American missionary, bragged about the killing squads under his command. The missionary, Ellsworth Faris, recorded the conversation in his diary:

> Each time the corporal goes out to get rubber, cartridges are given to him. He must bring back all those that have not been used; and for every one used he must bring back a right hand! ... As to the extent to which this is carried on, [Roi] informed me that in six months they, the State, on the Momboyo River had used 6000 cartridges, which means that 6000 people were killed or mutilated. It means more than 6000, for the people have told me repeatedly that the soldiers kill children with the butt of their guns.¹⁷

The government agents, who in the Congo took delivery of these severed hands and counted the number of used cartridges, were just "doing their job." Years later, working for a power that was equally criminal, other government agents too just "did their job" with similar dispassion and indifference. Most of them later stated they did their job without suspecting what its consequences were.

A transformation that knows no bounds

When the rule of terror is a key element of power, those who work for it very quickly go through a process of change that turns them into expert torturers. We remember Father Labat who upon arrival in the Martinique instinctively felt sorry for the Blacks he was shown who bore the scars left by the lashes of a whip. But soon enough, he began to feel more comfortable because, as he said, "one gets used to it." This was so true that in fact, some years later, when he had acquired the skills of torturers of Blacks, he would proudly say, speaking of the first time he landed in the Martinique: "There came on board a great many Negroes. Many of them bore on their backs the marks of the whip lashes they had received eliciting compassion from those who were not accustomed to this practice, but soon one gets used to it.[18]"

Hilberg takes us through the very rapid steps that change a man from someone who initially, to all intents and purposes, had no criminal inclinations, nor any willingness to commit mass crimes. Very quickly such a man can become an expert torturer of the kind much needed by any power founded on terror, be it in the Americas, in Africa or in Europe.

In June 1941, with the invasion of the Soviet Union, began what Hilberg calls "mobile killing operations.[19]" The wholesale, methodical extermination of the civilian population, the Jews, the Bolsheviks and others, presented some difficulties for Nazi officials. On the one hand, there were those who acquired huge gratification from killing as many people as possible, and on the other, there were civil servants trained only to do office work who were uncomfortable and had some hang-ups about taking on their new tasks as front-line killers.

> Even the Higher SS and Police Leader of Central Russia, Obergruppenführer von dem Bach-Zelewski, was brought into a hospital with serious stomach and intestinal ailments. He did not respond to treatment, and Himmler dispatched the top physician of the SS, Grawitz, to the bedside of his favourite general. Grawitz reported that von dem Bach was suffering from hallucinations in which he relived his experiences in the East, particularly the shooting of the Jews.[20]

After this first sweep of mobile killing operations to the East, there was a second sweep.

> During the second sweep, mobile killing operations were also carried out by the so-called 'anti-bandit' [anti-partisan] units (*Bandenkampfverbände*). The employment of these units derived from one of Hitler's orders, issued in the late summer of 1942, for the centralisation of anti-partisan fighting. Pursuant to the order, counter-insurgency operations in the *civilian areas* were to be organised by Himmler. In the military areas the same responsibility was to be exercised by the chief of the army's General Staff. Himmler appointed as his plenipotentiary Higher SS and Police Leader, Centre Region, von dem Bach and gave him the title Chef der Bandenkampfverbände [Chief of the anti-partisan units]. In his capacity as anti-partisan chief in the civilian areas, von dem Bach could draw upon army personnel (security divisions, units composed of indigenous collaborators, etc.), SS units, police regiments, and

> Einsatzgruppen, for as long as he needed them for any particular operation. [...] In the guise of anti-partisan activity the units killed thousands of Jews in the woods and in the swamps.[21]

It is nonetheless disquieting to discover that in a letter to Himmler dated September 5, 1942, "Von dem Bach recommended himself, as the most experienced Higher SS and Police Leader in the business, for the position.[22]" The letter sent to Himmler by Dr Grawitz explaining the causes of his nervous breakdown was dated March 4, 1942. One can only infer that it took just under six months for this member of a respectable family to become an expert persecutor so much sought after by the Nazi power.

In an environment where subjecting the "other" to terror and destruction is seen not just as normal but as the norm, the transformation of an individual is an apparently simple process. Let us go back to the case of Rochambeau. This was the son of a noble and respected father who as the messenger of the Enlightenment crossed the Atlantic with La Fayette to fight for the freedom and independence of White society in North America. Nothing in Rochambeau's career up to 1802 raised the slightest suspicion that he could possibly become the assassin he was in Saint-Domingue. There he massacred non-Whites just as von dem Bach-Zelewski massacred non-Aryans. But unlike his SS counterpart, Rochambeau increasingly revelled in torturing his victims and devised ever more sophisticated forms of cruelty and abuse. It is quite plausible that if Rochambeau had never dealt with beings he believed were clearly inferior – something between a monkey and a man – he would never have become the assassin he proved to be.

No finer an example can illustrate this than the self-assertiveness of a European working in the Congo for the government of King Léopold, quoted by Hochschild. This was one Georges Bricusse, a station chief, who on the grounds that he was White, could determine the life and fate of countless indigenous peoples. In 1895, in his diary he records the death of a man he ordered to be hanged because he had stolen a rifle:

> The gallows is set up. The rope is attached, too high. They lift up the nigger and put the noose around him. The rope twists for a few moments, then crack, the man is wriggling on the ground. A shot in the back of the neck and the game is up. It didn't make the least impression on me this time! And to think that the first time I saw the chicotte administered, I was pale with fright. Africa has some use after all. I could now walk into fire as if to a wedding.[23]

There is, after all, something to be said for Africa! Just like America and the Asian continent. There is something to be said for all these remote lands where just being White lends legitimacy to the relations of subordination and destruction forced on non-White populations through sheer military superiority. And just a few decades later, there was something to be said for Nazi Germany first, and then occupied Europe, particularly the eastern part of the continent where people as insignificant as Georges Bricusse, whose only noteworthy trait was that they belonged to the "Aryan race," were vested with the gruesome power of presiding over the lives of non-Aryans.

Let us not forget such superior thinkers as Martin Heidegger (whose scientific background and intellectual qualities remain unchallenged even today), who lived through the Nazi period without noticing that anything particularly bloodthirsty or contrary to the principles of humanity was going on. It can be inferred that to show indifference in the face of the destruction of non-Aryans was the least iniquitous thing one could do. To refrain from actively taking part in their annihilation was in itself a generous gesture, at a time when their inferiority was preached and every effort, including the "scientific approach," was made to identify them with a scourge that must be eradicated.

The Nazis were able to denounce the existence of "racially inferior" groups within the White race itself because the well-established principle of a racial hierarchy of human groups was by then practically indestructible. The reason many people, both in Germany and elsewhere and regardless of their political leanings, remained indifferent to the ordeal of the non-Aryan, in spite of the fact that the latter was subjected to discrimination, humiliated, persecuted, publicly hunted down and arrested before finally being killed, is that the destruction and annihilation of "inferior beings" was something one was permitted to contemplate within the European sociocultural fibre. The process of destruction and annihilation was a commonplace of sorts that made acceptable what, in principle, should have been energetically fought. This penchant for destruction that Daniel Goldhagen[24] believes he detected in Nazi Germany is not a prerogative of the Germans. It is characteristic of all groups that find themselves in a position of strength and ascendancy. It is wholly consistent with the culture of annihilation that was produced and nurtured by the modern barbarity that was set in motion in the Americas, repeated in Africa, implemented on the Asian continent, ruthlessly applied to the Aborigines on the Australian continent, spreading undeterred across Europe itself. The annihilation of "inferior" groups became a matter of course. The Nazis were well aware of this and for this reason were intent on having people believe that non-Aryans were "inferior beings." They relied on that "inferiority" to alienate all Aryans from the fate of those inferior beings.

As a result of King Léopold's enterprise in the Congo, the "population of the territory dropped by approximately ten million people.[25]" There is argument about the figures and no doubt, when the time comes for historians and specialised researchers to investigate this topic, their first finding will be that these figures are exaggerated. Whatever the actual number of Congolese put to death, King Léopold was to the populations of the Congo what Adolph Hitler was to the Jewish communities of Europe: the source of destruction and death. But that is where the comparison ends. A complete and unconditional military defeat was inflicted on Hitler's Germany, as a result of which the peoples who had been under its rule, rather than the occupiers, were able to maintain control over their history and its interpretation.

When in 1908 Léopold handed the Congo over to Belgium, the Belgian administrators took over from the king's superintendents. From that point onwards, "hands were no longer severed with the blessing of the authorities." But, notes Hochschild, "[i]t was legal for mine management to use the chicotte, and at the gold mines of Moto, on the upper Uele River, records show that 26,579 lashes were administered in the first half of 1920 alone.[26]"

Manipulating history to control memory

In the Congo just as everywhere else, the colonisers were the ones who wrote the history textbooks. Additionally, they monopolised the topic so that between 1908 and 1960, the Belgians, unhindered and enjoying complete impunity, were able to engineer the history of this country and teach the Congolese that it is their duty to pay tribute to the memory of King Léopold. As Hochschild reports:

> For example, a 1959 text for young Congolese soldiers studying to become NCOs in the Force Publique explained that history 'reveals how the Belgians, by acts of heroism, managed to create this immense territory.' Fighting the 'Arab' slavers, in three years of sacrifice, perseverance and steadfast endurance, they brilliantly completed the most humanitarian campaign of the century, liberating the decimated and exploited peoples of this part of Africa.' As for critics, who go unnamed: 'The criticisms emitted in the

course of defamatory campaigns undertaken by jealous foreigners were shown to amount to nothing.[27]

The disparity between the legal characterisation given to Hitler's atrocities and the absence of any definition of the Leopoldian atrocities is a reflection of the relative strength of the opposing parties. In the Congo, due to their military superiority, the persecutors maintained their power and control over how history is written and interpreted. Léopold determined that the rule of the Belgian government would succeed his own rule and, starting in 1908, in addition to the "benefits" of Léopold's rule, there would also be the "benefits" of Belgian rule. The Congolese were expected to heap praise not only on the king but also on the Belgian people as a whole. This brainwashing, which was a combination of concealment and falsification of the historical truth, was to last for half a century. Long enough to deprive a people of their history and of their memory.

On June 30, 1960, the Congo became independent and for the first time in its painful history, its people were able to choose a government. Patrice Lumumba was appointed Prime Minister of a government of national unity. He seemed to want to place the rights of the Congolese people above the interests of the groups, clans and elites that the White rulers had relied on until then. This was something Western democracies could not tolerate. Lumumba was de facto condemned to death. "Less than two months after Lumumba was named Congo's first democratically chosen prime minister, a US National Security Council subcommittee on covert operations, which included CIA chief Allen Dulles, authorised his assassination.[28]"

After several unsuccessful attempts, Western democracies (with the United States, Belgium and France in the lead) found a *chien de garde* in the person of Joseph Désiré Mobutu, who appeared best suited to protecting their interests. This former non-commissioned officer of the Force Publique who went on to become General Chief of Staff was given the assistance he needed to prepare the assassination of the person who embodied the hopes and trampled dignity of his people. The Swiss sociologist Jean Ziegler summarises: "On September 14, 1960, Lumumba was arrested. The North American Embassy, Joseph Kasa-Vubu (President of the Republic) and Mobutu (Chief of General Staff) decided to physically eliminate Lumumba.[29]" On January 17, 1961, Patrice Lumumba was tortured and then assassinated.

"A United Nations' committee of inquiry together with a correspondent of the daily *Le Monde,* Pierre de Vos, reconstructed Lumumba's last moments. A strange dialogue took place between the prophet and his assassins:

> "So, are you still invulnerable? Do you still spit out bullets?"
>
> Lumumba, drained of any strength after being tortured and losing blood, half-conscious, nods his head. Yes, he is still invulnerable.
>
> A White mercenary kneels on the prisoner's chest. He seizes his bayonet and slowly and methodically pushes it into Lumumba's breast. Colonel Weber, a Belgian officer, administers the coup de grace.[30]

This was the bloodbath that drowned the hopes of a people who, after first enduring the atrocities of Léopold and then the direct domination of the Belgian state, held on to the utopian belief that the time had come to assert themselves as human beings. According to Hochschild, "Richard Bissell CIA operations chief at the time later said 'The President [Dwight. D. Eisenhower] regarded Lumumba as I did and a lot of other people did: as a mad dog […] and he wanted the problem dealt with.[31]"

So the problem was dealt with. The criminal chosen by the United States, Belgium and France rendered excellent services and up to 1997 reigned over a starved, humiliated population that was carefully maintained in a state of utter ignorance. It is easy to see how the tragedy, the disaster that still afflicts the people of the Congo is largely the doing of the Western democracies.[32] In spite of this, no monument has so far been erected in memory of the several million Congolese exterminated under the administration of the king of the Belgians. And the Belgian state has not felt the need to officially express any inkling of remorse.

[After an 18-month parliamentary inquiry into Patrice Lumumba's killing,[33] on February 5, 2002, Belgium formally presented to Lumumba's family and the Congolese, "its profound and sincere regrets and apologies for the sorrow that was inflicted upon them by this apathy".[34] On June 30, 2018, Le square Patrice Lumumba was inaugurated by the city of Brussels.]

Notes

1. Brunschwig, Henri, *Le partage de l'Afrique*, Paris, 1971, p. 45 (quote translated from the French).
2. Ibid, p. 65.
3. Hochschild, Adam, *King Leopold's Ghost*, Basingstoke and Oxford, Pan Books, 2006, pp. 131–133.
4. Ibid, p. 106.

5. Ibid, pp. 110–111.
6. Kogon, Eugen, *L'État SS*, Paris, 1947, pp. 333–335 (quote translated from the French).
7. Hochschild, op. cit., pp. 111–112.
8. Ibid, pp. 160–161.
9. Ibid, p. 162.
10. Hilberg, Raul, *The Destruction of the European Jews*, Revised Edition, vol. 1, New York, Holmes & Meier, 1985, 187, Questia, Web, 6 July 2010.
11. Hochschild, op. cit., pp. 164–165.
12. Ibid, p. 165.
13. Las Casas, op. cit., *Isla española* (quote translated from the French).
14. Poliakov, Léon, *Auschwitz*, Paris, 1973, p. 62.
15. Hochschild, op. cit., p. 165.
16. Ibid, p. 226.
17. Ibid, pp. 226–227.
18. Schoelcher, *Des colonies françaises*, op. cit., p. 83.
19. Hilberg, Raul, op. cit. p. 177.
20. Ibid, pp. 215–216.
21. Ibid, p. 243.
22. Ibid, p. 243, footnote 4.
23. Hochschild, op. cit., p. 123.
24. Author of the best-seller *Hitler's Willing Executioners*, 1996. Translated and published in French as *Les bourreaux volontaires de Hitler* (1997), Paris, Seuil.
25. Hochschild, op. cit., p. 233.
26. Ibid, pp. 278–279.
27. Ibid, p. 299.
28. Ibid, p. 302.
29. Ziegler, Jean, *Main basse sur l'Afrique*, Paris, 1980, p. 119.
30. Ibid, p. 122.
31. Hochschild, Adam, *King Leopold's Ghost*, Mariner Books, 1999, p. 298.
32. For an in-depth study of the plot by Belgium aided by its Western accomplices to break the process of economic liberalisation and political democratisation engaged by the Lumumba government, see *L'Assassinat de Lumumba*, by Ludo de Witte, Paris, 2000.
33. Ian Black, "Belgium Blamed for Icon's Murder", *The Guardian*, 17 Nov 2001, https://www.theguardian.com/world/2001/nov/17/humanities.research
34. See https://www.independent.co.uk/news/world/europe/belgium-sorry-for-killing-of-lumumba-9195253.html

II
The Ideological Weight of White Supremacy

5

From the Exclusion of Non-Whites to the Exclusion of Non-Aryans

So inferior and liable for extermination

In 1913, when the German scientist Eugen Fischer published *Die Rehobother Bastards und das Bastardierungs problem beim Menschen (The Rehoboth Bastards and the Human Bastardization Problem)*, his intention was to provide scientific proof that Blacks were of an inferior race. At the end of his book, he asserts with the self-assurance of someone stating the obvious: "... and only idealists or fanatics can deny that Negroes, Hottentots, and many others are inferior.[1]" His theory received no criticism from his British, French or North American colleagues because they shared that view. Fischer's work was undertaken in the context of German colonisation in Africa and more specifically Namibia.

When the former slave-trading powers met in Berlin in 1885 to formally dismember Africa, Germany made sure it got possession of South-West Africa (now Namibia) and control over East Africa (the current area covered by Tanzania, Burundi and Rwanda), as well as Togo and Cameroon. One of the various populations established in Namibia are the Basters, a group of mixed bloods descended from European settlers that lived outside the Cape settlement and Nama women. The continual expansion of the settlement forced them to move. "This community of Basters was the last group to migrate to Namibia and had negotiated an agreement with the Nama chief Zwartboi allowing them to settle at Rehoboth in the centre of Namibia for a fee of one horse a year. This arrangement was confirmed when the Nama and the Herero chiefs concluded a peace treaty at Okahandja in 1870.[2]"

German colonisation in Africa lasted from 1884 to just after the war in 1918. But it was not until 1893 that the Germans actually took over and sought to entrench their domination over native populations in Namibia.

Under Lieutenant General von Trotha, who was appointed commander by order of the emperor on May 19, 1904 to replace General Theodor Leutwein, the war against the people of Namibia became wholesale extermination and destruction. There was a time when the annihilation of entire peoples was an official part of a power's plans to achieve supremacy.

In a letter dated November 5, 1904 and addressed to his predecessor, Trotha confirms his attitude towards Africans:

> I am fairly familiar with tribes in Africa. They are all alike in thinking that they will surrender only to force. Indeed, my policy has always been to exert such force by brutally instilling terror, and sometimes by cruelty. I annihilate the insurgent tribes in streams of blood because this is the only seed that will grow into something new and stable.[3]

He attacked the Herero people by encircling them so that their only escape route was to go into the desert. At the same time, he ordered poison to be put into the water holes. Trotha's report to the military high command in Berlin illustrates this man's unconcealed determination to annihilate:

> The pursuit of the defeated enemy brilliantly highlights the boundless energy of the German command. No efforts, no hardships were spared in order to deprive the enemy of his last reserves of resistance; like a half-dead animal he was hunted from water-hole to water-hole until he became a lethargic victim of the nature of his own country. The waterless Omaheke was to complete the work of the German arms: the annihilation of the Herero people. The sandveld barrier established with an iron will was to complete the work of annihilation (...) The drama was therefore played out in the sombre setting of the sandveld. When the rainy season returned, it shed light on the stage: as our patrols advanced up to the border with Bechuanaland, they discovered the awful image of armies that had died of thirst. The groans of the dying, the crazed cries had gone quiet in the sublime silence of eternity. The punishment had come to an end. The Hereros had ceased to be an independent people.[4]

The high command in Berlin states: "The ongoing racial battle can only be concluded by the annihilation of one party (...) as a result, General Von Trotha's intention may be approved.[5]" According to Diener, in two years of war, the Germans had exterminated three quarters of the Herero people, not counting the deaths among the Namas, Basters, Hottentots, etc. Clearly, the policy of wholesale annihilation of allegedly "inferior" peoples long preceded Hitler. The ground had been cleared for him. His innovation was to introduce this policy inside the borders of Europe and thereby bring to completion what in Africa and America had served as a dress rehearsal.

It was under the German domination of Namibia that Professor Fischer in 1908 conducted investigations among the Basters who had settled at Rehoboth on "the problem of bastardization in human beings." His frank and direct advice sends chills up the spine: "The Hottentots and the racially mixed population of German South-West Africa should only be allowed to live as long as they are doing useful work.[6]" This publication made Eugen Fischer's reputation. His fame spread beyond the borders and in 1929 he became Chairman of the International Genetics Congress. Quite naturally, when Adolph Hitler came into power in Germany in 1933, Fischer brought the prestige and authority attached to his worldwide reputation as a scientist into the service of the new State's racial policy. It is no coincidence that many eminent Nazis were the sons or nephews of people who had proved their worth in the undertaking directed at annihilating the indigenous peoples that had fallen prey to German rule in Africa. It is memorable that Goering, the commander of the Luftwaffe, was the son of Dr Heinrich Goering who between 1885 and 1890 was the first German governor of South-West Africa.[7]

We now know from the work of Benno Muller-Hill, a teacher and researcher in genetics at the University of Cologne, that Black people were the first to be the victim of the Nazi regime's eugenic measures. The "bastards of the Rhineland" – as were called the children born of Black soldiers in the French occupation army and German girls – were sterilised along with the mentally ill and other 'antisocial' elements. Benno Muller-Hill writes:

> A meeting of Working Group II of the Expert Advisory Council for Population and Race Policy was convened on March 11, 1935. The topic for discussion was the sterilisation of coloured children, overlooked when the law for the prevention of hereditary defects was drafted. […] Three possible approaches were considered: widening of the scope of the law, 'export,' i.e. deportation, and compulsory sterilisation without any basis in law. An expert opinion had to be obtained on each child. The experts included Dr Abel and Professor Fischer […] The 'material' was also 'scientifically' evaluated. The Gestapo then took 385 coloured children to university clinics, where they were surgically sterilised.[8]

Again we meet the ubiquitous Professor Fischer, the expert whose competence was by then indisputable. The Germans that gave a scientific shine and an orderly appearance to the Nazi plan had acquired their prestige essentially by working on the demonstration of the blacks' racial inferiority. The international scientific community shared their theories in this area. One such member was the French surgeon Alexis Carrel, a physician, sociologist and biologist who was awarded the Nobel Prize for medicine. During the First World War, he was instrumental in developing the Carrel–Daken method for antiseptic irrigation of wounds. In 1935, he published a best-seller: *Man, the Unknown* that was translated into 19 languages. In it he says: "Europe and the United States are thus undergoing a qualitative as well as quantitative deterioration. On the contrary, the Asians and Africans, as well as the Russians, the Arabs, the Hindus, are increasing with marked rapidity.[9]" He continues: "The suppression of natural selection, as already mentioned, has caused the survival of children whose tissues and consciousness are defective. The race has been weakened by the preservation of such reproducers.[10]" Needless to say, the cause of this degeneration is none other than democracy: "The democratic principle has contributed to the collapse of civilisation in opposing the development of an elite. The feeble-minded and the man of genius should not be equal before the law.[11]"

Dr Alexis Carrel is by no means short of ideas and after having observed that "natural selection has not played its part for a long while, many inferior individuals have been conserved through the efforts of hygiene and medicine,[12]" he finds the solution to rid the race of these inferior and hence harmful individuals: "Eugenics is indispensable for the perpetuation of the strong. A great race must propagate its best elements. However, in the most highly civilised nations reproduction is decreasing and yields inferior products.[13]" To remedy this degenerative trend, the researchers of the Third Reich entered into the employ of the Fuhrer. This is how these scientists solved the problem arising from the presence of a few "little niggers" on German soil, before going on to place their "scientific skills" in the service of the Jewish question. It was only natural then that Philippe Pétain should appoint Alexis Carrel in 1941 to establish and manage the French Foundation for the Study of Human Problems in Paris.

Conscientious, incorruptible scientists

When the certificate of Aryan race became the only means for escaping anti-Semitic persecutions, many among the wealthy businessmen affected by those measures attempted to get hold of this precious document through bribery. They sometimes succeeded when the "expert" was corrupt or corruptible. Sons or daughters of Jewish fathers and Aryan mothers could claim that their mothers had had an affair with an Aryan. The implicit desperation of this tactic reminds us that, earlier, in the concentration camp setting of America, a mixed blood seeking a position among the Whites was well-advised to get hold of a certificate that "proved" that he had been carried in the womb of a Native American rather than of a mulatto woman. According to Schoelcher, mulattoes who sought certificates that proved they belonged to the White race, "unless they actively made use of means of bribery in the offices of the metropolis were unsuccessful in obtaining the honour of having been carried in the womb of a Carib woman rather than that of a Negress.[14]" Which is why C.L.R. James, back in 1938, said "…we have lived to see the rulers of a European nation make the Aryan grandmother as precious for their fellow countrymen as the Caribbean ancestor was to the Mulatto.[15]"

For a half-Jew wanting a certificate of Aryan race, it must have been tragic to end up in the hands of a team of "experts" working under Professor Fischer's supervision. The diagnosis was a bolt from the blue. Fischer was the head of Emperor Wilhem's Institute of Anthropology. As the number of requests for "expert opinions" mushroomed, he asked his assistant, Professor Abel, to perform the "expert assessments on Jews." This makes for some very interesting statements by the latter during the interview he had with Muller-Hill, long after the war, on January 23, 1981:

> I had a telephone call from a gentleman from the Kaiserhof, who wanted to speak to me about an expert report. I was prepared to go to visit him, but he wanted to see me at the institute. At two o'clock, a big Maybach drove up to the institute, and the gentleman spoke to me about the expert report which had turned out to be unfavourable. I fetched it and said: "Judge for yourself, his father, whom I am supposed to exclude, looks like his twin brother." He then said: "Well, well. We can still do something about that. You're a young man, and you'll want to make anthropological research trips abroad, isn't that right? I would be happy to help with the expenses." I showed him the door. The result was a telephone call from the Reich Kinship Bureau. "But, Abel, are you crazy? Do you know whom you threw out? – No – The president of the German paper industry, worth sixty million marks." As a result of that, a letter came from Bormann to Fischer, transmitted through the Reich Kinship Bureau, saying that we should be lenient in writing our expert reports.[16]

On June 22, 1941, the German armies entered the Soviet Union, closely followed by the death commandos in charge of the mobile killing operations. Their task was to exterminate the Jews (men, women and children) together with the Bolshevik commissioners and all those who supported the Soviet regime. During August, the killings turned into mass slaughter. "During the first sweep the mobile killing units reported approximately one hundred thousand victims a month[17]" revealed Hilberg. It was at that point that "Professor Fischer travelled to Paris with the aim of convincing the French intelligentsia that Bolshevism and Jewry were identical and that the final solution was a scientific necessity".[18]

Fischer was not particularly anti-Semitic. In any case, no more than he was a negrophobe. He was just a scientist convinced that irrevocably inferior individuals exist and that society is entitled to rid itself of these undesirable elements. In his lecture on "The problem of race and racial legalisation in Germany," addressing his French colleagues, he states: "… the morals and actions of the Bolshevist Jews bear witness to such a monstrous mentality that we can only speak of inferiority and of beings of another species.[19]"

This scientist is true to himself. He uses the same principles and says the same thing apart from replacing the word "Negro" with "Jew" or "Bolshevik," to name those who belong to "another species." From that point onwards, their annihilation follows its course as determined by the needs of the dominant group and using the technological means of the time.

From the exclusion of non-Whites to the exclusion of non-Aryans

The anti-Jewish measures implemented by the Nazis starting in 1933, i.e. the segregationist laws and decrees that were designed to ostracize the Jews of Germany, were the first phase in a process that led to their destruction, not just in Germany but all over Europe. In 1933, it was not possible to forecast how many people that belonged to the Jewish, Gypsy and other communities would be murdered, nor the actual means chosen to annihilate them. However, no one whether in Germany or elsewhere, neither could nor should have misapprehended the fundamentally criminal nature of the National Socialist movement. This political movement openly advocated racial hatred and asserted, with the utmost violence, the racial superiority of some and the inferiority of others, vowing to annihilate the so-called inferior beings. The intellectuals, those distinguished scholars, who had already been working in the 1920s on understanding and interpreting political, social and historical events, could not have been unaware of the danger that the rise of a party that mobilised its troops with the additional promise of giving them the spoils of the inferior groups represented for humanity. Hilberg makes a distinction.

> These characteristics are reflected in five steps of the ghettoisation process: (1) the severance of social contacts between Jews and Germans, (2) housing restrictions, (3) movement regulations, (4) identification measures, and (5) the institution of Jewish administrative machinery [...] The dissolution of social relations began with the dismissals of Jews from the civil service and industry, and with the Aryanisation or liquidation of Jewish business establishments. These measures, however, were primarily economic. Their social consequences were incidental.[20]

This onslaught of discrimination, spoliation and persecutions against the Jewish population of Germany was viewed by Western democracies with a mixture of indifference and connivance reminiscent of the attitude of the North American authorities – a mixture of indifference and sympathy – towards the activities of the Ku Klux Klan. There is one difference however: in the United States, the activities of the Ku Klux Klan together with the lynching of Blacks in which the white population willingly took part from time to time right up to the 1930s, was just a leftover from the time when the case law of the Supreme Court established that: "Blacks had no rights that the White man was bound to respect."[21]

Not all Germans despised the Jews but, to varying degrees, they all accepted the various anti-Jewish measures applied by the National Socialist state. When the extermination of the Jews began in 1941, there was no show of hostility towards the dreadful treatment to which they were publicly subjected, no display of solidarity with the Jewish victims whose humanity was challenged by the state. Why was this? In the answer to this question, I find one of the most disastrous outcomes of the conventionalisation (sometimes the barely concealed justification) of Gorée, Saint-Domingue and other pinnacles of human suffering, that have been continuously ignored by history textbooks.

The conquest of America and its colonisation profoundly altered the relationships between Europeans and other peoples. They soon bridged the gap between difference and superiority. A racial hierarchy developed the feeling among Whites that they were plainly superior to non-Whites. The most decisive element in this process – and it led to the spiritual breakdown and moral collapse of Europe as exposed by Nazism – was that the feeling of superiority among Whites was concomitant with the devaluing of the life of allegedly inferior beings. In this way, while the primary goal of the relationships of subservience imposed by Europe on other peoples was not their complete extermination, destruction or annihilation, nonetheless, from the moment they were formally pronounced inferior onwards, these outcomes entered the realm of possibility. Worse still, for centuries, there was ideological justification and cultural acceptance of the idea that these "inferior" beings could be exploited at will, treated as objects and even removed if necessary. The material and psychological benefits deriving from being part of the superior group worked in favour of the acceptance of these givens that over the centuries became deep-seated cultural elements of Western civilisation. As a result, any empathy when confronted with the suffering of "inferior" beings was precluded. The system of terror that was concomitant with colonial rule was formative in the sense that barbarity was not just institutionalised but – as an ultimate mockery – presented as having a civilising effect. For generations, the Westerners' gratifying belief in the virtue and benefits of their mission took on the proportions of a collective belief, i.e. an axiom.

The advent of the National Socialist Party and Hitler's scheme to apply colonisation inside Europe itself radically altered the way some commonly accepted notions were used and applied. For instance, the criterion for establishing that a person belongs to the superior race was drastically revised. Hence, notions such as "Non-Whites" became obsolete; creating a new circumstance where belonging to the "White race" that was traditionally defined as the race of masters was no longer enough. The word "Jew" replaced "Black," and "Aryan" replaced "White."

The vast majority of Germans, happy to find themselves on the right side, accepted the *fait accompli*, i.e., the exclusion of non-Aryans, and even took full advantage of it. Since the Jew had become the "inferior" being, his destruction entered into the realm of possibility and there was no reason to get excited about it. And so, a horrible, gruesome conjunction took place between ideological factors and material interests. On the ideological side, very widespread anti-Semitism efficiently utilised the ideologies and theories that made the other an inferior being, one whose humanity may be denied and who can be worked to death or roasted alive, with the best of intentions and in the midst of the civilising crusade. The ideologists of the Third Reich made clever use of these commonplaces, the racial hierarchies that were opportunely devised by scholars and scientists to meet the ideological needs of colonisation and have been skilfully cultivated ever since. Until the Second World War, racism essentially spread within scientific communities, and from there onwards cloaked in the legitimacy and recognition bestowed by science. The very same scientists who had worked on demonstrating the inferiority of non-Whites in general and of Black people in particular, imperceptibly moved on to work on the selection and identification of Aryans versus non-Aryans. German scientists were not necessarily hardline anti-Semites; they were deeply convinced that racial hierarchies were founded and applicable within the White race.

In the nineteenth century, racism was "first and foremost a scientific doctrine, accepted throughout the West, professed in the universities and even reflected in primary education.[22]" This consensus among intellectuals and scientists in the Western world, at a time when scientism had acquired an unprecedented power of legitimation and conferred enormous prestige on the racist theories. In this way, racist theories spread and took root.

Léon Poliakov is quite right when he states how "important it is to underscore the responsibility of the whole of the West in the formulation and propagation of racism, of which the Third Reich was the extravagant but logical outcome.[23]" Unless proper consideration is given to the influence of all these ideological factors, any view or analysis and interpretation of Nazism and of its popularity in Germany and elsewhere is inevitably skewed.

Even under Nazi rule, Germany did not compare to the Congo or North America

People who look at Nazism ponder the insoluble conundrum whereby such a civilised country as Germany could sink into Nazi barbarity. To anyone who cares to check, it is obvious that up to 1945 no parliament in any democracy, no head of government, no representative of any major power, and indeed no officially certified historian ever solemnly stated that the annihilation of human groups, once they had been declared to be inferior and relegated to the condition of sub-humans, could be construed as barbarity. No official institution was created to develop a theory or an approach, which for educational purposes, set itself apart from institutionalised barbarity and strove to obtain the reinstatement (be it belated) of the humanity of the victims of white supremacy. What was missing was a gesture, or perhaps more than a gesture, indicating that the atrocities inflicted upon other peoples on the basis of their inferiority would never again be tolerated because they are contrary to civilisation and to the principles of humanity.

There was never any declaration that officially expressed a regret and, at the very least, a condemnation on principle that surely was warranted by the extermination of the indigenous peoples of America and Australia, as well as the wholesale destruction of all those who were raided in their native lands, deported and forced into slavery. Quite the contrary, the history of America continues to be the charming story of the European conquerors whose crimes were considered to be genuine feats. In the Congo, school textbooks for Africans sang the praises of King Léopold II and celebrated him for the civilising value of his enterprise. This continued unchanged until 1960.

In France, historians try to justify the "military genius" of a madman who at one time led the country. Napoleon, that small, cruel man who, as he admits himself, would have had anyone who went to Egypt to argue for the freedom of the Blacks or the Arabs hung from a high mast. Everything, absolutely everything, reinforced the legitimation, after the fact, of deeds that were in blatant contradiction with the principles of humanity. Nothing in politics or in the official doctrine of those who could have helped to shape opinions and change mentalities was undertaken to teach the peoples of Europe that there is no such thing as an outcast race or a higher people. Any prospect of delegitimising barbarity and banning this method in relations with "inferior peoples" hinged on such an act of repentance. No one questioned the degree of civilisation of the French Republic in 1931, during the Exposition Coloniale in Paris when the organisers "tastefully" put on exhibit, among other strange creatures, a group of Kanaks brought in straight from New Caledonia. "From a safe distance, visitors could admire a group of Kanaks locked up in a cage.[24]"

Since the 1870s, Europeans acquired the habit of crowding into human zoos where indigenous peoples from various colonies were exhibited like exotic animals for their curiosity.[25]

Scientific publications and literature together with history and anthropology textbooks before 1945 are explicit. At that time, the tone was blunt as anyone who cares to check can see.

Starting in 1933, in Nazi Germany, signs began to appear saying "No dogs or Jews," or "Aryans only." In spite of its policy of racial segregation, this country was chosen to host the 1936 Olympic Games, showing how pervasively exclusion and racism were integrated into Western thought. The casting out of a minority stated to be undesirable did not offend the sensibilities of the governments of Western democracies. In fact, during the Olympic Games, *The Nation* – a Liberal North American paper, in its August 1, 1936 edition – saw fit to spell out that in the streets of Germany "one sees no Jewish heads being chopped off. (...) People smile, are polite, and sing with gusto in beer gardens. Board and lodging are good, cheap, and abundant... Everything is terrifyingly clean and the visitor likes it all.[26]"

The reporter searched for gallows, but to no avail. Of course, in the concentration camp setting of America, the practice of decapitating one or several Blacks and nailing their heads to stakes became customary and lasted for as long as the system itself did. Some masters even adopted the practice of setting up stakes in front of their houses and nailing the heads of a few Blacks to them, claiming that this would discourage anyone from running away. This is a custom we also find in Africa under colonial rule. Some officials went so far as to paint their victims' heads to make them decorative.

In the Congo, a certain Léon Rom, station master in charge of collection at Stanley Falls was well-known for his fondness for decapitated heads. A British explorer-journalist passing through Stanley Falls describes the aftermath of a punitive military expedition against some African rebels: "Many women and children were taken, and twenty-one heads were brought to the falls and have been used by Captain Rom as a decoration round a flower-bed in front of his house![27]" Léon Rom died a natural death in 1924 "in Belgium, in his office at the Compagnie du Kasai.[28]" Nobody ever troubled him or asked him to provide any sort of justification for his ghastly habits. The question of whether Belgium was civilised or not was never for a moment entertained because these practices were consistent with the nature of the relationships that had been established with the "inferior" populations. In the United States, the white population demonstrated a taste for lynchings, but that does not mean the country was not civilised. In other words, these practices were fairly well integrated into 'civilisation.' It is therefore only reasonable that the reporter at *The Nation*, being from the United States, should look for decapitated or severely beaten up Jews, as evidence capable of convincing him that things were not going well for Jews. Even in 1941, when the extermination of Jews began in Germany, driving stakes into the ground in public places to exhibit decapitated heads was never contemplated. This did sometimes happen in the camps where a climate of terror was cultivated in a similar manner as in the concentration camp setting of America. Even under Nazi rule when Jews were persecuted, Germany did not have time to develop the tastes acquired by the white population of the United States where "the habit of lynching indeed became rooted as a tradition [...] so much so that long after slavery had officially ended, in the last decade of the nineteenth century, a Black [...] was hanged and torched by the crowds every other day.[29]"

Still in 1920, in Mississippi and Georgia, in Arkansas, Florida and Alabama, White crowds wholeheartedly gave themselves over to lynching Blacks without this ever, as far as I know, having attracted the attention of psychologists and other experts on the manifestations of violence. On a single day,

> "fourteen Blacks were burned in public, eleven of whom were still alive. An African American editor in Charleston, South Carolina", cried out: "There is scarcely a day that passes that newspapers don't tell about a Negro soldier lynched in his uniform. Why do they lynch Negroes, anyhow? With a White judge, a White jury, White public sentiment, white officers of the law, it is just as impossible for a Negro accused of crime, or even suspected of crime, to escape the White man's vengeance or his justice as it would be for a fawn that wanders accidentally into a den of hungry lions to escape with its life. So why not give him the semblance of a trial?"[30]

Considering these facts, even the German population's animosity towards the Jews in the 1930s never reached the height of popular hatred expressed in the United States. There were no American-style lynchings in public places with the accompanying explosion of racial hatred.

To illustrate the absence of any spontaneous manifestation of racial hatred in the streets of Germany, Finkelstein quotes the thoughts of Eva Reichmann:

> If those people who, under the influence of anti-Semitic propaganda, had been moved by outright hatred of the Jews, their practical aggression against them would have been excessive after the Jews had been openly abandoned to the people's fury. Violence would not then have been limited to the organized activities of Nazi gangs, but would have become endemic in the population as a whole and seriously endangered the life of every Jew in Germany. This, however, did not happen. Even during the years in which the party increased by leaps and bounds, spontaneous terrorist assaults on Jews were extremely rare ... In spite of the ardent efforts of the Nazi Party, the boycott against Jewish shopkeepers and professional men before the seizure of power was negligible, although this would have been an inconspicuous and safe way of demonstrating one's anti-Jewish feeling. From all this all but complete lack of anti-Semitic reactions at a time when the behaviour of the public was still a correct index to its sentiments, it can only be inferred that the overwhelming majority of the people did not feel their relations to the Jewish minority to be unbearable.[31]

In contrast to this German reserve, the White North-American society from the nineteenth century up to the 1960s considered lynching to be a healthy form of entertainment, decent enough for citizens to be perfectly willing to come forward and take a pose before a camera to immortalize these barbarian revelries.[32]

I am sometimes criticised, with a mixture of irritation and condescension, for spending too much time on a few aspects of local history in the United States whereas I claim to deal with the destruction of the Jews in Europe. It seems obvious to me, however, that if the ideological factors that contributed to the dreadful atrocities perpetrated by the Nazis are not taken into consideration, there can be no understanding or explanation. These ideological factors can no more be set aside than the political and economic factors, in combination with which they are crucial.

Civilisation and barbarity

The ideological factors that contributed to the normalisation of Nazi theories were not born in Germany and certainly did not wait for the advent of Adolph Hitler to prosper in the political arena. To pretend to believe this is part of the conceptual trickery that has been a constant throughout history, from the time the Europeans reached America to this day, particularly in the first half of the twentieth century when African American historians tried to uncover some of the manipulations of their White colleagues. This task has yet to be completed in spite of the colossal implications.

Western historians are not the only ones having been involved in rearranging history. African historians generally speaking are not yet able to historicise the responsibility of their elites who surrendered their peoples to the Europeans. As for Arab historians, including those most committed to the struggle against Western domination, they are neither demanding nor interested in research directed at establishing the damage inflicted on the peoples of Black Africa by the Muslim conquerors who were the first to introduce the trade of human flesh on this continent. Intent upon condemning the crimes committed against the Arab peoples who were subjected to Western colonisation for more than a century, they say nothing about the crimes perpetrated by the Arabs in the name of conquering Islam, in the form of several centuries of raiding. It is no coincidence that the word "abd" in Arabic means both "black" and "slave." In that culture, a Black person is equated to a slave. Cases of slavery are still found in Mauritania or Sudan, to mention only those most familiar to Western public opinion. The fact that from the nineteenth century Muslim countries too were subjected to European colonial domination must not obscure that "while Islam[sic] was under colonial rule for one century, it was colonialist and imperialistic for ten centuries without (so far) feeling the slightest pang of conscience.[33]"

An interpretation of history other than a purely dichotomous one has yet to be written. This is borne out by the reluctance of specialists of the Nazi issue to grasp the internal and dialectical relation between the various ideological factors that made the "final solution" possible. A true understanding of the Nazi phenomenon cannot afford to leave out an analysis of the responsibility that rests with the major powers for establishing racial hierarchies and theories that facilitated and then provided justification for the annihilation of other non-European groups. It will become more and more difficult to steer clear of this thus far studiously avoided analysis quite simply because there are more and more people who realise that Nazi barbarity and its attendant atrocities are the consummation of a process lasting more than four centuries.

The process goes back to the arrival of the Spaniards in the Americas. The Spaniards have the dubious distinction of having pioneered this enterprise of destruction (with the Portuguese hot on their heels, and the Dutch jealously trying to elbow their way in). This enterprise of barbarity soon achieved legitimacy, and was legally recognised when the French government, in 1685, adopted legislation that codified the banishment of Blacks from the human species and their enslavement. The English added a very British touch to this series of atrocities. Preferring a more expeditious method for their colonies, the British proceeded quite simply to exterminate the indigenous populations in spite of the fact that since 1215 they already had their Magna Carta – the precursor to the *habeas corpus*. Their standard practice was soon based on the idea that "a good Indian is a dead Indian." The ultimate literary expression of this conviction is to be found in *The Last of the Mohicans* by James Fenimore Cooper. His story is set in the regions that his father William Cooper colonised in the State of New York and the "bloodthirsty" criminals he describes are the indigenous populations his father annihilated aided by other pioneers who like himself had come bearing the gift of Western civilisation. This best-seller, a true apology for the elimination of "inferior races" was published in the first half of the nineteenth century and devoured by young Europeans.

The genocide perpetrated by the English against the Native Americans of North America paved the way for a White society that was structured around the systematic negation of non-Whites. This is how the "American nation" was built. When slavery was officially abolished, the Native Americans had already been annihilated and were not a problem, but the Blacks who had survived subjugation staked a claim to citizenship to which Whites only were eligible. Faced with this development, the racist ideology had to devise scientific, philosophical and political arguments not only to rationalise the exclusion of non-Whites from political and social roles, but also to confer suitable legitimacy upon a form of government that was to become universally accepted. Some considerable effort was therefore spent on rooting the conviction that Blacks were irretrievably inferior.

> Morton, Gliddon and Nott, who were leading figures at the American School of Anthropology, were firm advocates of Black slavery. In order to provide a scientific foundation for their opinions on this topic, they set about proving the natural inferiority of Blacks. They did this by developing a theory based on a new discipline: craniology.[34]

In the nineteenth century, French intellectuals and scientists for instance, made a significant contribution to disseminating those racist ideologies. Armand de Quatrefages, a French naturalist and anthropologist, was appointed to the chair of anthropology and ethnology at the National Museum of Natural History in 1855. He had gained fame through his work on the anatomy of the skull. As a disciple of the American school of anthropology, he was a pioneer in craniology in France. Using other criteria such as the angle of the face and shape of lips, the representatives of this discipline believed they had scientifically proven the inferiority of Blacks and categorised them as sub-human or an anomaly of nature, a view that Quatrefages himself asserts:

> The Negro is an intellectual monstrosity, this word being used here in its scientific sense. To produce it, nature has used the same methods as it does when it engenders those monstrosities, examples of which are plentiful in our premises. [...] To obtain this result, it is sufficient for certain parts of the being to stop developing at a certain level. This gives rise to these foetuses without heads or limbs, these children who enact the fable of Cyclops [...]. Well then! The Negro is a White whose body acquires the final shape of the species but whose whole intelligence is arrested on the way.[35]

Saint-Simon, who was convinced of racial inequality, said that "Blacks were at different levels of civilisation because they were biologically inferior to Whites.[36]" Victor Courtet de l'Isle, author of *La science politique fondée sur la science de l'homme* and a dedicated follower of Saint-Simon, wrote:

> In my view, the emancipation of the inferior races will never have the effect of putting them on an entirely equal footing with the superior races; and it is in anticipation of this inequality that will always weigh them down that I think the lawmaker must apply himself in the aftermath of abolition, not before.[37]

The principle of racial inferiority as a biological feature of entire human groups was firmly established, and the social inequalities it produced, because they derived from alleged natural inequalities, had the authority to become the immutable norm. The members of the groups in this way designated should naturally stay in their place. Against this backdrop, Ernest Renan's altogether reasonable discourse was quite acceptable:

> We aspire not to equality but to domination. The country of a foreign race must become once again a country of serfs, of agricultural labourers or industrial workers. It is not a question of eliminating the inequalities among men but rather of widening them and making them into a law. [...] The regeneration of inferior or degenerate races by the superior races is part of the providential order of things for humanity. [...] Nature has made a race of workers, the Chinese race; [...] a race of tillers of the soil, the Negro; [...] a race of masters and soldiers, the European race. Reduce this noble race to working in the ergastulum like Negroes and Chinese and they rebel. [...] Let each one do what he is made for, and all will be well.[38]

This is clearly the model that the leaders of the Third Reich tried to enforce against non-Aryans.

I believe that revisiting the commonplaces that characterised the Western mind-set at the time when Nazism came to power is crucial. It is time to shed the very common habit of scoffing at the role of theories that attempted to prove the inferiority of Blacks scientifically and face up to the fact that these theories existed as axiomatic truths. The scorn of historians is just a ploy to avoid having to conduct a disturbing analysis. It is a trick whereby the causal relation between the theories developed to justify the exclusion of non-Whites and the favourable reception given to the theories that justified the exclusion of non-Aryans are conjured away.

Germany had reached a degree of civilisation that should have been enough to preclude any descent into barbarity. This was a highly civilised country in 1904 when the Commander in Chief for South-West Africa, General Lother von Trotha, received an order from Wilhem II to exterminate the Herero: "Do not spare a single man, woman or child, kill them all.[39]" This was no metaphor; it was the death warrant of an entire people. General von Trotha handed down the extermination order to his men: "Within the German boundaries every Herero, whether found with or without a rifle, with or without cattle, shall be shot.⁴⁰" Ninety per cent of the Herero people were exterminated. This was no secret, but nonetheless not a single Western democracy came forward to protest that this wanton destruction was contrary to civilisation.

No one disputes the fact that the British killed the indigenous peoples they came in contact with in North America and also, in the nineteenth century, exterminated the Aborigines on the Australian continent. In spite of this, they were never banished from the entente between civilised nations. Their enterprise of annihilation was never declared to be contrary to civilisation or incompatible with the customs of the country to which we owe the *habeas corpus*, i.e. a historical step forward which since the seventeenth century has better protected individual freedoms than any other declaration of intent. The White North American society that had succeeded in imposing a democratic model that worked solely with and for the people of the superior breed and had established racial laws that enabled it to maintain the sub-humans of the inferior breed at the margins of society was nevertheless highly respected among civilised nations.

Let us consider the atrocities perpetrated in the French colonies at the end of the nineteenth century. From 1885 to 1895, the indigenous people of Tonkin had to endure seeing their kinsfolk's heads put on display on posts at the entrance of villages. At the time, "French soldiers would send their families who had stayed back in France some curious postcards depicting decapitated heads either lying on the ground or displayed on boxes.⁴¹" Exhibiting heads nailed to stakes was a lasting feature of the concentration camp system in America as well as of the various colonial dominions of Africa and Asia. In Madagascar, "witnesses of the conquest saw a hundred times stakes topped with heads that were ceaselessly being replaced just as they were at the entrance to Tonkin villages.⁴²" These were serious atrocities, but even more serious was the fact that they were conventionalised and elicited no reaction among inhabitants of the metropolis. Some children in France learned to read with the comic book *Les aventures du capitaine Ratapoil*: "Having on his own one day captured twenty Bedouins who had attempted to take the station by surprise, he had them all kneel down in a row in front of him and using his sabre like a scythe chopped off the darkies' heads in one fell swoop, much to their annoyance.⁴³"

And that is how the twentieth century began. Thereafter, not one government, whether left- or right-wing, ever felt the obligation to condemn those atrocities and declare them to be contrary to civilisation or unworthy of the land of human rights. This has not prevented France from being labelled a civilised country, remembering that some inhabitants of the metropolis were able to keep their hands clean but only because there were others who did the dirty work in these genocidal enterprises. Still a century later, the vast majority of the people of France, regardless of their political leanings, are far from being convinced that their debt is as heavy and indefeasible as the one owed by the Germans to their victims. And yet, the difference lies only in the legal characterisation of the victims.

In the light of these observations, what peculiar feature or miracle could possibly have made the German people in the 1930s the only European people who, against the ideological and cultural tradition of civilisation in general, rise up as one against the exclusion, subjugation and bestialisation of "inferior" beings? To this day, ever since the Spaniards reached America, there has never been a precedent of this type. No one suspected that a civilised people could not allow its government to perpetrate the exclusion, enslavement and extermination of other so-called inferior peoples, without itself sinking into the most savage barbarian madness. Quite the contrary. It is easy to ascertain that, in those countries that were historically implicated in these enterprises of enslavement and destruction, the vast majority felt no compassion and were indifferent. At worst, what we find in the publications that express the thinking of those who shape society's opinions and ideological representations, is a venomous discourse directed at the groups considered inferior and targeted at justifying their annihilation.

A common misconception is racial hierarchy. This is the essential premise and prerequisite for any enterprise of enslavement and destruction. Racial hierarchy has never been truly opposed in Western civilisation. Even among humanists, fighting this scourge never became a matter of principle nor a profound necessity.

Western experts pretend they do not understand that the people of Germany adopted more or less the same attitude as all the other European peoples whose government at some point in their history were involved in the annihilation of other peoples: pretending to know nothing of the atrocities while reaping as much benefit as possible from it. Once the Jews were declared to be inferior, once they had been relegated to the sub-human condition, the power of racial hierarchies and the traditional inability to identify or empathise with these individuals created the same mixture of indifference and hostility among Germans as had already been displayed in earlier times by other European peoples towards more distant foreign victims. This notion of inferiority was to play a key role in the ordeals suffered by the victims. In many instances, the Nazis' treatment of prisoners varied depending on the category or status assigned to each group within the racial hierarchy adopted by the thinkers of the Third Reich. For instance, British prisoners sometimes received different treatment from Russian or Polish prisoners who were considered racially inferior. In the plan to achieve hegemony, the Nazis did not face Black or non-White peoples in Europe. Hence the lowest position on the racial scale was by necessity filled by new victims singled out from within the Whites. Jews – especially if they originated from Eastern Europe – received the most brutal treatment. They were hence subjected to the most barbaric deeds thus so far set aside for those considered to be in the lowest position of the racial hierarchy.

Notes

1. Muller-Hill, Benno, *Murderous Science: Elimination by Scientific Selection of Jews, Gypsies and Others*, Cold Spring Harbor Laboratory Press, 1997, p. 228.
2. Diener, Ingolf, *Apartheid! La cassure*, Paris, 1986, p. 46 (quote translated from the French).
3. Ibid. p. 103.
4. Ibid pp. 103–104.
5. Ibid.
6. Muller-Hill, Benno, op. cit., p. 123.
7. Cornevin, Robert, *Histoire de la colonisation allemande*, Paris, PUF, 1969, p. 42 and p. 85.
8. Muller-Hill, Benno, op. cit., p. 32.
9. Carrel, Alexis, *Man, the Unknown*, Harper & Brothers, United States, 1935. Retrieved June 8, 2010 from http://www.soilandhealth.org/03sov/0303critic/030310carrel/Carrell-toc.htm
10. Ibid.
11. Ibid.
12. Carrel, Alexis, *Man, the Unknown*. Retrieved June 8, 2010 from http://www.soilandhealth.org/03sov/0303critic/030310carrel/Carrel-ch8.htm.
13. Ibid.
14. Schoelcher, *Des colonies françaises*, op. cit., p. 169.
15. James, C.L.R., *The Black Jacobins: Toussaint L'Ouverture and the San Domingo Revolution*, New York, Random House, 1963, p.43. See also p. 42 et. seq. on

the legal battle conducted by Chapuzet de Guérin, lawyer in Cape. The local authorities, having proved that the Chapuzet family had a Black ancestor who went back 150 years, attempted to deny Chapuzet the privilege of belonging to the White race. He was fortunately able to prove that the undesirable ancestor was a Caribbean and not Black.

16. Muller-Hill, Benno, op. cit., p. 139.
17. Hilberg, op. cit., p. 208.
18. Muller-Hill, Benno, op. cit., p. 50.
19. Ibid, op. cit., p. 17.
20. Hilberg, Raul, *The Destruction of the European Jews*. Revised Edition Vol. 1. New York: Holmes & Meier, 1985. Questia. Web. 6 July 2010.
21. See Chapter 8 on the Supreme Court case law on the trial of Dred Scott in 1857 and that of the Plessy versus Ferguson in 1896.
22. Poliakov, Léon, *The History of Anti-Semitism: From Voltaire to Wagner*, University of Pennsylvania Press, 2003, p. 125.
23. Poliakov, Léon, "De la notion de race au génocide," in *La politique nazie d'extermination*, Paris, 1980, p. 56 (quote translated from French).
24. Nicolaidis, Dimitri, "La Nation, les crimes et la mémoire", in *Oublier nos crimes*, Paris, 1994, p. 18.
25. See "Ces zoos humains de la République coloniale" by Nicolas Bancel, Pascal Blanchard and Sandrine Lemaire, in *Le Monde diplomatique*, August 2000.
26. Friedlander, Saul, *Nazi Germany and the Jews*, Volume 1, Harper Perennial, New York 1998, p. 180.
27. This account was first published in *Century Magazine*, then reprinted by *The Saturday Review* on December 17, 1898, quoted by Hochschild, op. cit., p. 145.
28. Ibid. p. 284.
29. Paraire, Philippe, *Les Noirs Américains, généalogie d'une exclusion*, Paris, 1993, p. 93. (quote translated from the French).
30. Franklin, John Hope and Moss Alfred, Jr., *From Slavery to Freedom: A History of Negro Americans*, MacGraw Hill, Eighth Edition, 2000. p. 385.
31. Finkelstein, Norman and Birn, Ruth, *A Nation on Trial: the Goldhagen Thesis and Historical Truth*, p. 15, pdf file downloaded June 3, 2010 at jrbooksonline.com/PDF_Books_added2009-4/nationontrial.pdf
32. On the festive element in these mob lynchings carried out in the United States up to 1965 (25 years after Auschwitz), a book by Leon Litwack, Professor of history at the University of Berkeley and James Allen, antiques dealer in Atlanta, *Without Sanctuary, Lynching. Photography in America,* is enlightening. In addition to the analysis provided by Professor Litwack, the book contains reproductions of the 98 photographs collected by James Allen. They depict upright citizens and reputable public figures who had themselves

photographed next to the corpses just before the latter were dismembered. These snapshots were then used by these people to boast that they had taken part. Nazi barbarity played no part in this. The article *Sans Sépulture* by Anne Chaon in *Le Monde diplomatique*, June 2000, is also worth reading.
33. Barreau, Jean-Claude, *De l'islam en général et du monde moderne en particulier*, le Pré aux clercs, 1991.
34. Poliakov, Léon, *Le racisme*, Paris, pp. 78–79.
35. Ibid, p.79.
36. Cohen, William B. and Le Sueur, James D., *The French Encounter with Africans: White response to Blacks, 1530–1880*, Indiana University Press, 2003, p. 215.
37. See the book by Jean Boissel, *Victor Courtet, 1813–1867, premier théoricien de la hiérarchie des races*, Paris, 1972, p. 157.
38. Renan, Ernest, *La réforme intellectuelle et morale*, Paris 1871, quoted by Aimé Césaire in "Discourse on Colonialism", in *African Philosophy: An Anthology*, edited by Emmanuel Chukwudi Eze, Blackwell Publishing Ltd., p. 224.
39. Cros, Gérard, *La Namibie*, Paris, 1983, p. 35.
40. Hochschild, op. cit., p. 282.
41. Ruscio, Alain, in *Oublier nos crimes*, op. cit., p. 49 (quote translated from the French).
42. Ibid, p. 41.
43. Ibid, p. 50.

6

Business Comes First

Anything goes if there is something to gain

Ideological factors certainly facilitated the task of the Nazis but there is no doubt that this mass slaughter took place because "the persecution and destruction of Jews was capable of immediately and practically furthering the social and economic interests of a large portion of the population.[1]"

For instance, the removal of 5,000 non-Aryan civil servants from their positions pursuant to the civil service reform law dated April 7, 1933, met with support from much of society at all levels. German physicians welcomed the decree that stripped their non-Aryan colleagues of their right to practise medicine on Aryan patients. As for the legal profession, and although most Jewish lawyers had already been debarred since 1933, Hilberg recalls that in April 1938, Staatssekretar Franz Schlegelberger at the Ministry of Justice informed Friedrich Wilhelm Kritzinger at the Reich Chancellery that "[t]heir continued presence irked the legal profession, which demanded their removal.[2]"

People are not generally inclined to act against their own immediate interests. Many Germans were in favour of the anti-Jewish laws because they produced opportunities for taking over the vacated positions. This was the motivation that prevailed at all levels of society rather than other feelings such as solidarity or compassion.

> The most important of these anti-mixing ordinances was the Law against Overcrowding of German Schools of April 25, 1933, which reduced the admission of non-Aryans to each school or college to the proportion of all non-Aryans in the entire German population. The acceptance quota was accordingly fixed at 1.5 per cent, while enrolment ceilings were devised with a view to the progressive reduction of the Jewish student body as a whole.[3]

Once again, rather than eliciting hostility of any sort, this measure raised hopes among Aryans. Many German families blindly believed that their children would do better in school now that there were fewer Jews. Many students, particularly the underachievers, were convinced that they owed their own failure to such and such a Jew and therefore welcomed the law as a means of ridding them of their most formidable opponents.

The grievances that students and professors had against Jews can be traced back to 1869 when the law emancipating them was passed. For Jews to acquire these new constitutional rights and be entitled to equal treatment before the law was a major development that entirely altered their status. Education, as noted by Fritz Stern, became one of the focal points of this surge of development in the community.

> Traditional Jewish veneration for learning plus the new promise of social reward gave Jews a particular incentive to excel in German education. As a consequence, they were disproportionately represented in gymnasiums and universities; by the mid 1880s, nearly 10% of all the students enrolled at Prussian universities were seven times their proportionate number in the population. The disproportion was even higher in large-city gymnasiums, and the anti-Semitism of secondary school teachers, made more virulent by their occupational resentment at being so close to, yet so inferior to, university teachers, may also have been related to the palpable presence of so many Jewish children in their classes.[4]

Prior to 1869, Germans would have been less favourable to the expulsion of Jewish students and professors because it was one thing to have just a few Jews in the educational system and quite another to have the upsurge that followed their emancipation.

No less spectacular was the change in the economic circumstances of the Jewish community following their legal emancipation. Having experienced and suffered the throes of exclusion, Jews seized the opportunities presented by equality before the law and asserted themselves as a flourishing community in all sectors of the economy from which they were no longer excluded. They climbed the social and economic ladder at lightning speed. Although they represented only 1.25% of the population, their social role became considerable.

> In 1881 Berlin Jews made up 4.9% of the population, 0.4% of the civil servants, 8.6% of its writers and journalists, 25.8% of those engaged in the money market and 46% of its wholesalers, retailers and shippers. In many cities in Silesia, Jews constituted about 4% of the population and paid more than 20% of the taxes – an index of their disproportionate income. [...] And by the 1880s, a member of the British embassy in Berlin

had the impression that "the capital of the country was rapidly passing into the hands of a limited number of Jews of enormous wealth, as industry encroached upon the old agricultural interest".[5]

The financial might of a few Jewish business people was such that observers passing through Berlin appeared to be surprised that it did not elicit any hostility. Stern mentions a book by Shepard Thomas Taylor published in London. In it, the author, who stayed in Berlin between 1870 and 1871, expresses the belief that

> the Berlin Christian is a far more tolerant being than his English coreligionist. Whilst the Christians of Berlin have, as a rule, to bear the burden and heat of the day, a disproportionate share of the material loaves and fishes falls into the lot of the more fortunate Jew… [Jews] inhabit the best houses in the best quarters of town, drive about the parks in the most elegant carriages, figure constantly in the dress circle at the opera and theatres, and in this and other ways excite a great deal of envy in the minds of their less fortunate Christian fellow citizens.[6]

The tolerance of Christian Berliners apparently soon dried up and hostility against Jews was in fact gathering momentum. Indeed, in 1880, a movement made up of different groups together with some leading figures joined forces and organised a petition demanding measures to restrict application of equal treatment to Jews, seeking to ban them from public office and limiting Jewish immigration. Towards the end of the year, this petition was tabled before the Prussian Landtag and was the topic of a debate that lasted two days. The agitation and interest it aroused among the public were commensurate with the interests at stake. The controversy raised a furore and the public gallery were overflowing well before the scheduled time. During the debate, the anti-Semites led the offensive while the isolated progressives remained on the defensive.

> The right-wing progressive deputy, Dr Hänel, solicited the government's views regarding its demands "that aim at the elimination of complete constitutional equality of the Jews". Admitting to the many unpleasant characteristics of Jews, Hänel called nevertheless for the affirmation of their legal rights and warned that anti-Semitism had already taken a most perfidious turn by embracing racism, that irredeemable condemnation of individuals based solely on the accident of their birth. […] The Prussian vice-chancellor responded with a few aseptic sentences, culminating with the statement that "the state government does not intend to have the constitutional arrangements changed." […] The conservatives and most of

the center spokesmen heaped abuse and admonitions on the Jews: endless variations on the charges that, by usury and cheating, the Jews had attained a predominant position in the German economy to the detriment of all other sectors, that in other realms of public life Jews had also reached an equally pernicious power. [...] The imagery of Stoecker's [the spokesman for the anti-Semites] peroration told all: "Gentlemen, recently a corpse was found in a district not far from here. The corpse was examined – and at hand were a Jewish district physician, a Jewish surgeon, a Jewish judge, a Jewish barrister – only the corpse was German. [Much laughter]. Gentlemen, we do not want this fate for Berlin or for the other great cities; we want to keep our people alive through their own vital strength, and be assured that in this effort the people stands behind us".[7]

The members of Parliament who were against the anti-Semite petition that called for the constitutional rights of Jews to be repealed wanted the government to make an uncompromising statement energetically condemning this endeavour. As it turned out, the government said not a word to condemn the excesses played out in Parliament. According to Stern, "the record of the two debates gives a grisly picture of the atmosphere of the occasion: the anti-Semite catcalls, the vicious sarcasm, the pent-up hatred. The tone of the debate was more ominous than the words themselves. It was not a glorious moment for Parliament nor a reassuring moment for German Jewry.[8]"

This explosion of popular anti-Semitism that brought out into the open a growing hatred of Jews profoundly disturbed the Jews of Germany and those of the same faith in other countries. The benevolence of the government towards the anti-Semites was a bitter experience for them. Foreigners who occupied positions in Berlin and who were not necessarily prone to siding with the Jews, indeed who might even sometimes be highly critical of the social and economic position of the Jews in German society, were nonetheless dismayed by the government's attitude. Stern mentions the comment made by the famous Portuguese writer, José Maria Eça de Queiroz, who, disregarding the reserve expected of him as a diplomat, bluntly stated his impressions of the government:

"It leaves the Jewish colony unprotected to face the anger of the large German population – and washes its ministerial hands, as Pontius Pilate did. It does not even state that it will see that the laws protecting Jews, citizens of the Empire, are enforced; it merely has the vague intention, as vague as the morning cloud, of not altering them for the moment. [...] In the liberal professions, [the Jew] absorbs everything: he is the lawyer with more briefs and the doctor with more patients ... But if the Jew's wealth irritates [the German], the show the Jew makes of his riches absolutely maddens him... [The Jews] always talk loudly as if treading a conquered land... They cover themselves with jewels, all the trappings of their carriages are of gold, and they love vulgar and showy luxury... In Germany, the Jew has slowly and stealthily gained possession of two great social forces – the Exchange and the Press." Eça de Quieroz then lists all the social and economic grievances of Germans which in the old days Bismarck would have dispelled by a war. War was no longer feasible and, "therefore, with little chance of a war, Prince Bismarck distracts the starving Germans' attention by pointing to the prosperous Jew. Naturally, he does not allude to the death of Our Lord Jesus Christ. But he speaks of the millions of Jews and the power of the synagogue.⁹"

This social, economic and cultural influence of the Jews in German society was not a figment of the anti-Semites' imagination. Although the latter used and exploited it perfidiously, they did not make it up.

Irresistibly attractive opportunities

While in the following decades anti-Semitism in Germany was not as vicious as it was in France in the same period, there was a palpable unease between the Jews and the Germans. But it was the First World War and the crushing defeat of the Germans that untied tongues, giving rise to clichés of unprecedented violence. For instance, the leaders of the National Socialist movement spread the lie that Germany was the victim of a "knife in the back." And, needless to say, the culprits could only be Jews. The drastic conditions imposed upon Germany by the Treaty of Versailles worsened the already precarious circumstances of the population. Widespread unemployment and growing pauperisation sharpened feelings of bitterness and triggered the search for a scapegoat.

"Two months after Germany's defeat, the left-wing revolutionary Spartacists attempted to seize power in Berlin. The uprising failed and on the evening of January 15, 1919, its main leaders, Karl Liebknecht and Rosa Luxemburg, were arrested and shot.[10]" The anti-Semite right wing used the fact that most of the Spartacist leaders were Jews to "denounce the Jewish plot" to bring about revolution, take power and subjugate the Germans. At the same time, the clichés relating to "the Jewish influence," "Jewish finances" and the "power of the synagogue" became increasingly common and were unashamedly exploited. When they came to power, the Nazis claimed that it was only fair to "recover" from the Jews what "belonged to the German people," an attitude that suited a large majority, except the victims. It would be a mistake to believe that the population did not object to these spoliations because it had been terrorised.

The First World War and the ensuing defeat and humiliation of the Germans, along with the economic crisis and unemployment were all factors that the Nazis drew on to stimulate hatred for Jews, using them as the scapegoat for the misfortunes of the German people. Additionally, the anti-Bolshevists, who feared a revolution, denounced Bolshevism as the most dangerous of Jewish plots. They were so effective that it became common belief that the salvation of the German people depended solely on neutralising the "Jewish influence." This meant that the measures of exclusion taken and applied by the Nazi state were necessary or even legitimate (as Mrs Heidegger would put it).[11]

When, on top of segregation, it came to expropriating the Jews and taking possession of their riches, the potential beneficiaries outdid each other in greed. The activists in the National Socialist Party considered that it was for the party to take possession of these riches, the most senior officials wanted the State to do so, traders and craftsmen wanted to take over the property of former competitors. Even people who were not particularly hostile to Jews felt no compunction about receiving confiscated goods. In fact, Hilberg notes:

> German enterprises by the thousands were surveying the country in search of suitable Jewish firms. In German business parlance, Jewish enterprises had now become *Objekte* ('objects'). Since it was not always easy to find an *Objekt*, the process of searching became a specialised business in itself. The institutions which specialised in this business were the banks. It was a lucrative activity. The banks collected threefold profit from the Aryanisation transactions: They collected 2% commissions on the sales price having brought together buyers and sellers, they also took in the interest on loans extended to buyers, and finally they benefited from all subsequent business contracted between the bank and the Aryanised firm. (Such business usually derived from a provision in the contract between prospective buyer and bank, pursuant to which the buyer was to designate the bank as "principal banking connection" for his new acquisition.) Moreover, the banks were not only agents – steering *Objekte* to interested buyers – they were buyers themselves, and they missed no opportunity to buy out a Jewish bank or some choice industrial shares. Every type of German business was in the scramble, but the banks were in the very midst of it.[12]

This business was so profitable that the Deutsche Bank and the Dresdner Bank earned the equivalent of six billion francs between 1937 and 1945 just from the profits and commissions earned by selling Jewish undertakings and the loans granted to businesses operated by SS members.

Whatever their social, economic or cultural position in society, Germans tended to think that dismissing Jews from their jobs and expropriating them could be validly argued from the German standpoint. In Western culture, the idea of profit has been placed above any other value or standard. There was therefore no issue with the majority deriving the utmost benefit from the eviction of the Jews. In the final analysis, as Bettelheim notes:

> many Germans – by no means only Nazis – derived tangible benefits from the persecution of the Jews. The vast majority of Jews either owned business enterprises or held lucrative positions. They were deprived of these, which were handed over to the Germans. During the last year before the war, when the Jews emigrated they could take none of their possessions with them. The same was true during the war when they were first sent to the ghettos in Poland and later into the camps. Rather than see the Nazis acquire all their possessions, when they were forced to leave most Jews preferred to give their art objects, jewelry, valuable furniture and clothing and whatnot to gentile acquaintances, either as presents or for safekeeping. The end results were nearly always the same: the Jews died in the camps and nobody was left to claim what was left in safekeeping.[13]

This is not to say that the desire to take possession of Jewish wealth and take over their position in society was the sole motivation behind the Nazi policy of extermination. That would be simplistic and far from the truth, just as it is simplistic to say that German anti-Semitism alone explains the destruction of Jews and Gypsies and the way they treated the Slavs. Such a thesis would have us believe that Nazism was the consequence of itself, and that the racial theories – which the Nazis exploited but did not invent – are purely a creation of the Germanic mind. The fact that four centuries of white supremacy incorporated the annihilation of racially inferior beings into the cultural and ideological fabric of Western civilisation would then not come into the picture at all. Although this thesis is patently absurd, it was nonetheless favourably received on both sides of the Atlantic. Considering how useful this notion is, that comes as no surprise. As long as the Nazi policy of extermination can be explained by a specificity of the German mentality and German history, and as long as the ideological factors involved in the destruction of the Jews were self-generated and had the good manners to develop within the German borders, there is no reason for the countries that had instituted a policy of discrimination and had crushed so-called inferior peoples, well before the advent of Hitler, should feel any pangs of conscience. German specificity takes all the blame. It offers a convenient escape route for decent citizens and forgetful intellectuals in countries that in former times institutionalised the superiority of Whites and the exclusion of non-Whites.

The claim is that the economic factors and financial motivations used to explain but also – and that is quite a feat of cynicism – to justify the raiding and massacres perpetrated against other peoples far away from Europe did not apply in Nazi Germany. The Nazis are said to have a peculiarity: they were never interested in the economic benefits they could derive from the persecution or destruction of Jews. But facts are stronger. More than fifty years later, there is an abundance of proof. Many institutions and people hastened to offer their support to the leaders of the Third Reich not because they unconditionally backed the Fuhrer but because the persecutions conducted against the Jews offered attractive opportunities.

In Austria for instance, specifically in its capital city, Jews enjoyed an enviable economic and social position. "In Vienna, there were an estimated 1,600 lawyers out of a total of 2,100 were Jewish, and in "occupied-Austria 3,300 physicians out of a total of 7,000 were Jewish," writes Hilberg.[14] Clearly, the Austrian anti-Semites had good reason to believe that, in economic and social terms, the persecution of the Jews was a viable proposition. The anti-Semites did more than just take an interest in the benefits derived from these spoliations. When the Anschluss took place, Botz estimates that

> 70,000 apartments, i.e. 10% of all dwellings in Vienna were occupied at that time by Jews. In spite of its structural nature, the shortage of housing and the fact that the living space occupied by Jews was a significant economic factor converged to generate a special form of persecution. The surface area that the municipality had access to for the purposes of its housing policy was therefore a decisive element in Vienna. The evacuation of the Jews would make 70,000 apartments available, i.e. 6,000 more than the number of apartments that had been built between 1919 and 1933 under the subsidised housing policy the 'red' social-democrat town council of Vienna was so proud of.[15]

Just as in Germany, in Austria the Aryan population (regardless of social status) not only appreciated the policy of "re-housing," but also often exerted pressure so as to have these measures intensified. While it has not been established that these Austrians actively wanted the Jews exterminated, someone who has acquired confiscated property almost naturally hopes the owner will never return. Once the war was over, many Aryans who had "repossessed" property confiscated from Jews lived in fear and trembled that they might return.

In the Netherlands, under German occupation, "[…] in February 1942, the first deportation caused such an uproar that a general strike of several days' duration, something inconceivable under the Nazi boot, broke out spontaneously,[16]" writes Poliakov who mentions a note dated July 31, 1942 in which Bene, who was Ribbentrop's representative in the Netherlands, reports "some in temporary excitement was noticeable, particularly in Amsterdam." In spite of this initial generous fervour, Nazi propagandists were confident that the persecutions would end up by getting the better of the Dutch. The same Bene, in another note to his minister informs him with relief that "the Dutch population disapproves of the deportations, but seems to take an outwardly indifferent attitude." The population's change of mind is not entirely attributable to Nazi terror, although the latter did contribute, as can be inferred from yet another note from Bene on April 30, 1943: "The population, apart from friends made by mixed marriages, did not show any interest in the transports of Jews and seem to have become resigned to them. Circles that were previously pro-Jewish sometimes make some effort to acquire apartments evacuated by Jews.[17]"

If a profit can be made, it can't possibly be bad

One can appreciate why Jewish survivors who returned from the camps were given a disappointing and sometimes hostile reception. They had been the owners of shops or apartments which, in the meantime, were taken over by new owners, and they had every intention of recovering their property. This was a situation that prevailed in all the occupied countries, although during the Aryanisation campaign the most valuable assets were expropriated for the sole benefit of German trusts and the army.

Doctor Knochen, the head of the German police service in France, in a report made to the Germany military administration dated January 28, 1941 summarises the situation as follows:

> It is plainly almost impossible to cultivate in the French an anti-Jewish feeling based on ideological grounds, whereas the offer of economic advantages could more easily create sympathy for the anti-Jewish struggle…

> The internment of nearly 100,000 Jews living in Paris could give many Frenchmen the chance to pull themselves up into the middle classes.[18]

Far more than hatred for Jews was needed to enlist French Cartesianism in support of the forces that trampled its homeland. This encouraged Poliakov to say: "Although the economic motives, however large their part may have been in the formation of Nazi anti-Semitism, were surpassed by Hitlerism's religious fervour, they provide an essential key to the behaviour of individuals in the conquered countries.[19]"

In reality, the profit motive and economic rivalry were determining factors in the behaviour of the German population. The financial incentive was as strong for them as it was for the populations in the vanquished countries. If the Jewish community had lived in poverty prior to 1939, far fewer people would have been willing to act as the eager accessories of the authorities of the Third Reich. The spoils would have been far less attractive.

The example of Switzerland is also instructive. Switzerland claimed to be neutral, but its collaboration in the persecution of the Jews has since been proven. Anti-Semitism in the Swiss Confederation in the 1930s, however widespread, does not on its own explain this country's often criminal policy towards the victims of Nazi persecution. Ziegler recalls:

> The gnomes of Zurich, Basel and Bern were Hitler's fences and creditors. (…). In 1943, when the Allies began their terrible bombing of German cities and industrial and mining centres, Switzerland remained Hitler's only unscathed industrial area: one in which, without prejudice to the Third Reich, munitions, precision equipment, optical instruments, and many other items of military importance continued to be manufactured. The Buhrle-Oerlikon armaments firm delivered its last consignment of rapid-fire guns to the Wehrmacht in April 1945.[20]

This complicity was neither the result of any blind, unconditional allegiance to Hitler and his Reich, nor the manifestation of some hard-line, devastating anti-Semitism, nor the fear of being crushed by Hitler was the true motive. "The overwhelming majority of senior bank officials (…) were willing accomplices and eager henchmen.[21]" Daniel Bourgeois, in his book *Business helvétique et le IIIe Reich*, provides documented proof that the confederal and cantonal authorities gave in to pressure from business circles and from some captains of industry, becoming involved in industrial, financial, diplomatic and even military collaboration with the Third Reich's war effort. Fortunately for their peace of mind, the citizens of Switzerland (along with those of many other countries) can rely on a defence: they were not aware of the existence of gas chambers.

Since 1945, Western specialists have been obstinately focussed on making the gas chambers the symbol of Nazi barbarity. On that premise, once it is demonstrated that people did not know that the outcome of the intolerable ordeal of the victims was the gas chamber, it follows that their contribution to the genocide was nearly "insignificant." Thus, it is so essential and useful to be utterly persuaded and conviced that it was impossible to imagine or even to believe in the existence of the gas chambers. It was another of Hitler's strengths that he gave everybody in Germany and elsewhere, especially all levels of the bourgeoisie, a chance to actively participate in the destruction of Jews while enjoying the privilege of not seeing or hearing anything. How easy it is to be oblivious.

Thus, when Switzerland could no longer officially conceal the fact that many Jews were handed over to the Nazis by the Confederation's authorities, it was thankfully still able to hide behind the secret surrounding the gas chambers to argue that it had acted in good faith, unlike the perpetrators. One can only assume that the Swiss, and those elsewhere who collaborated with the leaders of the Third Reich, believed that the Nazis rounded up Jews just for the fun of it. Friedländer recalls:

> Eastern Europe's participation in the growing anti-Jewish agitation of the second half of the thirties took place within the context of its own traditions. The influence of Christian anti-Jewish themes was particularly strong among populations whose majority was still devout peasantry. Social resentment on the part of budding nationalistic middle classes of the positions acquired by Jews in commerce and the trades, light industry, banking, medicine and the law, created another layer of hostility. The latest addition and possibly strongest ingredient was the fierce anti-Bolshevism of regimes already oriented towards fascism, regimes for which identification of the Jews with Bolshevism was a common slogan, for example in Hungary, where the memory of the Béla Kun government remained vivid.[22]

This mixture of religious anti-Judaism, militant anti-Bolshevism, plus the prospect of material gain that people from all levels of society could expect from the persecution of the Jews worked in the Nazi occupier's best interests. In many cases, these sentiments prevailed even among nationalists who might have been expected to be hostile to the invader.

In Poland for instance the attitude of the popular masses towards the agony of the Jews, apart from a few acts of heroism, "was primarily one of indifference – while all active minorities assiduously gathered in the countless fruits of pillage and denunciation.²³" One example took place during the uprising in the Warsaw ghetto, when the Nazis were able to ignite the zeal of their Polish collaborators. SS and Police General J. Stroop, who led the German troops engaged in the destruction of the Warsaw ghetto, sent daily reports to his senior authorities, informing them about the means used to better secure the necessary contributions from the locals. In one report where he recaps the first few days of the rebellion, he writes: "The Polish police have been authorised to hand over to policemen one third of the cash assets of any Jew they capture in the Aryan neighbourhoods of the city. This measure has already proved largely successful.²⁴" And in a report on May 6, he adds: "The Police, with the incentive provided by the bonuses we have promised them, is doing its best to turn over to us any Jew who shows up in town. I am getting anonymous letters telling me of the whereabouts of Jews in the Aryan neighbourhoods.²⁵"

The road to Auschwitz should have been beset with obstacles for the Nazis. But no, quite the contrary. The rosy prospects offered by the persecution of the Jews smoothed the way. Everywhere in the occupied countries, these criminals found keen accessories, more than willing to take advantage of this unique opportunity to quench their thirst for revenge with no risk involved, to settle a rivalry and moreover to take possession of some coveted assets.

In a survey conducted among people who had in one way or another taken part in the Nazi enterprise of destruction, three German historians admit that indeed no one was compelled to take part in the massacres, quoting a police official from Neu-Sandez (Cracow District/General-Government):

> Members of the Grenzpolizeikommissariat were, with a few exceptions, quite happy to take part in the shootings of Jews. They had a ball! Obviously they can't say that today! Then, nobody failed to turn up... I want to repeat that today people want to give a false impression that the actions against the Jews were carried out unwillingly. There was great hatred against the Jews; people wanted revenge, and they wanted money and gold. Let's not kid ourselves; there was plenty that was up for grabs during these anti-Jewish operations! Everywhere we went, there was always something to be taken. The poor Jews were brought in, the rich Jews were fetched and their homes were scoured.'²⁶"

Silver and gold, forever and again silver and gold, and the benefits they produce. The appetite for gold and silver was one of the driving forces behind the killing of the indigenous peoples of the Americas and the annihilation of several million Black children, women and men. It was also one of the motivations of many of the people who voluntarily became a party to the destruction of Jews. Evaluating the extent to which the conquest of America and its repercussions altered the behaviour of Europeans in general, including in the countries that did not directly contribute to the destruction of the Native Americans, is a task still to be accomplished.

> Certainly the desire for riches is nothing new, the passion for gold has nothing specifically modern about it. What is new is the subordination of all other values to this one. The conquistador has not ceased to aspire to aristocratic values, to titles of nobility, to honours, and to esteem; but it has become quite clear to him that everything can be obtained by money, that money is not only the universal equivalent of all material values, but also the possibility of acquiring all the spiritual values.[27]

This subordination of all other values to the craving for gold, to the power of wealth and its side benefits, gradually developed, eventually giving rise to an economic mentality whereby the most terrifying crimes became acceptable as long as they were based on a sound economic foundation. Hence, committing evil acts for the sole purpose of inflicting misery and suffering on the victim was seen as contrary to the values and principles generally shared among the European societies. However, inflicting similar misery and suffering, not just for pleasure but to derive profit therefrom, especially large profits, was not only accepted but justified. It was through the power of money that many European families who had fed on the blood of Blacks like vampires were able to acquire their titles of nobility. This is how, in the European mentality, the pursuit of profit and of wealth reached this position of extraordinary power. So much so that after 1945, for the purpose of, at least in theory, wholeheartedly condemning the enterprise of destruction and death perpetrated by the servants of the Third Reich, it became necessary to invent the lie asserting that no social and economic factors whatsoever were involved in the crimes of National Socialism. By European standards, accepting that these factors did play a role might have been enough to erase or even justify this abomination. It will take time to demolish this absurdity.

Specialists are beginning to discover that the social base for the German National Socialist Party was broader, i.e. more popular, than is generally claimed. This explains why the working class remained passive, by and large, until mid-way through the war. Its continued support of Hitler was attributable to the economic recovery. It is increasingly difficult to believe and make others believe that the savagery of German Nazis and their accessories in the occupied countries was motivated by sadistic pleasure alone. If this were true, they would be the only conquerors impervious to the fascination of gold and of power. There is no foundation for these delusions.

Gérard Botz mentions an article published in a Viennese paper on April 26, 1938, just a month and a half after the Anschluss:

> Up to 1942, the Jewish element in Vienna will need to be rooted out [...] and made to disappear. At that point in time, not a single magazine or business should be in the hands of a Jew. Not a single Jew should be in paid employment. And apart from a few street where old Jewish men and women will be allowed to spend the money they have left – they are prohibited from exporting it – while they wait to die, nothing in this city should recall their presence [...] All those who know what the opinion of the Viennese is on the Jewish question can understand that the Viennese find these four years during which the economic death penalty will be executed exceedingly long. They find all this consideration and this caution that still protect Jewish assets surprising. They have had enough: "The Jew must go and his dough must stay".[28]

This type of rabble-rousing met with great approval among Austrians, because in Austria, like Germany, the Aryans, whether working-class or petty bourgeois, hoped that, as a result of Aryanisation of the economy and the housing sector, their own social and economic aspirations would be fulfilled. So much so that the reforms (or rather, the spoliations of the Jews) were fastracked due to the pressure from the people. The fact is that, to accomplish the Aryanisation of the economy and of housing, the Jews had to be physically removed.

These situations where the denial of a group's humanity is used as a substitute for an official policy encourage outbursts of violence and unleash sadistic behaviour. It is essential to carefully scrutinise the concentration camp setting of America so as to understand how ordinary folk became persecutors working for the Nazi machinery of destruction and death. Such a scrutiny should not consist in analysing for the umpteenth time what the economic effects of the genocidal policies in America on the metropolises. What it should examine is the scale of the psychological, ideological and cultural consequences on White people generally as a result of a practice which, although criminal, was nonetheless willingly accepted in the legal order.

Such a study should analyse the far-reaching changes that the exercise of terror as a system of domination inevitably generates among those who make use of it. This phenomenon spans several centuries and Europeans were massively involved. We know that even the more sensitive minds, always ready to shed a humanist tear or two, after denouncing the horror, cruelty and brutality that punctuated the agony of Blacks in the colonies, eventually ended up "getting used" to them to use the words of Father Labat who was not himself a brutal soldier. Cohen recalls:

> Bernardin de Saint-Pierre wrote movingly of Black slavery in his romantic novel *Paul et Virginie* and attacked slavery and prejudice against blacks in his *Voyage à l'Ile de France* but, while serving as an official at Ile-de-France, he put down his innermost feelings (now preserved in a manuscript). Of all the peoples he had ever seen, de Saint-Pierre confided, he had never seen a people more vicious than blacks; perhaps, he speculated, it was part of the order of nature that men who were superior should dominate Blacks. Moreover, de Saint-Pierre, who in France passionately denounced slavery, had been a slave-owner in Ile-de-France.[29]

All this argues in favour of gaining better knowledge about the moral debacle of Europeans caused by the uninterrupted exercise of institutionalised terror in America, the end result of which was the Nazi disaster. This is a long overdue task, one that needs urgent attention rather than dodging the issue forever to serve up the mercantile history of the former European powers.

Notes

1. Botz, Gerhard in François Bédarida, *La politique nazie d'extermination*, Paris: Albin Michel, 1980, p. 209.
2. Hilberg, Raul, *La destruction des Juifs d'Europe*, Tome 1, Paris, Gallimard, 1988, p. 221 (Quote translated from the French).
3. Hilberg, Raul, *The Destruction of the European Jews*, Revised ed., vol. 1, New York, Holmes & Meier, 1985, p 166, Questia, Web, 6 July 2010.
4. Stern, Fritz, *Gold and Iron*, New York: Vintage Books, 1979, p. 499.
5. Ibid. p. 499.
6. Ibid. pp. 466–467.
7. Ibid. p. 518.
8. Ibid. p. 519.

9. Ibid. p. 519
10. Friedlander, Saul, op. cit., p. 91.
11. Ibid, p. 53.
12. Hilberg, op. cit., 1961, p. 64.
13. Bettelheim, Bruno, *Surviving and Other Essays*, New York, Knopf, 1979, pp. 86–87.
14. Hilberg, Raul, *La destruction des Juifs d'Europe*, Tome 1, Paris, Gallimard, 1988, p. 220–21 (quote translated from the French).
15. Botz, Gerhard in Bédarida, op. cit., p. 218.
16. Poliakov, Léon, *Harvest of Hate*, Bestseller Library, 1960, p. 245.
17. Poliakov, Léon, *Bréviaire de la haine. Le troisième Reich et les juifs*, Paris, Calmann-Lévy, 1951, p. 430.
18. Poliakov, Léon, *Harvest of Hate*, Bestseller Library, 1960, pp. 71–72.
19. Ibid, p. 72.
20. Ziegler, Jean, *The Swiss, the Gold and the Dead*, New York, Harcourt Brace & Co., 1998, p. 18.
21. Ibid. p. 18.
22. Friedlander, op. cit, pp. 214–215.
23. Poliakov, op. cit., p. 243.
24. Borwicz, Michel, *L'insurrection du ghetto de Varsovie*, Paris, Editions sociales, 1979, p. 203 (quote translated from the French).
25. Ibid, p. 212.
26. Klee, Ernst, Dressen, Willi and Riess, Volker (editors), *The Good Old Days: The Holocaust as Seen by Its Perpetrators and Bystanders*, Connecticut, Konecky and Konecky, 1991, p. 76.
27. Todorov, Tzvetan, op. cit., pp. 142–143.
28. Botz, Gerhard, op. cit., pp. 210–211.
29. Cohen, William B. and Le Sueur, James D., *The French Encounter with Africans: White Response to Blacks, 1530–1880*, Indiana, Indiana University Press, 2003, p. 138.

7

The Weight of Racist Ideologies

They did not know

Following the military defeat of Nazi Germany, the Germans and all their collaborators in the occupied countries claimed that they did not know that so-called "inferior beings," the "useless mouths," were being gassed in extermination camps. In short, anyone who instead of taking advantage of the possibilities for "improving the race" (improving the race, one should recall, is something the Enlightenment adamantly believed in) had turned back and become "racially degenerate beings" to use a stock phrase at the time (as well as during the Enlightenment when much was made of degeneration) was concerned. They were not aware that prisoners in the concentration camps – some of which had begun to function as early as 1933 – were robbed of their humanity, reduced to the condition of sub-humans, and subjected to the barbarity and terror required to maintain them in that state. They had not been told.

What they perhaps did not know was that these people that were hunted down by the Nazi authorities, arrested by the Gestapo and deported to concentration camps were, in spite of official doctrine, actually human beings. It is quite likely that they did not know that there is no such thing as an outcast race, or a superior people. But failure to understand this and the consequent failure to properly assess what was happening was not confined to the Germans alone.

Prior to 1939, governments, authorities and the political leaders of Western democracies, as well as the vast majority of their populations, were not able to "understand" or "guess" that the Nazi regime was fundamentally criminal because, by its very nature, it was contrary to humanity. How did this inability to understand the dangers presented by a government that laid its "legitimacy on negating the other" come to be? How is it that reasonably intelligent people with no ill-intentions did not realise that a system that not only advocated but methodically applied exclusion to so-called "inferior" beings was contrary to humanity?

It seems to me that this is a fundamental question that calls for a much-needed answer. It brings to mind the statement made by an SS General, the supreme commander of the SS and of the police for Central Russia, at the Nuremberg trials. Erich von dem Bach-Zelewski was questioned about the essential task carried out by the Einsatzgruppen. He answered that their main task was to remove the Jews, the Gypsies and the political commissars. When he was asked whether when Himmler called for the extermination of thirty million Slavs in a speech, he was just expressing a personal opinion or whether it reflected the National Socialist ideology, he answered that in his view it was a logical conclusion of their ideology. To conclude, he added: "If for ten long years you preach that the Slavic peoples are an inferior breed, and that the Jews are sub-humans, it follows on logically that killing millions of these human beings will be accepted as a natural phenomenon. The road from *Mein Kampf* leads straight to the ovens of Auschwitz and to the gas chambers of Maïdanek.¹"

Von dem Bach-Zelewski is not saying that all those whose humanity is denied end up being gassed and then cremated. What he means is what history has already demonstrated: to advocate the racial inferiority of a group, to deny that it belongs to the human species puts that discredited group at great risk, including the risk of annihilation. This SS criminal was right and his words should have held the court's attention. It would have been a fine opportunity to seek out and analyse the set of conditions that helped bring to power a political party which had rallied its followers on the premise of racial superiority and the "reassuring" promise that the racially inferior groups would be put back into their rightful place. Since when could a government, inside its borders, decree the inferiority of any group it chose, legally challenge its humanity and remove its dignity, by law, as did the National Socialist government with the so-called Nuremberg laws?

Unfortunately, that historical opportunity was not seized. The members of the court represented powers that had themselves until very recently applied, or indeed continued to apply, special laws passed specifically to deal with "racially inferior" groups and keep them in their "place." In other words, the judges at Nuremberg were to hear and judge crimes which in many respects were the extension of, or a European variation on, the crimes that were legally perpetrated for centuries in the concentration camp setting of America by their own nations. The significant difference however was that because the victims of those precedent crimes were still in a position of weakness, these countries would never find themselves in the dock nor be required to account for their deeds.

Hitler was no theorist

In a special report published in the journal *L'Histoire* in March 1999, entitled "Hitler, historical portrait of a monster," the author writes:

> In reading the work [*Mein Kampf*], one is immediately struck by the intellectual inconsistencies. Take his racism for instance: he does not truly establish a hierarchy, he makes no mention of the Asians, refers only in passing to Blacks, and it is unclear what his stance is on non-German Aryans. In short, it is all rather messy; Hitler was no theorist.[2]

These statements reflect the confusion caused in European minds by the way Hitler chose to exploit racist ideology during his ascent to power. In the 1920s, when Hitler wrote *Mein Kampf*, the 'superiority' of Whites had already been amply proven. It was a given, it went without saying. Western theorists had already more than demonstrated white superiority so as to fulfil a specific purpose. These hierarchies were devised so as to meet a real necessity, namely providing a rational, objective explanation for the annihilation of other non-White peoples in America, Africa and elsewhere, and in any case far away from Europe. Contributions had been sought from scholars in all branches of science and thought, so as to support and exalt the racial hierarchy by capitalising on the prestige enjoyed by scientifically established truths. As for Hitler, he himself had little time for this racial hierarchy as it stood. For the purposes of his progression towards power, it was inadequate, if not useless. What he needed was a racial hierarchy that matched the requirements of the subservient relations he intended to establish.

The theory and demonstration of the inferiority of Blacks or Asians were not helpful to Hitler in excluding Jews from public life in Germany, robbing them of their rights and property, i.e., reducing them to animal status. Similarly, to take control of the territories in Eastern Europe and deport, oppress and exterminate thirty million Slavs, as was his plan, the conventional categories and concepts on racial hierarchy already embraced by Western culture, consistent though they were, were not suitable. The myth of a monolithic, superior White race, meaning that every single White was superior because of his whiteness, worked very well indeed as long as the aim was to contrast it with the inferiority of non-Whites. When

Hitler switched the scope of application of these racial theories to Europe itself, the conventional racial hierarchy no longer suited the purposes of his plans to rule over the peoples of Europe. This is why Hitler never made the inferiority of non-Whites the centrepiece of his discourse. What purpose could that serve? He decided to shift the manipulation of racist ideologies into high gear, and instead put the "Aryan race" at the centre of his discourse. This was the myth, the ideal to which men and women from all layers of society rallied round.

Hitler's successful shift from the "White race" to the "Aryan race" disturbed the comforting reassurance that every White until then derived from belonging to the race of masters. It dealt a fatal blow to that marvellous confidence that relied on the knowledge that belonging to the White race necessarily makes you superior. Necessity is the mother of invention. A much more daring conception of racial hierarchy than one that opposed Whites to non-Whites was needed to convince people of the necessity and legitimacy of reducing the Jews to the status of animals, and to repeat this exercise in respect of the Slavs once Europe had come to heel. Ever since, this shift has been at the root of misunderstanding and confusion in the minds of European intellectuals.

Hitler did not invent the Aryan myth although he was the first leader to use it officially, first to rally the support of the majority, and secondly to underpin his regime's power. It is true that Hitler took the manipulation of racist ideologies farther than anyone else. Other regimes that had institutionalised racial ideologies by incorporating them into the political systems they established in both America and Africa had always contented themselves with proclaiming the superiority of the White race as a whole, which was less 'restrictive', as it were.

The tradition of using these racial theories to justify the enslavement of other non-European peoples conditioned Western democracies to adopt their typically lenient attitude towards the racist persecutions perpetrated by the German National Socialist state as of 1933. This failing later became truly crippling. From it stems the ambiguities in the Allies' position towards the racist policy of extermination conducted by the Nazis. The Allies had to take great care to avoid putting themselves in an untenable position. They needed to be wary of irrevocable condemnations which could be turned against them; to avoid calling too much attention to the crime of racist persecutions or to ban all policies that discriminate against minorities. It was essential not to establish a precedent that would allow interference in the internal affairs of a country by exposing it to accusations of racist persecutions or racial segregation. Obviously, these considerations prevented the Allied powers from making any declaration stipulating that the annihilation of a minority was a crime, and consequently that the anti-Jewish laws passed before the war broke out were criminal too, let alone the crimes perpetrated against the Jews under cover of war.

Towards the end of 1942, when the extermination of Jews that had begun in Russia in June 1941, together with the deportations occurring all over Europe, became common knowledge (assuming that these massacres conducted openly and for all to see were ever a real secret), it became obvious that the Allies would have to take up a stance against racist policies of extermination. In any case, political leaders, international institutions and journalists could no longer be unaware of the fate reserved to the Jews by the Nazis and their servants.

The Allies trapped in their tradition of racist domination

In fact, the procrastinations of the Allied powers, in spite of available information, helped to obscure the facts and thus to keep the fate of Jews hidden from view. This tendency to obscure the facts actually persisted beyond 1945 and up to the end of the 1970s when, for reasons of political expediency, the United States president, Jimmy Carter, established a Presidential Commission on the Holocaust[3] with the goal of setting up a memorial. In passing it should be noted that the Gypsies did not have a powerful enough lobby so that they were not mentioned. Nor were the homosexuals who had also been targeted by the Nazi policy of extermination.

Before the war, the Germans brought all sorts of pressure to bear on Jews to force them to leave and abandon all their possessions. No government had the political will to offer them sanctuary. [Although there were various initiatives and attempts to get Jews out of Germany and Nazi-occupied Europe, most were fraught with tremendous difficulty and expense the world over, even with the efforts of organisations such as the World Jewish Relief. The contrasting outcomes of two cases, the Kindertransport which rescued nearly 10,000 Jewish children unaccompanied by their parents into safety in the UK nine months before the outbreak of the war in 1939, and that of the failed attempt of 901 refugees on the ship *MS St. Louis* to enter Cuba, the United States and Canada, are reflective of official policies of the time.] The preferred attitude today is to ignore the fact that racial discourse of the Nazi leaders was so similar to the conventional discourse of white supremacists that it was treated as commonplace in Western democracies.

A debate that took place in the French parliament on July 28, 1885 is enlightening. I have chosen to quote Jules Ferry, a figurehead to whom the French Republic owes, among other advances, the major reforms in state education that made primary school secular, free and compulsory, and opened secondary education to girls. He also helped establish essential public rights such as the freedom of association and freedom to form unions. Parts of this speech published in the Official Journal of July 29, 1885 are found in Raoul Girardet's *Le nationalisme français, anthologie 1871–1914*, while some lengthier excerpts are in Jean-Martin Mbemba's *L'autre mémoire du crime contre l'humanité*.

During this parliamentary debate on France's colonial mission, in reply to Camille Pelletan[4] who had just expressed his hostility to the colonial enterprise, Jules Ferry says:

> Gentlemen, there is a second point, a second order of ideas to which I have to give equal attention, but as quickly as possible, believe me; it is the humanitarian and civilising side of the question. On this point the honourable M. Camille Pelletan has jeered in his own refined and clever manner; he jeers, he condemns, and he says "What is this civilisation which you impose with cannon-balls? What is it but another form of barbarism? Don't these populations, these inferior races, have the same rights as you? Aren't they masters of their own houses? Have they called upon you? You come to them against their will, you offer them violence, but not civilisation." There, gentlemen, is this thesis. I do not hesitate to say that this is not politics, nor is it history: it is political metaphysics.
>
> ... And I challenge you – let me throw you down my challenge, M. Pelletan – to carry your argument to its logical conclusion, your argument that is based on the principles of equality, liberty and independence for inferior races. [...] Gentlemen, we must speak more loudly and more honestly! We must say openly that indeed the higher races have a right over the lower races [...]. I repeat, that the superior races have a right because they have a duty. They have the duty to civilise the inferior races.[5]

At that stage the member for the département of Haute-Loire, Jules Maigne, intervened to say how embarrassing it was to hear such things inside the Parliament of the country where human rights had first been proclaimed, to which Jules Ferry retorted that the Declaration of the Rights of Man "was not written for the black people of equatorial Africa.[6]"

One might object that Jules Ferry is not advocating the extermination of the so-called inferior races, but rather the right and duty of what he calls the superior races to civilise them through colonisation. Furthermore, the reactions of French politicians such as Jules Maigne, who clearly challenges the racialisation of human relations, must be taken into consideration. However, I would add that the stakes on which were nailed the heads of indigenous peoples who had resisted the benefits of civilisation provide a clear account of the colonial enterprise. As for Jules Maigne, his reaction is much to his credit, but the ideas advocated by Jules Ferry were the ones which won the day. What history remembers are the benefits associated with his name.

These parliamentary debates that took place at the end of the nineteenth century illustrate how the conviction that there are "racially inferior" human groups was firmly rooted in Western democracies. Resting on that foundation, there was nothing in the doctrine and policies of the Third Reich that could frighten these democracies. This is why for the entire span of the 1939–1945 war, the Allies never presented the fight against racism, anti-Semitism or racial discrimination and segregation as an integral part of their overall fight against Nazism. Atrocities committed against "racially inferior" groups did not have the greatest impact on public opinion, especially in societies that were themselves engaged in racial segregation. Renée Poznanski of the Beer Sheba University in Israel recalls that at the time "opinion surveys carried out by the US Office of War Information had revealed that the impact of information concerning the atrocities on the average American was seven times higher for atrocities in general than for the atrocities that were specifically mentioned as being directed at Jews.[7]"

Racial hierarchies played a damaging role in two respects. Not only were the ideologies they supported instrumental in spreading the racial theories propagated by the Nazis. They also crippled the reaction to the atrocities perpetrated against Jews, even during the war. Even the Allies' communication about these atrocities and the penalties risked by the culprits never referred to the Jews (or, for that matter, the Gypsies) as being a racial minority specifically targeted by the Nazis.

Hilberg rightly points out that the Moscow declaration of the three Allied powers, signed by Roosevelt, Churchill and Stalin and issued in October 1943 at a time when the Allies knew about the existence of the Auschwitz, Belzec, Treblinka and Sobibor camps, omits any reference to the Jewish disaster. This is particularly shocking in view of the warning the document plainly gives:

> Germans who take part in the wholesale shooting of Italian officers or in the execution of French, Dutch, Belgian or Norwegian hostages or of Cretan peasants, or who have shared in slaughters inflicted on the people of Poland or in the territories of the Soviet Union which are now being swept clear of the enemy, will know that they will be brought back to the scene of their crimes and judged on the spot by the peoples whom they have outraged.[8]

Of course, the Allies had no intention, once the war ended, of making any allowances for the top leaders of the German National Socialist Party. However, they were careful to avoid defining as punishable crimes the acts that led to the total or partial destruction of a group on the sole basis of race or religion. The British and the North Americans, as well as the French delegation, had every intention of bringing the Nazi criminals to trial and executing them, as long as there was no risk of allowing charges that might be turned against them.

In the interval between the Moscow declaration and the London meeting of the American, British, Soviet and Free France representatives that drew up the statute of the International Military Tribunal in charge of judging the "major criminals," Jewish leaders living in the United States became active in promoting the need for a legal definition of the deeds committed against the Jews of Europe.

> An interim commission established during the first session of the American Jewish Conference in London in 1943 stated succinctly that the trials were 'not a matter of vengeance or of punishment of the guilty in the ordinary sense;' they were a matter of "practical" import. The non-punishment of the Germans for their crimes against an entire people, said the commission, would "signify the acquiescence of the democratic nations in the act of Jewish extermination." [...] The commission therefore recommended to the State Department that annihilation of a people, including all acts whereby this aim was sought to be accomplished before and during the war, in Axis territories and occupied areas, be made a punishable crime.[9]

It is through Hilberg's work that we learn about the procrastinations of the Allies when it came to drawing up the tribunal's statute. They were willing to consider the recommendation presented by the American Jewish Conference, but did not, however, want to recognise the destruction of Jews as a *sui generis* crime. The head of the British delegation, Sir David Maxwell

Fyfe, was quite aware that, well before Hitler in the German political context, the UK had set up a political system for the peoples that had come under its rule to which discrimination and racial segregation were integral. He knew full well that the power he represented was not willing to renounce its policy of racial domination. So it was crucial to remain prudent and not take matters too far. As for the American representative, Robert Jackson, a Supreme Court judge, he too was well-advised not to venture too far into the maze of racial segregation since it was part of his own country's legal order. Perhaps he did not know that the rules of racial segregation were maintained and enforced among American troops sent to Europe to fight the Nazis and defend freedom and democracy. What he did know, however, was that in his country racial theories were an integral part of the political system and heavily influenced the workings of the judiciary, to the extent that discrimination determined how the death sentence itself was applied.

In other words, the racial policies of Western democracies that paved the way for the racial policy of National Socialism later largely shaped the "prudent" attitude of the Allies towards the specific issue of the crimes and atrocities committed by the Nazis against the Jews and the Gypsies.

Considerations that weighed heavily on the Nuremberg Court's statute

The underlying historical, political and moral motivations of the statute of the International Military Tribunal were particularly important because in theory the individuals accused of having committed crimes against humanity were to be judged in Nuremberg in the name of humanity as a whole, not in the name of the particular interests of two or three former slave-trading nations who were furthermore the victors. The positions of the British and the North Americans, and their approach to overcoming the difficulty raised by the demands of the Jewish organisations are briefly explained in the statements made by the leaders of the two delegations, which can be found in the minutes of the London conference as quoted by Hilberg.

Torn between the, to say the least, legitimate demands of the leaders of the Jewish community and their own need to entertain some ambiguity that would allow the Jewish demands to be satisfied without putting themselves in an untenable position, the British and North American delegates searched for appropriate phraseology. They "set up a series of acts which could be recognised as criminal *if they were a part or a product of the 'conspiracy' to commit an aggression or a war crime*.[10]" In short this was not an independent category of offenses." In other words, the very same acts committed elsewhere, by and against different players, would not qualify as criminal except under the stringent condition that they had been committed in connection with the preparation of illegal war activities or in connection with war itself. The use of the conditional tense here is by no means neutral or a question of semantics.

Sir David Maxwell Fyfe, Crown Prosecutor for His Majesty's Government, explained his government's proposal as follows:

> The preparation would in my view include such acts as the terrorisation and murder of their own Jewish population in order to prepare for war; that is, preparatory acts inside the Reich in order to regiment the State for aggression and regimentation. This would be important politically for us because the ill-treatment of the Jews has shocked the conscience of our people and, I am sure, of the other members of the United Nations as well; but we had to consider it at some stage, and I thought it was covered by this act in the preparation of this design. I just wanted to make it clear that we had this in mind because I have been approached by various Jewish organisations and would like to satisfy them if possible. I have in mind only such general treatment of the Jews as shown to be part of the general plan of aggression.[11]"

Along the same lines, the official policy of total or partial extermination of a population by a government that controls it would not qualify as a crime, unless these acts occurred "in preparation for war." This is a brilliant caveat because it precludes any comparisons with other policies of extermination and annihilation that never led to a war between "civilised" nations.

Justice Robert Jackson, head of the North American delegation – with the cynicism and self-confidence of those who wield the power of decision – crudely explained why the only possible basis for establishing the tribunal's jurisdiction could be a crime against peace, the crimes committed in preparation for war. It was out of the question that any unfortunate precedent should be created:

> It has been a general principle from time immemorial that the internal affairs of another government are not ordinarily our business; that is to say, the way Germany treats its inhabitants, or any other country treats its inhabitants, is not our affair any more than it is the affair of some other government to interpose itself in our problems. [...] We have some regrettable circumstances at times *in our own country in which minorities are unfairly treated.* We think that it is justifiable that we interfere or attempt to bring retribution to individuals or to states only because the concentration

camps and the deportations were in pursuance of a common plan or enterprise of making an unjust war in which we became involved. We see no other basis on which we are justified to consider the atrocities which were committed inside Germany, under German law, or even in violation of German law, by authorities of the German state.[12]

Between peers at least, it was possible to call a spade a spade. Powers are at liberty to exterminate and brutalise as they deem fit those groups that are under their domination (and who tend to be declared as racially inferior) without the interference of any other State.

In the third millennium, these same powers have a tendency to flaunt their penchant for human rights. We must not forget, however, that at the beginning of the twentieth century this was unthinkable. What would have happened if the scenario had been different? If in the 1930s, treating a population in a manner that could lead to its total or partial destruction or systematically destroying it had been considered punishable crimes justifying intervention by other States, there would have been pandemonium. At the time, the powers that ruled over the destinies of humanity were not yet primarily concerned with principles such as respect for human beings or the rejection of the modern barbarity that had gone on since the indigenous peoples of America were destroyed.

In retrospect, the least that can be said about this international context that was so sympathetic to conventional methods of racial domination that never ruled out the annihilation of "racially inferior" populations, is that the German Nazi government had plenty of elbow room to destroy the "inferior" groups as it deemed fit "without any State being allowed to interfere." It was therefore predictable that the targets of the Nazi extermination policy would not find support or protection from these powers in their fight against the murderous policy of the German National Socialist government. In August 1945, in spite of the horrifying discovery of the gas chambers, these same considerations and same fears weighed just as heavily on the characterisation of what was going to be considered a crime coming under the tribunal's jurisdiction. These powers had no difficulties with the definition of crimes against peace and crimes of war. And anyway, the acts perpetrated by the Nazi criminals were more than enough to warrant the death penalty. The only difficulty was that the definition of crimes against peace and crimes of war "did not automatically cover anti-Jewish measures wholly performed within Axis territories, nor did it reach the prewar decrees.[13]" It was no easy task to satisfy the legitimate demands of Jewish organisations while at the same time steering clear of an untenable position.

In the end, after fifteen drafts, the tribunal was established by the London Agreement of August 8, 1945 to examine and punish the major war criminals of the European Axis countries. It had jurisdiction to examine any of the following crimes:

(a) crimes against peace: namely, planning, preparation, initiation or waging of a war of aggression, or a war in violation of international treaties, agreements or assurances, or participation in a common plan or conspiracy for the accomplishment of any of the foregoing;

(b) war crimes: namely, violations of the laws or customs of war. Such violations shall include, but not be limited to, murder, ill treatment or deportation to slave labour or for any other purpose of civilian populations in occupied territory, murder or ill treatment of prisoners of war or persons on the seas, killing of hostages, plunder of public or private property, wanton destruction of cities, towns or villages, or devastation not justified by military necessity;

(c) crimes against humanity: namely, murder, extermination, enslavement, deportation, and other inhumane acts committed against any civilian population, before or during the war; or persecutions on political, racial or religious grounds in execution of or in connection with any crime within the jurisdiction of the tribunal, whether or not in violation of the domestic law of the country where perpetrated.

Through Professor André Gros, the French delegation suggested to no avail that "persecutions (on political, racial or religious grounds) be defined as an independent crime.[14]" As already demonstrated, it was impossible for the delegates from London and the United States to recognise the destruction of the Jewish population in Europe as a *sui generis* crime without running the risk of themselves being held accountable for similar crimes committed at other times, in other places and against other populations. This is why "murder, extermination, enslavement, deportation, and other inhumane acts committed against any civilian population, before or during the war; or persecutions on political, racial or religious grounds (could only be considered as crimes against humanity if committed) in execution of or in connection with any crime within the jurisdiction of the tribunal…" In other words, in connection with a crime against peace or a crime of war. In clear contradiction with the common sense expressed by André Gros who "did not think that the prosecution would be able to prove that the anti-Jewish persecutions had been inflicted in pursuit of aggression.[15]"

And indeed, he was right. During the trials, the prosecution established no connection between the anti-Jewish decrees that preceded the war and preparations for aggressive war.

> With regard to crimes against humanity, there is no doubt whatever that political opponents were murdered in Germany before the war, and that many of them were kept in concentration camps in circumstances of great horror and cruelty. The policy of terror was certainly carried out on a vast scale, and in many cases was organised and systematic. The policy of persecution, repression and murder of civilians in Germany before the war of 1939, who were likely to be hostile to the government, was most ruthlessly carried out. The persecution of Jews during the same period is established beyond all doubt. To constitute crimes against humanity, the acts relied on before the outbreak of war must have been in execution of, or in connection with, any crime within the jurisdiction of the tribunal (aggressive war). The tribunal is of the opinion that revolting and horrible as many of these crimes were, it has not been satisfactorily proved that they were done in execution of, or in connection with, any such crime. The tribunal therefore cannot make a general declaration that the acts before 1939 were crimes against humanity within the meaning of the charter, but from the beginning of the war in 1939 war crimes were committed on a vast scale, which were also crimes against humanity; and insofar as the inhumane acts charged in the indictment, and committed after the beginning of the war did not constitute war crimes, they were all committed in execution of, or in connection with, the aggressive war, and therefore constituted crimes against humanity.[16]

A step to counter horror seen from a different angle

Following the atrocities perpetrated by the Nazis, the Convention on the Prevention and Punishment of the Crime of Genocide, adopted by the United Nations General Assembly on December 9, 1948, was and continues to be a very important step towards combating barbarity, racist persecutions and impunity. It is the outcome of a fight led by Raphael Lemkin on an international scale. He was a North American Jew of Polish origin who was concerned with the absence of any provisions that could deter and punish the crime of genocide.

Article II of the Convention concerns the perpetrators of acts "committed with intent to destroy, in whole or in part, a national, ethnical, racial or religious group, as such." In Article IV, it is specified that "Persons committing genocide […] shall be punished, whether they are constitutionally responsible rulers, public officials or private individuals." In Article V, the contracting parties (i.e., the signatory states) "undertake to enact […] the necessary legislation […] to provide effective penalties for persons guilty of genocide." Finally, according to Article VI, persons charged of genocide shall be tried by a competent tribunal of the state in the territory of which the act was committed, or by the International Criminal Court if the person's government is itself implicated.

This Convention breaks through the straitjacket created by the Nuremberg tribunal. As a result the total or partial destruction of human groups became a *sui generis* crime. However this text, which was ratified by an overwhelming majority of the member states of the United Nations, was not apparently to the liking of all the democracies in the so-called free world. The United States Senate, in the midst of the continuous lynching of Blacks, had stood in the way of the draft of a federal bill designed "to assure to persons within the jurisdiction of every state the equal protection of the laws, and to punish the crime of lynching" and it opposed ratification of the Convention up to 1986. Is this not an inexplicable inconsistency for a democracy whose citizens are so eager to recall their contribution to crushing the hideous monster? Not at all – this is realpolitik. The unstated reasons for refusing continue to be the same: in the United States in the 1950s and 1960s, in spite of the Holocaust and all the lessons it taught, the upholders of white superiority were still unable to get rid of their habit of terrorising and trampling on the "inferior" race. But worse still, the racial discrimination that was at work in the judiciary allowed court tribunals to apply the death penalty on the basis of fundamentally racist criteria, at least up to 1972 if we are to believe the US Court of Appeals for the Eleventh Circuit.

Hilberg cites two hearings on January 23 and February 9, 1950 before a sub-committee of the US Senate Foreign Relations Committee on the subject of the Convention on Genocide. It is instructive (or astounding, depending on one's point of view) to learn that

> before the US Senate Foreign Relations Committee, fear had been expressed that, under Article 6 of the US constitution, the Convention [on the Prevention and Punishment of the Crime of Genocide] as "supreme law of the land" might be invoked by minority groups before the courts to strike down discriminatory laws of various state and local jurisdictions.[17]

The Weight of Racist Ideologies   143

No wonder then that the White establishment was alarmed when Malcolm X decided to bring the matter of racial discrimination in that country before the United Nations. In an interview on December 2, 1964, he explained:

> One of the organisations that we've formed, the Organisation of Afro-American Unity, has reached the conclusion, after a careful analysis of the problem, that approaching our problem just on the level of civil rights and keeping it within the jurisdiction of the United States will not bring a solution. It's not a Negro problem or an American problem any longer. It's a world problem, it's a human problem. And so we're striving to lift it from the level of civil rights to the level of human rights. And at that level it's international. We can bring it before the United Nations.[18]

Two months later on February 21, 1965, Malcolm X was shot dead.

The reason they had to be exterminated

On October 6, 1943, one of the most remarkable gatherings of party officials of the Third Reich was held in Posen. On that day, speaking to the Reichsleiter and the Gauleiter, Heinrich Himmler gave a very long speech from which I have taken the following passages:

> I am really asking you only to listen to what I have to say in this small circle, and never to talk about it. The question has arisen: What about women and children? I resolved to find an utterly clear solution for this as well. For I did not consider myself justified to eradicate the men – that means kill them or have them killed – and allow their children to grow up and avenge their deaths on our own children and grandchildren. Thus, the difficult decision had to be taken to make this people disappear from the face of the earth. For the organisation which had to carry out this task it was the most difficult one we had ever had. It has been carried out – I believe I can say this – without inflicting damage on the minds and souls of our men and their leaders. The danger that it might was a real one. The path between the two possibilities of either being too cruel and heartless and losing respect for human life, or too soft and so suffering distress to the point of a nervous breakdown – the strait between this Scylla and Charybdis is narrow indeed.[19]

Clearly, these reasons of security or of the state that were withheld from public view even during the war were not going to be invoked by Nazi officials before the tribunals they were brought to account for their acts following their military defeat. To the best of my knowledge, the only Nazi criminal prosecuted following the defeat of Nazi Germany who had the temerity to justify the decision to exterminate Jewish children in this way was SS Commander Otto Ohlendorf. His case is instructive in several respects because nothing in his education, further training or previous experience heralded the criminal who was willing to perform or order the extermination of entire populations. It teaches us about the approach and nature of many Europeans – sometimes from very good families, rather well-educated, fundamentally upright and, according to their friends and relatives, not lacking entirely in human feeling or qualities – who had no misgivings whatsoever about contributing to the murderous deeds committed in America, in Africa and elsewhere against other groups whose only crime was that they were not born in Europe. And all this so as to serve the overarching interests of their respective countries or quite simply their own personal interests, but at any rate an interest they set above the lives of their victims.

According to his affidavit of March 4, 1947, quoted by Hilberg, Otto Ohlendorf

> had studied at three universities (Leipzig, Göttingen, and Pavia); he held a doctorate in jurisprudence; and as a career man he had successfully worked himself up to a research directorship in the Institute for World Economy and Maritime Transport in Kiel. By 1938 he was also Hauptgeschäftführer in the Reichsgruppe Handel, the German trade organisation. While Ohlendorf had joined the party in 1925, the SS in 1926, and the SD in 1936, he regarded his party activities, and even his position as chief of SD-Inland, as a side job in his career. Actually, he devoted four years (1939–43) to full-time activity in the RSHA [Central Office of Security of the Third Reich], for in 1943 he became a Ministerialdirektor and deputy to the Staatssekretär in the Economy Ministry.

> Now Heydrich was a man who did not like subordinates with divided loyalties. Ohlendorf was too independent. Heydrich wanted no one who functioned ehrenamtlich "in an honorary capacity". He was determined to teach Ohlendorf a lesson. The "executive measures" to be taken in the Soviet Union were the kind of activity which required complete, undivided attention; thus it came about that the intellectual Otto Ohlendorf found himself in command of Einsatzgruppe D.[20]

During the Russian campaign, he had received orders to protect the army by killing Jews, Gypsies, Bolshevik officials and anyone who was a "threat to security." By his own account, at the end of the war, the group he had led totted up some 90,000 murders. When Ohlendorf was brought to trial before a bench of American judges, he "maintained that the Jews had to be destroyed. Even if they had not actually started the war, they had now been attacked, and after such an assault one could expect from them only the most dangerous reactions. Asked by Prosecutor Heath what had happened to the Jewish children, Ohlendorf replied 'They were to be killed just like their parents.'"

In other words, although all Jews did not fight with the same determination as Maurepas[21] in Saint-Domingue, these matters should not be left to chance. Questioned about the reason for such relentlessness, he said, "I believe that it is very simple to explain if one starts from the fact that this order did not only try to achieve security but also permanent security because the children would grow up, and surely, being the children of parents who had been killed, they would constitute a danger no smaller than that of their parents."[22]

Were it not that White society in the United States had chosen to ignore the stacks of corpses and the genocide on which it built its racial supremacy, Prosecutor Heath would have recognised the arguments raised by Ohlendorf for what they were, namely the same reasons as those called on several centuries earlier to justify the destruction of the indigenous peoples of America. Native Americans never achieved the position of victors in relation to their former tormentors, nor for that matter did the deported Africans or their descendants. As a result of this particular circumstance, those responsible for this twofold destruction were never held accountable. Even the tribunal of history did not condemn them, because history is written by the victors alone. It is therefore no coincidence that in the concentration camp setting of North America, any Black caught in the act of learning to read was severely punished by the law.

Otto Ohlendorf, Commander of Einsatzgruppe D, was sentenced to death by a North American bench at the military tribunal and executed in 1951, as he deserved. That being said, there is no doubt that, if Nazi Germany had won in 1945, Ohlendorf would have had every opportunity to spend the rest of his days living in peace, as did so many Spanish, British, French, Portuguese, Belgian and Dutch criminals after actively contributing to the genocidal enterprises of their countries. They spent the rest of their days with their close relatives, relishing the honours bestowed by wealth and the official recognition with which states sometimes reward their most faithful servants.

Notes

1. Adolf Hitler, *Mein Kampf*, Warning to the reader, publication of which was ordered by the Court of Appeals of Paris in its ruling of July 11, 1979, Paris, 1979, pp. 2–3.
2. In *L'Histoire*, March 1999, Issue No. 230, p. 27.
3. Hilberg, op. cit., p. 907
4. Camille Pelletan (1846–1915), one of the leading representatives of the radical opposition. He was to become Minister for Naval Affairs in 1902.
5. Ferry, Jules quoted by Kenneth Shadbolt and John Jensen in *The European Experience: Forces of Change*, A.H & A.W. Reed Ltd, 1971, p. 103. Retrieved March 24, 2010, from http://books.google.com/books.
6. Ibid, p. 104.
7. Poznanski, Renée, *Qui savait quoi?*, Paris, 1993, p. 40 (quote translated from the French).
8. Hilberg, op. cit., 1961, p. 681–682.
9. Ibid, p. 685.
10. Ibid, p. 686, my italics.
11. Ibid, p. 686.
12. Ibid, p. 686-687, my italics.
13. Ibid, p. 686.
14. Ibid, p. 687.
15. Ibid, p. 687.
16. Retrieved March 24, 2010, from http://avalon.law.yale.edu/imt/judlawre.asp
17. Hilberg, op. cit., 1961, p. 764.
18. Perry, Bruce (editor), *Malcolm X: The Last Speeches*, Pathfinder, 1989, p. 85. Retrieved March 24, 2010, from http://www.amazon.com/
19. Himmler, pdf file retrieved June 7, 2010, from openlearn.open.ac.uk/file.php/2091/doc4.pdf
20. Hilberg, op. cit., 1961, p. 187–188.
21. I have been criticised for covering the distance between Auschwitz and Saint-Domingue too hastily. The reader will however have noticed that the arguments used by Ohlendorf were used also by the torturers of Maurepas to justify exterminating the latter's children.
22. Hilberg, op. cit., 1961, p. 695.

8

The Racist Tradition of the United States

A society that excludes

The circumstances that give rise to the inception and growth of a nation cannot fail to influence its later development, particularly as regards the substance of human interactions. A nation in the making needs a number of unifying factors around which the identity of the community or the individuals that make it up is built and asserted. The American nation, i.e., the White society in the United States, was built on the corpses of its non-White victims, on a pool of their blood.

In the sixteenth, seventeenth and eighteenth centuries, the Europeans who landed on the lands now known as the United States were mostly English and Irish, but people from other parts of Europe also came. Although they came from the same continent, these people did not speak the same language or share the same religion. They had different customs and different historical and cultural traditions. One thing that did bind this assortment of people arriving from Europe in relation to the Native Americans, and soon afterwards to Africans was first of all that they all belonged to the White race. Inside Europe, this sense of belonging did not have the same bonding strength it had in North America as is proven by the fact that Adolph Hitler tried to introduce similar methods in Europe: he had to go further than the concept of "White race," which was wholly ineffective between Europeans, and resort to the concept of "Aryan race." Confronted with Native Americans and Blacks, Europeans developed what were to become the historical and cultural foundations of the United States: the sense of belonging to a "superior" race, the deep-rooted belief that by exterminating Native Americans they were doing the right thing, both by standards of justice and of reason, because this was essential to conquering their Lebensraum, they were justified in keeping an "inferior" race, i.e. Black people, in bondage.

For the sense of belonging to a "superior" race to counteract effectively the inconvenience and potential conflicts that could arise from differences in language and religion, which in Europe had been enough to ignite and fuel a number of unending wars, it had to be powerful. This sense of belonging to the White race needed to gain unprecedented efficiency to act as the unifying element capable of producing social cohesion. To acquire that efficiency required a cultivation of the mixture of hatred and contempt shown towards non-Whites whose dead bodies have served as the foundations of the "American dream." The result is a deeply racialised, fundamentally negrophobe society in which racism and violence mutually feed on each another.

To say that the instrument that unified Whites and provided the essential cement for building the American nation was their hatred and the negation of their victims might seem simplistic. But it is meaningful that the only serious and bloody confrontation between Whites – indeed one that put the nation at risk of rapid disintegration – arose when leaders in the North, for economic reasons, attempted to slightly alter, at least on paper, the subservient status of the Black race.

The split between the North and the South became apparent soon after 1812, when leaders in the North embarked on the process of industrialisation and began to question the benefits and the necessity of keeping Black people in bondage. In the decades that followed, as industry expanded in the North, the effectiveness of the unifying element that had hitherto ensured the social cohesion of the "American nation" was weakened. The captains of industry in the North (who were inclined to be protectionists) were increasingly hostile towards the landowners of the South who grew cotton as a cash crop intended for export and relied wholly on Black slaves, a situation which constituted 'unfair" competition. The economic stakes were very significant and so the question of maintaining or abolishing Black slavery became a source of tension and caused unprecedented clashes between the Whites who had settled in North America. According to Franklin,

> In the North, the practical abolitionists resolved to destroy slavery by encouraging runaways on and off the Underground Railroad. In the South the practical pro-slavery leaders resolved to keep the institution of slavery inviolate by destroying every vestige of thought that was at variance with it. ... Perhaps no decade in the history of the United States has been so filled with tense and crucial moments as the ten years leading to the Civil War; and closely connected with most of these crises was the problem of slavery.[1]

In 1860, the election of President Abraham Lincoln – an anti-slavery advocate, although not a radical abolitionist – stepped up the pace of events. South Carolina seceded followed by six other states before the President-elect was even sworn in. "When President-Elect Lincoln arrived in Washington late in February 1861, the nation he was to administer during the next four years was rapidly falling apart. Seven states in the lower South had already seceded, and there was talk of the same momentous step being taken in each of the other slave states.'" Soon afterwards the (pro-slavery) Confederation of eleven states was proclaimed under the presidency of Jefferson Davis. If the Northerners wanted to avoid the breakdown of the Union, they were going to have to fight for it. White unity in North America was challenged for the very first time.

Together, Whites began by exterminating the inidgenous peoples, thereby establishing the historical and cultural foundations of the American nation. They went on to cement their hegemony by reducing the Blacks to a less than human status and keeping them clapped in irons. Industrial development in the North altered the Whites' perception of how best to derive profit from the servitude of Blacks to the extent that they contemplated doing away with it. In the South, however, the conditions of cotton production made for a rigid perception by Whites of how best to use Black people. As they saw it, the only way to produce cotton was to maintain Black people in slavery; otherwise they would be ruined. Even the slightest change was liable to destroy the entente built on a perception and on a set of interests and objectives hitherto shared by all the members of the superior race.

This may be stating the obvious, but it should be remembered that, regardless of whether they were Northerners or Southerners, there was no change in the Whites' perception of the Blacks. This was not the issue. There was no question of challenging the superiority of the White race, or denying that Blacks were and would remain inferior beings regardless of their efforts. The change in perception that threatened the unity of the American nation was confined only to how the slave labour provided by a racially inferior group should be used. The idea of ending slavery was simply inconceivable for the Southern slave owners. No promises that the Blacks would not attain full American citizenship, a prerogative of the Whites, could alter that fact. So the seeds of civil war were inevitably sown. The radicalisation of the positions on the question of Black slavery led to a breakdown and a divide in the superior group, the Whites, who hitherto had been united. It is only natural that having built their unity on the inferiority of another race, tampering in any way with this notion would lead to chaos. As it turned out, the issue was settled by bloodshed; 617,000 lives were lost and thousands were left mutilated.

In the late nineteenth and early twentieth centuries, by which time slaughtering Blacks because they were Black was no longer permissible by law, lynching continued. A number of Black organisations began to seek legal protection from Congress.

> After carefully working to secure the support of senators and representatives, James Weldon Johnson, the secretary of the association, succeeded in 1921 in getting Rep. L.C. Dyer of Missouri to introduce in the House a bill "to assure to persons within the jurisdiction of every state the equal protection of the laws, and to punish the crime of lynching." After fierce opposition, the House of Representatives adopted the Johnson proposal. The task in the Senate was infinitely more difficult, and despite the fact that the NAACP doubled its efforts to achieve the Herculean task of securing passage of the bill there, the bill was abandoned. Numerous similar bills were later introduced, but all of them met a similar fate.[3]

These deeds continued into the 1960s, perpetrated not just by a few murderers such as Ku Klux Klan members. Nor can they be considered on a par with the racist crimes that still clutter the sundry news sections of modern-day newspapers in America. What we are talking about here is the carefully organised collective lynching of one or several Blacks, along with the traditional photo session, ending with a fine barbecue on the front lawn so that everyone could settle down and relax.[4]

Hence, in North American democracy, the "outcast" race, the allegedly inferior population, was forced to go begging for laws that would end the ingrained habit of killing Blacks because they were Black. To no avail. Even the Rosewood massacre in Florida failed to convince the US Senate that not only was it urgent to ban lynching, but also that an information campaign should be conducted so as to explain to the White population in that country that these were no longer institutionalised practices.

We are talking here about the democracy that Alexis de Tocqueville used as a model. The prophet (as some members of the French intelligentsia like to call him) went so far as to say: "We have seen how the customs of (American) society become more humane and gentle in proportion as men become more equal and alike.[5]" Well, naturally! Since non-Whites had been banished from the human family and reduced to a less than human condition, White North American society could thrive in a state of almost perfect equality. One of its founding fathers, Thomas Jefferson, a great admirer of Beccaria, went to the extreme of proposing a ban on cruel and degrading punishments. After all, it was a family affair.

As part of this process of mainstreaming iniquity, this democracy, which was considered "exemplary in many respects," succeeded in institutionalising the negation of the humanity of non-Whites without being discredited. The principle of the total enslavement of non-Whites was built into the political workings of the American democracy that was acclaimed as an example to be followed.

This model of racial domination developed in the American democracy morally bolstered Adolph Hitler's ambitions:

> North America, whose population consists in by far the largest part of Germanic elements who mixed but little with the lower coloured peoples, shows a different humanity and culture from Central and South America. [...] The Germanic inhabitant of the American continent, who has remained racially pure and unmixed, rose to be master of the continent; he will remain the master as long as he does not fall a victim to defilement of the blood.[6]

He was no doubt right. Now, at the beginning of the twenty-first century, White power in the United States, which "shows a different humanity," continues to be the master of the American continent and indeed of the planet.

Of course, Tocqueville did not know that many years later, so as to maintain that marvellous equality between the chosen people, the very same practices of exclusion introduced into Europe and applied to European citizens would produce Auschwitz. On the other hand, in 1981, the historian François Furet quite seriously suggests that "America offers him (Tocqueville) the society and culture of a pure democracy. With a tradition of collective local freedoms."

A time-honoured tradition of racial violence

The Rosewood massacre was again one of those "extreme situations" in which, alas, America, abounds, although "scientific research" and "rigorous analysis" have chosen to ignore them. This butchery took place when a horde of Whites, whom Las Casas would surely have described as being possessed by the devil, set fire to the houses of the three hundred Blacks in the community, razed them to the ground and at the same time lynched the inhabitants. Within five days, these vicious Whites went after every Black they came across – man, woman or child – and hung them, burnt them alive or shot them dead. Few Blacks were lucky to escape. To begin with, most of them were able to escape into the forest but they were soon surrounded and slaughtered.

What was the pretext? There is always a pretext. For the La Rubiera[7] massacre, the ostensible reason was that Native Americans might steal the cassava and pigs. In Rosewood, Florida, the pretext was salacious: it is the story of a White woman in the habit of two-timing her White husband. Five kilometres from Rosewood (a Black town) was Sumner, inhabited only by Whites. On January 1, 1923, while her husband was working, Fannie Taylor, aged 22, entertained her lover, who was White too and worked as an engineer close to Sumner, the White town where the Taylors lived. For some unexplained reason, the meeting turned brutal and Fannie was assaulted by her lover, who beat her so badly before fleeing the scene but seen by the servants. All that remained for Fannie Taylor was to tend to her wounds; but how was she to explain the blows to her husband? The young woman rushed outside screaming that a nigger had assaulted her. This was enough to trigger an anti-Black butchery that completely obliterated Rosewood. The Taylor household servants, who had witnessed the assault, stated that her lover, a White engineer, had beaten her. In the United States, as everyone knows, the word of one Black or a thousand Blacks is not worth the word of one White woman, regardless of whether she is known to be a compulsive liar. This is tautological with white superiority. White men and their dogs, led by the Sheriff, started out for Rosewood. The fate of its inhabitants was henceforth sealed.

Although he was informed of the "troubles", the Governor refrained from intervening: the Whites were not in danger. Armed Whites arrived from all over Florida to take part in the punitive expedition that had been announced by a Miami newspaper. Neither children nor the elderly were spared. Anything Black had to disappear. The handful of survivors did not even dare to file a suit. They were better advised to hide if they did not wish to be silenced once and for all. Not even a semblance of a trial took place. Officially, "only eight Blacks were killed," which in the judicial tradition of the United States democracy is not worthy of an in-depth investigation. In Florida, a specially appointed Grand Jury made up of Whites deemed there were no grounds for convicting anyone at all.[8] As a result, not a single White was in any way bothered, to the delight of those who in the United States from time to time get a kick out of "thrashing a Black."

Advancing backwards

In 1857, a Black man named Dred Scott managed to bring a case before the Supreme Court of the United States. In this trial, he faced Dr Emerson, a White man living in Missouri, who insisted on keeping him in bondage on the grounds that he was just a nigger. The Supreme Court handed down what is known as the Dred Scott vs. Sanford decision (1857). The majority opinion as expressed by the President of the Court, Chief Justice Roger Taney, states that:

> Blacks are excluded from the national community by the Constitution itself because they are an inferior and subordinate class of beings subjugated to the dominant race and [...] remain subject to its authority. We think they (the Blacks) are not included and have never been included under the title of 'citizens' in the Constitution; they can therefore claim none of the rights and privileges which that instrument provides for and secures to citizens of the United States.[9]

Thus, in 1857, the Supreme Court inaugurated a tradition of racial discrimination which was to become inherent to the workings of the North American judicial system.

A few decades later, in 1896, in the Plessy vs. Ferguson decision, the United States Supreme Court upheld the constitutionality of segregationist laws that remained in force until the 1950s.[10] These laws, like the segregationist laws enforced by the British in South Africa, provided a moral backing to the legal experts of the Third Reich who indeed used them to draft their own segregationist laws aimed at non-Aryans.[11]

Racial segregation therefore quite lawfully affected every facet of the daily lives of non-Whites, who were not entitled to any of the privileges set aside for the race of masters. Thanks to segregated schools, for instance, the American democracy was able to provide White children with a fairly satisfactory education, while dealing out some third-rate instruction to Black children. Franklin points out: "The current expenditures per White pupil averaged $37.87, while such expenditures per Black pupil averaged $13.09.[12]" Even during the war, the Black soldiers enlisted to fight Nazism were recruited into separate units.

> The policy of the War Department became clearer in the fall of 1940 when a statement was issued that African Americans would be received into the army on the general basis of the proportion of the African American population of the country. They were to be organised into separate units, however, and existing Black units that were officered by Whites would

receive no African American officers other than medical officers and chaplains.[13]

However, a combination of the memories left by the Nazi laws on racial segregation together with the atrocities that followed, led to a mobilisation of the forces hostile to racial hatred in the United States. And in 1954, the Supreme Court gave a historic decision, the Brown vs. Board of Education decision, which ruled that segregation in schools was inherently inegalitarian and therefore unconstitutional. This was by no means a foregone conclusion. The progress embodied in the Brown vs. Board of Education decision towards equality before the law for everyone did not conclusively settle the matter. Disregard for the rights of Blacks is solidly entrenched in the American judicial system and the road ahead for the non-Whites is still long and sinuous.

In a preparatory memorandum shortly before the decision, one of the members of the Court, Judge William Rehnquist, pleaded in favour of racial segregation at all levels. He concluded as follows: "I think Plessy vs. Ferguson should be reaffirmed... I realise that it is a position that is neither popular nor humanitarian, which has caused me to be excoriated by my 'liberal' colleagues.[14]" Because of Hitler and the atrocities he committed in Europe, the time was not ripe to conduct a nation-wide campaign in favour of maintaining the segregationist laws, but Judge Rehnquist, nevertheless, openly expressed his sympathy with the 1896 Plessy vs. Ferguson decision in which the Court had upheld the constitutionality of the segregationist laws which the Brown vs. Board of Education decision of 1954 struck down. Although his was a dissenting opinion, William Rehnquist felt justified in making this spine-chilling statement: "It is high time for the Court to face the fact that the White people in the South don't like coloured people.[15]"

This came a century after the Dred Scott decision in which through the voice of its Chief Justice, the court advocated the idea that neither the Africans nor their descendants could enjoy the rights set out in the Constitution since Blacks had no right that could be objected to a White. All this did not prevent William Rehnquist – apparently the most faithful representative of the judicial tradition begun in 1857 by Chief Justice Roger Taney – from becoming Chief Justice of the Supreme Court, i.e., the highest Court of the world's major power – the power that represents the free world and is engaged in a permanent crusade to enforce human rights! With William Rehnquist as Chief Justice of the United States Supreme Court, the Whites in that country who do not like coloured people could be sure that their judicial tradition would persist. All this sheds light on the violations uncovered by a few studies that have examined the relationship between race and death penalty sentencing by courts of the United States of America.

Legal murders

Rape was once punishable by death in Virginia. However, "between 1908 and 1972, only Blacks were executed under this statute, even though 45% of those convicted of rape were White. [...] In 1950, lawyers representing seven Black men appealed their rape convictions on the grounds that only Blacks were executed for the crime. The Virginia Supreme Court denied the appeal, [...] All seven were executed.[16]"

In the 1960s, the self-proclaimed guardians of the free world – the United States – were busy trying to gain recognition as lead international prosecutor of the communist regimes for human rights violations. Concomitantly, inside their own borders, the most progressive organisations protested against the tragic consequences of applying double standards to defendants in criminal proceedings depending on their ethnic origin. Leaders of the Black community, including Martin Luther King, criticised the great American power for being unable to guarantee impartial application of the law to Blacks brought to trial. Some people contemplated bringing the matter before the Human Rights Committee of the United Nations.

In 1972, the United States Supreme Court, in the Furman vs. Georgia case, took a crucial decision about the right to life. The Court invalidated all the state laws concerning the death penalty on the grounds that their application was unacceptably arbitrary and unconstitutional.

At last!

Considering that American authorities have never directly admitted to having executed innocent people during this century, it is unfortunate that in 1972 no one saw fit to order an investigation of the topic. For the last twenty years at least, it would have been worthwhile to find out how many people have been sentenced to death and executed even though their guilt has never been established or because they were condemned for reasons linked to racial profiling. The findings of such an investigation would probably have helped better understand the soundness and crucial importance of the Court's decision in the Furman vs. Georgia case.

Only four years went by before the Supreme Court backtracked. Several states adopted new laws stating that capital punishment should be applied with discernment, as opposed to the usual practice up to 1972. In 1976, "In Gregg vs. Georgia, the US Supreme Court upheld the 'guided discretion' procedures for death sentencing established by the Georgia legislature. These procedures became the general constitutional model for other retentionist US states to follow.[17]

On several occasions, Amnesty International has expressed its concern about the racially discriminatory practice of American courts. In 1985, for instance, 48 per cent of all death penalties were decided against Blacks or members of other minorities, whereas they accounted for only 12 per cent of the population – 66 per cent of prisoners sentenced to death in Alabama are Black.

> In the cases when the death sentence has been imposed, important disparities are revealed when the race of the victim is taken into consideration. Out of 66 prisoners executed between 1977 and 1985, 59 (or 89%) were sentenced for murdering Whites. In 1985, the percentage was 77% for the whole the United States. The percentage is higher in the states of the South where the disproportion seems even wider since Whites and Blacks are practically guilty of the same number of homicides. It would seem that Blacks convicted of murdering Whites are more often sentenced to death than any other category of people; conversely, Whites are rarely sentenced to death for having murdered Blacks.[18]

The mechanics of justice in criminal cases are such that Black lives are inevitably undervalued while those of Whites are overvalued.

The system and the procedures for selecting jurors allows the attorney-general to reject prospective jurors. It has been established that prosecutors very commonly use this method to remove prospective jurors who are against the death penalty. "Georgia lawyers told Amnesty International that 80 per cent of Black prospective jurors in capital trials are routinely excluded from the initial jury pool under Witherspoon and that, after peremptory challenges as well, the final trial jury may have no members of the Black population, even though they constitute 20 to 30 per cent of the state population.

> Lawyers from the state of Georgia have told Amnesty International that, in 1985, 80% of Blacks likely to be judged in a trial which may lead to a death penalty are commonly excluded from jury pre-selection. It happens that final juries do not include any Black although 20 to 30% of the population

of the state (of Georgia) is Black. In Louisiana, all executed Black people were sentenced by all-White juries.[19]

Once the prosecutor has successfully barred Blacks from being jurors along with anyone who opposes the death penalty, any Black accused of murdering a White, even if there is no conclusive evidence against him, is not likely to escape the death sentence.

I should mention two studies on the subject of racial discrimination in US courts highlighted by Amnesty International:.

> One of these studies compares statistics on all the criminal homicides committed in Florida, Georgia, Texas and Ohio. The statistics include all the death sentences inflicted between 1972, after the Georgia Supreme Court had rendered its verdict in the Furman vs. Georgia affair, and the month of December 1977. Death sentences in the four states accounted for 70% of all the death sentences imposed nationally during that period. It is noticeable that in Florida and Texas, Blacks guilty of killing Whites ran the risk of being sentenced to death five and six times more often respectively than Whites who had murdered Whites. Among Black offenders in Florida, those who had killed Whites were 40 times more likely to get the death penalty than those who had killed Blacks. During the same period, no White offender in Florida had been sentenced to death for killing a Black person. The findings are identical for the states of Georgia and Ohio. These findings are consistent with the findings of a Florida study conducted in 1981. In 1976 and 1977, out of 326 murders perpetrated between people of different races, 5.4% of the cases in which the victim was Black led to a death sentence; conversely, the per centage reaches 14% when the victim was White. The study also demonstrates that in 53.6% of the cases when the victim was Black, a verdict of murder with qualifying circumstances was reached; whereas, if the victim was White this percentage climbed to 85%.[20]

Studies conducted at the beginning of the 1980s on the application of capital punishment in Georgia are relevant for two reasons: not only do they provide the most detailed analysis of racial disparities in the application of the death penalty, but furthermore, the Court called upon to pass judgment on the findings of the investigation could neither contest the relevance of this work, nor even challenge a single piece of evidence presented to expose the influence of racism in the way in which the judicial system operates in the United States. The research team, headed by Professor David Baldus, an authority on race and the death penalty in the United States, in collaboration with a statistician, George Woodworth, aimed to discover why killers of White victims in Georgia during the 1970s had received the death penalty approximately eleven times more often than killers of Blacks, taking into the possibility that different levels of aggravation within potentially capital murders could explain the difference in sentencing. [...] they subjected each case to a series of rigorous tests, matching the known facts against all possible factors which might play a role in determining the sentence. More than 230 control factors were identified, including statutory and non-statutory aggravating and mitigating circumstances, weight of evidence, the defendant's background and prior record, race of defendant and victim, geographical area, and chance. [...] They found that no significant racial disparities in sentencing appeared in the most highly aggravated cases (a relatively small number of homicides involving three or more statutory aggravating circumstances such as a serious additional felony, multiple victims and torture). However, the team identified a mid-range of cases with intermediate levels of aggravation, in which death sentences were also imposed. These cases in which there was most room for discretion – comprised the bulk of the 400 potentially capital cases. In this range of cases, Professor Baldus found that offenders with White victims were twenty times more likely to receive death sentences than those with Black victims, at similar levels of aggravation. In fact, the victim's race at this level was more important than several of Georgia's 10 statutory aggravating circumstances. The team also found at this level that Black defendants were more likely to receive a death sentence than similar White defendants.[21]

These studies show that in spite of the guarantee of discernment invoked by the State of Georgia in its law on the death penalty, the latter is applied exactly as it was prior to 1972. And no wonder! The district attorneys there have the same huge power that they had prior to the Furman vs. Georgia case. Most of them are elected to this office by predominantly White voters many of whom, according to the polls, are in favour of the death penalty. As locally elected representatives, district attorneys are not accountable for their decisions except towards public opinion for the purpose of being re-elected. For instance, "In late 1994 the District Attorney of Oklahoma City campaigned for re-election on his record of having 'sent 44 murderers to death row.[22]'" This may explain (although by no means justify) the relentlessness of so many district attorneys in murder cases, some of whom are willing to go as far as to conceal evidence that might clear the accused.

In any case, the fact that the authorities have the power to score political points by choosing whether or not the death penalty will be sought in any particular case, combined with the discretionary power to select or reject jurors, creates an extremely serious situation where prosecutors are not subject to judicial oversight. Such oversight would not make up for all the shortcomings of the system, it would at least limit its most alarming failings. Examples of alarming circumstances are revealed in an article titled "The Flip Side of a Fair Trial" published in the *Chicago Tribune* on 13 January 1999:

> Michael Goggin, a former prosecutor for Cook County, Illinois, recently admitted that the District Attorney's office ran a contest to see which prosecutor could be the first to convict defendants whose weight totalled 4,000 pounds. Men and women upon conviction were marched into a room and weighed. Because most of the defendants were Black, the competition was known by local officials as 'Niggers by the Pound.'[23]

The racial composition of the judicial body does not help to avert ascertained misconduct of this type: "In 1998, for example, of the 1,838 District Attorneys (prosecutors) in states with the death penalty, 22 were Black, 22 were Latino, and the rest were White.[24]" The training given to prosecutors was an added element:

> The Assistant District Attorney for Philadelphia made a training videotape for the city's prosecutors. On the video, he describes how to select a jury more likely to convict, including the removal of potential Black jurors: "Let's face it, Blacks from the low-income areas are less likely to convict. There's resentment to law enforcement... You don't want those guys on your jury... If you get a White teacher in a Black school who's sick of these guys, that may be the one to pick." The video also instructed the trainee prosecutors on how to hide the racial motivation for the rejection of prospective jurors in order to evade claims of racial discrimination from defence lawyers. The tape did not become public until 1997.[25]

This method would seem to apply almost everywhere, as it is apparent from statements made by Alan Greiman, a judge at an Illinois Court of Appeals, published in the previously mentioned article "The Flip Side of a Fair Trial". Judge Greiman inventoried the many fanciful arguments presented by state prosecutors to reject Black jurors:

> too old, too young, divorced, unkempt hair, freelance writer, wrong religion, social worker, renter, lack of family contact, single, lack of maturity, improper demeanour, improper attire, lives alone, lives in an apartment complex, misspelled place of employment, unemployed, employed as a part-time barber, spouse employed as school teacher, failure to remove hat, living with girlfriend, deceased father.[26]

Since the publication of the research led by David C. Baldus, other work on the connection between the application of the death penalty and race have yielded similar results. In an article entitled "Race and the Death Penalty in Kentucky Murder Trials," published in 1995 in the *American Journal of Criminal Justice*, Thomas J. Keil and Gennaro F. Vito, two researchers from the University of Louisville, come to the following conclusion: "Blacks and Whites in the USA are the victims of murder in almost equal numbers, yet 82% of prisoners executed since 1977 were convicted of the murder of a White person. In Kentucky, for example, every death sentence up to March 1996 was for the murder of a White victim, despite over 1,000 homicide victims in the state being Black.[27]"

A step forward according to the appeals court

The Georgia findings were used in support of an appeal to the Court of Appeals for the Eleventh Circuit brought by the LDF on behalf of Warren McCleskey, a Black man sentenced to death for killing a White Atlanta police officer. Warren McCleskey claimed that the discriminatory application of Georgia's death penalty statute violated both the Eighth Amendment's prohibition of cruel and unusual punishment and his Fourteenth Amendment right to equal protection of the law. In a nine-to-three decision given in January 1985, the appeals court rejected the claim that Georgia had unconstitutionally discriminated against the petitioner on account of race. The court, which reviewed the Georgia study in some detail, did not dispute its findings, stating: "The statistics show there is enough discernible correlation between the race-of-the-victim and the imposition of the death sentence in cases to be statistically significant in the system as a whole", but "the magnitude cannot be called determinative in any given case". The court held that, because there was no proof that the state had intentionally discriminated against the defendant, there could be no constitutional violation of his rights. Indeed, the court went on to say that: "The marginal disparity based on race of victim tends to support the state's contention that the system is working far differently from the one which Furman condemned. In pre-Furman days, there was no rhyme or reason as to who got the death penalty and who did not. But now, in the vast majority of cases, the reasons for a difference are well-documented." Three judges, Judges Johnson, Hatchett and Clark, filed separate dissenting opinions [...]. Judge Hatchett found that the 20 per cent racial disparity among the middle range of cases, in which "decision on the proper sentence is most difficult and the imposition of the death penalty most questionable". He said: "To allow this system to stand is to concede that in a certain number of cases the consideration of race will be a factor in the decision whether to impose the death penalty".[28]

Thanks to the admissions of the Court of Appeals for the Eleventh Circuit, we can be certain that what others have condemned on many occasions but without indisputable evidence such as that provided by David Baldus and his team is true. No one ever again can pretend these allegations to be a leftist conspiracy designed to damage the image of the criminal justice system in the United States.

In 1987 in the US, there were 1,788 inmates in death row, waiting to find out whether they would be electrocuted, asphyxiated, poisoned, hanged or shot: men, women, sick and mentally retarded people. Nearly half of these prisoners, i.e., roughly 850 people, were Black; 20 per cent of these had been sentenced to death on the basis of racial criteria. For the appeals court, this is a "marginal disparity" which translates into a figure of 170 Blacks. Just 170 Blacks! In 1999, twelve years later, 3,565 convicts awaited execution.

In 1998, Attorney-General Janet Reno requested the National Institute of Justice (NIJ), an entity that is part of the Federal Department of Justice, to form a national expert committee on developments in the area of DNA testing so as to "identify the means to maximise the value of DNA in our criminal justice system". At the end of September 1999, after 18 months of work, this committee of eighty judicial, scientific and academic experts handed over its report. It states that "The strong presumption that verdicts are correct, one of the underpinnings of restrictions on post-conviction relief, has been weakened by the growing number of convictions that have been vacated because of exclusionary DNA results.[29]" Most of the convicts are too poor to pay for DNA tests (that cost between 3,000 and 5,000 dollars) and often have to call on charity organisations that work with convicts.

At the Cardozo Faculty of Law in New York for instance, there is a legal aid programme called Innocence Project, funded by various charities. This programme provides free legal aid to convicted prisoners who may be able to prove their innocence through DNA tests. For Jane Siegel Green, who heads this programme, the use of this technology "is a major development in the American legal system, it is an enormous change. […]. For the first time, it offers victims of miscarriages of justice an effective tool enabling them to prove their innocence". She deplores the lack of political will of the competent authorities to solve this problem and argues that it is not that expensive to exonerate these people. There are probably thousands of innocent people in prison, but the number of these who may be able to prove their innocence by DNA testing is only in the hundreds. To help them prove their innocence would likely cost no more than two or three million dollars. The problem is not money, it is a matter of political will.[30]

It is alarming to see that in the United States there is a growing tendency to reverse the 'burden of proof' principle: prisoners sentenced to death whose innocence might be proven by DNA tests are left to seek out the help of charitable organisations. If they are really lucky, they might escape execution. What a pity it is, as Jane Siegel Green herself admits, that there are so few such lucky ones. The others, the "thousands of innocent inmates" whose innocence cannot be proven by means of DNA tests must just wait for their day of execution to arrive. That's how things go in the North American democracy.

One can only imagine the solitude and powerlessness of these faceless people sentenced to death on the basis of race and executed in an environment of utmost indifference. From time to time, among their numbers, an emblematic figure emerges such as the African American journalist and activist Mumia Abu-Jamal, former president of the Philadelphia branch of the National Association of Black Journalists and former Black Panther activist. Accused of killing a White policeman, Abu-Jamal, whose nickname is the "voice of the voiceless", was sentenced to death in June 1981 following a typically American trial. To start with, the trial was presided over by Justice Albert Sabo, who had been deputy sheriff in Philadelphia for sixteen years before being appointed judge. He became famous because he was "responsible for imposing 31 death sentences – the highest total for any US judge since the reintroduction of the death penalty in the USA.[31]" As for the prosecutor, he had attracted attention in another case (Commonwealth vs. Connor) where he was successful in having an innocent person sentenced to death, who then had to spend years on death row before proving his innocence.

Mumia Abu-Jamal, who had decided to defend his case himself, was deprived of the right to provide his own defence in the middle of the jury selection process. Because he insisted on asserting this right, and on his right to avail himself of the assistance of John Africa, he was expelled from the courtroom and assigned a counsel who was not familiar with the file and reluctantly took over the case. Thereafter, "the prosecution used 11 of its peremptory challenges to exclude potential Black jurors.[32]" To make matters worse, the judge decided to remove an already selected Black woman and replace her with an older White man who was not inclined towards the idea of equality.

In fact, Mumia Abu-Jamal was sentenced to death because of his political past and his revolutionary convictions. In a May 1999 document, Amnesty International expressed its fears:

> Amnesty International is concerned that the level of hatred for Mumia Abu-Jamal by the law enforcement community and the lack of inde-pendent and impartial arbiters in Pennsylvania's appeal court system mean Mumia Abu-Jamal may be prevented from receiving a fair and impartial hearing for the legal claims he has made concerning his original trial.[33]

And indeed, on 4 October 1999, the Supreme Court refused to review the case in spite of the recommendations given by the National Committee established by the Minister of Justice. The Committee's report, in view of the exorbitant number of innocent people sentenced due to a miscarriage of justice, suggested that fewer restrictions should be placed on reopening closed cases. As for the Governor of Pennsylvania, who was elected on a campaign for reinstating the death penalty, promising the mobs that he would step up the planned execution rate,[34] he rushed to sign the order for the execution of Mumia Abu-Jamal on 13 October 1999. The date set for him to be legally lynched was 2 December 1999, later postponed because his file had just been referred to a federal court.

[After international protests and activism on Abu-Jamal's cause and numerous appeals and review, on December 7, 2011, in agreement with the prosecution, his death sentence was commuted to life imprisonment without parole, and reaffirmed on July 9, 2013.]

The Supreme Court of the United States declares its willingness to accept racial discrimination in death penalty sentencing

In 1987, the Supreme Court had to make a public pronouncement on the issue of racial disparity in death sentencing. The attorneys representing Warren McCleskey, relying on a statistical analysis of sentencing practices in Georgia, were convinced that the arguments raised by the Court of Appeals for the Eleventh Circuit contradicted its decision. They therefore entered an appeal before the Supreme Court.

The Supreme Court determined that it had jurisdiction to review the McCleskey case, reopened the investigation, and after examining the evidence, admitted the validity of most of its conclusions. However, by five votes to four, it handed down a ground-breaking decision:

> The racial disparities revealed in the Baldus study were insufficient to show that Georgia's capital sentencing system was operating 'irrationally' or 'arbitrarily.' The [...] apparent disparities in sentencing are an inevitable part of our criminal justice process, and ... any system for determining guilt or punishment has its weaknesses and potential for misuse.[35]

Since disparities in sentencing were accepted as inevitable in any criminal justice system, the Supreme Court of the United States affirmed the decision of the Court of Appeals for the Eleventh Circuit: "In a 5–4 opinion written by Justice Lewis Powell, the majority maintained that McCleskey had not demonstrated that the decision-makers in his particular case had discriminated against him.[36]"

However, a minority of the members of this court was certainly aware of the legal monstrosity supported by the highest court in the United States in the McCleskey vs. Kemp case. In the opinion written by Justice Brennan, this minority expresses the view that:

> the risk that race influenced McCleskey's sentence is intolerable by any imaginable standard [...]. It has been scarcely a generation since the court's first decision striking down racial segregation...We cannot pretend that in three decades we have completely escaped the grip of a historical legacy spanning centuries...We remain imprisoned by the past as long as we deny its influence on the present.[37]

Even though this position of principle adopted by a minority of the judges of the court in the McCleskey vs. Kemp case could not contain the racist and inevitably deadly abuses of the American judicial system, it is nonetheless to the credit of these four judges that they so clearly expressed their disagreement.

Many years later, Justice Lewis Powell, who was no longer a member of the Supreme Court, had the nerve to explain his position in the McCleskey vs. Kemp case: "My understanding of statistical analysis ranges from limited to zero," he admitted, adding that nowadays he would have voted against the death sentence as a matter of course. "I have come to think that capital punishment should be abolished.[38]" The least one can say is that Lewis Powell's change of heart comes a little too late: first, because he no longer sits on the Supreme Court; and secondly, because Warren McCleskey was executed on 25 September 1991. The Court's tragic leap backwards could have been avoided if only Powell had added his vote to that of his other dissenting colleagues.

The gradual acceptance of an inherently inhuman policy by those who apply it even though they do not endorse it is alarming. Not just in the United States, but in the other so-called civilised countries, public opinion is aware that in North America, a Black person accused of murdering a White can only escape the death penalty if he proves his innocence. When the convict is not a member of the superior race, the White judiciary can naturally dispense with the burden-of-proof rule that requires it to seek out the truth and establish the accused's responsibility beyond reasonable doubt. This is by no means an imaginary situation; many people recognise this but do not seem to be troubled. Why is that?

Clearly, people do not like to be reminded that the legal system of the Third Reich, which was not fond of non-Aryans, applied the very same racial criteria that are currently reflected in the majority opinion of the highest court in the American system of justice. The mistake the German legal authorities made was to be in the employ of a state, which after antagonising all the major powers ended up by being defeated in 1945. In contrast, in the United States, the judges serving white supremacy do so in the name of the foremost world power. That is the difference, and indeed a considerable one.

For a more uniform ethnic structure

Following the Supreme Court's ruling in the McCleskey vs. Kemp case, people who found the inevitability of racial discrimination in the application of capital punishment unacceptable turned to Congress. It was asked to use its authority to prohibit any unjustified racial disparity as ascertained by conclusive statistical evidence. In 1988, a draft law called the Racial Justice Act was introduced. Pursuant to this law, defendants would be able to challenge a death sentence if they could provide hard figures as evidence of discriminatory practices.

Two years went by before the House of Representatives adopted this draft law. When the draft reached the Senate, it received the same treatment as the draft law against lynching in 1921. It was presented once again to the Senate in 1991, as a provision that was part of another law. "President Bush made it clear that he would prevent passage of the entire bill if the Racial Justice Act was not removed; [...] Proposed again in 1994, the Racial Justice Act once more failed to become law.[39]" One of the arguments of the opponents to this draft was that it could turn into a law abolishing the death penalty.

It is commonly accepted that nothing is more difficult than bringing about changes in mind-sets. But it is distressing to see that the United States of America, the most technically accomplished and technologically efficient White society, has remained so backward, prisoner of the unbending ideology of the 1850s. Furthermore, this society, that is so comfortably settled in a state of ideological backwardness, has no intention of breaking out of the psychological limitations that prevents it from acquiring a different perception of humans, one, for instance, that is less conditioned by the racial hierarchies that reigned supreme among Westerners until the advent of Nazism and its consequences.

This determination not to evolve towards a degree of humanism or just plain humaneness is illustrated by a letter sent by Senator Mike Everett of Arkansas to a member of Amnesty International on the topic of the death penalty, on 1 July 1997, expressing his profound belief that:

> What is moral and what is legal are often a matter of perspective. Nations, like humans, evolve. America is not so far removed from the frontier as Austria [where his Amnesty International correspondent lives]. Your country is much older, its culture more developed, more ethnically and socially unified, further from its history of un-civilisation, than ours. From our perspective, the death penalty is both moral and legal. From your perspective, it is not. The day will come when our acceptance of the death penalty will change, but it is still decades, and probably centuries, away. Our attitude toward the death penalty will change when our attitudes toward gun control, racial differences, religion, poverty, and other fundamental values, change.[40]

In the meantime, as we wait for the ethnic structure of American society to become more uniform, Senator Everett feels he must spell out that "77% of Arkansas people favour (the death penalty). That is enough said. If 77% of Arkansas people want it, they will have it.[41]"

Not long ago, it was still customary to lynch Blacks because they were Black, and terror seemed a good way of keeping them at bay. Between 1890 and 1930, at least 3,000 Blacks were lynched. The brutality that accompanied these barbaric deeds reflected a mentality that has yet to be thoroughly investigated by psychiatrists and psychologists who specialise in criminal conduct and behaviour.

Norman Finkelstein, professor of political science at Hunter College, City University of New York, refers to the description given by the *New*

York Tribune of a lynching that happened in Georgia at the turn of the twentieth century:

> Sam Hose [...] was burned at the stake in a public road, one and a half miles from here. Before the torch was applied to the pyre, the Negro was deprived of his ears, fingers and other portions of his body with surprising fortitude. Before the body was cool, it was cut to pieces, the bones were crushed into small bits and even the tree on which the wretch met his fate was torn up and disposed of as souvenir... Those unable to obtain the ghastly relics directly, paid more fortunate possessors extravagant sums for them. Small pieces of bone went for 25 cents and a bit of liver, crisply cooked, for 10 cents.[42]

One can reasonably surmise that the lynching of Sam Hose had been planned ahead since aficionados in the area, including those from the capital, had the time to arrange for the spectators to travel to the spot. If we are to believe Professor Litwack:

> On a Sunday afternoon, April 23, 1899, more than two thousand White Georgians, some of them arriving from Atlanta on a special excursion train, assembled near the town of Newman to witness the execution of Sam Hose, a Black Georgian. [...] Before Hose's body had even cooled, his heart and liver were removed and cut into several pieces and his bones were crushed into small particles. [...] Newspaper reporters noted the active participation of some of the region's most prominent citizens. [...] One of the participants reportedly left for the state capitol, hoping to deliver a slice of Sam Hose's heart to the governor of Georgia.[43]

These popular manifestations of racial hatred along with this particular brand of ferocity made in the USA were something even the most fanatical Nazis never dared express on the streets of Hitler's Germany. If we are to believe Ian Kershaw, quoted by Hobsbawm: "Jews who escaped from newly occupied Vienna to Berlin in 1938 were astonished at the absence of street anti-Semitism. Here violence came by decree from above, as in November 1938.[44]" The mere fact that there were no spontaneous lynchings does not of course mean that non-Aryans had no reason to be terrified. My point is simply that, in the democracy of America, not long before the Nazis were in power, this decidedly terrifying taste for cruelty and for barbaric deeds should draw attention and foster some serious thinking about the pathogenic components of American society and the destructive mentality they generate.

This destructive mentality is reflected as active animosity and is particularly disquieting because, unlike Germany after the war, the United States has never been forced to officially condemn the extreme violence displayed towards "racially inferior" groups. Nor has it been compelled to eradicate, to the extent possible, the negrophobia which has traditionally characterised a large majority of this country's population. The consequences of this differentiated treatment of similar ills are by no means insignificant. For instance, the German government, whatever its political leaning, could not possibly allow the neo-Nazis to parade the streets of Berlin, clamouring their support for Hitlerism. It is easy to imagine the (justified) outcry that such a provocation would trigger. In the United States, regardless of whether the President is a Democrat or a Republican, the Ku Klux Klan is allowed to organise mass demonstrations championing white superiority. On October 23, 1999, while in France a few thousand people marched in the streets of Paris expressing their support for Mumia Abu-Jamal and demanding a fair trial, in the United States, the Ku Klux Klan marched in the streets of New York, complete with permission from the authorities, to assert the right for the White race to maintain its privileges...

This is the murderous mentality, aided by an ideology which surreptitiously replicates itself, that makes this country, the United States of America, the only democracy in the Western world where candidates campaign on the promise they will restore the death penalty or step up the pace of executions, depending on whether the coveted position is that of governor or state attorney.

The need to end the misapplication of the death penalty in the United States has been amply demonstrated. Even the Subcommittee on Civil and Constitutional Rights of the US Congress said so quite explicitly in a report published on this topic in 1993. Having examined some forty recent cases of people who had been sentenced to death but then released because they were innocent, the authors of the report reached the following conclusion:

> Americans are justifiably concerned about the possibility that an innocent person may be executed. Capital punishment in the United States today provides no reliable safeguards against this danger. Errors can and have been made repeatedly in the trial of death penalty cases because of poor representation, racial prejudice, prosecutorial misconduct, or simply the presentation of erroneous evidence. Once convicted, a death row inmate faces serious obstacles in convincing any tribunal that he is innocent.[45]

In actual fact, the risk that an innocent person might be executed is not a concern for the majority of Americans. Indeed, the majority in this country appears to be more interested in restoring its segregationist tradition than in the number of innocent people executed every year. This hankering back is expressed more and more openly, legally validated and even orchestrated by the most senior court of the United States. "For example, in Board of Education of Oklahoma City Public Schools v Dowell (1992), the Court ruled that a district court decree ordering desegregation of public schools could be terminated, despite a new policy by the local school board in which half of the elementary schools would have almost entirely White or entirely Black enrolment.[46]" To the alert reader, it is immediately apparent that jurisprudence thus takes a huge, one-century leap backwards. The court revives its 1896 Plessy vs. Ferguson decision that upheld the constitutionality of segregationist laws that remained in force until 1954 at a time when memories of the Nuremberg segregationist laws and the destruction of non-Aryans were still fresh in people's minds and racial segregation had yet to be reinstated.

Fifty-eight years went by between the Plessy vs. Ferguson decision (ruling that racial segregation was constitutional) and the Brown vs. Board of Education decision (ruling that segregation in schools was unconstitutional). It took the Supreme Court far less time in 1992 to quash the 1954 decision and invalidate laws that banned segregation in public schools. The reasons for the Board of Education vs. Dowell judgment are found in the decision itself. "The Chief Justice wrote the majority opinion, finding that court orders arising out of Brown vs. Board of Education to prevent one-race schools were a temporary measure to remedy past discrimination.[47]" We remember that, at the time, Justice Rehnquist had brilliantly argued in favour of maintaining racial segregation in the constitutional charter. We also remember that when he was outvoted, the judge angrily expressed his powerlessness and warned that it was high time that the Court faced the fact that the White people of the south did not like coloured people.

The relentlessness of prosecutors

The tragic leap backwards that was taken in 1987 when the Supreme Court, in the McCleskey decision, publicly declared its acceptance of racial discrimination in the application of the death penalty on the grounds that manifest disparities in sentencing are inevitable in any criminal justice system has turned the American judicial system into an institution unique in the Western world. Here is a small selection among the numerous cases for which there is undisputed evidence. Any reader who wishes to investigate the sentencing and execution of innocents in the United Sates more thoroughly can usefully refer to Amnesty International's publications on the topic.

In October 1982, a Mexican national, Ricardo Adalpe Guerra, was found guilty of murdering a police officer, sentenced to death and sent to death row in Texas. After clamouring his innocence consistently for ten years, in 1992 he was granted a stay of execution, just 3 hours before it was planned to take place. "In 1994 a US District Judge threw out the conviction and ordered a new trial because of police and prosecutorial misconduct. The judge stated that police and prosecutors had intimidated witnesses into accusing Adalpe Guerra and had manipulated evidence to ensure a conviction." Two years later, this judgment was upheld in August 1996 by the Fifth Circuit Appeals Court and Adalpe Guerra was transferred to a detention centre to await retrial.

"However, when at pre-trial hearings the trial judge ruled that [...] there was "overwhelming evidence" that Adalpe Guerra was not the gunman; the Harris County District Attorney dropped the prosecution.[48]"

Adalpe Guerra was aged thirty-five when he was sentenced for a crime he had not committed. When he was released from prison at the end of a 15-year ordeal on death row in 1997 he was fifty.[49] Although it was established that the police and the district attorney had tampered with the evidence to secure a conviction, none of those responsible for such misconduct were ever prosecuted.

> In 1980, a 16-year-old White pupil was raped and murdered at a Texas school. The police suspected that the crime was committed by one of the school janitors. Of the five janitors, only Clarence Brandley was Black. On the day of the murder, Brandley and another janitor were interviewed by a police officer. According to the other janitor, the officer said, "One of you two is going to hang for this." Turning to Brandley he added, "since you're the nigger, you're elected." [...] His trial, composed of an all-White jury, resulted in a conviction and death sentence. In 1986, a woman approached the prosecutor claiming that her husband had confessed to the murder for which Brandley was sentenced to death. The prosecutor refused to act on the new information. Eventually, in 1990, after the unreliability of the evidence and testimony at the original trial had been conclusively established, Clarence Brandley was released from death row and his conviction was overturned.[50]

In spite of his misfortune, Brandley was "lucky" that it was incidentally discovered that there was a deliberate intention on the part of his tormentors to have him executed because he was Black. As usual, neither the police nor the district attorney were held accountable, although the judge that recommended his release wrote: "…the investigation was conducted not to solve the crime, but to convict Brandley. [...] The Court unequivocally concludes that the colour of Clarence Brandley's skin was a substantial factor which pervaded all aspects of the State's capital prosecution against him.[51]" Ten years on death row just for being Black and working in a school where a White girl was raped and murdered: a heavy penalty indeed.

It is telling that in 1994 Harry Blackmun, the United States Supreme Court's highest-ranking judge, said that "Even under the most sophisticated death penalty statutes, race continues to play a major role in determining who shall live and who shall die.[52]" To make matters worse, an additional hurdle that an innocent person sentenced to death must overcome is that the states that "impose death sentences mandate time limits on the admissibility of new exonerating evidence following a conviction.[53]" In Virginia, this time limit is 21 days!

Earl Washington is a Black man sentenced to death by a court in Virginia after being found guilty of raping and murdering a White teenager named Rebecca Williams in 1982.

> In October 1993 the Attorney General of Virginia ordered that a new form of DNA testing be carried out on a vaginal swab from the victim. The results raised strong doubts concerning Washington's guilt: since the DNA could not have come from him, another perpetrator must have been involved. The victim's dying testimony had been that she was attacked by a single assailant. But the new evidence could not be heard in court, under the conditions of Virginia's "21-day rule".[54]

In November 1998, during a conference held in Chicago where Amnesty International issued its report on the sentencing to death of innocents, Earl Washington was still in prison, five years after having been cleared by the DNA test.

Enquiries carried out by various organisations have uncovered a tendency for American authorities to use torture against murder suspects so as to extract confessions. It is often the case when evidence, either probative or rigged, is unavailable, the defendant is sentenced on the basis of confessions extracted by police officers in charge of interrogating him. This happened to Aaron Patterson, a Black man who was convicted and sentenced to death for the murder of an elderly couple. "No physical evidence linked Patterson to the crime; fingerprints and footprints from the crime scene did not belong to him and no eyewitnesses placed him there. He was convicted almost solely on the strength of a "confession" extracted by the officers interrogating him. Patterson alleges that he was tortured during the interrogation (that lasted twenty-five hours).[55]"

In its report on the sentencing to death of innocents, Amnesty International published Patterson's version. It is consistent with the information received from various sources by the organisation, according to which the detectives in Area Two in Chicago mistreated suspects to extract confessions from them.

> Other death row inmates have alleged that they were beaten into "confessing" to murders in Chicago. They include Ronald Jones, sentenced to death for rape and murder in 1989. Jones recently won a new trial after DNA testing established that semen found inside the victim was not his. The prosecution then suggested that the semen came from the victim having sex with her fiancé shortly before her murder and that Jones raped her but did not ejaculate. However, further DNA tests ruled out the fiancé as the source of the semen.[56]

Flying in the face of the obvious, the public attorney refused to let go of his prey. Ronald Jones, the seventy-ninth death row inmate to be declared innocent, was freed two years after his innocence had been unequivocally established and after spending 8 years awaiting execution in Illinois.[57]

Human rights not for all?

In the trials instituted by the district attorney of Cook County, Dennis Williams, Verneal Jimerson and two other young Blacks were found guilty of a crime they had not committed. These four boys were accused of murdering a couple in 1978 and sentenced to death at the end of a patently flawed trial.

> Very often, innocent people on death row have been spared only thanks to the untiring efforts of a few individuals who were ready to spend a considerable amount of their time, their energy and personal resources. This was notably the case of Verneal Jimerson and Dennis Williams. [...] Their attorneys had worked on the case free of charge for six years; journalism students from Northwestern University had uncovered evidence of the men's innocence as part of a class project.[58]

With the help of a private detective, the students discovered the identity of the true culprits much to the district attorney's displeasure. The latter nonetheless tried to hinder the release of these wrongly condemned boys.

When they were eventually released, in July 1996, someone asked Dennis Williams why, in his opinion, he had been unjustly condemned. "The police just picked up the first four young Black men they could find and that was it. They didn't care if we were guilty or innocent," he replied.[59]

Such relentless hounding by public prosecutors continue to produce cases of legal injustices to such an extent that the Justice of the Supreme Court Harry Blackmun, in spite of the fact that he had approved the death penalty in 1976, expressed a dissenting opinion at the Callins vs. Collins case in 1994, saying:

> Twenty years have passed since this Court declared that the death penalty must be imposed fairly, and with reasonable consistency, or not at all, [...] Despite the effort of the states and courts to devise legal formulas and procedural rules to meet this daunting challenge, the death penalty remains fraught with arbitrariness, discrimination, caprice, and mistake. [...] I feel morally and intellectually obligated simply to concede that the death penalty experiment has failed.[60]

One wonders how, in 1976, Justice Blackmun could believe that the new laws that restored capital punishment subject to them being applied "with discernment" would be enough to prevent arbitrary application of such punishment in the United States. Disillusioned by the result, he even added in his 1994 dissenting opinion: "From this day forward, I no longer shall tinker with the machinery of death."

In response to this, Mumia Abu-Jamal, who has been on death row since 1982, replied "His principled refusal to further 'tinker with the machinery of death' comes after the machine has been fine-tuned and stripped to its malevolent best, after all of its bugs have been purged and a pit crew installed to keep it running well into the next century.[61]"

In the United States, negrophobia is so widespread and its consequences so devastating that it goes so far as to make it possible for the defence council of a Black man accused of murder to mistake one brief for another and ask the jury to vote in favour of capital punishment.[62] "In California, Melvin Wade was represented by an attorney who used defamatory language against Blacks (including his client), who failed to present adequate evidence of the childhood abuse suffered by Wade, and who asked that his own client be sentenced to death". Wade was indeed sentenced to death.

> Examples of prejudiced representation abound from across the USA. For example, Ramon Mata, a Hispanic man was convicted and sentenced to death in Texas in 1986 by an all-White jury after his attorney, in agreement

with the prosecutor, consented to the removal of all potential non-White jurors. Although the trial judge was aware of this highly irregular arrangement, the appellate courts ruled that Mata's right to a fair trial had not been impaired [...] During closing arguments, Gary Burris, a Black man, executed in Indiana on 20 November 1997, was described to the jury by his White attorney as an "insignificant, snivelling little street person".[63]

In 1998, during the "Save Mumia Abu-Jamal" campaign, the state-owned radio channel France-Culture broadcast a programme on the death penalty featuring Julia Wright. André Kaspi, a historian specialised in the United States, in a very even, academic voice, explained that one might not agree with the application of the death penalty but that in the United States a large majority of both Whites and people from ethnic minorities were in favour of capital punishment. Moreover, he stressed, the judicial system in that country offers mechanisms that enable defendants to seek all the remedies that ensure their rights to adequate defence. Perhaps Professor Kaspi is unaware that

> while there are a multitude of factors contributing to mistaken death sentences in the USA, a deadly pattern emerges from the cases of individuals who were later exonerated. These recurring factors include the inadequate performance of defence attorneys and misconduct by prosecuting authorities eager to gain a conviction at any cost.[64]

In most cases, innocents who are released after being wrongly sentenced to death owed their freedom to lawyers affiliated to pro-bono post-conviction defender organisations. These PCDOs were established in 1988 by Congress to guarantee that people sentenced to death are provided with adequate defence before federal and state courts. When Kaspi sang the praises of the guarantees afforded by the United States judicial system, he was perhaps forgetting that "in 1995, Congress voted to eliminate the $20 million annual budget for PCDOs nationwide, leaving the majority of the centres with insufficient funding and forcing their closure.[65]" Kaspi's attitude is in stark contrast with his demands for transparency when in 1982 he complained that the truth about the Jews during the Nazi period was hidden from view and that textbooks, encyclopaedias, history books and plays said nothing about their fate.

At the beginning of January 2000, legislators in the State of Florida voted "by an overwhelming majority in favour of allowing lethal injections to replace the electric chair, whose faulty operation had been responsible for some unfortunate incidents lately, as a method of execution.[66]" This decision by the two chambers of the State of Florida is considered a step forward because henceforth death row inmates will be "free to choose" between the electric chair and a lethal injection. Black elected representatives attempted to bring the "problem of racial inequality in the face of capital punishment" into the discussion. Their attempt was drowned in the general enthusiasm stirred up among the majority by Governor Bush[67] when he offered to "shorten the time for appeals and so reduce the time convicts spend on death row.[68]" Florida hence entered the new millennium with a debate on the technicalities of putting human beings to death and the quickest way of speeding up executions.

For a long time, I have felt strongly about differentiating between the often bloodthirsty politics of the United States and the immense majority of the population in that country which – or so I believed – could not be held accountable for the injustices committed by its government, whether through its internal or its foreign policies. However, to maintain its policy of domination, as Herbert I. Schiller, professor of communication at the University of California, San Diego, notes, the government of the United States requires "the active or passive support of some 270 million Americans […] which never fails it." In defence of the Americans, it can be said that this support is "the product of a system that combines indoctrination, starting from the cradle, with a practice of selection and retention of information that is aimed at maintaining and reinforcing the United States' enterprise of planetary domination.[69]"

After all, the United States Constitution establishes the Electoral College in charge of appointing the President – as reflected in the episode of the face-off between Bush and Gore in Florida – not on the basis of the aggregate number of votes all over the country, but by banishing certain human groups considered to be racially inferior from the ranks of humanity: according to the 1790 census, the population of the United Sates came to approximately 4 million, of whom more than 750,000 were Black and considered to be less than human. These 19 per cent of the population, largely in the southern States, belonged to the White citizens who demanded and obtained a constitutional guarantee allowing them to maintain slavery. The Electoral College therefore took into account the number of slaves owned by each citizen to establish the total number of representatives to which each State was entitled. The 1787 Constitution thus established the principle whereby a Black counted for only 3/5ths of a White. This monstrous equation is still the basis for calculating the political weight carried by the former slave states. Section 2 of Article 1 of the Constitution of the United States indeed lays down that: "Representatives and direct Taxes shall be apportioned among the several States which may be included within this Union, according to their respective Numbers, which shall be determined by adding to the whole Number of free Persons, including those bound to Service for a Term of Years, and excluding Indians not taxed, three fifths of all other Persons." While the wording allows for Blacks who belong to their owners, it quite simply erases Native Americans. They cannot be taken into consideration because they are not part of the human livestock owned by American citizens.

After denying the humanity of non-Whites in this way, the Constitution offered as a model of democracy to the world concerns itself with settling the question of the representation of slave states in presidential elections. Their political weight must take into account a sort of qualitative majority, i.e., the volume of the human livestock in the hands of each owner, the number of citizens being incremented on the basis of the number of slaves owned in a set proportion: one Black is worth three-fifths of a White. This shameful, biased demographic basis continues to weigh in the balance between the states and on presidential elections. This system, built on the foundation of exclusion of non-Whites and still true to that foundation today, continues to be called a democracy.

Notes

1. Franklin, John Hope and Moss, Alfred Jr., *From Slavery to Freedom. A History of African Americans*, McGraw Hill, Eighth Edition, 2000. p. 214.
2. Ibid, p. 221.
3. Ibid, pp. 392–393.
4. Grotesque, one might say. Horrendous too. It is enough to take a look at *Lynching Photography in America*. For instance, the picture of Jesse Washington's dead body, lynched on May 16, 1916 in Robinson, Texas. His mutilated body, hanging from the branch of a tree is surrounded by a crowd merrily posing for the camera. On the other side of the photograph, used as a postcard and sent by Joe Meyer to his parents, we see written: "This is the barbecue we had last night. My picture is to the left with a cross over it. Your son Joe."
5. Tocqueville de, Alexis, *Democracy in America*, Volume I. Retrieved January 12, 2011 from xroads.virginia.edu/~HYPER/DETOCK/ch4_06.htm
6. Hitler, Adolph, *Mein Kampf*, 1926. Retrieved June 8, 2010 from http://history.hanover.edu/courses/excerpts/111hitler.html
7. See Chapter 9 and after.

8. Behar, Henri, *Le Monde*, April 10, 1997, p. 12 (translated from the French).
9. Dred Scott vs. Sanford Ruling of the US Supreme Court (1857). Retrieved June 8, 2010 from http://www.encyclopedia.com/doc/1G2-3498200072.html
10. Amnesty International, *Killing with Prejudice: Race and the Death Penalty in the USA*, Retrieved April 15, 2010 from http://www.amnesty.org/en/library/info/AMR51/052/1999/en
11. For further insight into the attention paid by the leaders of the Third Reich to how the Anglo-Saxon racial policy towards non-Whites was formulated in legal terms, see Alexandre Kum'a N'Dumbe, *Hitler voulait l'Afrique*, op. cit., p. 241 et seq.
12. Franklin, op. cit., p. 446.
13. Ibid, p. 478.
14. Kluger, Richard, *Simple Justice*, quoted by Amnesty International, in op. cit. Retrieved April 15, 2010 from http://www.amnesty.org/en/library/info/AMR51/052/1999/en.
15. Abu-Jamal, Mumia, *Live from Death Row*, New York: Perennial 2002, p. 27.
16. Rise, Eric W., *The Martinville Seven: Race, Rape and Capital Punishment*, quoted by Amnesty International. Retrieved April 15, 2010 from http://www.amnesty.org/en/library/info/AMR51/052/1999/en
17. Amnesty International, op. cit. Retrieved April 15, 2010 from http://www.amnesty.org/en/library/info/AMR51/052/1999/en
18. Amnesty International, *United States of America: The Death Penalty*, Amnesty International Publications, 1987, p. 54.
19. Ibid, pp. 39–40.
20. Ibid, pp. 55–57.
21. Ibid, pp. 57–59.
22. Amnesty International, USA, *Rights For All: Human Rights in the United States of America*, AI Index AMR 51/40/98. Retrieved April 15, 2010 from http://www.amnesty.org/en/library/asset/AMR51/040/1998/en/ac314ed9-d9ea-11dd-af2b-b1f6023af0c5/amr510401998en.html
23. Amnesty International, *Killing with Prejudice: Race and the Death Penalty in the USA*. Retrieved April 15, 2010 from http://www.amnesty.org/en/library/info/AMR51/052/1999/en
24. Study conducted by Jeffrey Pokorak, professor at St. Mary's University Law School (Texas) and quoted by Amnesty International, Ibid.
25. Amnesty International, Ibid.
26. Amnesty International, Ibid.
27. Amnesty International, USA, *Rights For All: Human Rights in the United States of America*, AI Index AMR 51/40/98, op. cit.

28. Amnesty International, *United States of America: The Death Penalty*, Amnesty International Publications, 1987, pp. 59–61.
29. National Institute of Justice, Washington, *Postconviction DNA Testing: Recommendations for Handling Requests*. pdf file downloaded June 8, 2010 at http://www.ojp.usdoj.gov/nij/pubs-sum/177626.htm.
30. In *Le Monde,* Oct. 16, 1999, p. 2.
31. Amnesty International, *Killing with Prejudice: Race and the Death Penalty in the USA*, op. cit.
32. Ibid.
33. Ibid.
34. He most certainly fulfilled the hopes of his constituency since, after he took office in mid-January 1995, Thomas Ridge has had the pleasure of signing 170 death warrants.
35. Amnesty International, "United States of America: The death penalty – Warren McCleskey (Georgia)." Retrieved April 15, 2010 from http://www.amnesty.org/en/library/info/AMR51/024/1991/en.
36. Amnesty International, *Killing with Prejudice: Race and the Death Penalty in the USA*, op. cit.
37. Amnesty International, USA, *Rights For All: Human Rights in the United States of America*, AI Index AMR 51/40/98, op. cit.; and *Killing with Prejudice: Race and the Death Penalty in the USA*, op. cit.
38. Biography of Justice Powell, quoted in Amnesty International, *Killing with Prejudice: Race and the Death Penalty in the USA*, op. cit.
39. Ibid.
40. Amnesty International, USA, "A Macabre Assembly Line of Death", *Death Penalty Developments in 1997*. Retrieved April 15, 2010 from http://www.amnesty.org/en/library/info/ AMR51/020/1998/en.
41. Ibid.
42. Finkelstein & Birn, op. cit, reference to Tolnay, Stewart and Beck, E.M., *A Festival of Violence: An Analysis of Southern Lynching,* University of Illinois Press, Chicago, 1995, p.23.
43. Litwack, Leon, *Without Sanctuary: Lynching Photography in America,* Sante Fe: Twin Palms Publishers, 2000, p. 9.
44. In Hobsbawm, Eric, *The Age of Extremes*, New York: Vintage Books, 1996, p. 120.
45. Amnesty International USA, *Fatal Flaws: Innocence and the Death Penalty in the USA,* Retrieved April 15, 2010 from http://www.amnesty.org/en/library/info/AMR51/069/1998/en.
46. Amnesty International, *Killing with Prejudice: Race and the Death Penalty in the USA,* op. cit.
47. Ibid.

48. Amnesty International, USA: "A Macabre Assembly Line of Death": *Death Penalty Developments in 1997*, op. cit.
49. Ibid.
50. Amnesty International USA, *Fatal Flaws: Innocence and the Death Penalty in the USA*. This report was published at a memorable conference held in Chicago in November 1998, attended by nearly half of the 75 prisoners who since 1976 had been wrongfully sentenced and released from American death rows.
51. Ibid.
52. Supreme Court of the United States, Callins vs. Collins, 114 S. Ct. 1127, 1135 (1994) (Blackmun, J. dissenting from the denial of certiorari). Retrieved April 22, 2010 from http://www.law.cornell.edu/supct/html/93-7054.ZA1.html
53. Amnesty International USA, *Fatal Flaws: Innocence and the Death Penalty in the USA*, op. cit.
54. Ibid.
55. Ibid.
56. Ibid.
57. In *L'Actu*, May 21, 1999, Issue 193, p. 2.
58. Amnesty International USA, *Fatal Flaws: Innocence and the Death Penalty in the USA*, op. cit.
59. Amnesty International, *Killing with Prejudice: Race and the Death Penalty in the USA*, op. cit.
60. Supreme Court of the United States, Callins vs. Collins, 114 S. Ct. 1127, 1135 (1994) (Blackmun, J. dissenting from the denial of *certiorari*). Retrieved April 22, 2010 from http://www.law.cornell.edu/supct/html/93-7054.ZA1.html
61. Abu-Jamal, op. cit., p. 94.
62. Amnesty International, *Killing with Prejudice: Race and the Death Penalty in the USA*, op. cit.
63. Ibid, See also USA, *The Death Penalty in Georgia: Racist, Arbitrary and Unfair*, AI Index: AMR 51/25/96.
64. Amnesty International USA, *Fatal Flaws: Innocence and the Death Penalty in the USA*, op. cit.
65. Ibid.
66. Kauffmann, Sylvie, "La chaise électrique ne sera plus le seul moyen d'exécution en Floride", in *Le Monde*, January 9–10, 2000.
67. One should remember that in 1994 his brother, George W. Bush, who at the time was running for governor of the state of Texas, campaigned in favour of lowering the eligibility age for the death penalty from seventeen to sixteen, according to Marie-Agnès Combesque, a journalist for *Le Monde diplomatique* quoted in an Appendix to the French edition of *Live from Death Row: Mumia Abu-Jamal, En Direct du couloir de la mort*, Paris 1996, p. 128–129.

68. Kauffmann, op. cit., p. 2.
69. Schiller, Herbert I., "Décervelage à l'américaine", in *Le Monde diplomatique*, August 1999, p. 15.

9

The Consequences of Normalisation

Always liable for extermination

Colombia, a former Spanish colony, together with Venezuela and Argentina, are among the first countries in the Americas to free themselves from Spanish domination. Although the struggle against colonial domination was waged by all social groups (Native Americans, Blacks, Mestizos and Creoles), the benefits of independence were rapidly monopolised by the Creole elites who worked hard to maintain the status quo. People referred to as Criollos were Spaniards born in the New World. They had nothing against the mass deportation of Africans to the Americas, or keeping them in bondage, nor did they object to the policy of casting out the Native Americans. Had the Crown applied a less foolish policy to the Creoles, they certainly would not have rebelled. Even Creoles who descended from Native Americans on their mother's side identified with Spain and were just as contemptuous of Native Americans as they were of Blacks. To their great frustration, the Crown did not allow them to share in the privileges and responsibilities apportioned to metropolitan Spaniards alone, who hence monopolised the levers of power. The local elites found the overt contempt that metropolitan Spaniards displayed towards them hard to take. Matters were made worse by the fact that the Spaniards from Europe dispatched there by the Crown were often not as cultured as these Creoles they despised because they were born in the Americas rather than in Spain. After having tried in vain to get involved in public affairs, the Creoles realised that independence was the only way they could gain power. Hence their sudden discovery of the grandeur of patriotism that motivated them to fight bravely for their country's independence.

Once they had removed the Spaniards, the patriots maintained the institutions that had been set up by their predecessors and reneged on the promises they had made to Blacks and Native Americans in consideration of their contribution to the war effort against colonial domination. This is how, following independence, Blacks were entered as assets in the inventory of the young Republic of Colombia, i.e., the property of the Creoles who took over the positions of power from the Spaniards. As for the Native Americans, in the new republic, they were given the status of perpetual minors, precluded from ever coming of age.

Five centuries after the arrival of Spaniards in the Americas, indigenous peoples are still liable to be exterminated because, in North, Central and South America, there are too many ignorant fools who still fail to understand that Native Americans are human beings and killing them is prohibited by law.

"La matanza de La Rubiera", i.e., the massacre of La Rubiera, named after the farm where it took place, is a story that will go down in the judicial history of Colombia for a long time to come. This particular killing occurred in 1967, forty-eight years after independence. What is the particular relevance of this story compared to the many other massacres that have been perpetrated since the mid-1980s? What does white supremacy have to do with the fact that Colombians slaughter one another at an alarming rate? It seems to me that this episode comprehensively answers those questions.

On December 25, 1967, Anselmo Aguirre, a Venezuelan, and Marcelino Jimenez, a Colombian, are out fishing. They see three canoes with eighteen Native Americans aboard, no doubt from the village of El Manguito nearby. Anselmo Aguirre suggests to his companion that they should "kill those creatures there on the spot." Marcelino Jimenez thinks about this for a few seconds and then says: "Not here, some of them might escape." Aguirre and Jimenez quickly put together an effective plan. They approach the Native Americans, make friendly conversation and before departing invite them to the La Rubiera farm where, they promise, they will receive gifts and a generous meal. Back at the farm, they warn Luis Enrique Morin, the overseer: "There are a few Native Americans coming, for sure to steal our cassava and pigs. We should kill them." They assemble the other employees, Elio Torrealba, Celestino Rodriguez, Eurodo Gonzalez, Luis Ramon Garrido, Cupertino Sogamosa and Pedro Ramon Santana. Together, they agree on a plan.

On the afternoon of 27 December, the Native Americans reach La Rubiera. They ask for food and sit down in front of the large house. The two women who work at the farm, Maria Gregoria Lopez and Maria Helena Jimenez, go to the kitchen to prepare a meal.

They return with a huge plate of rice indicating to the Native Americans that they should eat. At the agreed signal, the slaughter begins. Only two Native Americans, Antuco and Ceballos, are able to escape. They hide in a tree from where they can follow the progress of the massacre. The news reaches El Manguito through them. They file a complaint. The murdered Native Americans are Ramon aged 30, Luis aged 20, Cirila aged 45, Luisa aged 40, Chain aged 19, Doris aged 30, Carmelina aged 20, Guafaro aged 15, Bengua aged 14, Aruse aged 10, Julio aged 8, Aiddé aged 7, Milo aged 4, Alberto aged 3 and a baby still suckling his mother Doris.

Eighteen days later, an investigating team led by Judge Carlos Gutierrez Torres goes to the La Rubiera farm. What follows are the confessions of the perpetrators of the massacre, taken from the book *Colombia amarga* written by journalist Germán Castro Caycedo.[1]

To the investigating judge, Luis Morin states:

> The meal was served at the table in a large platter because they did not need cutlery. Indians eat with their fingers and if there is soup they don't need a spoon. When they went to the table, I went into the sitting room and knocked three times, which was the agreed signal. The others then went out by the door and the windows. That is when the Indians tried to escape but then we began to kill them. Well, the first one I killed was a small Indian. I dealt him a blow with my machete. The second one, I killed with Garrido using a pistol. The third one I killed with Anselmo Aguirre: that one was injured and so I stabbed him with a knife. I shot him twice with the revolver. I also killed the little Indian girl with a shot in the back ...

As for Cupertino Sogamoso, who was the last to come out of hiding to join in the slaughter, he declared:

> I had a club and ran after an Indian who had been injured by a bullet. I hit him on the side with the club to knock him over. I stepped into this Indian's path and finished him off by stabbing him. After that, I ran after a little girl and stabbed her in the belly. She fell down just like that.

A little girl who was trying to hide beneath a table falls into Eurodo Gonzalez's hands. He declares:

> She got in my way so I hit her on the head with my machete and she fell down. I then struck her three times with my machete to finish her off. To begin with she moaned because she was dying and that is when I hit her three times with the machete. This little Indian girl was around 8 years old. When I went back to the house, I came face to face with another girl who wanted to escape through a gap in the fence. But I quickly caught up with

> her and hit her on the head with the club and she fell to the ground. And there, on the ground, I hit her with the club four times in succession and she died. That one didn't moan. After the first blow I gave her, she stopped moving. She was more or less 18 years old, dressed in yellow and black... The first Indian women I killed was wearing a wrap. Afterwards I sat down at table, ate supper and went to bed.

Some of the Native Americans had a hard time dying and their moans could be heard in the house. "So then," states Luis Morin again,

> Anselmo called me to deliver the final blow to the wounded Indian behind the house. I went to see the Indian who was lying on his stomach and I could see he was doing his best to stand up; so I stabbed him in the back with a knife and punctured his left lung. I pushed the knife in four fingers deep and so the Indian turned over with all fours in the air and finally died... This one was about 24 years old. But I want to add that I killed the little Indian boy who was roughly 8 years old because I saw he was still alive and since I had no bullets left, I hit him with a club too. I managed to catch a little Indian girl aged more or less 7 who was running away fast, but I hit her first on the head and she fell to the ground. Then I finished her off. I didn't know it was wrong to kill Indians.

The next morning, they hid the corpses because even though the Native Americans are peaceful, it is better for them not to find out what happened to their beloved ones. The killers did not realise that Antuco and Ceballos had escaped. Using four mules, they hauled away the corpses and chose a place where they set them in a pile. Maria Helena Jimenez remembers: "When we were fastening the corpses to move them, I heard a little Indian girl moaning because she had been stabbed in the chest. Then Elio Torrealba finished her off with a blow of the machete on the head, on her forehead and after that she didn't budge."

And since she had to help to haul away the corpses of another native and another woman, she adds:

> He was already old, 40 or 45 years, and quite tall. He wore trousers and a shirt but I don't remember the colour of his skin because this creature was very dirty. The woman was a fairly old Indian, 38 or so. She was wounded by a bullet that had entered through her back and exited through her belly. We roped them together by the legs so as to drag them away, and we stacked them about one metre high. The small ones were placed on top of the pile, above all the other corpses. The farm men went to fetch dry wood that they threw onto the bodies. They added straw too and then sprinkled

gasoline over them and set them on fire. It took more than a day to burn them... Then we mixed them with the bones of dead cattle so as not to draw suspicion from other Indians. Eighteen days later, the government came along and arrested us.

And indeed, they were arrested and held in custody at the prison of Villavicencio. As is usual in an investigation, the investigating judge questioned the suspects several times. Here are some excerpts:

> Judge Gutierrez Torrez: You don't think killing Indians is a crime?
>
> Accused Cupertino Sogamoso: No. I didn't think it was bad to kill them since they were Indians. Of course, the Indians in our parts are not very aggressive. They won't hurt people but they kill the animals.
>
> Judge Gutierrez Torres: What motivated you to kill these Indians?
>
> Accused Eudoro Gonzalez: Because we were told that they were likely to steal from us. Of course, when they came they seemed friendly. They greeted us and asked us if there was any food.
>
> Judge Gutierrez Torres: Were they carrying any weapons?
>
> Accused Eudoro Gonzalez: No, there was just one who carried a knife. None of the others had anything.
>
> Judge Gutierrez Torres: Had you already killed other Indians before this?
>
> Accused Elio Torrealba: Yes, in 1960 I killed 6 Indians and buried them in a place called El Garcero.
>
> Judge Gutierrez Torres: Who, among the people you know, have taken part in massacres of Indians?
>
> Accused Elio Torrealba: Rosito Arenas who lives in Mata Azul close to Lorza, José Parra, Deca de Lorza and Esteban Torrealba, my uncle.
>
> Judge Gutierrez Torres: Is it customary in this area to kill Indians?
>
> Accused Eudoro Gonzalez: I heard that in the past Mr Tomas Jara ordered the killing of Indians. That's why I killed those Indians because I knew the government had no interest in them.
>
> Judge Gutierrez Torres: Why did you slaughter these natives?
>
> Accused Pedro Ramon Santana: Because I didn't know it was wrong to kill Indians and that we could be punished. If I'd known I would never have done it.

It is the inevitable consequence of the normalisation of the destruction of the Native Americans over the centuries that their lives should be so depreciated.

Who are they?

Who are these men who killed sixteen peaceful, defenceless indigenous peoples in cold blood? They come from some of the most disadvantaged social strata in Colombia. These people are peasants who are born, live, work and die without once seeing a doctor or a nurse. All they have ever known is the land they do not own where they toil day after day until their premature deaths.

They have no idea that they are entitled to a few days' holiday or that they should be paid a pension. They do not know how to read or write and cannot identify their own names. Electricity and running water were things unknown to them before they were taken into custody at Villavicencio prison.

They conscientiously kept to the rules they were taught as children. For instance, fear of God. Stealing, even to feed themselves, was unthinkable because at a very early age they learned that their master's property is as sacred as God. They also learned that they should not kill anybody and that killing is a serious sin. These very simple souls are incapable of wrongdoing. It is just that, for centuries now, they have internalised the idea that the Native Americans are not Christians and so killing them is not sinful. From one generation to the next, they learn that Native Americans are vermin, that they are a true scourge. This explains the "naivety" of these men when representatives of the law came to La Rubiera to conduct the investigation. When questioning began, they all tried to win credit for killing the most Indians because they sincerely believed "that the government was going to reward them." Judge Gutierrez Torres could not believe his ears or eyes. He never forgot his first conversation with the accused Luis Morin: "Doctor, don't forget, I was the one who killed the one by the chicken coop… as well as the other one close to the kitchen. And I was the one to finish off the one right by the fence: two and a half are mine, Doctor!"

When it gradually begins to dawn on the suspects that they would not be rewarded for their "good work" and instead perhaps be punished, they literally collapsed. It just did not make sense to them. They became totally disorientated. Being illiterate does not mean one has no standards or values. Their confusion was pitiful. Weighed down by sorrow and unable to comprehend how they came into this misfortune, the prisoners remained as polite as they always had been. Even the prison authorities considered them with a mixture of pity and sympathy. A committee was formed by a group of charitable people to seek permission from the authorities to teach the prisoners to read and write.

Four and a half years after the La Rubiera massacre when the trial before the court was about to begin, these people's vision of the world and their perception of what they were experiencing had changed enormously. Before they were brought before the court, Germán Castro Caycedo managed to interview them. These are some excerpts:

> Castro Caycedo: What do think of what happened at La Rubiera now?
>
> Luis Morin: Very differently from what I thought before. This time spent in prison has been very useful to me. I didn't know how all these laws worked before even though I thought I did.
>
> Castro Caycedo: What did you think of the Indians?
>
> Luis Morin: I thought that it was a good opportunity to kill them. But now, I know it is a very bad thing to do.
>
> Castro Caycedo: What were you taught about the Indians?
>
> Luis Morin: The truth is that out there they're considered as wild animals.
>
> Castro Caycedo: Who taught you that the Indians were animals?
>
> Luis Morin: To tell the truth, I learned that when I was very little. I was taught that they are very different from us in the way they dress and all the rest too. But today, thanks to civilisation, we know that they are as Christian as we are. And that I did not suspect before.
>
> Castro Caycedo: Why did you kill those natives?
>
> Pedro Ramon Santana: Because I was always taught they were vermin and that they did harm to people. I was taught to hate them because, over there, there is no civilisation like here. But when you start to think, you realise what life means. We live down there in a forsaken region. I have come to realise this here in prison because I have begun to overcome my ignorance.
>
> Castro Caycedo: Why did you allow yourselves to be arrested?
>
> Luis Morin: Because we didn't know that to kill Indians was a crime. So we stayed on at the farm, all of us going about our business for the eighteen following days. When we were arrested, we thought it was a hoax.

We were asked questions and we answered the truth. We denied nothing, we hid nothing. Why? Because we didn't know we had done anything wrong. But now, things are different... Now, we have thought about this and we realise we committed a crime... Here in the prison, we have learnt a great deal from those who are here because they stole or for other reasons, and we now understand that we lived far away from civilisation, that we were completely absent.

Castro Caycedo: How did you perceive Colombia as a whole before?

Luis Morin: The way I saw it, everything was like it is in my region, because from one village to the next, the road is a very very long one, and they were all in ruins. But here I discovered that there are some more developed villages and I realised that one can devote one's time to reading the newspapers and journals. Here, we have realised that to get on in life, you have to have an education. Here in the prison, we looked for teachers to teach us, because it is a sorry state of affairs when you have to sign papers using your finger prints. The time I had to sign the attorney's proxy, I didn't know how to write my name. Nowadays, that is no longer a problem for us.

Castro Caycedo: Do you resent your parents for not having sent you to school?

Luis Morin: No, I am not angry against my parents because they would have sent me to school. But unfortunately, the area was very much neglected and abandoned. There was no school... No, what I would say today is that I cannot forgive the government for forsaking our region, its indifference towards us, even though our region too is part of Colombia. Why were we forgotten like that?

Castro Caycedo: What do you think today concerning your three children?

Luis Morin: I hope for just one thing for them: for them to get a real education and learn a lot, learn and learn. But I am very poor. When I get out of here, I will work so that they can study... Several years ago, before coming here, I didn't think we could be educated because I thought we were too stupid for that. Now I know that we can, that it is possible and that getting an education is the only thing that can be of any use to us...

Castro Caycedo: When you were little, what did you hope to become later?

Luis Morin: I wanted to learn how to break in horses because ever since I was born I saw the men in my region breaking in horses. I didn't know that a book could be useful. Imagine, sitting down to read but not knowing how to get a bull down or how to swim.

Castro Caycedo: Why did you kill these Indians?

Luis Ramon Garrido: I only killed the little Indian girl and the two Indians who were already half dead. But you know, when I was little, what I saw was that everyone killed Indians. Down there in the whole region, the police, the army and the navy killed Indians and there was never any punishment. We are the only ones that have to pay.

Castro Caycedo: What have you learnt in prison?

Marcelino Jimenez: That if we had received an education, we would not have been down there, on a remote farm toiling away because we were ignorant. Now I realise that we lived in a different world to farming. Out there, just producing a little food for yourselves is back-breaking. You have to work day and night, starting at one in the morning non-stop. On the other hand, here in the city, there is electricity, water from taps and also cars. Out there, it costs a huge amount just to leave the village.

Castro Caycedo: What do you think?

Maria Gregoria Lopez: The Indians have always been nasty to us. I think it is time for me to be released because I have greatly suffered from being confined here.

Castro Caycedo: Do you know how to read?

Maria Gregoria: No, sir. I am learning but what's happening is that I have always been a bit slow on the uptake. Learning has required huge efforts. I learn to count but it doesn't sink in. For heaven's sake, Doctor, don't ask me anything else. I'm too stupid.

Castro Caycedo: And you, do you know how to read?

MJimenez: Yes, I do. It took me eight months to learn to read. Before I knew neither how to read nor write because out there, there was no school to go out and learn.

Castro Caycedo: What do you think of the Indians now?

Jimenez: Well! Now I think they are our equals because they are people. The only thing they are lacking is a mind. Because they don't have the same intelligence as us. They are equal to a Christian but they are lacking something we have, which is civilisation.

Castro Caycedo: Since when have you become civilised?

Maria Helena Jimenez: Well, here in prison. Now I already know how to read and write.

These statements speak for themselves, but a few remarks are in order. Between January 1968, when they were arrested and questioned by the investigating judge, and May 1972, when the journalist Germán Castro Caycedo was able to interview them, their way of reasoning had changed. They lost none of their spontaneity. Thanks to the efforts of the people who taught these peasants to read and write and sought to educate them, their perception of the Native Americans was somewhat altered. Nonetheless, what Luis Morin, Pedro Ramon Santana, Ramon Garrido, Marcelino Jimenez, Maria Helena Jimenez, and Maria Gregoria Lopez say does not express a radically changed perception of the Native Americans. What they have really acquired is knowledge about the judicial consequences of murdering Native Americans. In other words, these peasants followed the same pattern as the rest of their society: They still do not see Native Americans as fellow human beings or still less their brothers, but that is no longer sufficient grounds for killing them. Others cannot be killed just because they are inferior; and by the way killing them is prohibited by law. The fact that we have reached a stage of human development that permits some culturally backward people to be taught that it is not good to kill Native Americans is perhaps reason to rejoice or at least something we can chalk up as a victory. The murderous ideology that white supremacy continues to rage and refuses to die. This, is a spectre that haunts me.

The victims of the victims

In 1972, before the trial began, the disciplinary board of the Villavicencio prison where these prisoners were held together with four hundred and seventy others sent a report to its senior authorities stating that the behaviour of the La Rubiera prisoners had been exemplary. As the trial date loomed closer, tensions were mounting among those who for reasons of humanity or as a matter of principle take an interest in those who are at the greatest disadvantage. The La Rubiera massacre was a troublesome affair and opinions diverged. The torturers were the victims of a system where inequality, social injustice and misery at its most sinister are the pillars of the economic and political power of the ruling class that is convinced of the legitimacy of its privileges and always poised to defend them using any means, however violent or expeditious. Sentencing the La Rubiera defendants to a long prison term was not therefore the most effective way of getting to the root of the evil. Even the judge who had investigated the case and was no longer in charge of it at the time of the trial said: "Condemning these people will not solve a problem that was born when our history began. Instead, the State should develop social action in that environment."

When Gutierrez Torres, who by then was a member of the public prosecutor's office at Villavicencio, says that the problem was born "when our history began," he is – unwittingly – reinforcing what everybody learns at school, i.e., that the history of America began when the Whites got there. The implication is that those who were there before played no active part in their history, and their existence, if established, was meaningful only in relation to the newcomers. That being said, it is very commendable that this judge dared to posit a causal relationship which though obvious is often left unsaid. And he goes even further: "Those who in this case seek out objective reality will find that this is not a recent phenomenon but a problem that began in 1492 and has continued to exist throughout the life of our institutions."

When the Creole elites rid themselves of colonial domination, the departing colonisers did not take their prejudices with them. These had already widely permeated colonial society. The La Rubiera criminals, like all the peoples of South America, are, to varying degrees, of mixed Native Americans, White and Black descent. Poorly educated people are less likely to realise that they descend from those Native Americans that they have despised ever since childhood. This is what makes the words of Maria Helena Jimenez, herself a mestiza descended from Native Americans, so unbearable.

The discussions surrounding the La Rubiera massacre remained confined to the more militant segments of progressive circles. Nonetheless, the debate was harrowing. Even those who called for exemplary punishment knew that the greatest share of guilt fell upon the state. To hold the state responsible meant forfeiting requital from flesh-and-blood individuals. Defence counsel sought compassion from the jury asking its members to give the defendants an opportunity to be socially rehabilitated. On 27 June, 1972, a civilian jury, in conscience, determined that the defendants were innocent and they were acquitted. The verdict, which caused great indignation among Native Americans and their supporters, gave rise to a major problem. Since time immemorial killing Native Americans was commonplace, as simple as lynching Blacks in the United States. But this time there had been an investigation. To acquit the perpetrators on the grounds that at the time of the deed they did not know that killing Native Americans was a crime created a situation even more untenable than if there had been no investigation at all. Counsel for the plaintiff appealed and a re-trial was conducted eighteen months later in another town. At the end of the second trial on November 6, 1973, the defendants, with the exception of the two women, were sentenced to twenty four years' imprisonment to be served in full. Appearances were saved. The advocacy groups for Native Americans could not uphold that exterminating Native Americans in Colombia is not punishable by law.

The prejudices inherited from the conquest and colonial domination continue to exist. The stereotypes which, ever since the Whites came to the Americas, have portrayed Native Americans as the lowest of the lowly whom no one – not even the most deprived – wants to resemble still prevail. In 1980, on Bogotá, Colombia's capital city, small illustrated notices were displayed in public transportation vehicles and stations urging travellers to be well-mannered. They bore these words: *No sea indio* (Don't be Indian). It is common to hear: *Sea negro pero decente* (You can't help being Black, but at least be decent). There is a song with a refrain that says: *Aqui donde Usted me ve, soy un Negro decente, yo sé respetar la gente* (Here, where I stand, I am a decent Black. I know how to respect people). People are heard to say in fun: "What is even more grotesque than an affluent Black: an Indian wearing a tie."

The absence of Native Americans in their own history is just one of the consequences of the normalisation of the atrocities to which they fall prey and which endures today. This normalisation has been so successful and Native Americans have been so completely evicted that even as consistent a humanist as Hobsbawm, whose moral integrity and intellectual honesty together with his qualities as a researcher have been amply demonstrated, nonetheless wrote in good faith: "To this day the Civil War of 1861–1865 remains the bloodiest conflict in U.S. history.[2]" It is as if the history of the United States was just the history of the Europeans who settled there. In actual fact, the history of that country involves the destruction of several million children, men and women who made the mistake of not being European and hence paid the price of European domination with their lives, true to the very Anglo-Saxon conviction that "a good Indian is a dead Indian."

Ideological lies, once they are draped in the neutral apparel of scientific truth, become fearsomely efficient as a result of the credibility and prestige generally associated with the scientific approach, as if researchers working in the different areas of science were not themselves dependent and often prisoners of the social and cultural representations and mind-sets they inherit.

Take the very respectable *Encyclopaedia Universalis*. In version 4 (corrected and updated in 1998), under the article "United States History," the editors shamelessly state: "The history of the United States is the account of an extremely rapid ascent of colonies that were under British domination to the status of leading world power [...] This is a unique example in history.[3]" Ideological clichés become scientific swindles.

Notes

1. All quotes taken from the book by Germán Castro Caycedo, *Colombia amarga*, Bogota, 1986, pp. 45–51.
2. In Hobsbawm, Eric, *The Age of Extremes*, New York, Vintage Books, 1996, p. 44.
3. *Encyclopædia Universalis*, Cd-Rom version 4.0, 1998.

III

Apartheid – A Crime against Humanity...
But the Other One

10
When Nazism Becomes the Sort of Thing With Which One Can Associate

Very commonly shared beliefs
The Black people of South Africa are striving to heal their deep, excruciating wounds caused by apartheid – the crime against humanity that was an extension of the Nazi policies beyond European borders. It is necessary to understand how and why, in South Africa, just after 1945, former accomplices of the Third Reich for several decades successfully operated a system that had been unanimously condemned by the civilised world when it was applied by Hitler. This is proof that, in spite of Nazi Germany's military defeat and the death of Adolph Hitler, the famous "foul beast" remained alive and kicking.

The institutionalisation of racial segregation in South Africa in the name of the superiority of the White race, and moreover, the support this regime received from Western democracies from the start and up to the 1980s are a terrifying illustration of the fact that Hitler's policies and methods of destruction were subject to criticism only inasmuch as they were applied in Europe against Europeans, both Jew and non-Jew.

The idea of setting up "native reservations" where Africans would be parked and prevented from ever leaving, except to go out to work for Whites, goes back nearly to the time of the colonisation of South Africa by the Europeans. The Dutch set up the prerequisite conditions for achieving this goal. However, it was the British, who starting in 1894 once they had taken over from the Dutch, established a nation-wide network of native reservations. They wanted to drive home the idea that Blacks were naturally intended to serve the White race, the race of masters. The Africans being unwilling to submit to the system of subordination erected by the British, the latter had to result to inventing the "Hut Tax" (the Glen Grey Act of 1894) which enabled them to force even the most recalcitrant Africans to go and work for Whites for at least three months every year. Under this system, an African who would not "reasonably" offer his services to White masters was subject to a heavy fine; and those who did not accept the tasks the White authorities assigned to them were tracked down and punished as criminals. In order to lay down the foundation for white supremacy once and for all and in all areas, and block off any opportunity for social betterment for non-Whites, His Gracious Majesty's government passed the "Colour Bar" Act in 1911, i.e., the Mines and Works Act, that set aside some of the specialised and semi-specialised jobs in the mining sector for Europeans. These provisions regulating African labour was supplemented by the Apprenticeship Act of 1922 which extended the Colour Bar to several other branches of industry. As a result, Blacks were banned from becoming joiners, masons, electricians, etc.

There are some noticeable similarities between the South African 1911 Colour Bar and the 1922 Apprenticeship Act when compared to the 6 July 1938 law regulating the professions in the Third Reich.

This law passed by the Nazi regime in Nuremberg banned Jews from certain professions and trades that were explicitly set aside for Aryans only. Among the banned professions, Article 1 of the Nazi law mentions surveillance, real estate trading, trading by contract and the profession of managing estates and houses. This was supplemented by the 20 September 1939 law on hereditary farms, whereby "only those of German blood or descended from a German family are entitled to be peasants" and "anyone who has Jewish blood or blood of a coloured person among their paternal or maternal ancestors are not of German blood or descended from a German family."

People who have researched the topic of fascism – and there have been many of them since these regimes became established in the heart of Europe itself – have found a regular pattern of institutionalised racial domination in the legal arsenal of these regimes.

To protect, at least from the legal standpoint, the purity of the race of masters, the British government passed the Immorality Act in South Africa in 1927. This law forbade marriage between Whites and non-Whites, as well as sexual intercourse between people of different race:

> Any European male who has illicit carnal intercourse with a native female, and any native male who has illicit carnal intercourse with a European female, in circumstances which do not amount to rape, an attempt to

commit rape, indecent assault, or a contravention of section two or four of the Girls' and Mentally Defective Women's Protection Act, 1916 (Act No. 3 of 1916) shall be guilty of an offence and liable on conviction to imprisonment for a period not exceeding five years.

This conception was taken up by the Nazi leaders and embodied in the legal arsenal of the Third Reich, specifically in the Nuremberg Laws, "Law for the Protection of German Blood and German Honour" of 15 September 1935. The text upholds exactly the same principle, i.e., the purity of the race of masters:

"Article 1.

1. Marriages between Jews and citizens of German or related blood are forbidden. Marriages nevertheless concluded are invalid, even if concluded abroad to circumvent this law.

2. Annulment proceedings can be initiated only by the State Prosecutor.

Article 2.

Extramarital relations between Jews and citizen of the state of German or related blood are forbidden.

[...]

Article 5

1. Any person who violates the prohibition under Article 1 will be punished with prison with hard labour.

2. A male who violates the prohibition under Article 2 will be punished with prison or prison with hard labour..."

The Nazi leaders never made any attempt to conceal their racist ideology nor their determination to crush the "racially inferior" groups. On this point, there was absolutely no doubt. The mistake Western democracies made lay elsewhere. They were not quick enough in understanding that the fascist methods of racial domination advocated by the Nazis would not be confined to the groups that were conventionally considered to be inferior. Of course that is difficult and embarrassing. True, even most of the victims openly targeted by the Nazi policy of extermination made the same incorrect assessment: to believe that barbarity would affect only the others, i.e., those who according to prejudice were the riff-raff, the ones at the very bottom of the social ladder. This sort of mass delusion that was so useful to the Nazis is illustrated by the testimony of David Cohen, quoted by Hilberg. Cohen was a Zionist Jew, the former chairman of the

Dutch Jewish Council. In 1947, he stated: "The fact that the Germans had perpetrated atrocities against Polish Jews was no reason for thinking that they behave (sic) in the same way toward Dutch Jews, firstly because the Germans had always held Polish Jews in disrepute, and secondly because in the Netherlands, unlike Poland, they had to sit up and take notice of public opinion.[1]"

The fact that the victims shared the same cultural heritage and sometimes the same ideology as their oppressors hindered them from correctly assessing the danger. As a result, their psychological ability to fight and defend their right to life were considerably weakened. The notion of racial purity was nothing new or foreign and there was nothing shocking about trying to justify it. Sometimes, as Friedlander notes "Here and there some Jewish voices even pleaded for 'racial purity of the Jewish stock' and for investigations according to the rules of 'racial science' for more ample and precise information regarding 'the extent of the miscegenation between Jews and Christians [sic], thus between the Semitic and Aryan race.[2]"

This concern with racial purity and the enhancement of the racial heritage was fairly widespread, making it easy for the Nazi government to legislate on these matters. For instance, on 14 January 1933, "the law for the prevention of progeny with hereditary defects is proclaimed. It allows for compulsory sterilisation in cases of 'congenital mental defects, schizophrenia, manic-depressive psychosis, hereditary epilepsy... and severe alcoholism.'" Even some scientists who had every reason to reject these eugenic measures approved them enthusiastically and proposed a number of extensions. One example is Doctor Kallmann, a Berlin psychiatrist, who thought the law was inadequate. "Dr Kallmann advised compulsory sterilisation of healthy, heterozygous carriers of the abnormal gene for schizophrenia, for which he postulated recessive inheritance.[3]" At the International Congress of Population Problems from 26 August to 1 September 1935 in Germany, Doctor Kallmann claimed that "it is desirable to extend prevention of reproduction to relatives of schizophrenics [...] and, above all, to define each of them as being undesirable from the eugenic point of view at the beginning of their reproductive years.[4]" In spite of his zeal, Kallmann was dismissed because he was Jewish. He immigrated to the United States in 1936 where he continued to carry out research on hereditary schizophrenia, thus making his talent available to the higher race of his country of adoption.

Polite society today underscores the irrationality and absurdity of the racial theories championed by the Nazis and scoffs at it. This only covers up the fact that these theories were approved by academics, not necessarily mere ideologists of Nazism or members of the party. Worse still, their colleagues in the Western democracies shared and approved those theories.

Language dictionaries are universally considered as a prestigious and authoritative source. No one suspects them of making cheap propaganda. *The Grand Dictionnaire universel du XIXe siècle*, a major work by Pierre Larousse, published from 1866 to 1880, includes an article called 'Negro':

> Attempts by a handful of philanthropists to prove that the Negro race is as intelligent as the white species have proved fruitless. Some very rare exceptions are by no means adequate proof that they have significant intellectual faculties. One indisputable fact, indeed a compelling one, is that their brains are narrower, lighter and smaller than those of the white species and [...] this fact is sufficient to prove the superiority of the species over the black species.[5]

The Nazis put these lies dressed up in scientific frills pertaining exclusively to the Blacks to good use by reversing the logic. Blacks, whose laziness had been made incontrovertible, could work themselves to death because they were lazy. Jews, who were incapable of doing work because they were lazy, just stole the work done by the Aryans and therefore they had to be disposed of. But, before doing so, a definition of 'Jew' that would more effectively despoil them was needed.

Sir Julian Sorell Huxley, a British biologist, philosopher and humanist, was UNESCO's first Director General from 1946 to 1948. So it was that a man who "in 1941 found it opportune to commend eugenics and attributed inferior intelligence as a hereditary trait of "authentic negroes" (sic) was appointed to oversee an organisation one of whose aims is to "fight racism." In 1941, Auschwitz had not begun operating, but the Germans were already practising by gassing their mentally ill patients openly and publicly.[6]" The task of analysing the impact of these stereotypes on the attitude of both opponents and victims of Nazism is still pending. The nature of the historical events that took place immediately after 1945 in South Africa proves that such an analysis is sorely needed. It was here that erstwhile adversaries and even victims of the evildoers came together to form an alliance (that some people inanely describe as "unholy") to restore the superiority and the supremacy of the White race over the "racially inferior" peoples. This dirty work was made all the more urgent by the fact that under Nazi domination in Europe a great many Europeans had been relegated to the condition of sub-humans and – the ultimate crime – treated like niggers. It was high time to go back to the racial normality that guarantees that every White belongs to the superior race and to turn one's back on these absurd Nazi theories that took exclusion a little too far.

Fervent Nazis who meant business

During the Second World War, South Africa officially sided with the Allies and fought Nazi Germany. This occurred because of the relative weakness of the South African National Party, which was pro-Nazi, as compared with the pro-British group. Even before the armed conflict began in 1939, the South African nationalists, whose sympathies lay with the Third Reich, launched a campaign in favour of Nazi Germany. When the time came, the South African government debated on whether to take part or adopt a position of neutrality in the world conflict.

On 4 September 1939, Parliament remained in session for more than ten hours and the pro-British group won the day by eighty votes against the National Party. On 6 September 1939, South Africa broke off diplomatic ties with Germany. What weighed most heavily on the decision was Germany's clearly stated ambition that, once the war was over, it would claim South Western Africa, which was placed under South African mandate after the First World War. Among the fascist organisations active in South Africa before and after the war, the most heavily committed towards Nazi Germany in political and military terms was Ossewabrandwag. It was formed in 1939 by Hans Van Rensburg at the start of the war. This paramilitary organisation undertook major terrorist actions on behalf of Nazi Germany. In 1936, Van Rensburg had been invited to Germany where he "watched the Olympic Games, attended the National Socialist Party Congress in Nuremberg, and by invitation from the Wehrmacht, took part in military manoeuvres. There, he met Hitler, Goering, von Ribbentrop and other leaders. During the war, Ossewabrandwag received money and military equipment via German submarines or through agents sent out by Germany.[7]" One of the most dangerous terrorists that belonged to this organisation was John Balthazar Vorster who was a member of its General Staff. He held the rank of General and performed his assignment of providing intelligence to the Nazi forces very well. In 1942, the British ended up by sentencing him to seventeen months imprisonment for pro-Nazi activities. "Both Vorster and Swart were jailed along with members of Ossewabrandwag for sabotaging South Africa's military contribution to the war against Germany.[8]" Like many other pro-Nazi activists, Vorster was to become a leading figure in the South African National Party that came into power in 1948.

Another reputable South African politician, Hendrik Frensch Verwoerd, a professor of psychology at the University of Stellenbosch, was a keen Nazi supporter. In 1936, at his first public event, together with five other professors from the same university, he called for the expulsion of the Jews who had arrived in South Africa to flee racial persecution in Nazi Germany. Verwoerd's anti-Semitic and pro-Nazi stance earned him a position as editor-in-chief of the nationalist newspaper *Die Transvaaler* in 1937 which he filled until 1948 when he was elected senator. Throughout the war, Verwoerd systematically misrepresented the news from Europe in his paper, carrying out the task of indoctrination on behalf of the Third Reich. "When another South African paper commented on his pro-German bias, Dr Verwoerd sued for damages – and lost. The judge ruled that he had knowingly given support to the enemy.[9]"

Verwoerd's support for the Third Reich did not however interfere with his political career. It began in 1948 and led him to the position of Minister for Foreign Affairs from 1950 to 1958 when he went on to become Prime Minister, a position he retained until 1966. His pro-Israeli policy was much appreciated by several members of the Israeli Parliament. And when, "in October 1966, Professor Abrahams, the [Chief Rabbi of the United Council of Orthodox Hebrew Congregations (Cape Province and South-West Africa and Northern Rhodesia)], pronounced the eulogy for South African Prime Minister Verwoerd, he described him as a sincere, profoundly honest man whose politics had been inspired by his moral standards and who was the first to give apartheid a moral [sic] foundation.[10]"

Mixing with former Nazis

At the parliamentary elections, underground paramilitary groups that had collaborated closely with the armed forces of the Third Reich, and in particular the former terrorists that belonged to Ossewabrandwag, entered the South African parliamentary arena. They campaigned within the National Party with the slogans: "against the Black Peril," "to defend the white race." Former activists and backers of the Nazi cause won the elections on 26 May 1948. The Nazification of power officially named apartheid took place out in the open without any attempt by the leaders of the Nationalist Party to conceal the ideological choices they were already advocating before 1939. One of the first laws passed by the apartheid regime was to ban mixed marriages (Prohibition of mixed marriages Act, 1949). There was really no necessity for this law since, back in 1927, the British government had already banned marriages between Whites and non-Whites as well as intercourse between people of different race with the Immorality Act.

But at that stage the aim was to reorganise the legal framework so as to acquire legal and effective control over the "racially inferior" groups in all areas and ensure that nothing whatsoever could escape White control. To do so, the domination by the superior race over all the non-Whites was reinforced by all possible means, and any doubt whatsoever about the grounds for creating this situation or about how long it would last were erased. The South African lawmakers (like their German counterparts in 1933) began frenetically to churn out legislation to regulate these subhuman, racially inferior groups and debase them with almost manic meticulousness. Within less than two decades, apartheid's legal arsenal amounted to no less than two hundred laws, decrees, orders and resolutions, each of which was applied routinely, as standard practice, and sometimes ruthlessly.

There is an internal logic to the laws passed by the South African parliament. There is a red thread that passes through them all: to imprint, finally and unconditionally, the superiority of the White race on to reality and in the minds of non-Whites. The Population Registration Act No. 5 (1950) regulated how individuals are categorised into racial groups: White, Black, or Coloured. Indians were later added to represent those from South Asia, former British India. The classification was performed on the basis of the census survey and the law determined which racial group may settle where. The laws known as the Group Areas Act, passed in 1950, amended in 1955 and made even more restrictive in 1957, allow the government to classify residential districts by racial group and to order the expulsion of those who must settle elsewhere. This law also makes it illegal and a punishable offence for a White and a Black to have coffee together in a bar, unless they have obtained prior authorisation. This laughable ban loses its comic appeal when one remembers what became of the Blacks who were thrown into prison for infringing this law.

Verwoerd's successor as Prime Minister in 1966 was no better company than he was. He was Vorster, the former Ossewabrandwag terrorist. He continued in this position until 1978 and then became President of the Republic. When the South African Union left the Commonwealth and the Nationalist Party proclaimed the South African Republic in 1961, the first President of this young Republic was C.R. Swart, a former Ossewabrandwag terrorist, an activist for the Nazi cause during the war and former crony of Vorster in the organisation's general staff.

No more bickering

Just as they had done before in 1933 when the Nazis came to power in Germany, the Allied forces stood by and watched as the South African Nazis took over and settled in. The first reason for this attitude was their patent anti-Communism. Secondly, the apartheid regime had removed some of the aberrations in the Nazi theories and therefore gave an impression of gentility. As long as this regime, unlike the criminals of the Third Reich, sought to impose the hegemony of the Whites over the non-Whites, rather than of the Aryan race over the non-Aryans, it received the unflagging support of the powers of the free world (the United Kingdom, the United States, France, etc.). This fine difference was enough for eminent personalities in the Western world, who have earned respect by fighting Nazism, not only to identify with former South African Nazis but also to use their available prestige to assist apartheid leaders in building up their respectability.

Take the example of General Charles de Gaulle, the man who in France is the incarnation of the resistance against Nazi barbarity. It was under his authority nonetheless that "military cooperation began between France and South Africa with an invitation from de Gaulle to South African officers to come to Algeria.[11]"

This was a momentous invitation. Indeed, Major General Rademayer, who in South Africa had become the regime's strongman following the attempted assassination of Prime Minister Verwoerd in 1960, sent a number of his officers to Algeria where for the last five years the French had been engaging in Gestapo-like practices against the African population. "There the South Africans learned the technique called in French *ratissage*, involving the surrounding of a village and the systematic beating up of its inhabitants. Renamed *Kragdadigheit*, this brutal method was applied by Rademeyer in Cape Town and, in particular, in the African suburb of Nyanga.[12]" The Black people of South Africa were later to have ample opportunity to assess first-hand how useful the assistance furnished by the country of human rights was to the Pretoria regime that negated the humanity of non-Whites.

As for the United Kingdom, there was no way the British government could seriously object to the racial policy applied to non-Whites by the apartheid regime for a very obvious reason: it was the UK that laid the foundations for this system at the end of the nineteenth century. As for the United States of America, suffice it to recall that at the same time the Blacks under the leadership of people like Martin Luther King and other proponents of racial equality were being battered in the streets and thrashed in police stations by the law enforcement agencies. The dignity of non-Whites was as trampled upon by Uncle Sam as it was in the country of apartheid.

In short, the South African Nazis were given free rein as long as they acted democratically, i.e., in compliance with the principle of racial equality within the White race. Thanks to the apartheid regime, the position of overall superiority of the White race was restored along with its unity, which for a time, had been challenged by Nazi madness.

Zionists and former Nazis – a fascinating partnership

The state of Israel, whose leaders use the price paid by the victims of Nazi barbarity as the basis for their legitimacy, is a clear instance of this ideological difficulty that has stood in the way of drawing logical conclusions from Auschwitz. Because its legitimacy derives directly from the destruction of the Jews of Europe, the Israeli government was able to pocket the money paid by the Federal Republic of Germany by way of reparations. This state of affairs has stood in the way of the critical assessment of the various positions adopted by the state of Israel, which, through the voice of its governments, has consistently presented itself as the rightful claimant of the rights granted to the victims of the Shoah.

After 1948, the members of the Jewish community in South Africa, many of whom came there to escape racist persecution by Nazi Germany, discovered, with a few exceptions (all the more remarkable that they were few and far between), that – all things considered – perhaps there was some "moral foundation," to use the words of Professor Abrahams, Grand Rabbi of South Africa,[13] for racial segregation when it is aimed solely at non-Whites. The leaders of the state of Israel undertook the responsibility of providing the Pretoria regime with the military and technological aid needed for apartheid to operate effectively. At the same time, the Jewish community of South Africa exerted pressure on international Zionist organisations in order to obtain favourable treatment for the former collaborators of the Third Reich. In exchange, the government of apartheid made a special exemption to the rules applying to currency[14] and allowed the Jewish community of South Africa to transfer considerable amounts to Israel every year through the Zionist federation of South Africa. Everything is negotiable.

Some commentators described this choice as realpolitik because it enabled "the South African Jewish community, some of the richest in the world in terms of *per capita* income, to contribute to the cause of Israel more than any other Jewish community in the world, not excluding the American community.[15]" One example occurred during the June 1967 Arab–Israeli conflict when the financial support for Israel extended beyond the South African Jewish community as

> South Africa provided material support for the Israeli war effort in 1967, most importantly by relaxing controls on the transfer of funds. The sum involved, though never officially disclosed, is estimated to have been over R21 million. [...] collection of funds and support activities were carried out by all sections of the White community, not just Jewish groups.[16]

And during the 1973 war the support the apartheid regime gave to the state of Israel was even greater. "Although the total amount was not disclosed, press reports have indicated that it may have been as high as $30 million.[17]"

The South African Jewish press studiously avoided criticising the racial segregation that was institutionalised by the South African fascists. At the same time, Zionist organisations, which by then were the instruments of apartheid propaganda, decided "the Jewish community should take steps to explain South Africa's position to Jews overseas and at home.[18]" Actually, the intention was to ratify a position that had already been advocated by South African Zionists for a long time. For instance, at the 8th international conference of the World Union of Jews in London in July 1953, Rabbi M.C. Weiler who spoke on behalf of the South African Jewish community explained with some brazenness that:

> The Jews as a community had decided to take no stand on the native question, because they were involved with the problem of assisting Jewry in other lands. South African Jewry was doing more to help Israel than any other group. The community could not ask for the government's permission to export funds and goods and at the same time, object to the government.[19]

But even without Rabbi Weiler's explanations, it is not hard to see that South African Zionists and the state of Israel became heavily involved in supporting the apartheid regime, not just because of their ideological affinities, but also for economic, political and strategic reasons that made this partnership worthwhile for both parties. We know that the reason the Nazis were able to find so many partners in Germany, Austria and elsewhere is that, to begin with, their policy provided concrete, satisfactory solutions to very large portions of the population. Ideological motives are not always enough to maintain the momentum of commitment.

In any case, the ties established between the state of Israel and the former accomplices of Nazi Germany became closer and eminent persons in high positions from Israel regularly went to the country of apartheid. In 1969, Ben Gurion was warmly welcomed there: "He praised the superiority of the Israeli technique for expelling the indigenous population and declared that if it had been applied by the South African community it would have 'preserved South Africa from any internal subversion.[20]'" This visit by the founding father of the state of Israel to South Africa right at the time when former Nazi South Africans reigned supreme is startling to say the least, not only because Ben Gurion always claimed to be the spokesman for "world Judaism" but more importantly because he fought tooth and nail to assert that the state of Israel "speaks on behalf of all murdered Jews.[21]"

When bringing Eichmann to trial was being envisaged, some Jews in the diaspora expressed the wish that he should be brought before an international court rather than an Israeli one. For instance, the President of the World Jewish Congress, Nahum Goldmann, after having stated that there was no doubt about Israel's right to try Eichmann, went on to say: "since Eichmann and the Nazis exterminated not only Jews, it would be worthwhile to invite those countries, many of whose citizens were also killed by him, to send their own judges. I emphasised that the president of the court must be an Israeli judge and that the trial itself must take place in Israel.[22]" Ben Gurion's reaction to this proposal clearly illustrates the self-attributed role he played in respect of the Jewish victims of Nazi barbarity. In an open letter addressed to Goldmann, he writes: "The publication of your proposal in a newspaper aimed at world opinion is, whether you intended it or not, a harsh and serious blow to the sensibilities of the people of Israel (and I think not only in Israel) and to the country's honor.[23]"

According to Ben Gurion, Israel's right to try Eichmann arose from its status as representative, even owner, of the memory of the victims of Auschwitz. This is also apparent in an answer he sent to Proskauer, Honorary President of the American Jewish Congress, in response to a letter the latter had sent him, along with an editorial by the *Washington Post* that alleged that Israel was not accredited to speak on behalf of the Jews of other countries:

> The Jewish state (which is called Israel) *is the heir to the six million who were murdered*, the only heir; for these millions, the opinion of the *Washington Post* notwithstanding, regarded themselves as sons of the Jewish people and only as sons of the Jewish people. If they had lived, the great majority of them

would have come to Israel. The only historic prosecuting attorney for these millions is Israel. For reasons of historic justice, it is the duty of the Israeli government, as the government of the Jewish state, whose foundations were laid by millions of European Jews and whose establishment was their dearest hope, to try their murderers.[24]

This determination of Israeli leaders to be considered the sole heirs of the six million assassinated Jews in the face of international public opinion and history might have been more credible if they had not simultaneously established the Israeli–South-African racist alliance with the former Nazis making the Israeli state the most active ally of the apartheid regime. This shameful haggling in the name of the victims is intolerable and the duty of memory towards them would have been better served if the Jews in the diaspora had, through their organisations, expressed their disagreement with the state of Israel's racist compromises and their objections to Israel's instrumentalisation of the Shoah. Adopting this approach (which unfortunately did not happen) would have cleared up the confusion between Zionism and Judaism. The lonely voices of a few particularly brave Jews who were anti-Zionist activists did condemn the damage the state of Israel caused to Judaism by confusing the two.

It is just business

This is how it came to be that in 1948 the Black people of South Africa – a country that in 1939 had wholeheartedly joined ranks with the Allied powers – not only found themselves in the grip of racial domination orchestrated by South African ex-Nazis, but also delivered into their hands by the very powers alongside those Black soldiers had fought as well as by the very people who had been the Nazis' prime targets.

Ignorance sometimes serves as a powerful alibi, but it cannot serve to justify entering into devious dealings with South African former Nazis. Their commitment towards the Nazi armed forces during the war was no secret and they never subsequently disowned their ideological beliefs. In 1965, in answer to the sarcasms of an opposition member of Parliament on this topic, Vorster said: "I do not disown my past. If it were to be redone under the same conditions, I would not hesitate to do the same.[25]" Neither the Israeli leaders nor Israelis in general could possibly have been unaware of their past. In fact, "the German newspaper, *Die Welt*, had described Vorster's cronies as South African Nazis who had come out of hiding to take up key positions in the state's repressive machinery.[26]"

As for the Western anti-racists in the United States, the United Kingdom and France who condemned the devastation created by apartheid, they were told to clean up their own backyard. Let us not forget that, no European is in a historically comfortable position to give Israel advice about racism and racial persecutions.

Deals were therefore efficiently struck by the Israeli leaders who, on one side, did some good business with South African former Nazis,[27] and at the same time cashed in on the political and financial advantages associated with being the sole representatives of the victims of the genocide. Together with the extra bonus of the benevolent silence of the media and the right to brandish the accusation of anti-Semitism against anyone bold enough to condemn their shady dealings.

In this way, many Zionists, who tended to be uncritical or unwillingly critical of apartheid, talked about anti-Semitism in the United States so as to better discredit the Blacks who were bold enough to bring out into the open the complicity of Zionism.

> [...] Jewish neo-conservatives figured prominently in the assault on the poor. Playing the Holocaust card to deflect criticism, they wrapped themselves in the cloak of virginal innocence and bandied about the claim of "black anti-Semitism". In addition, former Jewish leftists joining the political mainstream exploited the Holocaust as they tarred the New Left with charges of anti-Semitism.[28]

In this context and on this topic, the attitude of Elie Wiesel, Nobel Peace Prize winner, is characteristic. He considers Blacks to be ungrateful:

> The people who take inspiration from us attack us in the vocabulary of the Holocaust, terms such as "ghetto", "genocide", "mass murder", do not thank us but attack us. [...] There is one thing they need to learn from us, it is gratitude. [...] If you are against Israel today, you are ipso facto anti-Jewish. And if you are a Jew against Israel, you are a renegade. You cannot have it both ways. When you see among the New Left so many kids, so-called intellectuals, [...] they must be proclaimed openly and publicly renegades of the Jewish people. Let them do what they want. But they should not be part of the Jewish people. They are not.[29]

Squabbles quickly patched up

In 1960, seventeen former African colonies became independent states and immediately joined the United Nations. They anticipated relying on the "one country, one vote" principle so as to have their voice heard in this forum. Many Blacks, including Professor Richard Stevens, who were profoundly hostile to the apartheid regime, and appalled by the complicity of Zionist circles, on many occasions denounced the shady dealings of Israel with the South African Nazis. African peoples and the descendants of deported Africans are not accountable for the destruction of the European Jews and as such could not be blackmailed by Israeli leaders who made a regular habit of using Auschwitz to quash the voice of anyone hostile to their racist policy. It was at that stage that the Israeli leaders began to contemplate establishing closer ties with these new African states.

Israel became a member of the United Nations in 1950 and always managed to avoid voting on any anti-apartheid resolutions, which did not prevent its UN spokesperson from denouncing information about the relations between the Israel and South Africa as "slanderous.[30]" From 1960 onwards, with the onslaught of new African countries, the issue of the criminal nature of the apartheid regime was raised more and more frequently. As a result, evading the resolutions became an almost impossible balancing act. In October 1961, Israel voted in favour of the resolution condemning apartheid as reprehensible and detrimental to the dignity of peoples and individuals. There were several subsequent occasions when Israel voted in favour of resolutions that were hostile to South Africa. Due to the pressure exerted by African countries, the struggle against the crime of apartheid became a priority on the UN General Assembly's agenda. Needless to say, this apparent turnaround by Israel produced a fierce response from Pretoria, crying traitor and discontinuing the special permission allowing unrestricted transfers of funds collected by the South African Zionist Federation to Israel. The Jewish community of South Africa deeply saddened by the "irresponsible" attitude of Israel and concerned by the retaliatory measures announced by the South African government "expressed its regret that the Israeli delegate to the United Nations did not content himself with abstaining from the vote like the other Western nations.[31]"

The chill in relations between the State of Israel and the apartheid regime caused ripples on both sides: "The Jews from South Africa, in an attempt at repairing what was almost considered as a serious blunder by Israel, sought to divert international criticism towards South Africa. This was especially to be noticed at the UN where, upon lobbying by the Council of South African delegates and the Jewish Organization, Jewish bodies refrained from officially condemning apartheid.[32]" These family squabbles did not last long since, as already mentioned, during the June 1967 Arab–Israeli war, Israel received financial support from South Africa beyond contributions from the South African Jewish community. Not to mention the dividends reaped by Israel as a result of this incident. For instance, after the "courageous" decision by Israel at the UN, some respectable anti-racist activists who were sympathetic towards Israel explained: "The state of Israel has not hesitated to sacrifice valuable sympathies it encountered in the South African government by adopting a vigorously anti-apartheid stance.[33]"

Pitilessly subjected to the annihilating power of subordination of apartheid, the non-Whites of South Africa, often paying the heavy toll of bloody repression, opposed this policy of destruction that challenged human dignity itself. The South African government could high-handedly go ahead with its policy of destruction aimed at "racially inferior" groups because it was broadly supported by the former Allied powers with the exception of the USSR. White South African society felt no need to unleash their violence against Black people in the ostentatious style of North American lynchings conducted by White mobs. Equipped with a system of laws and repression that would have been the envy of lawmakers working in the service of the Third Reich, the apartheid regime made sure it had the instruments to quite legally hang or put in chains anyone who interfered with its operation.

Notes

1. Raul Hilberg, *The Destruction of the European Jews*, Revised ed., vol. 1 (New York, Holmes & Meier, 1985) 23, Questia, Web, 6 July 2010.
2. Saul Friedlander, *Nazi Germany and the Jews, Volume I: The Years of Persecution, 1933–1939*, Harper Perennial, 1998, p. 119.
3. Benno Muller Hill, *Murderous Science: Elimination by Scientific Selection of Jews, Gypsies and Others,* Cold Spring Harbor, Laboratory Press, 1998, p. 10.
4. Ibid, p. 11.
5. Léon-François Hoffmann, *Le Nègre romantique,* Paris, 1973, p. 6.
6. André Pichot, researcher in epistemology and the history of science, in *Le Monde*, October 4, 1996.
7. Alexandre Kum'a N'Dumbe, *Hitler voulait l'Afrique*, Paris, L'Harmattan, 1980, p. 326–329.
8. Norman Phillips, *The Tragedy of Apartheid: A Journalist's Experiences in the South African Riots,* New York, David McKay Company, Inc., 1960, p. 123.
9. Abdelkader Benabdallah, *Israël et les peuples noirs*, Quebec, 1979, p. 73.

10. Marianne Cornevin, *L'Apartheid, pouvoir et falsification historique*, Paris, Unesco, 1979, pp. 33–34.
11. Marianne Cornevin, *L'Afrique du Sud en sursis*, Paris, Hachette, 1977, p. 162.
12. Phillips, op. cit., p. 160.
13. See p. 203 his funeral oration for Prime Minister Verwoerd in 1966.
14. See UN documentation, 5/77, for special dispensations to currency regulations granted by South Africa in favour of the South African Zionist Federation.
15. *Relations Between Israel and South Africa*. Reprint of the Report of the United Nations Special Committee Against Apartheid, No. 5/77, Feb. 1977, p. 7.
16. Ibid, p. 13.
17. Ibid, p. 13.
18. Ibid, p. 8, quoting *Jewish Chronicle*, London, December 1962.
19. Ibid, p. 7.
20. Benabdallah, op. cit., p. 73.
21. Segev, Tom, *The Seventh Million: The Israelis and the Holocaust*, New York, Henry Holt and Company, 2001, p. 332.
22. Ibid, p. 329.
23. Ibid, p. 329.
24. Ibid, pp. 330-331.
25. *Afrique-Asie*, 10 August 1971, Paris, in Benabdallah, op. cit., p. 20.
26. Ibid.
27. See in Chapter VI of Report of the United Nations Special Committee against Apartheid, No. 5/77, February 1977, on trade between Israel and the apartheid regime, and Chapter VII on investments made by the apartheid regime in Israel, and vice-versa.
28. Finkelstein, Norman and Birn, Ruth, *A Nation on Trial: the Goldhagen Thesis and Historical Truth*, p. 53, pdf file downloaded June 3, 2010 at jrbooksonline.com/PDF_Books_added2009-4/nationontrial.pdf
29. Finkelstein, Norman, *The Holocaust Industry*, Verso, 2000, p. 53; Wiesel, Elie, *Conversations*, University Press of Mississippi, 2002, p. 20.
30. UN document, Special Committee against Apartheid A/AC.115/L.285 add 3, 21 May 1971. Benabdallah, op.cit., p. 140.
31. Benabdallah, op. cit., p. 145.
32. Richard P. Stevens, op. cit., p.216
33. Paraf, Pierre, *Le racisme dans le monde*, Paris, 1981, p. 114.

11

Back Full Circle to the Exclusion of Non-Whites

The exclusion of non-Whites – An acceptable form of segregation

On December 5, 1956, just after dawn, the security police raided houses and arrested many anti-apartheid Blacks. Among the first was Nelson Mandela and in the next few days even Albert Luthuli, the venerable, indeed venerated, chief of his people, was thrown into prison. The regime charged them with high treason and a nationwide conspiracy to use violence to overthrow the present government and replace it with a communist state. This was a particularly serious accusation because, as a legacy of its Dutch past, under South African law, high treason is punishable by the death penalty.

Albert Luthuli, who later won the Nobel Peace Prize in 1960, became President of the ANC in 1952 after being the ANC President for Natal. He was also elected chief by his community in the region of the Groutville mission in 1935 with the approval of the government. When Luthuli became President of the ANC, the apartheid government made it known to him through the Native Affairs Delegate that he should resign, or else he would be removed from his chieftainship. He refused to comply and was therefore dismissed as chief of the Umvoti Mission Reserve. But so great was the respect for Luthuli among the population that, in spite of the authorities' repeated demands, they refused to appoint a successor.

People like Luthuli, Walter Sisulu, Mandela and many others were tried for high treason. High treason was defined by the apartheid regime as "a hostile intention to disturb, impair, or endanger the independence or safety of the state.[1]" They were accused of having supported or contributed to drafting the freedom charter adopted at the people's congress in Kliptown,

Johannesburg on June 25–26, 1956. The public prosecutor quoted the charter, vowing he would prove its criminal nature and demonstrate that the accused had planned to topple the government.

The apartheid system relied entirely on the exclusion of non-Whites, which was itself founded on the negation of the humanity of Blacks. In this context alone, the freedom charter, filled with claims for the Blacks, certainly undermined the stability of the regime. It states:

> "We, the people of South Africa, declare for all our country and the world to know:
>
> that South Africa belongs to all who live in it, black and white, and that no government can justly claim authority unless it is based on the will of all the People;
>
> [...] The rights of the people shall be the same, regardless of race, colour or sex;
>
> [...] All national groups shall have equal rights! There shall be equal status in the bodies of the state, in the courts and in the schools for all national groups and races;
>
> [...] All apartheid laws and practices shall be set aside. [...] People shall not be robbed of their cattle, and forced labour and farm prisons shall be abolished.
>
> [...] The courts shall be representative of all the people;
>
> [...] All laws which discriminate on grounds of race, colour or belief shall be repealed.
>
> [...] All shall enjoy equal human rights!
>
> [...] All laws involving travel passes, authorisations and other laws restricting freedom of movement shall be abolished;
>
> [...] Education shall be free, compulsory, universal and equal for all children;
>
> [...] Fenced locations and ghettoes shall be abolished and laws which break up families shall be repealed.'"

A criminal system like that of the Third Reich in Germany or apartheid in South Africa cannot be reformed. A single one of the measures mentioned above is clearly enough to shake its foundations, which is why the determination of the ANC members, in spite of being keen advocates of peaceful means, did indeed constitute a serious threat for the regime.

I have already noted that in 1939 South African Blacks willingly sided with the Allied powers to fight Nazism. But that is not the whole story. At a time when there was still uncertainty about the outcome of the war and White power was being hounded from the inside by the terrorists working in Hitler's forces, the government made a gesture in favour of the Black people. In 1942, Deputy Prime Minister Deneys Reitz hosted a delegation led by Alfred Xuma and James Calata, the President and Secretary General of the ANC, who had rallied the Blacks to fight Nazism. He assured them that from now on the police would no longer require them to show travel passes and the revocation of a number of the most degrading laws was discussed.

In Europe, the Nazis needed a yellow star to be able to control their victims; in Africa, the White authorities needed passes. This method that had been introduced into South Africa by the British was also very effective in the concentration camp system of America for several centuries. The abolition of this degrading instrument was something all its victims longed for. When the war ended with Germany's defeat, not only did the South African Nazis enjoy impunity for their activities during the war; their erstwhile white opponents also helped them establish the most coercive system of racial domination in modern times.

One may well imagine the anxiety, not to speak of the anger, of these Black leaders who were accused of high treason by a prosecutor who had once been a Nazi, while they had not hesitated to offer the sacrifice of their lives to their nation. Nearly forty years later, Nelson Mandela, with his customary restraint, remembers:

> In January [1958], when the government was scheduled to sum up its charges, the Crown brought in a new prosecutor, the formidable Oswald Pirow, was a former minister of justice and of defence and a pillar of National Party politics. He was a long time Afrikaner nationalist, and an out-spoken supporter of the Nazi cause; he once described Hitler as the "greatest man of his age". [...] The appointment of Pirow was new evidence that the state was worried about the outcome and attached tremendous importance to a victory.[3]

And indeed, Oswald Pirow, "the Minister for the Defence of the White Race", as the German papers described him at the time, was highly valued by the Nazi hierarchy. They gave orders to have the most relevant parts of his speeches before the South African Parliament translated and published. Pirow enjoyed prestige that he derived from being a member of the Germany–South Africa Society. To illustrate the interest the German Nazis took in the South African racial policy, Kum'a N'Dumbe quotes an article published in Issue No. 7 of the *Rassenpolitische Auslandskorrespondenz* paper in 1937:

> During a public meeting at Winburg, the South African Minister for Transport and Defence Oswald Pirow mentioned inter alia the problems faced by the population and specially emphasised the major accomplishments of the Vortrekkers in the area of racial policy. It is to them alone that we owe the fact that South Africa is a White state... This racial doctrine shaped the African policy into an exclusive policy of white domination. The Vortrekkers were portrayed as having created something that bore abundant fruit well after their death. Minister Pirow went on to state that the role of Africa in world politics would be determined by its position on Blacks. It depends almost entirely on one question, i.e., whether the White man will continue to maintain his domination.[4]

And Kum'a N'Dumbe adds:

> When Pirow visited Hitler in November 1938, he was given a triumphant welcome by the (German–South African) Society. A grand reception for 80 guests was held in his honour. The February 1939 report states that the coverage given by both the German and South African press to the Society's work so far is highly encouraging.[5]

More than 77,000 South African Blacks volunteered to join forces with England to fight Nazism. Notwithstanding, the Allied powers, the very ones that brought the people who were guilty of treating Europeans like niggers to trial, instead chose to support those who in South Africa had actively championed Nazi Germany! As it happens, the choice of the Allies is coherent and consistent with their difficulties in drafting the statute of the International Military Tribunal.[6]

Black, therefore sub-human

When Chief Luthuli appeared before the court in 1960, he was accused first of having burned his reference book, the appalling pass; secondly, of having disobeyed the law by protesting; thirdly and last, of having encouraged his fellow countrymen to follow his example. Luthuli had taken part in organising the campaign against the system of farm jails that were run by Whites based on the pass laws. C.R. Swart, an accomplice of Vorster within Ossewabrandwag's leadership,

> Governor-General of the Union, made it his custom, while he was Minister of Justice, to open *farm gaols* officially. He was loud in their praise. They relieve the country of the expense of accommodating offenders, they

Back Full Circle to the Exclusion of Non-Whites   219

> help farmers – and they rehabilitate criminals! [...] Pass offenders – half a million men a year – are drafted out of gaols into the safe-keeping of farmers. Both gaolers and farmers are delighted with the arrangement. The system helps to keep down the gaol population, and it provides the farms with an unending flow of beasts of burden deprived of any and all rights.[7]

The number of people who died in these farm jails has never been established. The death rate of those subjected to torture or to the daily brutalities inflicted upon prisoners is not known. Nor is anything known about the numbers that died from sheer exhaustion and lack of nutrition. Prisoners who died were buried without any requirement to inform their families. In fact, very often families were not even aware that a prisoner had been transferred to a farm gaol. Abolishing this abominable legislation was a core element in the claims of Black South Africans. On this point and in spite of his advanced age, Chief Luthuli defied the regime. Mandela never forgot:

> Chief Luthuli had been in the middle of his deposition, and Judge Rumpff asked for an explanation for his absence. [...] Later we discovered that after his arrest, the chief had been assaulted. He had been walking up some stairs when he was jostled by a warder; this caused his hat to fall on the floor. As he bent to pick up the hat, he was smacked across the head and face. This was hard for us to take. A man of immense dignity and achievement, a lifelong devout Christian, and a man with a dangerous heart condition, was treated like a barnyard animal by men who were not fit to tie his shoes.[8]

Oppenheimer cannot understand why Black people want the "one man, one vote" principle

While he was in prison, Harry Oppenheimer, a White South African, the son of a German Jew who had immigrated to Kimberley, paid Chief Luthuli a visit. He was the richest man in the country and also the most liberal of the captains of industry in South Africa. Chief Luthuli reports from this meeting that:

> Through the good offices of the Institute (of Race Relations) a few of us had a meeting also with Mr Harry Oppenheimer, the mining magnate. After a preliminary declaration of his understanding of the African point of view, he took us to task over what he saw as the excessive nature of our demands and methods – such things as the demand for universal adult suffrage and the methods of public demonstration and boycott. If I sum up his thought correctly, his plea was that the "extremism" of our demand

for recognition made it difficult for him and others like him to persuade 'liberal-minded people' of his own group of the justice of our demands.⁹

Fifteen years after Auschwitz, it was therefore possible for a Jew – the son of a German immigrant – to express doubts about whether it was reasonable for these people, who had been brutalised, to reclaim their status as human beings. Just like the rest of the White community in South Africa, Zionist Jews and confused Christians alike, Oppenheimer felt strongly about maintaining the privileges reserved to the superior race. His loyalty to the principles of the apartheid regime never waned throughout the period during which this crime against humanity was being committed. Again on May 18, 1976, speaking before an audience of some hundred bankers and business people at the London Stock Exchange, he stated:

> Government by a Black majority would lead to the destruction of the system of free enterprise and parliamentary government as we conceive it. [...] *The 'one man, one vote' system means the end of democracy* and, to a great extent, of the capitalist system. And no White in South Africa or in Rhodesia would tolerate such a form of government.[10]

Chief Luthuli's steadfastness and dignity shaped the men who were to follow in his footsteps: Mandela, Walter Sisulu, Govan Mbeki, Robert Sobukwe, Oliver Tambo and many others. These excerpts are from the statement Chief Luthuli prepared for the court that tried him is a further illustration:

> I stand before you, Your Worship, charged with the destruction of my reference book (or pass) and because of that with the crime of inciting my people to do the same. I have pleaded legally not guilty to all the charges.
>
> "What I did, I did, because I, together with the overwhelming majority of my people, condemn the pass system as the cause of much evil and suffering among us. We charge that it is nothing less than an instrument of studied degradation and humiliation of us as a people, a badge of slavery, a weapon used by the authorities to keep us in a position of inferiority.
>
> It cannot be very easy for you, sir, to understand the very deep hatred all Africans feel for a pass. [...] We are deeply conscious of, and grateful for, the fact that there is a growing number of fellow white South Africans who appreciate our situation and feel deeply about it; but they, too, can never fully understand the depth of our suffering. Can anyone who has not gone through it possibly imagine what happened when they read in the press of a routine police announcement that there has been a pass raid in a location? The fear of the loud, rude bang on the door in the middle of the night,

the bitter humiliation of an undignified search, the shame of husband and wife being huddled out of bed in front of their children by the police and taken off to the police station. [...]

Each year half a million of my people are arrested under the pass laws. Government annual reports tell of this tragic story. But statistics can tell only half the tale. The physical act of arrest and detention with the consequence of a broken home, a lost job, a loss of earnings, is only part of this grim picture. The deep humiliation felt by a black man, whether he be a labourer, an advocate, a nurse, a teacher or a professor, or even a minister of religion, when, over and over again, he hears the shout, 'Kaffir, where is your pass? – *Kaffir, waar's jo paas*?' fills in the rest of this grim picture.

[...] In the war years the late Mr Deneys Reitz, then Minister of Native Affairs, spoke publicly of the need to repeal these laws, and in fact, for a time, virtually suspended the system of summary arrest on which these laws are based.

[...] It has been a cause of regret and even bitterness amongst our people that in spite of such widespread condemnation, internal and external, of the inhumanity of these laws, the present government has not seen it fit to curtail or abolish them, and has even extended and intensified them, cancelling all exemptions from these laws and, to add insult to injury, it has extended them, for the first time in the history of our country, to our womenfolk. [...] There comes a time, sir, when a leader must give as practical a demonstration of his convictions and willingness to live up to the demands of the cause as he expects of his people. I felt that was the hour in our history, and in my life, for this demonstration. I am not sorry or ashamed of what I did. I could not have done less than I did and still live with my conscience. I would rightly lose the confidence of my people, and earn the disrespect of right-thinking people in my country and in the world, and the disdain of posterity. (Insisting on the abolition of the pass laws, he goes on): It is my firm belief that it is the duty of all right-thinking people, black and white, who have the true interest of our country at heart, to strive for this without flinching.[11]

The limits of non-violence in the face of barbarity

Faced with the barbarity of the Europeans in South Africa, Mandela reconsidered the virtues of non-violent protest. In spite of his attachment to this principle, he felt responsible for having discouraged anti-apartheid activists who were tempted to resort to violence to defend themselves and who were becoming increasingly exasperated by the brutality of White power. Their trust in him began to waver. They began to wonder whether it might not be more useful to put an end to the peace and quiet of the masters' race by a few deadly attacks. For the ANC leaders who wanted to avoid a civil war between Blacks and Whites at all costs, this was an extremely harrowing situation. The need for an organisation capable of offering an alternative that could channel the latent violence began to be felt.

When, at the end of the trial, Mandela was declared innocent along with the other accused thanks to their very efficient team of lawyers, he went underground and worked on creating an organisation that was to be in charge of the actions taken against apartheid. It was set up in November 1961 and initially allowed only acts of sabotage that did not endanger human life. Men in charge of sabotage undertook to act without weapons to ensure that situations remained under control and that strong discipline was enforced. Mandela and his companions believed this was a way to channel the violence of the victims of white barbarity. They hoped that the tormentors would realise that the people could endure only so much, so that the potential for the future relationship between the races might be preserved. Unfortunately, the response of the White community was both swift and brutal. Additional laws were added to the legal and repressive arsenal of apartheid and sabotage too became punishable by death.

The leaders of Umkhonto we Sizwe MK, the organisation in charge of sabotage, realised that the selective raids conducted against military facilities, power plants, telephone lines and means of transportation were not enough to make the whites reconsider their racial hegemony or bring them to the negotiating table with representatives of the African people. A switch to armed struggle must be organised. On the advice of his companions, Mandela left the country secretly to lead the ANC delegation that was to take part in the Addis-Ababa Conference in February 1962 organised by the West, Central and Southern Pan-African Liberation Movement. When he returned to South Africa, he was arrested on 5 August 1962, accused of having illegally left the country. He acted as his own defence counsel:

> I do not believe, Your Worship, that this court, in inflicting penalties on me for the crimes for which I am convicted should be moved by the belief that penalties will deter men from the course that they believe is right. [...]
>
> I am prepared to pay the penalty even though I know how bitter and desperate the situation of an African in the prisons of this country is. I have been in these prisons and I know how gross the discrimination against Africans is, even behind the prison wall... Nevertheless these considerations

> do not sway me from the path that I have taken nor will they sway others like me. [...] More powerful than my fear of the dreadful conditions to which I might be subjected in prison is my hatred for the dreadful conditions to which my people are subjected outside prison throughout this country…
>
> I have done my duty to my people and to South Africa. I have no doubt that posterity will pronounce that I was innocent and that the criminals that should have been brought before this court are the members of the government.[12]

Mandela received a three-year prison sentence for having encouraged people to strike and two years for having left the country without a passport. A five-year prison sentence without appeal. During the trial, he describes an incident that illustrates how disastrous, in human terms, fundamentally criminal systems such as those of the Third Reich or apartheid are for their victims, and sometimes for the individuals that serve those systems. It happened on the day the verdict was given, the morning before the court session began.

> I was in an office off the courtroom talking with Bob Hepple, who had been advising me on the case, and we were praising the fact that the day before, the UN General Assembly had voted in favour of sanctions against South Africa for the first time. [...] We were in the midst of this discussion when the prosecutor, Mr Bosch, entered the room and then asked Bob to excuse himself.
>
> "Mandela,' he said, after Bob had left, "I did not want to come to court today. For the first time in my career, I despise what I am doing. It hurts me that I should be asking the court to send you to prison." He then reached out and shook my hand, and expressed the hope that everything would turn out well for me. I thanked him for his sentiments, and assured him that I would never forget what he had said.[13]

Civil servants doing their work

In a civilised country where legislation establishes the right to life and human dignity, Prosecutor Bosch, who so uncompromisingly sought application of the letter of the law, could have become the advocate of the human rights to life and dignity. But in this case, his function was quite different. Under the apartheid regime, he served a criminal system in the name of a law that established a legal order premised upon the right of White people to enslave and maintain non-Whites in a state of enslavement. From the moment Parliament gives these practices its blessing, they are accepted and applied with no questions asked, even when their application "hurts." The law is the law.

Starting in 1960, in order to escape the pressure being brought to bear against South Africa, Verwoerd decided to "rid his country" of the surplus Black population which did not fit the needs of the White economy. His government created the Bantustans to make international opinion believe that the Bantus preferred to have their own "States." There were two main parts to the plan: establishing reservations that had no economic prospects but provided a permanent pool of slave labour and massively deporting "surplus" Africans who did not voluntarily go to the reservations where most of them had never set foot.

With the complicity of just a few chiefs, the apartheid government created the Bantustans of Bophuthatswana, Ciskei, Gazankulu, KwaZulu, Lebowa, Qwaqwa, Transkei and Venda. Fine men such as Prosecutor P.J. Bosch, in their capacity as magistrates and in the name of the law, had several million Africans deported there in spite of the patently life-threatening conditions that prevailed in those areas. Between 1960 and 1970, according, to the South African Institute of Racial Relations, 1,820,000 Africans were deported to the Bantustans by stringent application of the Bantu Laws Amendment Act of 1964 which allowed "endorsement out of the urban areas (i.e. the White areas) under pass law offences...[14]" Between 1970 and 1974, removals were considerably stepped up and in 1974, again according to the Institute of Racial Relations, the number of Africans deported reached approximately 4,169,000.

Victims were distributed as follows:

Bophuthatswana	496,000
Ciskei	413,000
Gazankulu	264,000
KwaZulu	1,029,000
Lebowa	705,000
Qwaqwa	25,000
Transkei	1,032,000
Venda	205,000[15]

Some additional 3.8 million Africans were expelled from White areas under a "land consolidation" plan announced in 1972. What is even more terrifying is the indifference of Western democracies that allowed the apartheid regime to "cleanse" the country basing itself on its economic needs.

The exact toll paid by the victims for this coldly devised and pitilessly applied policy has not so far been established by a body capable of performing such an assessment. However, in 1972, Barbara Rogers reported:

> Kupagani, a voluntary organisation aimed at boosting nutrition, circulated a request for information on conditions in the Bantustans at the end of 1972. The responses indicate that hundreds of people in the Transkei, Ciskei and Namaqualand are starving. Malnutrition was reported as the rule; 75–80 per cent of the children examined at two hospitals in Pond land, in the Transkei, were found to be suffering from it. Many of the children died or were permanently brain-damaged as a result. . . .
>
> Dr Trudi Thomas, who had practised for 25 years in the Ciskei, has found: 'About half of all the children in the Ciskei are being stunted in their growth through malnutrition.' In KwaZulu, a study of malnutrition warns that it is changing the people's physique; people are becoming small, stunted and mentally enfeebled.[16]

When presented with these results, the apartheid authorities responded:

> "Mr Froneman (Deputy Minister of Justice, Mines and Planning) announced that the South African government was under no obligation to prepare accommodation for people it was deporting from their homes: 'The removal of these superfluous Bantu from the White Homelands is not dependent on the development of the Bantu Homelands. . . . In the words of one Bantu Affairs Commissioner, the camps contain 'redundant people . . . (who) could not render productive service in an urban area men who had lost their jobs and could not find new employment; old and infirm people; unmarried mothers.'[17]"

This is a patent case of a policy that systematically imposes living conditions on a people that threaten the survival of the group either in part or in its entirety on racial grounds. In plain words, this is a genocidal policy. True, it was implemented in a legal framework by men acting in the name of the law who were doing their duty, often with the help of the law enforcement agencies. These men were neither any better nor any worse than Adolph Eichmann and so many others that did their "duty" within a legal framework.

However, some anti-racist Europeans quite seriously explained that: "A number of leading reporters have observed that the resettlement of the Bantus is not evocative of Nazi concentration camps. No one claims that there are any gas chambers in the Transkei. Racism there is of the cold and methodical kind, typical of businessmen who still believe this attitude pays off.[18]" As if the only way of effectively destroying a group, either wholly or partially, was to use gas chambers! It seems to me that in Rwanda, the Hutu extremists, trained – lest we forget – by French engineers,[19] exterminated between 600,000 and 1,000,000 Tutsis and moderate Hutus within a very short time in spite of the absence of gas chambers.

And the same author adds: "This cheerless combination of workers' estate and African village development nevertheless appeared to be quite habitable and reasonably priced: 3,500 old francs per month for a ground floor, three rooms, kitchen, small yard, for a tenant earning a monthly salary of 25,000 old francs.[20]"

These could just as well have been the words of a propaganda sheet on the payroll of Pretoria.

Notes

1. Mandela, Nelson, *Long Walk to Freedom*, Back Bay Books, 1995, p. 203.
2. Retrieved on 19 January 2011 at http://scnc.ukzn.ac.za/doc/HIST/freedomchart/freedomch.html
3. Mandela, op. cit., p. 213.
4. Kum'a N'Dumbe III, Alexandre, *Hitler voulait l'Afrique*, Paris, 1980, pp. 2 (Translation).
5. Ibid., p. 225.
6. The difficulties encountered by the American and British delegates in criminalising the Nazi policy of extermination of the Jews while steering clear of qualifying the annihilation of a group on racial grounds as a *sui generis* crime.
7. Luthuli, Albert, *Let My People Go*, Fount Paperbacks, 1984, pp. 195 and 194.
8. Mandela, op. cit., p. 244.
9. Luthuli, op. cit., pp. 153–154.
10. Cornevin, *L'Afrique du Sud en sursis*, op. cit. p. 51.
11. Luthuli, op. cit., pp. 219–220.
12. Mandela, op. cit., p. 332.
13. Mandela, *Long Walk to Freedom*, Abacus, London 1995, pp. 389–390.
14. Rogers, B., *Divide and Rule*, International Defence and Aid Fund, 1980, p. 58.
15. Ibid, p. 30–31, 45
16. Ibid, p. 51, 67.
17. Ibid, p. 61.
18. Paraf, Pierre, *Le racisme dans le monde*, op. cit., p. 114 (Translation).
19. See Braeckman, Colette, *Rwanda, histoire d'un génocide*, Paris, pp. 159–160, the testimony of Janvier Afrika, former member of the Interahamwes (Hutu extremist militia, death squad) trained by French soldiers.
20. Paraf, Pierre, op.cit., p. 114.

12

Never Again! Well..., Not in Europe Anyway

A prosecutor worthy of the Third Reich

It was therefore with the law entirely on its side that White power was poised to carry its racial policy to its logical conclusion and to suppress the slightest attempt by non-Europeans to stand up for freedom or racial equality. Repression was rampant everywhere. The government acquired the legal means to put any person suspected of hostility towards the regime under house arrest. The noose tightened around those anti-apartheid leaders who had so far escaped being thrown into jail.

On 11 July 1963, the police raided the farm where the senior command of Umkhonto we Sizwe (MK) had gathered. They were all arrested and although the police found no weapons, the documents there proved sufficient. Mandela, who had served nine months of his five-year prison term, was taken out of his cell to appear in court together with his comrades at what came to be referred to as the Rivonia Trial.

Lead Defence Counsel, Bram Fischer, was one of the few South African Europeans who like Ruth First, Joe Slovo or Denis Goldberg spent their lives fighting for the freedom of the people, for human dignity and for a democratic and non-racial South Africa. When the accused and their lawyers were permitted to meet, Bram Fischer announced that prosecution was going to seek the death penalty. Indeed, the public prosecutor chosen for this trial was tailored to the task. He was as forbidding as Oswald Pirow, the former South African Nazi who had preceded him. Thus, Walter Sisulu, Govan Mbeki,[1] Ahmed Kathrada, Andrew Mlangeni, Bob Hepple, Raymond Mhlaba, Elias Motsoaledi, Denis Goldberg,[2] Rusty Bernstein, Jimmy Kantor and Mandela found themselves facing Dr Percy Yutar. Many years later, Mandela would say:

> De Wet was one of the last judges appointed by the United Party before the Nationalists came to power and was not considered a government lackey.

> [...] The prosecutor was Dr Percy Yutar, deputy attorney general of the Transvaal, whose ambition was to become attorney general of South Africa. He was a small, bald, dapper fellow whose voice squeaked when he became angry or emotional. He had a flair for the dramatic and for high-flown if imprecise language.
>
> Yutar rose and addressed the court, "My Lord, I call the case of the state against the National High Command and others." [...] Yutar handed in the indictment and authorized that we be charged immediately and tried summarily. This was the first time we were given a copy of the indictment. The prosecution had kept it from us, though they gave it to the *Rand Daily Mail*, which had splashed it all over that day's edition of the paper. [...]
>
> Bram Fischer stood up and asked the court for a remand on the grounds that the defence had not had time to prepare its case. [...] The state had been preparing for three months, but we had only received the indictment that day. Justice de Wet gave us a three-week adjournment [...]
>
> We went on the attack immediately – Bram Fischer criticized the state's indictment as shoddy, poorly drawn and containing absurdities such as the allegation that I had participated in certain acts of sabotage on dates when I was in Pretoria Local (as a prisoner). Yutar was flummoxed. Judge de Wet looked to him to reply to Bram's argument, and instead of offering particulars he began to give what the judge derided as 'a political speech.' De Wet was impatient with Yutar's fumbling and told him so. "The whole basis of your argument as I understand it, Mister Yutar, is that you are satisfied that the accused are guilty." De Wet then quashed the indictment and gavelled the session to a close. [...]
>
> This was a blow to the government; for it now had to go back to the drawing-board in the case it was calling the trial to end all trials.[3]

The Rivonia Trial continues to be the most important political trial in South Africa. The prisoners wanted to use it as a platform for protest. In agreement with his comrades, Mandela decided to read out a statement from the dock rather than testifying as a witness; in this way he was able to make a representation to the Court that would otherwise have been censored. The drawback was that a witness statement made from the dock does not carry the same weight as one made from the witness stand. Defence Counsel warned Mandela about the situation in which he was placing himself. With some disdain, Mandela explained: "I wanted very much to cross swords with Percy Yutar, but it was more important that I use the platform to highlight our grievances.[4]

Never Again! Well..., Not in Europe Anyway

As an unflagging servant of the criminal system to which he belonged, Dr Percy Yutar ordered the room where the accused met with their lawyers to be tapped. Mandela and his comrades had enough of a sense of humour to mock him.

> We even used the state's eavesdropping to our advantage by supplying them with disinformation. We gave every indication that I was going to testify so that they would spend their time planning their cross-examination. In a staged conversation, I told our attorney Joel Joffe that I would need the treason trial record to prepare my testimony. We smiled at the notion of Yutar poring over the hundred or so volumes of the treason trial transcripts.[5]

In the days that followed, Nelson Mandela worked in his cell on this statement, which was to be (and remains to this day) the most moving political address and the most composed lesson of history and dignity uttered in South Africa. For four hours, Mandela quietly explained the legitimacy of his people's struggle. He showed how in every aspect of life, the Blacks were only barely able to survive whereas the Whites enjoyed a high standard of living and were determined to maintain things as they were.

> On Monday April 20, under the tightest of security, we were taken to the Palace of Justice, this time to begin our defence. [...] Then, in his soft voice, Bram said, "The defence case, My Lord, will commence with a statement from the dock by Accused No. 1, who personally took part in the establishment of Umkhonto, and who will be able to inform the court of the beginnings of that organization." At this, Yutar popped up from the table and cried, 'My Lord! My Lord! He was distressed that I would not be testifying, for he had undoubtedly prepared for my cross-examination. "My Lord," he said rather despondently, "a statement from the dock does not carry the same weight as evidence under oath."
>
> "I think, Dr Yutar," Justice de Wet responded curtly, "that counsels for the defence have sufficient experience to advise their clients without your assistance." Yutar sat down.
>
> "Neither we nor our clients are unaware of the provisions of the criminal code," replied Bram. "I call on Nelson Mandela."[6]

Hence, to Dr Yutar's dismay, Mandela, Accused No. 1, gave a memorable speech that ended with this sentence, that later became a paragon: "During my lifetime I have dedicated myself to this struggle of the African people. I have fought against White domination, and I have fought against Black domination. I have cherished the ideal of a democratic and free society in which all persons live together in harmony and with equal opportunities. It is an ideal which I hope to live for and to achieve. But if needs be, it is an ideal for which I am prepared to die."⁷

Three decades later, Mandela recalls:

> At this point I placed my papers on the defence table, and turned to face the judge. The courtroom became extremely quiet. I did not take my eyes off Justice de Wet […] When I finished my address and sat down, it was the last time that Justice de Wet ever looked me in the eye… Accused No. 2, Walter Sisulu, was next. Walter had to bear the brunt of the cross-examination that Yutar had prepared for me. Walter withstood a barrage of hostile questions and rose above Yutar's petty machinations to explain our policy in clear and simple terms.[8]

Preserving the master race

The South African historian Francis Meli sums up the cross-examination conducted by the prosecutor in this trial for the purpose of preserving the privileges of White people:

> Yutar: You have called them (the cabinet ministers) amongst other things, criminal?
>
> Kathrada: That's what they are.
>
> [According to Meli, Yutar found it hard to keep his temper, especially when Kathrada refused to answer questions about other people and their activities.]
>
> Yutar: Sisulu adopted that attitude in the box and you are doing the same.
>
> Kathrada: Is there anything wrong with that?
>
> Yutar: Don't ask me… I am telling you that you are adopting the same attitude as Sisulu.
>
> Kathrada: That's obvious.
>
> Yutar: And this political organisation to which you owe this loyalty; does it also include the African National Congress?
>
> Kathrada: Yes.
>
> Yutar: It also includes the Umkhonto?
>
> Kathrada: If I knew anything about the Umkhonto, I would not tell you. If the fact of it was to implicate anybody, I would not tell you.
>
> Yutar: Then how am I to test your story and what you are telling us?

> Kathrada: I feel very sorry for you Dr, but I am unable to help you there.
>
> Yutar: How is his Lordship to test the accuracy of your evidence?
>
> Kathrada: I am afraid I have no suggestions.
>
> [So it went on. In his irritation, Yutar picked upon one of Mandela's captured diaries in which there had been some entries referring to a certain 'K'.]
>
> Yutar: Are you sometimes referred to as K?
>
> Kathrada: I am not referred to as K.
>
> Yutar: Never?
>
> Kathrada: I don't know anybody who refers to me as K.
>
> Yutar: Do you know anyone else who goes under the initial K?
>
> Kathrada: Yes.
>
> Yutar: Who?
>
> Kathrada: Mr Khrushchev. [There was laughter in the court. Yutar bellowed: "So you are trying to be funny at my expense," and Kathrada replied that Yutar had asked him of a 'K' he knew of and he had replied.⁹]

In the end, Mandela and his comrades were not charged for high treason because in the case of a crime subject to capital punishment, the public prosecutor is required to prove this accusation beyond reasonable doubt. To do so, he needed two witnesses per charge. Instead, the public prosecutor chose the charge of sabotage because the Sabotage Act of June 1962 puts the onus of proof of innocence of the accused on the defence. Mandela tells us:

> On 20 May, Yutar handed out a dozen blue leather-bound volumes of his final speech to the press and one to the defence. Despite its handsome packaging, Yutar's address was a garbled summary of the prosecution's case and did not explain the indictment or assess the evidence. It was filled with ad hominem insults. "The deceit of the accused is amazing", he said at one point. "Although they represented scarcely 1 per cent of the Bantu population they took it upon themselves to tell the world that the Africans in South Africa are suppressed, oppressed and depressed." Even Judge de Wet seemed mystified by Yutar's speech, and at one point interrupted him to say, "Mr Yutar, you do concede that you failed to prove guerrilla warfare was decided upon, do you not?"
>
> Yutar was stunned. He had assumed precisely the opposite. We were surprised as well, for the judge's question gave us hope. Yutar haltingly told the court that preparations for guerrilla warfare were indeed made.

"Yes, I know that," de Wet replied impatiently, "the defence concedes that. But they say that prior to their arrest they took no decision to engage in guerrilla warfare. I take it that you have no evidence contradicting that and that you accept it?"

"As Your Worship wishes," Yutar said in a strangled voice.

Yutar finished by saying that the case was not only one of high treason par excellence, but of murder and attempted murder – neither of which were mentioned in the indictment. In a fit of bluster, he proclaimed, "I make bold to say that every particular allegation in the indictment has been proved." He knew, even as he uttered those words, that they were patently false.

Defence counsel Arthur Chaskalson rose first to deal with some of the legal questions raised by the prosecution. He rejected Yutar's statement that the trial had anything to do with murder and reminded the court that MK's express policy was that there should be no loss of life. When Arthur began to explain that other organizations committed acts of sabotage for which the accused were blamed, de Wet interrupted to say that he already accepted that as a fact. This was another unexpected victory.

Bram Fischer spoke next and was prepared to tackle the state's two most serious contentions: that we had undertaken guerrilla warfare and that the ANC and MK were the same. Though de Wet had said he believed that guerrilla warfare had not yet begun, we were taking no chances. But as Bram launched into his first point, de Wet interjected somewhat testily, "I thought I made my attitude clear. I accept that no decision or date was fixed upon for guerrilla warfare".

When Bram began his second point, de Wet again interrupted him to say that he also conceded the fact that the two organizations were separate. Bram, who was usually prepared for anything, was hardly prepared for de Wet's response. He then sat down; the judge had accepted his arguments even before he had made them. We were jubilant – that is, if men facing the death sentence can be said to be jubilant. Court was adjourned for three weeks while de Wet considered the verdict.[10]"

In spite of these circumstances – a poorly prepared indictment and a judge who knew that the grounds for the most serious accusations were lacking – the prisoners were not acquitted. All over the world, nonetheless, progressive forces rallied, calling for the annulment of the trial and the prisoners' release. At the UN, the countries that were against the imperialist policies of the major powers demanded that the government of Pretoria respect the lives of Mandela and his comrades. The reasoning for the sentence handed down by the judge is astonishing to say the least:

On Friday 12 June 1964 we entered court for the last time.

[…] De Wet […] seemed absorbed in his own thoughts. […] He nodded to us to rise. I tried to catch his eye, but he was not even looking in our direction.

His eyes were focused on the middle distance. His face was very pale, and he was breathing heavily. […] And then he began to speak.

'I have heard a great deal during the course of this case about the grievances of the non-European population. The accused have told me and their counsel have told me that the accused who were all leaders of the non-European population were motivated entirely by a desire to ameliorate these grievances. I am by no means convinced that the motives of the accused were as altruistic as they wish the court to believe. People who organize a revolution usually take over the government and personal ambition cannot be excluded as a motive.

De Wet paused for a moment as if to catch his breath. His voice, which was muted before, was now barely audible.

'The function of this court, as is the function of the court in any other country, is to enforce law and order and to enforce the laws of the state within which it functions. The crime of which the accused have been convicted, that is the main crime, the crime of conspiracy, is in essence one of high treason. The state has decided not to charge the crime in this form. Bearing this in mind and giving the matter very serious consideration I have decided not to impose the supreme penalty which in a case like this would usually be proper penalty for the crime, but consistent with my duty that is the only leniency which I can show. The sentence in the case of all the accused will be one of life imprisonment'.[11]"

The irony of this was that Dr Percy Yutar had been President of the South African Education Council and President of the United Hebrew Congregation of Johannesburg. As it turns out, his zeal was not entirely pointless since although he did not succeed in accomplishing his dream of becoming Attorney General for South Africa, he did manage to get appointed Attorney General of the Orange Free State in 1968.

A long and difficult struggle

The effect of the cynicism and infamy of the Rivonia Trial was to radicalise those who were against apartheid at the UN General Assembly. Countries from the South repeatedly proposed sanctions that were systematically countered by the Western powers. Passed resolutions carry some moral weight but have no binding force unless they are Security Council resolutions.

As a result, the position adopted by France, the United Kingdom and the United States was morally untenable. Using their vetoing powers, these countries systematically opposed the adoption of radical economic sanctions against apartheid. The Special Committee against Apartheid published communiqués that were poorly circulated and rarely caught the attention of those who decide what information should be fed to international opinion.

In the meantime, as noted by Indres Naidoo:

> loans and direct investment originating from France, the United States, Britain and Germany (in the country of apartheid) came to the enormous amount of thirty billion dollars. This economic aid and its technical, scientific and military extensions enabled Pretoria to establish powerful armed forces used both against anti-apartheid combatants internally, and, beyond its borders, against neighbouring African countries that the racist regime is seeking to destabilise.[12]

In spite of the manoeuvring by the powerful sponsors of the apartheid regime,

> On 30 November 1973, the General Assembly of the United Nations adopts and submits the International Convention on the Suppression and Punishment of the Crime of Apartheid to the states parties for ratification and adherence. Under Article 1 they declare *apartheid to be a crime against humanity*. Article 2 defines the crime of apartheid as including similar policies and practices of racial segregation and discrimination as practised in southern Africa, and applying to the following inhuman acts committed for the purpose of establishing and maintaining domination by one racial group of persons over any other racial group of persons and systematically oppressing them. The following acts are mentioned:
>
> (a) denial to a member or members of a racial group or groups of the right to life and liberty of person;
>
> (b) deliberate imposition on a racial group or groups of living conditions calculated to cause its or their physical destruction in whole or in part;
>
> (c) any legislative measures and other measures calculated to prevent a racial group or groups from participating in the political, social, economic and cultural life of the country and the deliberate creation of conditions preventing the full development of such a group or groups, in particular by denying to members of a racial group or groups basic human rights and freedoms, including the right to work, the right to form recognized trade unions, the right to education, the right to leave and to return to their country, the right to a nationality,

the right to freedom of movement and residence, the right to freedom of opinion and expression, and the right to freedom of peaceful assembly and association;

(d) any measures, including legislative measures, designed to divide the population along racial lines by the creation of separate reserves and ghettos for the members of a racial group or groups.[13]"

While peoples all over the world attempted to establish means to eliminate and punish the crime of apartheid, the governments that backed this crime against humanity were busy reinforcing their alliance with the apartheid regime. Menahem Begin, whose constant references to the Nazi genocides were aimed at gaining a monopoly over indignation, perhaps even over suffering, went to South Africa at the end of October 1971 to meet Prime Minister Vorster. The latter "expressed deep understanding of the situation in Israel and his willingness to entertain friendly ties between South Africa and Israel.[14]"

The Committee against the Crime of Apartheid formed at the initiative of the UN General Assembly embarked on an information campaign and expressed its concern with the strengthening of political, economic and military ties between Israel and the apartheid regime. In resolution 3151 G (XXVIII) dated 14 December 1973, the UN General Assembly condemned this alliance.[15] This resolution was given little publicity and so had limited impact.

Pierre Vidal-Naquet, who objected to the instrumentalisation of the Shoah by Israeli leaders, said:

> The genocide of the Jews ceases to be a historical reality as an existential experience and becomes a common instrument for political legitimation exploited with equal readiness both to achieve political adherence domestically and to put pressure on the diaspora and make its elements unconditionally toe the line with the slightest twist in Israeli policy. There is a paradox in using genocide both as a sacred moment in history and a very secular argument, or even as an opportunity for tourism and trade.[16]

An eternal legacy

In 1976, when the anti-racist forces in the world were rallying to support the South African people, Prime Minister Yitzhak Rabin of Israel extended an invitation to South African Prime Minister J.B. Vorster. While on a four-day visit to Israel, this former member of the Ossewabrandwag received a royal welcome. He "held talks with the President of Israel, the

Prime Minister, the Foreign Minister, the Defence Minister and other high officials in the Israeli Government. He toured strategic areas in the southern Sinai (reportedly the first foreign Prime Minister to do so), and visited a military aircraft factory.[17]" Whilst this former Nazi terrorist was visiting Israel, the apartheid regime and the state of Israel entered into a broad-based agreement on economic, scientific and industrial cooperation. "The subsequent announcement that Israel was building two missile boats for the apartheid regime made it clear that military co-operation is being rapidly strengthened following Mr Vorster's visit.[18]"

This agreement roused protests from the anti-racist movements but was welcomed with almost hysterical satisfaction by most parts of the White community. Some Zionist organisations "hailed Vorster as 'an outstanding statesman' and called the pact 'a most imaginative act of statesmanship on the part of both countries.'[19]" The *Star of Johannesburg*, in its weekly issue dated 17 April 1976, made the following comment: "Clearly the pact goes well beyond the usual trade and co-operation agreements which normally round off a state visit between friendly countries. [...] at the root of the pact is a mutual exchange of materials and military know-how which both countries desperately need[20]" The *Rand Daily Mail* of Johannesburg, on 14 April wrote:

> There is no gainsaying the signal nature of Mr Vorster's triumph this week. By achieving a publicly announced economic, scientific and industrial pact with Israel he has done far more than merely formalize bonds that have, in any case, been growing stronger. He has, in fact, acquired for South Africa a public friend, an avowed ally, at a time when this country confronts an increasingly hostile world and an increasingly aggressive black Africa.[21]

At these heights of cynicism, even the powers that protected the apartheid regime, the very same ones that also sponsored the state of Israel, were irritated by the "insouciance" of the Israeli authorities. The struggle against the crime of apartheid indeed gained considerable legitimacy. The International Convention on the Suppression and Punishment of the Crime of Apartheid was massively approved by the UN General Assembly on 30 November 1973. It recognised that apartheid was a crime against humanity. But the political instrumentalisation of the Shoah gave the Israeli leaders a sort of moral impunity.

This moral impunity enabled the Israeli lawmakers to adopt overtly discriminatory measures without the press ever mentioning the fact. At the

Eichmann trial in Jerusalem in 1961, some people were certainly irritated to hear Hannah Arendt recall that

> in Israel, where rabbinical law rules the personal life of Jewish citizens, in such a way that no Jew can marry a non-Jew; that marriages concluded abroad are recognised, but children of mixed marriages are legally bastards (children of Jewish parentage born out of wedlock are legitimate), and if one happens to have a non-Jewish mother he can neither be married nor buried [...]. There was certainly something breath-taking in the naïveté with which the prosecution denounced the infamous Nuremberg Laws of 1935, which had prohibited intermarriage and sexual intercourse between Jews and Germans. The better informed among the correspondents were well aware of the irony, but they did not mention it in their reports. This, they figured, was not the time to tell the Jews what was wrong with the laws and institutions of their own country.[22]

Israel's racist policy spurred the UN General Assembly to adopt resolution 3379 (XXX) on 10 November 1975. On this occasion, the assembly recalled its resolution 1904 (XVIII) of 20 November 1963 that proclaimed: "Any doctrine based on racial differentiation or superiority is scientifically false, morally condemnable, socially unjust and dangerous." It also expressed concern over "the manifestations of racial discrimination still evident in certain parts of the world, this discrimination being sometimes imposed by certain governments by means of legislative, administrative or other measures." Finally, it recalled that in resolution 3151 G (XXVIII) dated 14 December 1973, the General Assembly had condemned the alliance between South African racism and Zionism and "defined Zionism as a form of racism and racial discrimination".[23]

In 1975, Unesco had already condemned Israel for its racist practices in the cultural sphere. The government's response was to identify Judaism with Zionism and Jews with Zionists. The logical conclusion was that anti-Zionism was necessarily anti-Semitism.

We are family

As early as the end of the 1920s, the Zionist movement acknowledged its family ties with German National Socialism, when it found the party's political programme concerning the Jews to be pro-Zionist. "… only Zionists had any chance of negotiating with the German authorities," states Arendt, "for the simple reason that their chief Jewish adversary, the Central Association of German Citizens of Jewish Faith, to which 95% of organised Jews in Germany then belonged, specified in its bylaws that its chief task was the "fight against anti-Semitism;" it had suddenly become by definition an organisation "hostile to the State.[24]" This happened before the security police established its dictatorial authority over the organisation and turned it into "an integral part of the machinery of destruction.[25]"

The Nazi leaders saw the Zionists as the only trustworthy Jews with whom they could embark on negotiations:

> In the spring of 1933, they invited Baron Leopold Itz von Mildenstein, an engineer and journalist of Austrian extraction and one of the first members of the SS, to come to Palestine with his wife, to write a series of articles for *Angriff*, newspaper founded by Joseph Goebbels. The von Mildensteins came accompanied by Kurt Tuchler and his wife. Tuchler was active in the Zionist Organization of Berlin and was in charge of relations with the Nazi party. [...] Von Mildenstein toured the country from one end to the other [...] His articles titled "A Nazi Visits Palestine," exuded sympathy for Zionism.
>
> The *Angriff* attached such importance to this series of articles that it cast a special medallion to commemorate von Mildenstein's journey: one side displayed a swastika and the other a Star of David. Von Mildenstein also took several recordings of Hebrew songs back with him; Tuchler heard one of the records playing during one of his visits to Gestapo headquarters. Von Mildenstein did more than promote Zionism to the German public. From time to time he also passed on useful information to Tuchler. [...] Von Mildenstein headed the Office of Jewish Affairs; on his staff was a man who would be his successor: Adolf Eichmann.[26]"

Thus, the alliance between the state of Israel and the apartheid regime ruled by former South African Nazis – far from being unholy as some are apt to believe – was coherent. In the words of a history textbook for secondary school pupils in the country of apartheid, the Second World War was "an unfortunate misunderstanding between Western powers that led to weakening of the colonial powers.[27]" With that nasty incident disposed of in 1945, naturally one could go back to the good old days and revive family ties.

Ever since the United Nations resolution that defines Zionism as a form of racism and racial discrimination, some major changes have occurred in the world, including the fall of the Berlin wall, the release of Mandela and his accession to power in South Africa, negotiations between the Israeli government and the PLO represented by Yasser Arafat. Throughout, the Israeli policy of discrimination remained unchanged. According to a report submitted to the United Nations in March 1998, "seventeen laws that discriminate against the Arab citizens of Israel have been inventoried in that country.[28]" Not to mention, the alarm sounded by Amnesty International against the practice of systematic involvement of medical doctors in the torture of Palestinian prisoners in Israeli jails.[29]

Notes

1. In June 1999, his son Thabo Mbeki succeeded Mandela and became the second President of a freed post-apartheid South Africa.
2. Denis Goldberg, the youngest member of the group, was a Jewish social campaigner and activist in the struggle against apartheid and for the cause of freedom and human dignity.
3. Mandela, Nelson, *Long Walk to Freedom*, London: Abacus, 1995, pp. 418–421.
4. Ibid, p. 430.
5. Ibid, p. 430.
6. Ibid, pp. 431–432.
7. Ibid, p. 438.
8. Ibid, pp. 438–439.
9. Meli, Francis, *A History of the ANC. South Africa Belongs to Us*, London: James Currey Ltd, 1989, p. 157.
10. Mandela, op. cit., pp. 440–442.
11. Ibid, pp. 446–448.
12. Naidoo, Indres, *Dans les bagnes de l'apartheid*, Paris, 1986, p. 11.
13. UN pdf file downloaded 11/01/11 at http://search.un.org/search?ie=utf8&site=un_org&output=xml_no_dtd&client=UN_Website_English&num=10&lr=lang_en&proxystylesheet=UN_Website_
14. Benabdallah, Abdelkader, op. cit., p. 86.
15. United Nations Special Committee Against Apartheid, No. 5/77, February 1977.
16. Vidal-Naquet, Pierre, *Les assassins de la mémoire*, Paris, 1987, p. 130.
17. *Relations between Israel and South Africa*. Reprint of United Nations Special Committee Against Apartheid, No. 5/77, February 1977, p. 10.
18. Ibid, p. 11.
19. Ibid, p. 11.
20. Ibid, p. 11.
21. Ibid, p. 11.
22. Arendt, Hannah, *Eichmann in Jerusalem: A Report on the Banalization of Evil*, New York: Penguin Books, 2006, pp. 7–8.

23. *Sionisme et racisme*, op. cit., p. 314. See also Report on relations between Israel and South Africa adopted by the UN Special Committee against apartheid, August 19, 1976
24. Arendt, op. cit., p. 59.
25. Hilberg, Raul, *The Destruction of the European Jews*, New York, Harper & Row, 1961, p. 123.
26. Tom Segev, op.cit., p. 40–41.
27. *La France et l'apartheid. Documents de la commission d'enquête sur l'apartheid en Afrique du Sud*, Paris, 1977, p. 84.
28. *Le Monde diplomatique*, May 1999, p. 19.
29. See Report by Amnesty International, *"Under Constant Medical Supervision" – Torture, Ill-Treatment and Health Professionals in Israel and the Occupied Territories*, published in August 1996. See also *Le Monde diplomatique*, January 1997, p. 8.

13

They Did Not Realise Blacks Are Humans

Ordinary persecutors

On May 25, 1999, the Franco-German TV channel, Arte, broadcast a programme on South Africa and presented excerpts from some 2,700 testimonies heard by the Truth and Reconciliation Commission formed in South Africa. The survivors and relatives of victims were willing to testify along with former persecutors who, in exchange for an amnesty, were willing to confess their crimes.

All of these Whites, who had become persecutors for a good cause before going on to confess, individually sent the Commission a statement through the attorney representing them.

These men simply called the attention of the commission and of the competent authorities to the fact it would be a great injustice if they were sentenced. They had only done their duty by obeying orders and had not at any moment acted of their own initiative or in pursuit of personal gain. They stated they had acted as patriots. It had been their responsibility to prevent the forces hostile to the government from prospering or developing. Their performance was assessed by their capacity to suppress individuals that were harmful to the proper operation of the state machinery. And although these people were torturers, they were conceivably sincere in their arguments.

> We were brought up under apartheid. We were taught by the Church that it was approved by God, that our participation in the Special Forces was justified to maintain apartheid. We were taught that the Blacks were inferior, that their needs, emotions and aspirations differed from ours. We were taught that we were superior, that our differences justified apartheid. We understand this was wrong. We supported the National Party until 1994. We always acted in its interest, to further its goals. We believed in its policy, we believed that we had a duty to support it. What we say now is that the party

has abandoned us and more or less thrown us overboard. We are alone in shouldering the responsibility of confronting our past, of justifying our acts, of presenting the views of the Afrikaners about the conflict. The former government and our superiors must account for the orders about which we will be testifying and admit that they approved illegal acts as shown by our actions and the fact that they were authorised. We will testify about the time of conflict and will show that our acts were all strictly tied to a political objective: maintaining the government, the National Party and apartheid, fighting communism, preventing liberation and democracy for all in South Africa![1]

As the "Black Peril" grew, these men had to alter their strategy, and engage in repression and preventive elimination. From the confessions of Lieutenant Hechter, who to his credit was willing to shoulder responsibility for what his men had done, it is apparent that rather than waiting for people to return covertly, it was decided that they would be removed before leaving the country to go into military training abroad. This new strategy, referred to as "preventive elimination" led to Black children, particularly secondary school pupils, being slaughtered. Police officers, who were often Black themselves, were tasked with approaching them and offering them the option of leaving the country covertly to join the ANC and receive military training, added to which they would be paid a very good salary. Afterwards, special force groups, the death squads, would dispose of the teenagers that had fallen into the trap. When questioned by the Commission on the ultimate fate of nine students who were burned alive at Kwandebele, Lieutenant Hechter who was the former commander for preventive elimination explained: "They were activists. And they wanted to go abroad for training. Their elimination was a preemptive action to prevent trained people from returning.[2]" When asked whether the children of Kwandebele had died because they had committed acts of sabotage or because they wanted to leave the country, Lieutenant Hechter replied that preventive elimination was justified because they all intended to leave the country.

We should remember that on the eve of the nineteenth century in Saint-Domingue, Rochambeau consulted with his men to decide whether they should kill Maurepas' children to avert the risk that they might become a threat to white power when they grew up. We should also remember that, nearly a century and a half later, when questioned about the extermination of Jewish children, Otto Ohlendorf explained to the prosecutor that as they grew up they would become as serious a danger as their parents had been.

A few decades later, Lieutenant Hechter took up the same argument. These children must be killed so that they do not become a danger to the state.

One of these perpetrators noted that if their work had been arbitrary or done unbeknownst to the people who were governing the country, how was it that they had received all those tributes and honorary distinctions? Their worth was measured on the basis of their performance in fighting the enemy. Another perpetrator calmly declared that, ever since they had been small, they had been educated to believe that a Black was just a *Kaffir*, a *caffer* or something like that, but not a man because inferior in every way. They had been told that *caffers* were dangerous and that there was no such thing as degrading or cruel treatment of them. He did not say he had changed his mind and did not express any remorse.

In 1960, Indres Naidoo was a young anti-apartheid activist. His father, grandfather and grandmother before him were acquainted with South African jails. Arrested and sentenced to ten years imprisonment and then banished upon being released, Naidoo published his testimony. An extract illustrates the type of indoctrination a White child received under the apartheid regime:

> There were more than a thousand of us in dirty, ill-fitting and scanty clothes, our caps looking strange on our hairless heads, and we marched in four silent columns across the island to the old quarry.
>
> Our feet were uncomfortable [...]. It was a little after six in the morning, and we were off to work. No one sang. No one whistled. No one spoke. Four long columns, moving without a sound.
>
> A house stood completely on its own, fenced in and guarded by an armed warder, and in the doorway we could see the figure of Robert Sobukwe, leader of the PAC [...]
>
> A little further on we saw women chatting in little groups and children playing: we were excited to be approaching civilian life, the first we had seen in all the months since our imprisonment. As we trooped quietly past, the children started shouting at us: '*Kaffirs... coolies*', and some even began to throw stones. One little boy of about five was standing on a small platform built in his yard, pointing a homemade toy rifle at us and yelling in his little voice: '*Kaffirs, ek skiet julle* – *kaffirs*, I'm shooting you'. We felt very bad to see these young kids brought up to hate us like that.[3]

This was happening in 1963–1964 – is there any reason that by the time these children became adults they would have any misgivings about shooting down Blacks? Hardly surprising, just a natural consequence.

What is not quite so logical is that after 1945, the Allied powers gave their support to former Nazis of South Africa for reasons that are easy to identify: the victims were not Whites, specifically Blacks, i.e., "inferior" beings. Not only would the culprits of this crime preserve the superiority of Whites in South Africa but these staunch anti-communists would also protect the interests of international capitalism. That being the case, human rights could be dispensed with.... in some places. At that time, Western powers had embarked on something of a crusade against the human rights violations perpetrated in countries with regimes that claimed to be communist.

A state above the law

Were similar developments inevitable in the relationship of domination imposed by the Israelis on the Palestinian people? The Israelis treat the non-Jews much in the same way as the country of apartheid treated non-Whites. The judicial system applies differently depending on whether the accused is a Jew or a Palestinian.

In criminal cases for instance, as noted by Amnon Kapeliuk,

> when the authorities conduct investigations, there is blatant discrimination between Jews and Arabs especially when someone has died. When a Palestinian kills a Jew, the investigation is thorough and the accused receives the heaviest sentence (life imprisonment), his family's house is blown up or sometimes put under seal. If a Jew kills a Palestinian, the police takes its time before beginning the investigation. The investigation drags on and in most cases the offender is not prosecuted. (...) In 1993, in fourteen cases of Palestinians being murdered by Jews, the investigation was closed without any indictment being issued.[4]

This policy of belittling the lives of the members of a group while magnifying those of the members of the dominant group considered to be superior in every way, is a permanent feature of regimes that have built-in classifications of inferiority and superiority for individuals based on the group to which they belong.

For as long as the concentration camp environment of America lasted, the Europeans that managed it, independently of language or religion, established a system of law and order in which individuals were assigned legal status on an explicitly racial basis. In the 1670s for instance, when a Black was worth between 600 and 1,000 pounds, "the nineteenth century historian Peytraud revealed a scale of punishments for slave owners who abused their slaves: thus, the fine for having cut off a slave's hands was two pounds; for having burnt a slave alive sixty pounds, for having cut out a slave's tongue, six pounds.⁵" A century later, although the status of freeborn and emancipated mixed bloods was not as bad as that of the Blacks, they continued to suffer discrimination under racial laws that assigned them a non-White status:

> In 1767 a free man of color was sentenced to be flogged, branded, and sold into slavery for assaulting a White. The principle that Whites were inviolate and should not be struck – even in cases of self-defense – was considered essential for the security of the colony.⁶

This principle was essential to the security of the concentration camp system.

The consequence of this tradition of applying and administering justice using criteria of racial discrimination, as we discussed previously, is still visible in the way the death penalty is applied in the United States. It is enlightening that in Israel, the most extremist elements, those who openly express their racism, come from the United States. This is where Baruch Goldstein came from. He was a Jewish doctor who, at daybreak on 25 February 1994, in the middle of Ramadan, massacred some thirty Palestinian worshippers at prayer in the Hebron mosque. At the Bronx faculty of medicine, where Goldstein had been educated, he was known for advocating that all Arabs be slaughtered.

> "In 1982, after finishing his medical studies, Baruch Goldstein emigrated to Israel," explains Kapeliuk. During his three years of military service as a doctor, Goldstein made no secret of his racist feelings. At the cadet school, he openly declared that "all Arabs should be killed." Indeed, during his military service, in particular in Lebanon, Goldstein refused to tend to injured Arabs. [...] However because of his devotion to the army, the military authorities looked the other way and he was able to continue to serve.⁷

Jonathan Goldberg, one of Igal Amir's three lawyers, also comes from the United States. Igal Amir is the young Jew who on 4 November 1995 assassinated Yitzhak Rabin, the Israeli prime minister.

> He [Goldberg] was one of the most markedly right-wing lawyers in Israel. He is rumoured to have represented a young man accused of having set fire to the Christian churches of Jerusalem, including the Gethsemane Church at the foot of the Mount of Olives, as an act of Jewish religious zealotry. The young man repented; the lawyer persuaded him that the

Rabbis approved of his action as conforming to rabbinic law, and so he retracted his repentance.[8]

After the attack that cost Prime Minister Rabin's life, "the Israeli authorities realised that fanatical American Jews were joining the ranks of the extreme right in Israel, using the Law of Return to sow hatred and conduct their antidemocratic activities.[9]" These Jews who were an unadulterated product of the White American culture where contempt and even violent suppression of inferior beings are well-rooted, were not the ones to sow the seeds of hatred in Israel. This hatred was already widespread; they simply discovered the ideal circumstances there to serve their cause, i.e., the modus operandi of Israeli society and institutions side by side with the vilification of the Palestinians.

The Palestinian Fedayeens were depicted as less than human by the Israeli authorities. In front of the Knesset on 8 June 1982, the Israeli Prime Minister describes them as "animals with two legs.[10]" A flood of abuse ensued. And what to think of the words of Golda Meir, who as "Prime Minister after the 1967 war was wont to say that the Palestinian people do not exist, that it is the invention of a few 'warped' Jews.[11]" Such an attitude could not be helpful in tempering hatred.

"Immigrants from the United States played an important role in the activities of the Zo Artzeinu (It's our country) movement which has ramifications in several American cities.[12]" Often the activists that belong to these groups make no attempt to conceal their nostalgia for Nazism. For instance the leader of the Zo Artzeinu movement, Moshe Feiglin, makes no secret of his admiration for the Fuhrer and thanks to Kapeliuk, we discover that:

> on the 8th of December 1995, in an interview published in the highly respected daily *Haaretz*, Feiglin says: "Nazism promoted Germany from a low to a fantastic physical and ideological status. The ragged, trashy youth body turned into a neat and orderly part of society and Germany received an exemplary regime, a proper justice system and public order. Hitler savored good music. He would paint. This was no bunch of thugs."[13]

For Feiglin and for many other Israelis, the Palestinian people does not exist: "There is no Palestinian nation. There is only an Arab-speaking public which has suddenly identified itself as a people. They are only parasites, inferior people. Neither do you have peoples amongst Africans, only tribes.[14]" Indeed, Feiglin is an extremist, but he voices racist attitudes that are not unusual in Israel. Large sections of society at all levels identify with these theories that assert the superiority of some and the implicit inferiority of others. The fanatics among them express those convictions in an unrefined or crude manner; but that is just a matter of form, not of substance. One example: "Abba Eban, the Minister for Foreign Affairs, who had the reputation of being a moderate, [...] too intellectual and distinguished for the political class.[15]" Before becoming Prime Minister, he was the Israeli Ambassador to the United States, the Minister for Education and even Deputy Prime Minister. Throughout his career, Abba Eban earned the respect of one and all including his opponents who recognized the uprightness of this brilliant jurist and former Cambridge scholar who was seen as "a politician in combination with a true intellectual.[16]" The statement he gave to the Israeli press in 1974 is particularly striking considering his habitual moderation:

> Just a few weeks ago a study by Professor Baker was published in Great Britain which, among other things, compares the history of Jews and of the Blacks in the United States, showing the differences in development, under similar circumstances, between the races that differ in terms of intelligence and other traits, Benabdallah reports. The question raised is whether the inferiority of Blacks is the outcome of the difficult circumstances they experienced for generations (chronic malnutrition, etc.) or whether it is their cause. In spite of the objections made by the progressives, who describe studies of this type as 'racist,' it appears that there is a hereditary difference in the intellectual level of a person whose father lived in the jungle and that of another whose ancestors were rabbis.[17]

To talk about "similar circumstances" applying to Blacks and Jews in America is one of those barefaced, blatantly dishonest lies. In the United States, just as in South Africa (which, incidentally, is where Abba Eban was born), all Whites were part of the superior race. As a result, they all, without exception and regardless of religion, availed themselves of the exclusive, legal, social and economic benefits and privileges set aside for the masters' race within a system of domination that relegated Blacks to the status of sub-humans. In other words, this is yet another instance of the widespread tendency among Westerners to forget that their privileges were obtained through a time-honoured hierarchy based on ethnicity.

When even the moderates and the most respected personalities in a society (and this applies to Israel) so outwardly support the theories that in the past brought the Nazis to power in Germany, one simply cannot expect any recognition of the right to life and to dignity for those whom they see as inferiors.

On 25 September 1994, Claude Lanzmann, on the strength of the prestige of his brilliant film, *Shoah*, presented *Tsahal* in Paris, a 5-hour long propaganda film about the Israeli army. Using the moral authority befitting a survivor of Hitler's genocides, Lanzmann made a point of showing that the Jewish army has special features that distinguish it from other armies. He avoids mentioning events that contradict his statement. For instance, "In the Israeli army, there is a death squad made up of units disguised as Arabs who summarily execute wanted Palestinian activists. The Israeli media have provided abundant material on this topic. But not a word of this is to be found in Claude Lanzmann's document.[18]"

Military cooperation between the apartheid regime and the state of Israel is not just a matter of selling military equipment. General Meir Amit, the former chief of the Israeli intelligence service, who went on to become CEO of Koor Industries, disclosed during a visit to South Africa in July 1975 that "senior Israeli military officers visit South Africa regularly and lecture African officers in modern warfare and counter intelligence techniques.[19]" Nor does Claude Lanzmann say anything about this either. Was he unaware that Marcia Freedman, who at the time was an opposition member of parliament in Israel, "asserted in June 1976 that hundreds of Israeli soldiers were attached to South African army units as instructors and participated in training maneuvers?[20]"

Testimonies of torture and sadism taken and made public by three members of the Knesset as described by Kapeliuk in his book, *Hebron, un massacre annoncé*, are all too similar to other events that took place in the German concentration camps, the torture rooms in the Congo under the rule of Léopold II and the prisons under the apartheid regime. Concerning the collective punitive expeditions undertaken by the army in the village of Halhoul close to Hebron, we are told:

> The men were taken from their homes as of midnight, wearing only pyjamas. It was winter and very cold. They were collected at the centre of the village on the square where the mosque is. They stayed there until morning. Meanwhile, the border police stormed the houses beating the occupants with sticks and hurling insults at them. The men herded to the mosque square received orders to urinate and defecate on one another.
>
> They were ordered to sing the Israeli national anthem and to chant "Long Live Israel!"[21] They were beaten tirelessly. Some fell to the ground. At dawn,

four trucks were requisitioned, into each of which more than a hundred inhabitants were crammed to be taken away to be interrogated at the Hebron military headquarters.

Here is another testimony: "On the day of the Holocaust Remembrance Day in April 1982, the prisoners were ordered to write a number on their arms just as the Germans had done with the Jews in the Nazi extermination camps. Then there was an endless game of slaps and blows with a stick. Every time a prisoner was slapped, the number of slaps his neighbour would get doubled. This sadistic game took place in the courtyard of the military headquarters in Hebron. Every evening, the duty officers would while away the time by brutalising the prisoners. They were taught to sing the Israeli national anthem. Those who did not sing properly had their genitals beaten.

This testimonial relates to the treatment to which the highest Muslim judge of Hebron was subjected. Cheikh Rajab Bayoud Tamimi states: "The settlers stopped me in the street and ordered me to remove a barricade of stones set up by some youths. These settlers from Kiryat Arba had recognized me, they knew who I was. They said to me: 'Clean the road' I refused saying that it was no task for a clergyman to remove stones from the road at which point they threatened me with their weapons. I asked the people around me to remove the stones, but the settlers from Kiryat Arba told them:

'Don't touch the stones.' They required me and me alone to remove them. I had no choice because they threatened me with their weapons and I remembered the photos where you see the Germans forcing Jewish clerics, who were bearded like me, to clean the streets. I shall never forget this humiliation."[22]

These methods were not unique to the Israeli army, and they are certainly not substantially different from those of their South African counterparts.

So what does Alain Finkielkraut, who is disgusted by the defence counsel's statements at Klaus Barbie's trial, think of this?

"Try to imagine for a moment at Nuremberg, the lawyers for the Nazis pleading the case of their clients (among others, Goering, Bormann, Frank, Rosenberg, Kaltenbrunner, Julius Streicher) by quoting from André Gide's *Voyage to the Congo* and by passionately invoking their own experience of racism or of European colonialism. Such a grotesque scene is unimaginable.[23]"

Let us follow Alain Finkielkraut's advice. Imagine being before the Nuremberg court, where defence counsel might have pleaded as follows:

You wish to judge these men and that is legitimate, first because the crimes they are guilty of are an attack against humanity as a whole, but also and more importantly because they were defeated and you were the winners. For your judgment to be consistent and credible not only in the eyes of the Western world but for mankind as a whole, on behalf of which you are claiming to judge them, I beg you, consider the annihilation of all those non-European peoples whose only sin was that they were not White and who one day found themselves under the domination of the powers you represent. Finally, provide the legal characterisation of that crime. Once you finally reinstate the contested humanity of all those anonymous victims, you will understand that Hitler and his lackeys – including the men appearing before you today applied, on a small scale, the scale of Europe, what you – I mean your people – applied on a global scale for more than a hundred years. To acquire the moral authority that will entitle you to speak on behalf of mankind rather than just Western kind you must necessarily condemn that crime. This is sine qua non to passing judgment on these men, whose crimes are horrible, in the name of humanity as a whole. Indeed, to be fair, their atrocities will have to be considered against the broader background of the atrocities perpetrated by their predecessors against other, non-European, peoples.

I speculate that this argument would have been considered inadmissible at Nuremberg but that does not mean it is irrelevant. It just means that fifty years ago and today likewise, it is not permissible to place victims whose humanity had never before been challenged on a par with those whose fathers (to take up Abba Eban's expression) lived in the jungle.

Non-scientific truths

Having heard them several times, I know what the reactions are: "One crime cannot justify another crime." "Your highly emotional position is sometimes moving but of no scientific relevance." I have never called on science to justify my position. I leave this label to the officially recognised eminent researchers working for political and ideological goals. Science is often used to silence dissenting voices. While the facts I rely on are not scientific, they are verifiable. When I state that the criminality of some acts stems from the identity of the victims, I do so because when these acts are committed in Europe against Europeans they are considered criminal, but when they occur elsewhere and the victims are no longer European, they are called by another name and become more or less acceptable. Let me take just one example. At the end of the First World War the triumphant powers shared out the spoils that had belonged to their defeated opponents. When the war booty was shared officially through the Treaty of Versailles, Germany's sovereignty over Namibia was handed over to South Africa where the English-speaking White minority represented the interests of His Gracious Majesty the King of the United Kingdom and the British Dominions, Emperor of India. For more than forty years, the people of Namibia were quite legally brutalised, subordinated and repressed, through the "mandate" and "sub-mandate" system, a notion that was introduced into international law by the Western powers to provide a legal expression for what was to remain a disguised form of colonialism. The en masse entry into the United Nations, as of 1960, of African states that had rid themselves of colonial domination altered the balance of power within that organisation and enabled the issue of the introduction by South Africa of the apartheid regime into Namibia to be raised in an altered setting. Resolution 2145 (XXI) dated 26 October 1966 ended South Africa's mandate and declared that South-West Africa would now come under the direct responsibility of the UN. Consequently, a Council of Nations for South-West Africa was formed to administer Namibia, a name chosen by the SWAPO liberation movement. Of all the 119 countries present when the resolution was submitted to the vote, only South Africa, Portugal, France, the United Kingdom and the puppet regime of Malawi were hostile to the position of the peoples of the South that initiated this resolution in favour of the people of Namibia.

As for the former Nazis of South Africa, they decided to quite simply annex Namibia, to reinforce the apartheid system and accelerate their policy of dismembering the territory, i.e., their Bantu areas policy. The UN General Assembly voted resolution 2248 (S–V) dated May 19, 1967, stating "everything shall be done for this territory to accede to independence." It requested the Security Council to take "any appropriate measures." Here again, the Allied powers felt no moral obligation to join this effort. Under the pressure of the ten non-permanent members of the Security Council, the latter did nonetheless vote in favour of the 12 August 1969 resolution that set out a deadline for South Africa to withdraw from Namibia. France refused to go along. Under growing pressure from the South, the Security Council, in spite of the abstentions of France and the United Kingdom, approved Resolution 276 of 29 July 1970 urging all governments to refrain from entering into relations with the South African government acting on behalf of Namibia. At the same time, the Council urged the International Court of Justice to rule on the following question: What are the legal consequences for states of the continued presence of South Africa in Namibia, in defiance of Security Council resolution 276 (1970)?

The struggle for the freedom and dignity of the people of Namibia was particularly difficult and the conditions highly adverse to the Blacks in this country because – in spite of the fact that the international community, i.e., the great majority of the peoples of the world, were clearly against the crime of apartheid – the Allied powers, with the exception of the USSR, continued to endorse and protect the South African regime by bringing their full weight to bear on its side. The Security Council is the only UN body that is permitted by the Charter to take coercive steps, providing its five permanent members agree to do so: United States, China, USSR, France and the United Kingdom. Every time the international community proposed a practical measure such as ending any form of military or technological cooperation with the apartheid regime, the UK, the United States or France opposed with a veto.

The reasons put forward by the UN General Assembly to demand that South Africa withdraw from Namibia were transparent and indisputable: racial segregation, exclusion for reasons of racial filiation, racist persecutions. These clearly conformed to the UN Charter. On the other hand, these Allies did not dare develop a discourse or any arguments to justify their obstruction. Having defeated Nazi Germany and held the Nuremberg trials to judge the leading Nazi war criminals in the name of humankind, these powers assumed a discretionary power of veto in the UN Security Council and used it inter alia to support and protect regimes that overtly acted against humanity or, at least, against non-Western humanity.

Under pressure from the ten non-permanent members, the International Court of Justice issued its advisory opinion on 21 June 1971. In essence, in answer to the question: "What are the legal consequences for states of the continued presence of South Africa in Namibia notwithstanding Security Council resolution 276 (1970)?", the Court was of the opinion,

> by 13 votes to 2,
>
> 1. that, the continued presence of South Africa in Namibia being illegal, South Africa is under obligation to withdraw its administration from Namibia immediately and thus put an end to its occupation of the Territory; by 11 votes to 4,
>
> 2. that Members State of the United Nations are under obligation to recognize the illegality of South Africa's presence in Namibia and the invalidity of its acts on behalf of or concerning Namibia, and to refrain

from any acts and in particular any dealings with the Government of South Africa implying recognition of the legality of, or lending support or assistance to, such presence and administration.[24]

It should be recalled that two judges at the International Court of Justice had been against demanding the withdrawal of the apartheid regime from Namibia from the very start. Naturally, these two judges represented two former Allied powers that had sat at the Nuremberg trials claiming to act on behalf of humanity: Sir Gerald Fitzmaurice for the United Kingdom and Professor André Gros[25] for France, the very same person who, in 1945, had rightly requested the international military tribunal to define racist persecutions as a separate crime. This time he "justified his decision arguing in particular that 'infringement of the rules set out in the Universal Declaration of Human Rights cannot be called upon as a reason for revoking the South West African Mandate.'[26]" How right Jules Ferry was to say before the French Parliament that human rights were not enacted for the Blacks of Africa. The French judge might well have added: 'no more so than for the Blacks of southern Africa.'

Thanks to the tenacity of the non-permanent members of the UN Security Council, resolution 301 dated 20 October 1971, that enshrined the opinion of the International Court of Justice, was adopted. France and the UK expressed their dissent as a result of which the resolution lost the force it would have carried if all five permanent members had upheld it. That is how Professor Gros' opinion was followed.

In 1976, at a time when the vast majority of people, through the United Nations General Assembly, had adhered to the International Convention on the Suppression and Punishment of the Crime of Apartheid, the governments of the United States, France and the UK, continued to use their power of veto to counter any effective measure against apartheid. This is an indication of the extent to which the interests of non-Western humanity and the rights of non-European peoples were trampled or even stifled by the force of the Allied powers.

In the light of these facts, the least one can say is that, between 1945 and 1976, the Allied powers not only did not represent the rights and aspirations of humanity in the name of which they had held trial in Nuremberg. Worse still, their actions continued to work against those peoples whose only sin was that they did not belong to the superior race. A scrutiny of less recent historical facts shows up that before, well before 1945, the policies of those Allies had never been favourable either to the dignity or the rights of the peoples of the world. It is high time that all these people understood the contortions whereby these very same powers could become, at the Nuremberg trials, the embodiment of their rights and aspirations.

In 1977, the UN Human Rights Commission set up a working group on the application of the International Convention on the Suppression and Punishment of the Crime of Apartheid. An effort was made to raise awareness among international public opinion about this crime against humanity. This is what just twenty years ago the former Allied powers objected to!

Hitler's posthumous victory

If the Western democracies had drawn the right conclusions from the Nazi catastrophe in 1948 and refused to enter into any deal with the shameless former Nazis of South Africa who, went on to set up a government founded on the exclusion and subordination of groups considered to be racially inferior, they would have made a significant contribution to the struggle against all forms of racism and segregation and to the fight for human dignity. Furthermore, this choice would have had beneficial effects on Europe too: Nazi nostalgics would have realised that that there was no longer any future for their ideals of racial supremacy.

Unfortunately, Western democracies took the opposite route. The support they gave to the apartheid regime administered a double defeat: both to the cause of humanity and to the non-Whites in South Africa struggling to gain recognition that they belong to humanity. Furthermore, that support was in a way a posthumous victory for Hitler. Indeed, in 1985, at a national gathering organised in Paris against apartheid, Andrée Franciscia told the assembly that "the openly Nazi South African army celebrates Hitler's birthday every year and hires (Nazi) defence commandos to suppress riots when it is unable on its own to fulfill its repressive function.[27]" In other words, the monstrous beast that so many believed had perished in 1945 had risen up again and indeed appeared to have been rehabilitated thanks to the support of the Western democracies.

The credibility of belated indignation

In the very last few days of January and first few days of February 2000, the national and international media turned their spotlight on to Austria where a coalition government between the conservatives and the extreme right was about to take power. For several days, they were inexhaustible on the topic of the xenophobic extreme right, on the sympathies of its leader, Jorg Haider, who called for respect for the SS and sang the praises of Hitler's employment policy, on the concern and protests this raised in Israel and other partners of Austria. I did not hear a single political commentator, observer or analyst explain why Jorg Haider's praise for Hitler's employment policy aroused far more feeling in 2000 than it did when he uttered it nine years before in 1991, extolling the benefits of "the employment policy under the Third Reich, which was well-structured." Of course, in 1991, the democracies in question were still supporting apartheid. Such is the inconsistency and cynicism that comes from choosing to condemn crimes depending on who the victims and who the perpetrators are. As Noam Chomsky points out: "The Western-backed crimes are no symbol of evil, and no blot on our record.[28]" Apartheid is an obvious example. Nobody dares to question that apartheid is a crime but people do not usually feel the same disgust and repulsion as they do in the face of Pol Pot's crimes which became "the very symbol of evil placed alongside those of Hitler and Stalin, where they remain in the approved list of twentieth century horrors.[29]" Can any credit whatsoever be given to the indignation of the former sponsors of apartheid confronted with Jorg Haider's overtly pro-Nazi stance, considering how they supported the former Nazi terrorists and endorsed the crime of apartheid for four decades?

As for the state of Israel, even at the end of the 1980s, not long before the Berlin Wall fell, it was still mired in its complicity with the crime of apartheid. This is apparent in resolution 41/35C approved by the UN General Assembly on 10 November 1986 relating to the relations between Israel and South Africa:

> The General Assembly,
>
> Reaffirming its resolutions on relations between Israel and South Africa,
>
> Noting with appreciation the efforts of the Special Committee to expose the increasing collaboration between Israel and South Africa,
>
> Reiterating that the increasing collaboration by Israel with the racist regime of South Africa, especially in the economic, military and nuclear fields, in defiance of resolutions of the General Assembly and the Security Council is a serious hindrance to international action for the eradication of apartheid, an encouragement to the racist regime of South Africa to persist in its criminal policy of apartheid and a hostile act against the oppressed people

of South Africa and the entire African continent and constitutes a threat to international peace and security,

1. Again strongly condemns the increasing collaboration of Israel with the racist regime of South Africa, especially in the economic, military and nuclear fields,

2. Demands that Israel desist from and terminate forthwith all forms of collaboration with South Africa, particularly in the economic, military and nuclear fields, and abide scrupulously by the relevant resolutions of the General Assembly and the Security Council.[30]

Can any credibility be ascribed to the indignation of the Israeli authorities in the year 2000 when confronted with the admiration expressed by Jorg Haider in 1991 for Hitler's employment policy? When the Israeli government announces that Jorg Haider will not be given an entry visa for Israel, what automatically springs to mind is former Nazi terrorist J.B. Vorster's visit to Israel at the invitation of the Israeli Prime Minister in 1976.

Notes

1. Broadcast on Arte, France, 25 May 1999.
2. Ibid.
3. Naidoo, Indres, *Island in Chains – Ten Years on Robben Island*, Penguin Books, London 2000, pp. 58–59.
4. Kapeliuk, Amnon, *Hébron, un massacre annoncé*, Paris, 1994, p. 131.
5. Cohen, William B. and Le Sueur, James D., *The French Encounter with Africans: White Response to Blacks, 1530–1880*, Indiana University Press, 2003, p. 56.
6. Ibid. pp. 105–106.
7. Kapeliuk, op. cit., pp. 3–39.
8. Kapeliuk, Amnon, *Rabin, un assassinat politique*, Paris, 1996, p. 95.
9. Ibid. p. 96.
10. Kapeliuk, Amnon, *Sabra et Chatila. Enquête sur un massacre*, Paris, 1982, p. 52.
11. Kapeliuk, Amnon, *Hébron, un massacre annoncé*, op. cit., p. 68.
12. Kapeliuk, Amnon, *Rabin, un assassinat politique*, op. cit., p. 94.
13. Quoted in Kapeliuk, Ibid, p. 94. Retrieved 27 January 2011 from http://en.wikipedia.org/wiki/Moshe_Feiglin
14. Retrieved on 27 January 2011 from http://www.haaretz.com/print-edition/news/yossi-sarid–feiglin-his-cronies-are-fascists-by-any-definition-1.259197
15. Greilsammer, Alain, *La Nouvelle histoire d'Israël*, Paris, 1998, pp. 352 and 358.
16. Kapeliuk, *Hébron, un massacre annoncé*, op.cit., p.112.
17. Benabdallah, op. cit., pp. 76–77.

18. Kapeliuk, Amnon, *Le Monde diplomatique*, November 1994, p. 14.
19. Report of the United Nations Special Committee Against Apartheid, No. 5/77, February 1977, p. 15.
20. Magubane, Bernard, "Israel and South Africa: The Nature of the Unholy Alliance". Retrieved 27 January 2011 from http://domino.un.org/unispal.
21. Gestapo torturers used to order their victims to shout "long live Hitler!" and French soldiers in Algeria used to oblige theirs to yell "long live France!"
22. Ibid.
23. Finkielkraut, Alain, *Remembering in Vain: the Klaus Barbie Trial and Crimes Against Humanity*, Columbia University Press, 1992, pp. 25–26.
24. Advisory Opinion of 21 June 1971, International Court of Justice. Retrieved on 27 January 2011 at http://www.mefacts.com/ cached.asp?x_id=11654
25. Ibid.
26. Inquiry Commission on Apartheid, *La France et l'apartheid*, Paris, 1978, pp. 114–115.
27. *Aujourd'hui l'Afrique*, No. 29, 1985, p. 19.
28. Chomsky, Noam, *Powers and Prospects. Reflections on Human Nature and the Social Order*, Pluto Press, 1996, p. 58.
29. Ibid. p. 57.
30. Retrieved on 3 March 2011 at http://www.un.org/documents/ga/res/41/a41r035.htm

Conclusion

Victims of a crime need and are owed recognition that addresses their pain and the injustice they have suffered. Failing to give this recognition has deadly consequences, particularly if the latter go unnoticed except by the victims who are locked in their forced silence, in a situation analogous to negation. It inevitably deprives the victims of the self-confidence necessary to establish a sound relationship with their immediate environment.

Think of the loss of self-confidence, self-respect and self-esteem that the Black people all over the American continent underwent as a result of being systematically and officially alienated from the human race for more than three and a half centuries. This was compounded by the devastating emotional and psychological effects of the various theories that were developed at all levels of consciousness to justify the suffering and time-honoured injustices they endured.

These theories lived on far beyond the concentration camp setting and the totalitarian system that produced them. They continued to oppress the survivors of this disaster and their descendants by heaping contempt upon them all the way into the first half of the twentieth century.

Blacks who were scorned as "descendants of slaves" had to live with the shame of being descended from those Africans who for so long were relegated to the status of sub-humans, of beasts of burden, of chattel. Being a victim of white supremacy does not produce any rights. Hence, Blacks are careful not to display this legacy of humiliation and suffering, aggravated by the wounds caused by the contempt and offensiveness that still pervade their day-to-day interaction with Whites.

Europeans have never accepted their responsibility for the damage their supremacy has inflicted on their victims. This has meant that the atrocities committed against these peoples have continued to be considered as a historical non-event. In contrast, immediately after 1945, crimes that were the follow-up to those atrocities – which themselves, through the centuries and up to the modern day, never qualified as crimes – suddenly, when they occurred in Europe, became the ultimate abomination, the crime of crimes.

In the concentration camp setting of America, we know that masters or mistresses who maim or kill their Black servants are at the worst just fined an amount of less than 12 per cent of the selling price on the market for the Black person. We also know that these thoroughly normalised deeds were consistent with the nature of a system that lasted – not twelve years – but three and a half centuries.

It was therefore practically inevitable that we perceive the reality of the gas chambers operating in the German extermination camps as another development in the technology used to annihilate anyone whose humanity is challenged. Consequently, the very Western claims of disbelief in the face of Nazi barbarity might elicit a smile from an American Indian survivor or a descendant of Africans who, looking at how their own people were annihilated, might well wonder what was so special about what Hitler did.

It might seem shocking and brutal to ask what was so special about what Hitler did, but for us it is a worthwhile question. As Aimé Césaire said back in 1948 in his essay *Esclavage et Colonisation*: "Nazi Germany simply applied on a small scale in Europe what Western Europe had applied for centuries to the races that were impudent or clumsy enough to get in their way.[1]

When the descendants of deported Africans and survivors of the Native Americans acquire an awareness of their own history and their very particular position in the history of humanity, they measure the atrocities perpetrated by the Nazis in occupied Europe with the yardstick of those committed against their ancestors. And using that yardstick, there is no abomination capable of superseding or even equalling the degree of horror to which their people were subjected – regardless of the element considered: the type of atrocities involved or the length of time when they were inflicted. I am not suggesting that to fall back on this position is the ideal response to the centuries of denial of justice and non-recognition that are still effective today.

In 1989, I went to Haiti to take part in a symposium on the French Revolution and its repercussions in Saint-Domingue. The participants were invited to a cocktail party at the French Embassy in Port-au-Prince. I engaged in a conversation with a group of people on the topic of the genocidal policy conducted by France in Saint-Domingue. In the middle of the conversation, one of the participants told me that the French had not been as clever as the English who wisely killed everyone they found on the spot and so did not encounter any further problems. He added with a rather friendly smile, "so you see, if we had done the same, you wouldn't have been here to criticise us."

When we left, I walked alongside Louis Sala-Molins. He looked at me for a moment and said drily: "You see, there are some jokes that we tell only to Blacks." I was deeply moved to hear him unequivocally express something I was and still am profoundly convinced of. That Frenchman's joke was hurtful like so many other clumsy remarks that we Blacks have swallowed in our dealings with Whites however well-educated they are.

Black people have to find ways of stifling their painful reaction every time they are confronted with these solecisms; otherwise they inevitably reach an impasse, even individually. What is certain is that some of these solecisms are targeted only at Blacks. Today, it is demanded of Germans (at least officially) that they never forget the atrocities perpetrated by Nazi Germany. On the other hand, our good French citizens, just as their English, Portuguese or Spanish counterparts, are not accountable for the atrocities that their people committed on the scale not of one continent only but of the world over and for several centuries.

The reason I was moved by Sala-Molins' comment to the extent that I still acutely remember it ten years later [1999], is that I have very rarely heard Europeans express a true recognition for the suffering and the memory of these millions of men, women and children who have paid for white barbarity with their lives.

I believe that even the most callous huckster or the most anti-Semitic German scum would no longer dare to openly ask public opinion whether the extermination of six or seven million Jews under the Third Reich was a good deal for Germany. I presume that such a scoundrel would not voice his thoughts if for no other reason than to avoid being charged for infringing the law that punishes attempts to justify crimes against humanity. Nonetheless, in the November 1997 issue of the journal *L'histoire*, Olivier Pétré-Grenouilleau, a lecturer in contemporary history, raises the question: "The Black Slave Trade – A Profitable Business for Europe?" Once again, the most chilling genocide in modern times is reduced to a financial analysis of the profits and losses for genocidal Europe. The reason this type of insult to the memory of the victims can continue to go unpunished is that their stolen humanity was never fully reinstated.

This denial of justice is staggering when even humanists who are known for their commitment to fighting certain forms of exclusion add their own little dose of contempt. Let me take one example amongst others.

The radio broadcast "Répliques" presented by Alain Finkielkraut on the France-Culture channel on Saturday 21 March 1998 dealt with the topic of "Proper use of remembrance." Finkielkraut's guests were Tzvetan Todorov, a research director at the Centre national de recherche scientifique (CNRS) and Richard Marienstras, emeritus professor at the Paris-VII University. The occasion was the publication of an article by Todorov in the journal, *Les Temps Modernes*. He had expressed some reservations about creating a Holocaust museum in Washington. This was hardly an incendiary article but it was because of the irritation it caused that the programme was broadcast. Professor Marienstras, who disagreed with Todorov's arguments, forcefully defended the legitimacy of the Holocaust museum, stressing the importance of passing on the memory of the Holocaust to the younger American generations before the last survivors die.

Todorov explained that he was skeptical about the educational value of such a museum. He thought it was more likely to ease the conscience of American youth quite simply because not only is their country not accountable for the crimes remembered by the museum, furthermore it fought the perpetrators. "On the other hand," he added, "if you really want to educate youth, what you need is a museum in memory of the destruction of the Native Americans or of the enslavement of Black people because these are crimes in which the United States were deeply implicated."

Professor Marienstras quickly retorted: "It is unreal to ask for such a monument to be established in the United States," adding, "It would be like asking France for a monument in memory of the war in Algeria."

Todorov then asked: "How is it that Germany has been required to build a monument to the Shoah?" Professor Marienstras's answer is staggering: "Oh no, Germany could not survive if it ignored the Holocaust. […]. But, the Blacks could do something like that if they wanted to, and the Native Americans too, because, after all, some of them have grown rich."

As Sala-Molins rightly says: "We do not even know who we disrespect, humiliate, trample on when our arrogance stifles, humiliates, scorns.²"

For many years, organisations in the United States have worked hard to do justice to the memory of Native Americans. They have succeeded in gaining acceptance that a National Museum of the American Indians be setup in Washington, the first brick of which was laid in October 1999. "This first museum," said a Kiowa lawyer "will help Americans to better understand what their ancestors did to us."

In other words, the time has not yet come to stop sifting out victims and rating the heinousness of the crimes committed against them depending on whether they rank either among those whose status as human beings has never been questioned or among those that European scientists had in their time defined as being something intermediate between a monkey and a man. The legacy of the Enlightenment, in spite of its claim to universality, is still fragmentary. More than three centuries of suffering and atrocities, regulated by an institutionalised system of barbarity, have not even earned a mention alongside the sufferings and atrocities perpetrated by the Nazis in Europe for twelve years…

The sometimes stifling burden of white supremacy on our unconscious must be made conscious. This is the only way we can identify that burden and, consciously, try to limit the damage it causes. You cannot cure the patient by ignoring the disease.

Some genuine humanists and convinced biologists have repeatedly said that, from a scientific standpoint, there is no such thing as race. But racial prejudice remains. And that only stands to reason. Hitler himself knew full well that there is no such thing as a race, but he nonetheless used it very deviously. He said,

> I know perfectly well, just as well as these tremendously clever intellectuals that in the scientific sense there is no such thing as a race. But you, as a farmer and cattle breeder, cannot get your breeding successfully achieved without the conception of race. And I as a politician need a conception which enables the order which has hitherto existed on historical bases to be abolished and an entirely new and anti-historic order enforced.[3]

These secrets confided by Hitler to his comrade and fellow traveller Herman Rauschning, were not intended for the public at large. In 1934, this person left the National Socialist Party and later, once he had left Germany, published a collection of his conversations with Hitler under the title *Hitler m'a dit*, which is far more useful to understand Nazism properly than the very official *Mein Kampf*. It is not enough to say there is no such thing as race to put an end to the demons of racism and their consequences. The fact that millions of Black men, women and children were officially and systematically banished into the vacuum of sub-humanity because they were Black cannot be disputed. But this matter is not on anybody's agenda and is always treated in the trivial manner of some minor news item.

Notes

1. Césaire, Aimé, *Esclavage et colonisation*, Paris, 1948, quoted by Jean-Martin Mbemba. *L'autre mémoire du crime contre l'humanité*, op. cit., p. 154.
2. Sala-Molins, Louis, *Le racisme et le microscope*, op. cit., p. 29.
3. Rauschning, Hermann, *The Voice of Destruction: Conversations with Hitler*, G.P. Putnam's Sons, 1940, p. 232.

Bibliography

Abrahams, P., 1956, *Je ne suis pas un homme libre*, Paris, Casterman.
Abu-Jamal, M., 1996, *En direct du couloir de la mort*, Paris, La Découverte.
L'actu, vendredi, 21 mai 1999, n° 193.
Alves Filho I., 1988, *Memorial dos palmares*, Rio de Janeiro, Xenon.
Amnesty International, 1987, *La peine de mort aux États-Unis, une horrible "loterie"*, Paris, AEFAI.
Amnesty International, 1991, *États-Unis. Des mineurs dans le "couloir de la mort"*, Paris, AEFAI.
Amnesty International, 1996, *Sous contrôle médical constant. Les professionnels de la santé face à la torture et aux mauvais traitements en Israël et dans les territoires occupées*, août.
Amnesty International, 1998, *États-Unis, La condamnation à mort d'innocents*, Paris, AMR 51/69/98.
Amnesty International, 1998, *Le paradoxe américain*, Paris, AMR 51/35/98.
Amnesty International, 1998, *États-Unis. Les enfants face à peine de mort*, Paris, AMR 51/58/98.
Amnesty International, 1998, *États-Unis, Des exécutions à la chaîne. La peine de mort en 1997*, Paris, AMR 51/20/98.
Amnesty International, 1998, *États-Unis. Utilisation de ceintures électriques neutralisantes*, Paris, AMR 51/45/98.
Amnesty International, 1999, *États-Unis, Des préjugés qui tuent*, Paris, AMR 51/52/99.
Arendt, H., 1966, *Eichmann à Jérusalem*, Paris, Gallimard.
Aujourd'hui l'Afrique, 1985, revue trimestrielle, n°29.
Bangou, H., 1987, *La Guadeloupe 1492–1848*, Paris, L'Harmattan.
Bangou, H., 1989, *La révolution et l'esclavage à la Guadeloupe*, Paris, Messidor.
Barreau, J-Cl., 1991, *De l'Islam en général et du monde moderne en particulier*, Paris, Le Pré aux Clercs.
Bastide, R., 1967, *Les Amériques noires*, Paris, Payot.
Bedarida, F. (sous la direction de), 1989, *La politique nazie d'extermination*, Paris, Albin Michel.
Benabdallah, A., 1979, *Israël et les peuples noirs*, Québec, Canada-Monde arabe.
Benot, Y., 1988, *La révolution française et la fin des colonies*, Paris, La Découverte.
Bensimon, D., 1987, *Les grandes rafles*, Toulouse, BHP.

Bernadac, C., 1979, *L'Holocauste oublié. Le massacre des Tsiganes*, Paris, France-Empire.
Bernal, Martin, 1999, *Black Athena. Les racines afro-asiatiques de la civilisation classique*, Paris, PUF.
Bettelheim, B., 1972, *Le cœur conscient*, Paris, Pluriel.
Bettelheim, B., 1979, *Survivre*, Paris, Robert Laffont.
Boissel, J., 1972, *Victor Courtet (1813–1867), premier théoricien de la hiérarchie des races*, Paris, PUF.
Borwicz, M., 1979, *L'insurrection du ghetto de Varsovie*, présentée par Michael Borwicz, Paris, Archives.
Bourgeois, D., 1998, *Business helvétique et IIIème Reich*, Lausanne, Page deux.
Bourne, P., 1953, *Tambores del destino*, Chili, Zig Zag.
Braeckman, C., 1994, *Rwanda, Histoire d'un génocide*, Paris, Fayard.
Braeckman, C., 1996, *Terreur africaine*, Paris, Fayard.
Brunschwig, H., 1971, *Le partage de l'Afrique*, Paris, Flammarion.
Burrin, P., 1989, *Hitler et les Juifs. Genèse d'un génocide*, Paris, Seuil.
Canot, T., 1989, *Confessions d'un négrier*, Paris, Phébus.
Carrel, A., 1935, *L'Homme, cet inconnu*, Paris, Plon.
Carriere, J-C., 1992, *La controverse de Valladolid*, Le Pré aux clercs.
Castro, Caycedo G., 1986, *Colombia amarga*, Bogotá, Planeta.
Cauna, J., 1987, *Au temps des isles à sucre*, Paris, Karthala.
Césaire, A., 1955, *Cahier d'un retour au pays natal*, Paris, Présence Africaine.
Césaire, A., 1955, *Discours sur le colonialisme*, Paris, Présence africaine.
Césaire, A., 1981, *Toussaint Louverture, la Révolution française et le problème colonial*, Paris, Présence Africaine.
Césaire, A., 1970, *La tragédie du roi Christophe*, Paris, Présence Africaine.
Césaire, A., 1972, *Une saison au Congo*, Paris, Présence Africaine.
Césaire, A., 1948, *Esclavage et Colonisation*, Paris, PUF.
Chaumont, J.M., 1997, *La concurrence des victimes*, Paris, La Découverte.
Chomsky, N., 1998, *Responsabilités des intellectuels, Démocratie et marché. Nouvel ordre mondial. Droits de l'homme*, Paris, Agone Éditeur.
Cochin, A., 1979 [1861], *L'abolition de l'esclavage*, Paris, Désormeaux.
Cohen, W., 1981, *Français et Africains*, Paris, Gallimard.
Cohen, W.B. & Le Sueur, J.D., 2003, *The French Encounter with Africans: White Response to Blacks, 1530–1880*, Indiana, Indiana University Press, p. 138.
Commission d'enquête sur l'apartheid, 1978, *La France et l'apartheid*, Paris, L'Harmattan.
Conan, E. & Rousso, H., 1994, *Vichy, un passé qui ne passe pas*, Paris, Fayard.
Cooper, J.F., 1978, *Le dernier des Mohicans*, Paris, Tallandier.
Cornevin, M., 1977, *L'Afrique du Sud en sursis*, Paris, Hachette.

Cornevin, M., 1979, *L'apartheid : pouvoir et falsification historique*, Paris, Unesco.
Cornevin, R., 1969, *Histoire de la colonisation allemande*, Paris, PUF, *Que sais-je?* n° 1331.
Courtois, S. et Rayski, A. (sous la direction de), 1987, *Qui savait quoi? L'extermination des Juifs, 1941–1945*, Paris, La Découverte.
Crete, L., 1989, *La traite des nègres sous l'Ancien Régime*, Paris, Perrin.
Cros, G., 1983, *La Namibie*, Paris, Que sais-je.
Cukierman, M., 1987, *Cap sur la liberté Afrique du Sud*, Paris, Messidor.
Charland, R., 1988, Devant l'Histoire : les documents de la controverse sur la singularité de l'extermination des Juifs par le régime nazi, Paris, Cerf.
Devyver, A., 1973, *Le sang épuré*, Bruxelles, Université de Bruxelles.
Diener, I., 1986, *Apartheid! La cassure – La Namibie, un peuple, un devenir*, Paris, Arcantère.
Dion, M., 1998, *Mémoires d'un candomblé*, Paris, L'Harmattan.
Do Nascimento, A., 1978, *O genocidio do negro brasileiro*, Rio de Janeiro, Paz e Terra.
Douglass, F., 1980, *Mémoires d'un esclave américain*, Paris, Maspéro.
Dvorjetski, M., 1973, *La victoire du ghetto*, Paris, France-Empire.
Elias, N., 1997, *Logiques de l'exclusion*, Paris, Fayard.
Encyclopedia Universalis, 1998, Cd Rom version 4.0, Paris.
Equiano, Olaudah, 1983, *La véridique histoire par lui-même*, Paris, Caribéennes.
Escalante, A., 1964, *El negro en Colombia*, Bogotá, Universidad Nacional.
Fabre, M., 1978, *Esclaves et planteurs*, Paris, Archives.
Fanon, F., 1961, *Les damnés de la terre*, Paris, Maspéro.
Fanon, F., 1952, *Peau noire, masques blancs*, Paris, Seuil.
Fanon, F., 1978, *Pour la révolution africaine*, Paris, Maspéro.
Ferro, M., 1994, *Histoire des colonisations, Des conquêtes aux indépendances XIII–XX siècle*, Paris, Seuil.
Finkelstein, N. et Birn, R., 1999, *L'Allemagne en procès*, Paris, Albin Michel.
Finkielkraut, A., 1989, *La mémoire vaine du crime contre l'Humanité*, Paris, Gallimard.
Fohlen, C., 1965, « Les Noirs aux États-Unis », Paris, PUF, *Que sais-je?* n° 1191.
Fonseca Junior, E., 1988, *Zumbi, a historia que não foi contada*, Rio de Janeiro, Christiano Editorial.
Fontette, F. de, 1982, « Histoire de l'antisémitisme », Paris, PUF, *Que sais-je?* n° 2039.
Franklin, J., 1984, *De l'esclavage à la liberté*, Paris, Caribéennes.
Friedemann, N., & Arocha, J., 1986, *De sol a sol*, Bogotá, Planeta.
Friedlander, S., 1997, *L'Allemagne nazie et les Juifs*, Paris, Seuil.
Girardet, R., 1983, *Le nationalisme français, anthologie 1871–1914*, Paris, Seuil.
Gisler, A., 1981, *L'esclavage aux Antilles françaises*, Paris, Karthala.

Goguel, A.M. et Buis, P., 1978, *Chrétiens d'Afrique du Sud face à l'apartheid*, récit et textes présentés par A.M. Goguel et P. Buis, Paris, L'Harmattan.
Goldhagen, D.J., 1997, *Les bourreaux volontaires de Hitler*, Paris, Seuil.
Greilsammer, I., 1998, *La nouvelle histoire d'Israël*, Paris, Gallimard.
Griffin, J.H., 1962, *Dans la peau d'un Noir*, Paris, Gallimard.
Grosser, A., 1989, *Le crime et la mémoire*, Paris, Flammarion.
Gutierrez, Azopardo I., 1980, *Historia del negro en Colombia*, Bogotá, Nueva america.
Haski, P., 1987, *L'Afrique blanche*, Paris, Seuil.
Herder, J.G., 1964, *Une autre philosophie de l'Histoire*, Paris, Montaigne.
Hilberg, R., 1988, *La destruction des Juifs d'Europe*, Tome 1, Paris, Fayard [trans. from the English, *The Destruction of the European Jews*, Revised ed., vol. 1, New York: Holmes & Meier, 1985, p 166, Questia, Web, 6 July 2010].
Hilberg, R., 1993, *Perpetrators Victims Bystanders–The Jewish Catastrophe 1933–1945*, New York, Harper Collins.
Himmler, H., 1974, *Discours secrets*, Paris, Gallimard.
Hitler, A., *Mon combat*, Paris, NEL.
L'Histoire, 1997, Revue n° 215, novembre.
L'Histoire, 1999, Revue n° 230, Mars.
Hobsbawm, E.J., 1999, *L'âge des extrêmes*, Bruxelles, Complexe, *Le Monde Diplomatique*.
Hochschild, A., 1998, *Les fantômes du roi Léopold II, un holocauste oublié*, Paris, Belfond.
Hoffmann L-F., 1973, *Le nègre romantique*, Paris, Payot.
Jackson, G., 1972, *Devant mes yeux, la mort*, Paris, Gallimard.
James, C.L.R, 1983, *Les Jacobins noirs*, Paris, Caribéennes.
Jaures, J., 1969, *Histoire socialiste de la Révolution, tome 1, II*, Paris, Messidor.
Joubert, E., 1981, *Le long voyage de Popie Nongena*, Paris, Belfond.
Journal officiel, 1885, Discours et Opinions, 29 juillet.
Kapeliouk, A., 1982, *Sabra et Chatilla, Enquête sur un massacre*, Paris, Seuil.
Kapeliouk, A., 1994, *Hébron, un massacre annoncé*, Paris, Seuil.
Kapeliouk, A., 1996, *Rabin, un assassinat politique*, Paris, Édition Le Monde.
Ki-Zerbo, J., 1978, *Histoire de l'Afrique noire*, Paris, Hatier.
Klee, E., Dressen, Riess, 1990, *Pour eux, "c'était le bon temps"*, Paris, Plon.
Kogon, E., 1947, *L'État SS*, Paris, Seuil.
Kom, A. et Ngoue, L. (sous la direction de), 1991, *Le Code Noir et l'Afrique*, Ivry, Nouvelles du Sud.
Kum'a N'dumbe III, A., 1980, *Hitler voulait l'Afrique: Les plans secrets pour une Afrique fasciste*, Paris, L'Harmattan.
Las Casas, B. de, 1966, *Brevísima relación de la destrucción de las Indias*, Buenos Aires.
Las Casas, B. de, 1951, *Historia de las Indias*, Mexico, Fondo de Cultura Económica.
Lelyveld, J., 1986, *Afrique du Sud, l'apartheid au jour le jour*, Paris, Presse de la Cité.

Le Monde, 4 octobre 1996.
Le Monde, 9–10 janvier 2000.
Le Monde diplomatique, janvier 1997.
Le Monde diplomatique, mai 1999.
Le Monde diplomatique, juin 2000.
Le Monde diplomatique, août 2000.
Lerner, G., 1975, *De l'esclavage à la ségrégation*, Paris, Denoël-Gonthier.
Lewis, B., 1993, *Race et esclavage au Proche-Orient*, Paris, Gallimard.
Limp, W., 1972, *Anatomie de l'apartheid*, Paris, Casterman.
Litwack, L., Allen, J., Als H.L., 2000, *Without Sanctuary: Lynching Photography in America*, Sante Fe, New Mexico, Twin Palms Publishers.
Livre blanc sur l'agression israélienne au Liban, 1983, Publisud / Association internationale des juristes démocrates.
Luthuli, A., 1963, *Liberté pour mon peuple*, Paris, Buchet-Chastel.
Malcolm, X, 1989, *Derniers discours*, Paris, Dagorno.
Mandela, N., 1995, *Un long chemin vers la liberté*, Paris, Fayard.
Mandela, W., 1986, *Une part de mon âme*, Paris, Seuil.
Mannix, D.P., & Cowley, M., 1968, *Historia de la trata de negros*, Madrid, Ed Cast Alianza.
Mannoni, O., 1951, *Psychologie de la colonisation*, Paris, Seuil.
Marchand, J., 1985, *La propagande de l'apartheid. Quand l'Afrique du Sud se crée une image de marque*, Paris, Karthala.
Martin, M.L. & Yacou, A. (sous la direction de), 1989, *Mourir pour les Antilles*, Paris, Caribéenne.
Mbemba, J-M., 1990, *L'autre mémoire du crime contre l'Humanité*, Paris, Présence africaine.
Meillassoux, C. (présenté par), 1975, *L'esclavage en Afrique précoloniale*, Paris, Maspéro.
Meli, F., 1991, *Une histoire de l'ANC*, Paris, L'Harmattan.
Mellon, J., 1991, *Paroles d'esclaves*, Paris, Seuil.
Mende, T., 1973, *De l'aide à la recolonisation*, Paris, Seuil.
Merle, M., 1968, *L'Afrique noire contemporaine*, Paris, Armand Colin, coll. U.
Metral, A., 1825, *Histoire de l'expédition des Français à Saint Domingue*, Paris.
Mina, M., 1975, *Esclavitud y libertad en el valle del rio Cauca*, Bogotá, Editorial Alternativa.
Morenas, J.E, 1828, *Précis historique de la traite des Noirs et l'esclavage colonial*, Paris.
Morrison, T., 1989, *Beloved*, Paris, Christian Bourgois.
Mouterde, P. & Wargny, C., 1996, *Après la fête, les tambours sont lourds; cinq ans de duplicité américaine en Haïti (1991–1996)*, Paris, Austral.

Muller-Hill, B., 1997, *Murderous Science: Elimination by Scientific Selection of Jews, Gypsies and Others*, Cold Spring Harbor Laboratory Press, p. 228.

Muller-Hill, B., 1989, *Science nazie, science de mort*, Paris, Odile Jacob.

Naidoo, I., 1986, *Dans les bagnes de l'apartheid*, Paris, Messidor.

Nations Unies, 1971, *Comité spécial Apartheid A/AC, 115/1285 add. 3*, 21 mai.

Nations Unies, 1976, *El apartheid en la practica, recueil de lois sud-africaines*, sollicité par le Comité apartheid des Nations Unies à M. Le Professeur L. Rubin, professeur de Droit comparé à Howard University, *États-Unies*.

Nations Unies, 1986, *Les Nations Unies et les droits de l'homme*, New York, Publication des Nations Unies, F84.1.6.

Nations Unies, 1977, *Rapport sur les relations entre Israël et l'Afrique du Sud, n° 5/77*, février.

Nations Unies, 1985, *Violation des droits de l'homme en Afrique australe, rapport spécial de la commission des droits de l'Homme*, E/CN 4/1985/14, 28 janvier.

Nicolaidis, D., (dirigé par), 1994, *Oublier nos crimes. L'amnésie nationale : une spécificité française?*, Paris, Autrement, n°144, avril.

Northup, S., 1980, *Douze ans d'esclavage*, Paris, Le Sycomore.

Paraf, P., 1981, *Le racisme dans le monde*, Paris, Payot.

Paraire, P., 1993, *Les Noirs américains*, Paris, Hachette.

Paxton, R.O., 1972, *La France de Vichy*, Paris, Seuil.

Phillips, N., 1962, *La tragedia del apartheid*, Mexico, Era.

Pluchon, P., 1984, *Nègres et Juifs au XVIIIème siècle*, Paris, Tallandier.

Poliakov, L., 1980, *Auschwitz*, présenté par Léon Poliakov, Paris, Seuil.

Poliakov, L., 1951, *Bréviaire de la haine*, Paris, Calmann-Levy.

Poliakov, L., 1971, *Le mythe aryen*, Paris, Calmann-Levy.

Poliakov, L., 1976, *Le racisme*, Paris, Scghers.

Rajsfus, M., 1980, *Des Juifs dans la collaboration*, Paris, EDI.

Rajsfus, M., 1987, *Israël Palestine. L'ennemi intérieur*, Paris, La Brêche.

Rajsfus, M., 1981, *Sois Juif et tais-toi!*, Paris, EDI.

Rauschning, H., 1979, *Hitler m'a dit*, Paris, Aimery Somogy.

La Révolution française et l'abolition de l'esclavage, textes et documents, Paris, EDHIS, tome I, II, III.

Rogers B., 1978, *Diviser pour régner*, Paris, Droit et Liberté.

Römer, L.F., 1989, *Le golfe de Guinée 1700–1750, récit de L.F. Römer, marchand d'esclave sur la côte ouest africaine*, Paris, L'Harmattan.

Rooney, D., 1990, *Nkrumah, l'homme qui croyait à l'Afrique*, Paris, Jalivres.

Rousso, H., 1987, *Le syndrôme de Vichy*, Paris, Seuil.

Ruscio, A., 1994, in *Oublier nos crimes. L'amnésie nationale : une spécificité française?*, dirigé par D. Nicolaïdis, Paris, Autrement, avril.

Saco, J.A., 1974, *Historia de la esclavitud*, Madrid, Jucar.
Saint-Ruf, G., 1977, *L'épopée Delgrès*, Paris, L'Harmattan.
Sala-Molins, L., 1988, "Le racisme et le microscope", *Lignes* 2, Revue n°3, Paris.
Sala-Molins, L., 1992, *L'Afrique aux Amériques. Le Code noir espagnol*, Paris, PUF.
Sala-Molins, L., 1987, *Le Code Noir ou le calvaire de Canaan*, Paris, PUF.
Sala-Molins, L., 1992, *Les misères des Lumières*, Paris, Robert Laffont.
Schoelcher, V., 1842, *Des colonies françaises*, Paris, Pagnerre.
Schoelcher, V., 1973 [1847], *Histoire de l'esclavage pendant les deux dernières années*, Paris, Pointe-à-Pitre, Desormeaux.
Schoelcher, V., 1889, *La vie de Toussaint Louverture*, Paris, Karthala
Schoelcher, V., 1882, *Polémique coloniale, tomes 1 et 2*, Paris, Desormeaux.
Segev, T., 1993, *Le septième million*, Paris, Liana Levi.
Semana, 1999, hebdomadaire colombien *n° 872*, Bogotá.
Soudan, F., 1987, *Mandela l'indomptable*, Paris, Jeune Afrique.
Souquet-Basiege G., 1979, *Le préjugé de race*, Paris, Désormeaux.
Steiner, J-F., 1966, *Treblinka*, Paris, Fayard.
Stern, F., 1990, *L'or et le fer, Bismarck et son banquier Bleichröder*, Paris, Fayard.
Symposium international sur le sionisme et le racisme, 1976, Paris, Le Sycomore.
Taguieff, P-A, 1988, *La force du préjugé*, Paris, La Découverte.
Tardieu, J-P., 1984, *Le destin des Noirs aux Indes de Castille*, Paris, L'Harmattan.
Theolleyre, J-M., 1985, *Procès d'après-guerre*, Paris, La Découverte.
Thibau, J., 1989, *Le temps de Saint-Domingue*, Paris, JC Lattès.
Thion, S., 1969, *Le pouvoir pâle ou le racisme sud-africain*, Paris, Seuil.
Tocqueville, A., 1962, *Œuvres complètes*, Paris, Gallimard.
Tocqueville, A., 1981, *De la Démocratie en Amérique, Tomes 1 et 2*, Paris, Flammarion.
Todorov, T., 1982, *La conquête de l'Amérique*, Paris, Seuil.
Tolnay, Stewart and Beck, E.M., *A Festival of Violence: An Analysis of Southern Lynching, 1882–1930,* University of Illinois Press, Chicago, 1995, p.23.
Torres, D., 1996, *Esclaves*, Paris, Phébus.
UNESCO, 1979, *La traite négrière de XVème au XIXème siècle*, Études et documents, Paris, UNESCO.
UNESCO, 1980, *Histoire générale de l'Afrique*, tome II, IV, VII, Paris, UNESCO/NEA.
UNESCO, 1982, *Introducción à la cultura africana en American Latina*, Barcelona, Serbal/Unesco.
Verger, P., 1968, *Flux et reflux de la traite des nègres entre le golfe du Bénin et Bahia de todos os santos*, Paris, Mouton & Co.
Verschave, F.X., 1994, *Complicité de génocide? La politique de la France au Rwanda*, Paris, La Découverte.

Vidal-Naquet, P., 1987, *Les assassins de la mémoire*, Paris, La Découverte.
Vissière, I. & J-L., 1982, *La traite des Noirs au siècle des Lumières*, Paris, Métailié.
Wismes, A. de, 1984, *La traite négrière vers le nouveau monde*, Rennes, Les documents Ouest-France.
Witte, Ludo de, 2000, *L'assassinat de Lumumba*, Paris, Karthala.
Woods, D., 1979, *Vie et mort de Steve Biko*, Paris, Stock.
Wyman, D., 1987, *L'abandon des Juifs*, Paris, Flammarion.
Zapata, Olivella M., 1972, *Chambacú, corral de negros*, Medellin, Bedout.
Zapata, Olivella M., 1986, *El fusilamiento del diablo*, Bogotá, Plaza et Janes.
Zavala, S., 1947, *Filosofía de la conquista*, Mexico, Fondo de cultura.
Ziegler, J., 1997, *La Suisse, l'or et les morts*, Paris, Seuil.
Ziegler, J., 1971, *Le pouvoir africain*, Paris, Seuil.
Ziegler, J., 1980, *Main basse sur l'Afrique*, Paris, Seuil.

Index

A

Abel, Dr 93, 95
abolitionist 29, 67, 148
Aborigines 83, 107
Abrahams, Israel 203, 206
Abu-Jamal, Mumia 162–3, 168, 173–9
Africa xi–xv, xviii, xx, xxii, xxviii, xxxiii, 1–8, 15, 18, 20, 42, 46, 51, 57, 58, 62, 69–77, 81–84, 91–94, 100–107, 111, 128, 131–134, 144–147, 154, 181, 197, 198, 201–208, 211–218, 220–224, 231, 234, 236, 240, 241, 246, 253, 256, 259, 260
Africa, John 162
African National Congress (ANC) 215–222, 232, 239, 242
Afrikaners 217, 242
Aguirre, Anselmo 182, 183
Alabama, US 102, 156
Algeria xxii, 205, 257, 262
alienation xxx, xxxiii, 25
Allied powers xxiv, 2, 12, 29, 122, 132–137, 202, 205, 209, 212, 216, 218, 244, 251–254
Aly, Gotz xxx
American Indians x, 262
American Jewish Conference 136
American Jewish Congress 208
Americas x, xi, xiv, xviii, 11, 12, 39, 70, 79, 81, 83, 104, 125, 181, 182, 191
Amiens peace treaty 59
Amir, Igal 245
Amit, Meir 248
Amnesty International 156, 157, 163, 166, 170–179, 239, 240
Anglo-Saxons xiv, 192

annihilation xx, xxi, xxiii, 1, 3, 11, 15, 27–58, 46, 72, 83, 92, 96–99, 104, 107, 108, 119, 125, 226, 250
Anschluss 120, 126
anti-apartheid xiv, xxxiv, 211, 212, 215, 221, 227, 234, 243
Antigua 35
Antilles xxvii, 57, 58
anti-Semitism xiv, xxi, xxx, 94, 96, 98, 102–122, 135, 167, 203, 210, 237, 238, 261
apartheid ix, xiv, xxii, xxv, xxxiv, 2, 197, 203–257
Apprenticeship Act of 1922 198
Arab–Israeli conflict 207, 212
Arabs xiv, xviii, xxvi, 61, 62, 84, 94, 100, 103, 207, 212, 239, 244–248
Arafat, Yasser 238
Arendt, Hannah 62, 64, 67, 237, 239, 240
Aristotle xx
Arkansas, US 102, 166
Aryanisation xxx, 97, 118, 121, 126
Aryans xxii, xxx, 21, 55, 56, 62, 67, 82–84, 91, 94–100, 106, 113, 120, 121, 124, 126, 131, 132, 147, 198, 200, 201, 205
Ashanti 5, 42
Asia xi, xiv, xv, xvi, xviii, 3, 94, 107, 131, 204
Augeard, Eugéne 67
Auschwitz xxi, xxiii–xxvii, 8, 49, 50, 79, 87, 110, 124, 130, 135, 146, 151, 201, 206, 208, 211, 220
Australia xi, xii, 83, 100, 107
Austria xxx, 29, 77, 120, 121, 126, 166, 167, 207, 238, 254, 255
Axis powers 12, 136, 139, 140
Ayala, Amilkar xxxiii

B

Bach-Zelewski, Erich von dem 81, 82, 130
Baeck, Leo 76
Baker, professor 247
Baldus, David 157, 158, 160, 161, 164
banality of evil 64, 66
banking 77, 118, 122, 123
Bantu 224, 225, 231, 251
Bantustans 224, 225
Barbados xx
barbarity xii, xxii, 4, 5, 6, 9, 15, 19, 27, 28, 30–33, 36, 42–45, 70, 72, 74, 79, 83, 98–104, 106, 111, 123, 129, 139, 141, 199, 205, 206, 208, 221, 222, 260, 261, 263
Barbie, Klaus 249, 257
Barri, commandant 65
Basters 91, 92, 93
Beccaria 151
Bédarida, François 127, 128
Begin, Menahem 235
Belair, Charles 62, 63
Belgium 20, 72–87, 101, 136, 145
Belle Epoque xiii
Belzec 135
Benabdallah, Abdelkader 212, 213, 239, 247, 256
Ben Gurion, David 208
Berlin Conference 69
Berlin Wall 255
Bernal, Martin xiii
Bernardin de Saint Pierre 127
Bernstein, Rusty 227
Bettelheim, Bruno 34, 36, 40–42, 45, 57, 119, 128
Biko, Steve x
Bismarck, Otto von 69, 117
Bissell, Richard 86
Blackmun, Harry 171, 173
Black Panther 162
Black Peril 203, 242
Board of Education vs. Dowell 169
Boer xiv
Bolshevism 81, 96, 118, 123, 144
Bophuthatswana 224
Bormann, Martin 95, 249
Bosch, P.J. 223, 224
Botz, Gerhard 120, 126, 127, 128
Bourgeois, Daniel 122
Bourne, Peter xxxiii, 37, 57
Braeckman, Colette 226
Brandley, Clarence 170, 171
Brazil xv, 23, 24
Brennan, Justice 164
Bricusse, Georges 82, 83
Brown vs. Board of Education 154, 169
Brunet, General 60, 61
Buchenwald 29, 37
Buffon xxiii
Burris, Gary 174
Burundi 91
Bush, George 165
Bush, George W 175, 179
Bush, Jeb 175
business 113–128, 202, 261; profit-making motive 3, 4

C

Calata, James 217
Callins vs. Collins 173, 179
Cameroon 91
Canaan xx, xxxiv, 67
Canada xii, 133
Cañete, Marquis 51
Canisius, Edgar 70
Caonao massacre 19
capital xv, xvi
capitalism ix–xvi, 244
capitalist modernity x, xi, xvi
Caribbean 17, 95, 110
Carrel, Alexis 94; Carrel–Daken method 94
Carter, Jimmy 133
castration 51
Castro Caycedo, Germán 183, 187–189, 193
Caucasians xiv
Cayenne 54
Central Association of German Citizens of Jewish Faith 237

Index

Césaire, Aimé xiv, xxii, xxvi, xxxiii, 60, 67, 68, 111, 260, 263
Chamberlain, Neville xviii
Chapuzet de Guérin 110
Charleston, US 102
Chaskalson, Arthur 232
Chaumont, Jean-Michel 5, 8
Chicago 171, 172, 179
Chicago Tribune 159
China xiv, 106, 252
Chomsky, Noam 255, 257
Christianity xvii, xix, xx, xxii
Christians xiv, xviii–xxii, 18, 19, 22, 72, 74, 79, 115, 123, 186–189, 200, 219, 220, 245
Churchill, Winston xxvii, 135
Ciskei, SA 224, 225
civilisation ix, xxix, 15, 62, 66, 69–72, 74, 98–108, 119, 134, 135, 166, 187–189
civil service 55, 56, 113, 223
Civil War (US) 47, 148, 149, 192
Cohen, Albert xxvii
Cohen, David 199
Cohen, William 54, 57, 127, 128
Cook County, US 159, 172
collateral damage 3, 12, 52
Colombia xix, 12–15, 23, 24, 51, 181–183, 186, 188, 191–193
colonial conquest xiii
Colonial Exhibition xxii
colonial justice 30, 53
colonisation xv, xxxi, 3, 12, 14, 15, 20, 91, 97, 98, 103, 109, 135, 197, 249, 251, 263
"Colour Bar" Act 198
Coloured x, xiv, 51, 54, 204
Columbus, Christopher xx
Combesque, Marie-Agnès 179
Commonwealth vs. Connor 162
communism 155, 205, 215, 242, 244
Compagnie du Kasai 101
compensation 8, 35, 52, 65, 66
concentration camps 5, 17, 22, 27–51, 54, 56, 59, 67, 95, 101, 107, 126, 129, 130, 135, 138, 141, 145, 217, 225, 244–8, 259, 260
Congo Free State xxii, 70, 72, 73, 77
Congo, the xxvi, 69, 70–86, 99–101, 248, 249
conquest x, xii, xiii, 3, 11–16, 20, 66, 70, 79, 97, 107, 125, 191
conquistadores 11, 14, 15, 17, 19
Cooper, James Fenimore 104
corporal punishment xvii, xxv, xxvi, 35, 41–45, 50–53, 75, 80, 81, 84
cotton 51, 75, 148, 149
Courtet de l'Isle, Victor 105
Court of Appeals for the Eleventh Circuit (US) 142, 160–164
craniology 105
Creole xii, 181, 182, 191
crimes against humanity ix, xii, xv, xvi, xxxi, 2, 49, 75, 137, 140, 141, 261
Cuba xvii, 19, 64, 133
culture xii, 1, 4, 22, 31, 34, 83, 103, 119, 131, 151, 166, 246

D

Dachau 29, 34, 41
Dahomey 5
Davis, Jefferson 149
Davoust 33
death penalty 126, 155–179, 215, 227, 245
death row 158, 161, 162, 168, 170–175
death sentence 137, 156–174, 232
Debelle, Jean-François Gen 63
decapitation 53
de Chèvres, M. 17
Declaration of Human Rights 31, 253
Declaration of the Rights of Man 134
De Gaulle, Charles 23, 205
de Gobineau, Arthur xiii
democracy ix, xiii, 94, 99, 107, 137, 142, 150–153, 162, 167, 168, 176, 220, 242
demography 77, 176
deportation xi, xviii, 1, 5, 7, 42, 67, 77, 93, 121, 140, 181
de Quatrefages, Armand 105
Der Angriff 238

Dessalines, Jean-Jacques 62
de Wet, Quartus, Justice 227–232
Diderot, Denis 23
Diener, Ingrid 92, 109
Die Transvaaler 203
Die Welt 209
"discovery of America" ix
discrimination xiv, 83, 97, 120, 135, 137, 142, 143, 153, 157, 159, 163, 165, 169, 173, 222, 234, 237, 238, 244, 245
"Divide and Rule" 46
DNA testing 161, 162, 171, 172, 178
dog platoons 18, 30, 47, 48, 64, 65, 152
Dominicans 17, 18, 21, 22
Do Nascimento, Abdias xxxiii
Douglass, Frederick 37, 38, 40, 48, 57, 58
Doumas, Régis xxxiv
Dred Scott vs. Sanford 153, 177
Dulles, Allen 85
Dutch Jewish Council 200
Dyer, L.C. 150

E

East Africa 91
Eastern Europe 109, 123, 131
Eban, Abba 247, 250
Eça de Queiroz, José Maria 116, 117
education xxviii, 12, 67, 99, 114, 134, 144, 153, 154, 169, 188, 189, 216, 233, 234, 247
Egypt 62, 100
Eichmann, Adolf 64, 67, 208, 225, 237–239
Einsatzgruppen 82, 130
Eisenhower, Dwight. D. 86
electric chair 174, 175
Encyclopaedia Universalis 192
Engels, Friedrich xi
Enlightenment xiii, xxiii, 22, 32, 64, 82, 129, 263
eugenics xxi, xxii, 94, 200, 201
Eurocentrism x, xi, xiii, 12, 13, 53
Europe ix–xv, xviii, xx, xxii, xxix, 1, 2, 3, 7, 8, 12, 16, 20, 21, 27, 28, 29, 34, 42, 45, 46, 47, 54, 57, 66, 76, 77, 81, 83, 84, 93–103, 109, 120, 123, 127–140, 144, 147, 148, 151, 154, 181, 197–201, 203, 206, 217, 227, 250, 254, 259–263
evangelisation 14
Everett, Mike 166
exclusion 9, 91–111, 215–226
extermination xxix, xxx, 1, 12, 49, 54, 64, 65, 79, 81, 91, 92, 97–101, 107, 108, 110, 119, 121, 127–140, 144, 181, 199, 226, 242, 249, 260, 261

F

Fanon, Frantz xxvi, xxxiii
Faris, Ellsworth 80
fascism xv, 11, 123, 198
Feiglin, Moshe 246
Ferry, Jules 134, 135, 146, 253
Fiévez, Léon 80
"final solution" 22, 96, 104
Finkelstein, Norman 102, 110, 166, 178, 213
Finkielkraut, Alain 249, 262
First, Ruth 227
First World War xxiii, 94, 117, 118, 202, 250
Fischer, Bram 227–229, 232
Fischer, Eugen 91, 93, 95, 96
Fitzmaurice, Gerald 253
Florida, US 102, 150, 152, 157, 174, 175
Force Publique 70, 76, 84, 85
France x–xxiii, xxvii–xxx, xxxiv, 5, 18–24, 29, 30, 33, 36, 39, 49, 52, 57–69, 72, 75, 85–87, 91, 93, 94, 96, 100, 104–111, 117, 121, 122, 127, 128, 134–136, 140, 145, 146, 150, 168, 174, 177, 179, 205, 210, 226, 234, 240, 251–257, 260–262
Franciscia, Andrée 254
Franklin, John 110, 148, 153, 176
Freedman, Marcia 248
French Guyana xxvii
French Resistance xxxiv
French Revolution xiii, xxx, 260
Friedlander, Saul 110, 128, 200, 212

Froneman, Mr. 225
Frossard, Benjamin 35
Fukuyama, Francis; "the end of history" ix, xiii
Furet, François 151
Furman vs. Georgia 155, 157, 158
Fyfe, David Maxwell Sir 137, 138

G

Garrido, Louis Ramon 182, 183, 188, 189
gas chamber xxvi, 2, 20, 79, 123, 130, 139, 225, 226, 260
Gazankulu, SA 224
General Assembly 233–237, 251–256
genocide ix, xi, xix, xxiv, xxv, xxix, 1, 2, 7, 8, 11, 12, 49, 54, 66, 67, 79, 104, 106, 107, 123, 130, 139, 141, 142, 145, 210, 235, 260, 261
Georgia, US 102, 155–158, 160, 163, 164, 167, 178, 179
Germany xxvi, xxx, 2, 5, 7, 8, 12, 27, 29, 50, 66, 69, 74, 83, 84, 91–110, 116, 117, 120–123, 126, 129, 131, 133, 138–145, 167, 168, 197, 200–208, 212, 216–218, 234, 238, 246–252, 260–263
Germany–South Africa Society 217, 218
Gestapo 36, 77, 93, 129, 205, 238, 257
ghetto 124, 128, 210
Gide, André 249
Girardet, Raoul 134
Gliddon, George 105
Glissant, Édouard xxii
Goebbels, Joseph 238
Goering, Heinrich 93
Goering, Hermann 74, 93, 202, 249
Goggin, Michael 159
Goldberg, Denis 227, 239
Goldberg, Jonathan 245
Goldhagen, Daniel 83, 110, 213
Goldmann, Nahum 208
Goldstein, Baruch 245
Gonzalez, Eudoro 182, 183, 185
Gore, Al 175
Gorée, Senegal xvii–xxviii, 8, 97

Grawitz, Ernst-Robert 81, 82
Great Britain x–xv, xix, 18, 59, 91, 101, 104, 107, 109, 114, 136, 137, 153, 192, 197, 198, 201–205, 217, 226, 234, 247, 251. *See also* United Kingdom
Greece xiii, 50
"Greek miracle" xiii
Green, Jane Seigel 161, 162
Gregg vs. Georgia 156
Greiman, Alan 159
Gros, André xxiii, 140, 253
Group Areas Act 204
Grunfeld, Jacqueline xxxiv
Guadeloupe 30, 35, 63
Guerra, Adalpe Ricardo 170
Gutierrez Torres, Carlos 183–186, 190
Gypsies 30, 96, 109, 119, 130, 133, 135, 137, 144, 212

H

Haaretz 246
Haider, Jorg 255, 256
Haiti xxxiii, 65. *See* Saint-Domingue
Hamilton, Thomas 40
Hänel, Albert 115
Hanke, Lewis 19
Hatchett, Joseph 160
Heath, prosecutor 145
Hebron 245, 248, 249, 256
Hechter, Lt. 242, 243
Heidegger, Martin xxi, 83, 118
Hepple, Bob 223, 227
Herero 91, 92, 106, 107
Heydrich, Reinhardt 144
Hicks, Giles 38
Hilberg, Raul 45, 46, 57, 67, 76, 81, 87, 96, 97, 110, 113, 118, 120, 127, 128, 135–137, 142, 144, 146, 199, 212, 240
Himmler, Heinrich 74, 81, 82, 130, 143, 146
Hindus 94
Hirsch, Otto 76
historiography xi, 3, 4, 53, 67, 97, 103
Hitler, Adolph xiv, xxi, xxii, xxv–xxvii, xxx, 7, 25, 51, 54, 61, 62, 64, 66, 74,

81, 84–87, 92, 93, 98, 103, 120, 122, 123, 126, 131, 132, 137, 146, 147, 151, 154, 167, 176, 177, 197, 202, 212, 217, 218, 226, 246, 248, 250, 254–257, 260, 263, 264
Hobsbawm, Eric 167, 178, 192, 193
Hochschild, Adam 70–78, 82–87, 111
Holocaust 128, 142, 210, 213, 249, 262
Hose, Sam 167
Hottentots 91, 92, 93
humanists xxi, 6, 15, 66, 108, 127, 192, 201, 261, 263
human rights ix, xxii, xxvii, 31, 108, 134, 139, 143, 154, 155, 205, 216, 223, 234, 244, 253
Humbert, Gen. 63
Hungary 123
Hut Tax 198
Huxley, Julian Sorell 201

I

Ilanga 70
Illinois, US 159, 172, 178
Immorality Act 198, 204
India x, xi, xiii, xv, xxii, 204, 251
"Indian problem" 22
indigenous peoples x, xi, xii, xx, 1, 5, 11, 14, 16, 17, 24, 25, 79, 82, 93, 100, 107, 125, 135, 139, 145, 182, 186
industrial revolution xi
"inferior groups" xi, xxix, 1, 2, 20, 21, 31, 32, 74, 82–84, 91–101, 104–109, 114, 119–130, 134, 135, 139, 142, 147, 149, 150, 153, 168, 175, 190, 199, 201, 204, 212, 241, 243, 244, 246, 254
inferior races xxix, 104, 106, 134, 135
Innocence Project 161
Interahamwe 226
International African Association (AIA) 69
International Congress of Population Problems 200
International Convention on the Suppression and Punishment of the Crime of Apartheid 234, 236, 253, 254

International Court of Justice 251–253, 257
International Criminal Court 142
International Military Tribunal 136, 137, 218
interpretation 4, 7, 8, 12, 13, 15, 84, 99, 104
Ireland 147
Isert, Paul Erdman 42, 43, 44
Islam xiv, 70, 103, 104, 249
Israel xx, xxv, 56, 135, 203, 206–213, 235–240, 245–249, 255, 256, 257

J

Jackson, Robert 137, 138
James, C.L.R. 95
Japan xiv, xv
Jefferson, Thomas 17, 151
Jimenez, Marcelino 182, 189
Jimenez, Maria Helena 182, 184, 189, 191
Jimerson, Verneal 172
Joffe, Joel 229
Jones, Ronald 172
Judaism xxiii, xxxiv, 123, 208, 209, 237
judicial system 153, 154, 157, 164, 169, 174, 244
Jüdisches Nachrichtenblatt 77
jury 102, 156, 157, 159, 162, 170, 173, 174, 191
justice xxiii–xxv, xxviii, 21, 30–33, 40, 42, 43, 53, 72, 102, 147, 156, 161–165, 169, 209, 217, 220, 245, 246, 260–262
justification 3, 4, 28, 43, 66, 97, 98, 101, 104

K

Kallmann, Dr 200
Kaltenbrunner, Ernest 249
Kanaks xii, 100
Kantor, Jimmy 227
Kapeliuk, Amnon 244–246, 248, 256, 257
Kasai 77, 78, 101
Kasa-Vubu, Joseph 85

Kaspi, André 174
Kathrada, Ahmed 227, 230, 231
Keil, Thomas J. 160
Kemp, Ralph 164, 165
Kershaw, Ian 167
Khrushchev, Nikita 231
Kindertransport 133
King, Martin Luther xxvi, 155, 205
Kiryat Arba 249
Kogon, Eugen 20, 29, 30, 37, 46, 47, 56, 57, 74, 87
Kragdadigheit 205
Kritzinger, Friedrich Wilhelm 113
Ku Klux Klan 97, 150, 168
Kun, Béla 123
Kwandebele, SA 242
KwaZulu, SA 224, 225

L

Labat, Jean-Baptiste 22, 36, 80, 127
labour xi, xxvi, 5, 14, 17, 34, 41, 42, 45, 46, 48, 73, 77, 78, 140, 149, 198, 199, 216, 224
La Fayette, Marquis de 82
Lamartinière, Gen. 63
language x, xiv, xix, xxvii, 13, 15, 21, 23, 46, 147, 148, 173, 201, 228, 244
Lanman, Thomas 37
Lanzmann, Claude 248
La Rubiera 152, 182–191
Las Casas, Bartolomé de 13, 14, 16, 17, 19, 20, 25, 78, 79, 87, 151
Latin America xii, xiv, xv, 14, 70. *See also* South America
law x, xviii, xxiii–xxviii, 18, 27, 28, 31, 33, 39, 40, 53, 55, 56, 65, 72, 74, 93, 94, 97, 102, 106, 110, 113, 114, 123, 130, 139, 140, 142, 145, 146, 150, 154–160, 163, 165, 179, 182, 186, 190, 191, 198–205, 215, 218, 223–227, 233, 237, 244, 246, 251, 261
Law of Return 246
Law for the restoration of the professional civil service 55–56
Law Olmsted, Frederick 34, 57

Laws Commission xxvii, xxviii
Lebensraum 147
Leclerc, Charles, Gen 59–64
Le Code Noir xxxiv, 52, 67, 99,
Lemkin, Raphael 12, 141
Le Monde 86
Léopold II, King 69–86, 100, 248
Le Pen, Jean-Marie 67
lethal injection 174, 175
Leutwein, Theodor 92
"liberal" discourse xv
Libya xiii
Liebknecht, Karl 117
Lincoln, Abraham 149
Lindqvist, Sven xxix
Litwack, Léon 110, 167, 178
London Agreement 140
London conference 137
Lopez, Maria Gregoria 182, 189
Louverture, Paul 62
Louverture, Toussaint 59, 60, 62, 63, 67
Lumumba, Patrice 85, 86, 87
Luthuli, Albert 215, 218–220, 226
Luxemburg, Rosa 117
lynching xxiii, xxiv, 97, 101–103, 110, 142, 150, 151, 163–167, 176, 178, 191, 212

M

Madagascar 107
Magna Carta 104
Maigne, Jules 134, 135
Malawi 251
Malcolm X xxvi, xxxiii, 143, 146
Mandate Rule 251, 253
Mandela, Nelson xxv, 215, 217, 219–232, 238, 239
Marienstras, Richard 262
Maroons xix
Martinique 31–35, 38, 52, 53, 55, 62, 63, 80, 81
Marx, Karl x, xi
Mascarene xviii
master–slave relationship 79
Mata, Ramon 173

Maurepas, Jacques 63, 64, 145, 146, 242
Mauritania 103
Mauthausen 42
Mbeki, Govan 220, 227
Mbeki, Thabo 239
Mbemba, Jean-Martin 134, 263
McCleskey, Warren 160, 163–165, 169, 178
Mein Kampf 130, 131, 146, 176, 263
Meir, Golda 246
Meli, Francis 230
memory xxiv, xxx, xxxiv, 37, 42, 50, 84, 85, 86, 123, 208, 209, 261, 262
Mendez, Denise xxxiv
mentality 4, 37, 43, 96, 100, 119, 125, 166–168
Métral, Antoine 60, 67
Mexico xiii, 12
Mhlaba, Raymond 227
Michaux, Oscar 70
Middle East xv, 207, 244, 248
Mildenstein, Leopold Itz von 238
Millares Carlo, Augustin 19
Millot de Girardière 30
mind-set 3, 106, 121, 166, 192
miscegenation 13, 54, 200
missionary 36, 77, 80
Mississippi, US 102, 213
mixed blood 12, 48, 49, 55, 95
mixed marriages 56, 121, 203, 237
Mlangeni, Andrew 227
Mobutu, Joseph Désiré 85
Montesquieu 23
Morenas, Joseph Eleazar 29, 30, 33, 53, 56, 58
Morin, Luis Enrique 182–189
Morton, Samuel George 105
Motsoaledi, Elias 227
MS St. Louis 133
mulatto 39, 55, 56, 95
Muller-Hill, Benno 93, 95, 109, 110
Murrain, Vincente xxxiii
mutilation 51, 52, 77, 78

N

Naidoo, Indres 234, 239, 243, 256
Nama 91
Namibia 91–93, 251–253
Nantes, France 67
Napoleon Bonaparte 59, 61, 62, 63, 100
National Association for the Advancement of Colored People (NAACP) 150
National Socialism 125, 137, 237
National Socialist Party 96–98, 118, 125, 130, 132, 136, 202, 263
Native Americans ix, 11, 11–26, 95, 104, 105, 125, 145, 147, 152, 176, 181–186, 189–192, 260, 262
natural selection 94, 200; *See also* eugenics
Nazi xiii, xiv, xxx, xxxi, 1, 2, 5, 6, 8, 28, 29, 45, 46, 47, 51, 54, 56, 76, 79, 83, 84, 93, 96, 103, 109, 113, 117–126, 132, 133, 135, 137, 141, 167, 168, 199–211, 217, 238, 247, 249, 251, 254, 260, 263
Nazism ix, xiii, xxi, xxiv–xxvi, xxix–xxxii, 1, 2, 5, 6, 7, 8, 12, 20, 29, 33, 34, 36, 56, 66, 74, 76, 77, 81–83, 93, 94, 97–106, 110, 111, 118–127, 129, 133–136, 139, 143, 145, 153, 154, 166, 174, 197–209, 212, 216–218, 225–227, 235, 236, 238, 244, 246, 249, 252–256, 260, 261, 263
N'Dumbe, Kum'a 11, 25, 177, 212, 217, 218, 226
Negro xiv, xxii, 31, 32, 33, 35, 38, 39, 42, 43, 44, 52, 53, 66, 77, 81, 91, 96, 99, 102, 105, 106, 110, 143, 167, 192, 201
negrophobe 96, 148
negrophobia xxi, 168, 173
Netherlands, The x, 16, 18, 20, 33, 41, 43, 49, 104, 121, 136, 145, 197, 200, 215
New Caledonia xii, 100
New England, US xii
New York Tribune 166
Nicaragua 17

Index   281

Noailles, Louis Marie, Viscount 64
non-violent protest 221–223
normalisation 66, 103, 181–194
North America 11, 51, 64, 72, 82, 99,
    104, 107, 136, 137, 145–149, 151, 165
North Atlantic Treaty Organization
    (NATO) xiii
Nott, Josiah, C. 105
Nuremberg xxi–xxiv, 54, 75, 130, 137,
    142, 169, 198, 199, 202, 237, 249,
    250–254
Nuremberg Laws 169, 198, 199, 202, 237
Nuremberg trials xxi–xxiv, 75, 130,
    136–139, 249, 250, 252–254

O

occupied territories 77
Ohio, US 157
Ohlendorf, Otto 144, 145, 242
Okahandja peace treaty 91
Olympic Games 100, 202
"one man, one vote" 219
Oppenheimer, Harry 219, 220
Ortiz, Tomas 21
Ossewabrandwag 202–204, 218, 235
Oviedo y Valdés, Fernandez 21, 22, 79

P

Palestine xxvii, 238, 239, 244–248
Palestine Liberation Organization (PLO)
    238
Panama 51
pass 74, 157, 218, 220, 221, 224
Patterson, Aaron 171, 172
Pelletan, Camille 134, 146
persecution 113, 119–124, 141, 203, 206
Peru 24, 51
Pétain, Philippe 94
Pétré-Grenouilleau, Olivier 261
Peytraud, Lucien 58, 244
Philadelphia, US 159, 162
Pirow, Oswald 217, 218, 227
plantations xi, xxv, 28, 35, 37, 41, 44–47,
    50, 70
Plato xviii, xx

Plessy vs. Ferguson 153, 154, 169
Plumelle, Frédéric xxxiv
Plumelle-Uribe, Rosa Amelia ix–xi, xix,
    xx, xxii–xxix
Poland 45, 77, 119, 123, 136, 200
Poliakov, Léon 79, 87, 99, 110, 111, 121,
    122, 128
Pol Pot 64, 255
population xviii, xxx, 12, 30, 34, 36, 45,
    46, 59, 60, 65, 70–77, 81–86, 91, 93,
    97, 101, 102, 104, 113–123, 134, 150,
    151, 153, 156, 168, 175, 205, 207,
    208, 215, 218, 219, 224, 231, 233, 235
Population Registration Act No. 5 (1950)
    204
Port-au-Prince, Haiti xxiii, 39, 260
Portugal x, 18, 20, 23, 33, 49, 104, 116,
    145, 251, 261
Powell, Lewis 164
Poznanski, Renée 135, 146
Prohibition of Mixed Marriages Act,
    1949 203
prejudice 67, 127, 168, 199, 263
Presidential Commission on the
    Holocaust 133
"preventive elimination" 242
prison xxv, 37, 162, 170, 171, 185–190,
    199, 204, 215, 219, 222, 223, 227
profit-making motive 3, 4
pro-Nazi 2, 202, 203, 255
Proskauer, Joseph 208
Pruneau de Pommegorge, Antoine 35
punishment xxi, 28, 31, 34, 44, 45,
    50–53, 63, 92, 136, 151, 156, 157,
    160, 164, 165, 168, 173–175, 188,
    191, 231, 244

R

Rabin, Yitzhak 235, 245, 246
"race of masters" xxii, 54
racial domination 54, 66, 137, 139, 151,
    198, 199, 209, 217
racial hierarchy xiv, xx, xxiii, 1, 83, 97,
    108, 109, 131, 132
Racial Justice Act 165

racial superiority xxi, xxii, 1, 16, 20, 21, 24, 27, 39, 43, 77, 83, 96–98, 106, 107, 120, 127, 129–135, 147–149, 165, 202, 204, 220, 241, 244, 247, 253
racism xii, xiii, xx–xxv, xxvii, xxxiv, 1, 12, 98–100, 115, 131, 135, 148, 157, 201, 210, 237– 238, 245, 249, 254, 263
Rademayer, C.I. 205
Ramel, Jean-Pierre 65
Rand Daily Mail 228
rape 13, 43, 48, 155, 172, 198, 199
ratissage 205
Rauschning, Herman 263
Rehnquist, William 154, 169
Rehoboth, Namibia 91, 93
Reichmann, Eva 102
Reichsvereinigung 76, 77
Reitz, Deneys 217, 221
religion 13, 22, 43, 69, 136, 147, 148, 159, 166, 221, 244, 247
Rémion-Granel, Christiane xxxiv
Renan, Ernest 106, 111
Reno, Janet 161
reparation viii, xxviii, 4, 206
repression 141, 212, 227, 242
Réunion xxvii
revolution xi, xiii, xxxiii, 14, 117, 118, 233
Rhineland xi, 93
Ribbentrop, Joachim von 121, 202
Ridge, Thomas 178
Rivonia Trial 227–233
Rochambeau, Donatien de 63, 64, 65, 82, 242
Rodriguez, Celestino 182
Rogers, Barbara 225
Roi, Simon 80
Rom, Léon 101
Roosevelt, Franklin D. 135
Rosenberg, Alfred 249
Rosewood massacre 150, 151, 152
Rousseau, Jean-Jacques 23
rubber 75, 76, 78, 80
Rumpff, Frans Lourens 219
Russia xii, 81, 94, 130
Rwanda 91, 226

S

Sabo, Albert 162
sabotage 222, 228, 231, 232, 242
Sabotage Act 231
Saint-Domingue xiii, xvii–xix, xxv–xxviii, 8, 32, 35, 37–39, 59–68, 82, 97, 145, 146, 242, 260
Saint-Lucia 35
Saint-Simon, Comte de 105
Sala-Molins, Louis xvii, xxxiv, 54, 58, 61, 67, 261–263
Samoyeds xii
Santana, Pedro Ramon 182, 185, 187, 189
Schiller, Herbert I. 175, 180
schizophrenia 200
Schlegelberger, Franz 113
Schmelt, Albrecht 46
Schoelcher, Victor xxviii, 28, 29, 56–58, 65, 67, 68, 87, 95, 109
scholarship ix, 3, 4, 29, 96, 98, 131
Schutzstaffel SS 20, 27, 29, 31, 33, 34, 37, 40, 41, 45–49, 56, 74, 76, 79, 81, 82, 87, 119, 124, 130, 144, 238, 255
science x, xix–xxi, xxx, 6, 21, 99, 105, 106, 109, 131, 166, 192, 200, 212, 250–254
Scott, Dred 110, 153, 154, 177
Second World War xxix, xxxi, 98, 135, 202, 238
Security Council 85, 233, 251–256
segregation xxii, 2, 100, 118, 133, 135, 137, 153, 154, 164, 169, 197, 206, 207, 215, 234, 252, 254
Senegal xxiii, xxv, xxviii, 35
settlers 4, 11, 62, 66, 91, 249
shared responsibility 4, 5
Sheppard, William 77, 78
Shoah 206, 209, 235, 236, 248, 262
Sisulu, Walter 215, 220, 227, 230
Slave Narratives 47
slavery ix, xii–xiv, xix, xxvii, xxviii, xxx, 7, 13, 16, 29, 35, 47, 48, 50, 51, 59, 62, 63, 64, 70, 71, 100, 101, 103, 105, 127, 148, 149, 175, 220, 244, 245; abolition of

Index

slavery xii, xiii; Arabo-Islamic brand xx; Biblical history xx
slave trade ix, xi, xix, xx, xxviii, xxxi, xxxii, 4, 7, 29, 54, 55, 67, 73, 91, 261
Slavs 119, 130, 131, 132
Slovo, Joe 227
Smith, Amir xxxiii
Sobibor 135
Sobukwe, Robert 220, 243
Sogamoso, Cupertino 183, 185
South Africa xiv, xxii, xxv, 2, 50, 153, 197–257
South African Institute of Racial Relations 224
South African National Party 202
South America 11, 13, 14, 151, 182, 191
South Carolina, US 102, 149
South East Asia xv
southern Africa 234, 253
South-West Africa 91, 93, 106, 202, 203, 251
South West Africa People's Organisation (SWAPO) 251
Soviet Union xii, 81, 95, 133, 136, 144, 212, 252
Spain x, xii, xx, xxii, 13, 18–24, 33, 47, 49, 51, 52, 64, 70, 71, 78, 104, 108, 145, 181, 182, 261
Spartacists 117
Stahl, Heinrich 76
Stalin, Josef x, 64, 135, 255
Star of Johannesburg 236
Stedman, Jean-Gabriel 16, 18, 41, 43, 44
sterilisation 93, 200
Stern, Fritz 114–116, 127
Stevens, Richard 211
Stoecker, Adolf 116
Streicher, Julius 249
Stroop, J. 124
Sudan 103
sui generis crime 136, 140, 142, 226
Swart, C.R. 202, 204, 218
Switzerland 72, 122, 123, 128
Syracuse, Sicily 42

T

Tambo, Oliver 220
Tamimi, Cheikh Rajab Bayoud 249
Taney, Roger 153, 154
Tanzania 91
Tardieu, Jean-Pierre 51
Taubira, Christiane xxvii, xxviii
Taylor, Fannie 152
Taylor, Shepard Thomas 115
Teodoro, Jovina xxxiii
Texas, US 47, 157, 170, 173, 176, 177, 179
Thiaroye, Senegal xxiii
Thibaudeau, Antoine Claire 62, 67
Third Reich xxiv, xxx, 54, 55, 56, 64, 94, 98, 99, 106, 109, 113, 120–125, 135, 143, 144, 153, 165, 177, 197–206, 212, 216, 223, 227, 255, 261
Thomas, Trudi 225
Tierra Firme 51, 52
Timur xvi
Tocqueville, Alexis de 66, 68, 150, 151, 176
Todorov, Tzvetan 12, 17–22, 25, 128, 262
Togo 91
Toledo, Francesco de 51
Tonkin 107
Torrealba, Elio 182, 184, 185
torture xviii, xix, xxi, 18, 30, 31, 34–38, 40, 50, 52, 158, 171, 219, 239, 248
Transkei 224, 225
trans-Saharan Slave Trade xx
Treblinka 135
Trotha, Lother von 92, 106, 107
Truguet, Laurent Jean-François 62
Tuchler, Kurt 238

U

Umkhonto we Sizwe MK 222, 227, 232
Umvoti Mission Reserve 215
UNESCO 201, 237
United Hebrew Congregation of Johannesburg 233

United Kingdom xii, xiv, 18, 20, 33, 49, 62, 107, 109, 133, 137, 145, 147, 205, 210, 234, 251, 252, 253, 260, 261. *See also* Great Britain
United Nations xxiii, xxxiv, 86, 138, 141–143, 155, 210–213, 234, 238, 239, 251–253, 257; General Assembly 141, 211, 223, 235, 255; Human Rights Commission 254
United States ix–xii, xiv, xvi, xxiv, 3, 11, 17, 34, 37, 47, 69, 72, 74, 75, 77, 85, 86, 94, 97, 101–103, 109, 110, 133, 136, 140–180, 191, 192, 200, 205, 210, 234, 245–247, 252, 253, 262
untermenschen xxii
US Supreme Court 97, 110, 137, 153–157, 163–169, 171, 173, 177, 179
utilitarian motive xxxi

V

Van Rensburg, Hans 202
Veil, Simone 5
Venda 224
Venezuela 51, 181
Versailles Treaty 117, 251
Verwoerd, Hendrik Frensch 203–205, 213, 224
victims xiv, xvi, xix, xxv, xxvi, xxix, xxxi, 1–8, 12, 16, 20, 21, 27–29, 33–54, 61, 65, 66, 72–79, 82, 96–101, 108, 109, 118, 122, 123, 131, 144, 147, 148, 158, 160, 161, 190, 199–210, 217, 222–225, 241, 244, 250, 255–263
Vidal-Naquet, Pierre 235
Virginia, US 155, 171
Vissière, Isabelle 42
Vissière, Jean-Louis 41, 42, 57, 68
Vito, Gennaro F. 160
Voltaire 23, 110
Vorster, J.B. 202, 204, 209, 218, 235, 236, 256
Vortrekkers 218
Vos, Pierre de 86

W

Wade, Melvin 173
Warsaw ghetto 124
Washington, Earl 171
Washington Post 208
weapons of mass destruction xvi
Weber, Guy 86
Weiler, M.C. 207
Weldon Johnson, James 150
West, Central and Southern Pan-African Liberation Movement 222
Western democracies 85, 86, 97, 100, 129, 132–135, 137, 197, 199, 201, 224, 254
West Indies xviii, xx, 22, 36
white supremacy xxxi, 4, 6, 12, 22, 24, 34, 41, 42, 49, 50, 52, 54, 72, 99, 119, 165, 182, 190, 198, 259, 263
Wiesel, Elie 210
Williams, Dennis 172, 173
Williams, George Washington 72–74
Williams, Rebecca 171
Windward Islands 55
Wismes, Armel de 29, 56
wood thieves xi
Woodworth, George 157
World Jewish Congress 208
World Jewish Relief 133
World Union of Jews 207
Wright, Julia 174

X

Xuma, Alfred 217

Y

Yugoslavia xv
Yutar, Percy 227–233

Z

Ziegler, Jean 85, 87, 122, 128
Zionism xxxiv, 199, 206–211, 213, 220, 236, 237, 238
Zo Artzeinu 246

"Rosa Amelia Plumelle-Uribe's book needed to be written; now it must be read. The magnitude of the crimes described in detail in this book cannot be disputed. ...In my view one might be tempted to say all this belongs to the past. But it should not be an excuse to forget history and the questions that still affect the reality of our world. The year 1492 is not a random date. Not the year of the 'discovery of America'. The year 1492 is when the conquest and destruction of the Americas by Europeans began. Plumelle-Uribe is right to say that the ferocity of the Nazis is not an anomalous, inexplicable occurrence. It is integral to the rationale for implementing ferocity, which, I once again stress, is inherent to capitalism. To understand where this ferocity originates, look at the logic of capital: accumulate, accumulate, regardless of the price (in human terms)."

– *Samir Amin (1931–2018)*
Professor of Economics and former Director of
Third World Forum, Dakar, Senegal

"Rosa Amelia Plumelle-Uribe's work will be struck down by those who glancing through it will form their opinions on the basis of the table of contents, and those who spending just a little more time, but not much, will in one fell swoop dismiss that this Black woman writing about Black people has the distance allowed to anyone speaking about the history of the calamities which have happened where they come from."

– *Louis Sala-Molins,*
Emeritus Professor of Political Philosophy,
Université Paris 1 and Université de Toulouse 2, France

www.ingramcontent.com/pod-product-compliance
Lightning Source LLC
Chambersburg PA
CBHW050857300426
44111CB00010B/1287